Analyzing Security, Trust, and Crime in the Digital World

Hamid R. Nemati
The University of North Carolina at Greensboro, USA

A volume in the Advances in Information Security, Privacy, and Ethics (AISPE) Book Series

An Imprint of IGI Global

Managing Director:	Lindsay Johnston
Production Editor:	Jennifer Yoder
Development Editor:	Erin O'Dea
Acquisitions Editor:	Kayla Wolfe
Typesetter:	Michael Brehm
Cover Design:	Jason Mull

Published in the United States of America by
  Information Science Reference (an imprint of IGI Global)
  701 E. Chocolate Avenue
  Hershey PA 17033
  Tel: 717-533-8845
  Fax: 717-533-8661
  E-mail: cust@igi-global.com
  Web site: http://www.igi-global.com

Library of Congress Cataloging-in-Publication Data

Analyzing security, trust, and crime in the digital world / Hamid Nemati, editor.
     pages cm
  Includes bibliographical references and index.
  Summary: "This book explores techniques and technologies used to secure data and prevent intrusion in virtual environments, providing meaningful research on intrusion detection and authentication techniques in order to further defend their systems and protect the information therein"-- Provided by publisher.
  ISBN 978-1-4666-4856-2 (hardcover) -- ISBN 978-1-4666-4857-9 (ebook) -- ISBN 978-1-4666-4858-6 (print & perpetual access) 1. Information technology--Security measures. 2. Computer security. 3. Data protection. 4. Computer crimes. I. Nemati, Hamid R., 1958-
  HF5548.37.A527 2014
  005.8--dc23
                              2013042581

This book is published in the IGI Global book series Advances in Information Security, Privacy, and Ethics (AISPE) (ISSN: 1948-9730; eISSN: 1948-9749)

Advances in Information Security, Privacy, and Ethics (AISPE) Book Series

ISSN: 1948-9730
EISSN: 1948-9749

MISSION

In the digital age, when everything from municipal power grids to individual mobile telephone locations is all available in electronic form, the implications and protection of this data has never been more important and controversial. As digital technologies become more pervasive in everyday life and the Internet is utilized in ever increasing ways by both private and public entities, the need for more research on securing, regulating, and understanding these areas is growing.

The **Advances in Information Security, Privacy, & Ethics (AISPE) Book Series** is the source for this research, as the series provides only the most cutting-edge research on how information is utilized in the digital age.

COVERAGE

- Access Control
- Device Fingerprinting
- Global Privacy Concerns
- Information Security Standards
- Network Security Services
- Privacy-Enhancing Technologies
- Risk Management
- Security Information Management
- Technoethics
- Tracking Cookies

IGI Global is currently accepting manuscripts for publication within this series. To submit a proposal for a volume in this series, please contact our Acquisition Editors at Acquisitions@igi-global.com or visit: http://www.igi-global.com/publish/.

Titles in this Series

For a list of additional titles in this series, please visit: www.igi-global.com

Analyzing Security, Trust, and Crime in the Digital World
Hamid R. Nemati (The University of North Carolina at Greensboro, USA)
Information Science Reference • copyright 2014 • 300pp • H/C (ISBN: 9781466648562) • US $195.00 (our price)

Research Developments in Biometrics and Video Processing Techniques
Rajeev Srivastava (Indian Institute of Technology (BHU), India) S.K. Singh (Indian Institute of Technology (BHU), India) and K.K. Shukla (Indian Institute of Technology (BHU), India)
Information Science Reference • copyright 2014 • 279pp • H/C (ISBN: 9781466648685) • US $195.00 (our price)

Advances in Secure Computing, Internet Services, and Applications
B.K. Tripathy (VIT University, India) and D.P. Acharjya (VIT University, India)
Information Science Reference • copyright 2014 • 405pp • H/C (ISBN: 9781466649408) • US $195.00 (our price)

Security Engineering Techniques and Solutions for Information Systems Management and Implementation
Noureddine Boudriga (Engineering School of Communications, Tunisia) and Mohamed Hamdi (Engineering School of Communications, Tunisia)
Information Science Reference • copyright 2014 • 359pp • H/C (ISBN: 9781615208036) • US $195.00 (our price)

Trust Management in Mobile Environments Autonomic and Usable Models
Zheng Yan (Xidian University, China and Aalto University, Finland)
Information Science Reference • copyright 2014 • 288pp • H/C (ISBN: 9781466647657) • US $195.00 (our price)

Network Security Technologies Design and Applications
Abdelmalek Amine (University of Saida, France) Otmane Ait Mohamed (Concordia University, USA) and Boualem Benatallah (University of New South Wales, Australia)
Information Science Reference • copyright 2014 • 361pp • H/C (ISBN: 9781466647893) • US $195.00 (our price)

Security, Privacy, Trust, and Resource Management in Mobile and Wireless Communications
Danda B. Rawat (Georgia Southern University, USA) Bhed B. Bista (Iwate Prefectural University, Japan) and Gongjun Yan (University of Southern Indiana, USA)
Information Science Reference • copyright 2014 • 577pp • H/C (ISBN: 9781466646919) • US $195.00 (our price)

Architectures and Protocols for Secure Information Technology Infrastructures
Antonio Ruiz-Martinez (University of Murcia, Spain) Rafael Marin-Lopez (University of Murcia, Spain) and Fernando Pereniguez-Garcia (University of Murcia, Spain)
Information Science Reference • copyright 2014 • 427pp • H/C (ISBN: 9781466645141) • US $195.00 (our price)

www.igi-global.com

701 E. Chocolate Ave., Hershey, PA 17033
Order online at www.igi-global.com or call 717-533-8845 x100
To place a standing order for titles released in this series, contact: cust@igi-global.com
Mon-Fri 8:00 am - 5:00 pm (est) or fax 24 hours a day 717-533-8661

This book is dedicated to the loving memory of my mother:

my guiding light, my shining star,

forever.

Table of Contents

Detailed Table of Contents

Chapter 1
Hodjatollah Hamidi, K. N. Toosi University of Technology, Iran

The authors present a new approach to Algorithm-Based Fault Tolerance (ABFT) for high performance computing systems. The Algorithm-Based Fault Tolerance approach transforms a system that does not tolerate a specific type of faults, called the fault-intolerant system, to a system that provides a specific level of fault tolerance, namely recovery. The ABFT techniques to detect errors rely on the comparison of parity values computed in two ways; the parallel processing of input parity values produce output parity values comparable with parity values regenerated from the original processed outputs can apply convolutional codes for the redundancy. This method is a new approach to concurrent error correction in fault-tolerant computing systems. This chapter proposes a novel computing paradigm to provide fault tolerance for numerical algorithms. The authors also present, implement, and evaluate early detection in ABFT.

Chapter 2
Amanda Eisenga, Florida Gulf Coast University, USA
Walter Rodriguez, Florida Gulf Coast University, USA
Travis Jones, Florida Gulf Coast University, USA

Investing in Information Technology (IT) security is a critical decision in the digital age. In most organizations, it is wise to allocate a significant amount of resources to IT infrastructure. However, it is difficult to determine how much to invest in IT as well as to quantify the maximum threshold, where the rate of return of this investment begins to diminish. The main research question is: How much and what financial resources should be allocated to IT security? This chapter analyzes different practices and techniques used to determine the degree of investment in IT security and recommends some suitable methods for deciding how much should be invested in IT security.

Chapter 3
Hossein Arsham, The Johns Hopkins University, USA
Veena Adlakha, University of Baltimore, USA

Models transform the managerial inputs into useful information for managerial decision. The Project Evaluation and Review Technique (PERT) is the most widely used model for project management. However, it requires three estimates for the duration of each activity as its input. This uncertainty in the input requirement makes the Critical Path (CP) unstable, causing major difficulties for the manager. A linear programming formulation of the project network is proposed for determining a CP, based on making one estimate for the duration of each activity. Upon finding the CP, Sensitivity Analysis (SA) of Data Perturbation (DP) is performed using the constraints of the dual problem. This largest DP set of uncertainties provides the manager with a tool to deal with the simultaneous, independent, or dependent changes of the input estimates that preserves the current CP. The application of DP results to enhance the traditional approach to PERT are presented. The proposed procedure is easy to understand, easy to implement, and provides useful information for the manager. A numerical example illustrates the process.

Chapter 4

Inge Hermanrud, Hedmark University College, Norway

Authenticity means that the closeness of observation matters for acceptance of new knowledge. The social norm of authenticity can have positive effects of colleagues to appreciate "better" knowledge within opportunity structures for knowledge sharing. However, how ICT influences authenticity in knowledge sharing needs more attention in research on knowledge sharing through online networks. This chapter reports and discusses recent finding of how ICT (here the interactive tool GoToMeeting™) facilitates authenticity.

Chapter 5

Regina Connolly, Dublin City University, Ireland

Information privacy concerns are a dominant concern of the information age, a concern that results from tension between the correct use of personal information and the individual's desire for their information to be private. That tension has extended to the computer-mediated work environment as employees' awareness of the ways in which management can employ technologies to monitor their email and Internet interactions has increased. These concerns have the potential to negatively impact organisational productivity and employee morale. The aim of this chapter is to outline some of the key issues relating to workplace surveillance and provide a balanced perspective that identifies the emerging issues and subsequent privacy concerns from the employees' perspective as well as the rationale underlying managements' decision to employ monitoring technologies in the workplace. In doing so, it attempts to progress academic understanding of this issue and enhance practitioners' understanding of the factors that influence employees' technology-related privacy concerns.

Chapter 6

John Lindström, Luleå University of Technology, Sweden
Claas Hanken, Nemetschek Bausoftware GmbH, Germany

This chapter discusses information security challenges encountered during the wearIT@work project and selected legal aspects of wearable computing. Wearable computing will offer interesting opportunities to improve and reengineer work processes in organizations, but can introduce alignment problems as users in organizations may adopt the new technology before organizations are prepared. Further, alignment problems posed by the emerging trend "Bring Your Own Device" (BYOD) are discussed. In addition, needed supportive legal frameworks have not yet fully addressed the new wearable computing technology. Different alignment concepts for how such challenges can be managed are discussed in the chapter.

Chapter 7

Mahmud A. Shareef, Carleton University, Canada
Vinod Kumar, Carleton University, Canada
Uma Kumar, Carleton University, Canada

There are many collection and application sources of identity theft. The Internet is one of the vulnerable medias for identity theft and is used, especially, as an application source of identity theft. This chapter has two objectives. As the first objective, it develops a conceptual framework to prevent/control identity theft of E-Commerce (EC) in conjunction with different sources of identity theft. From this framework and shedding light on the recent literature of sources of identity theft, the authors identify global laws, controls placed on organizations, publications to develop awareness, technical management, managerial policy, risk management tools, data management, and control over employees as potential measuring items to prevent identity theft in EC. All EC organizations are struggling to control identity theft. This chapter argues that control mechanisms of identity theft have both positive and negative impacts on EC. This chapter sets its second objective to explore the integrative effect of overall identity theft control mechanisms on consumer trust, the cost of products/services, and operational performance, all of which in turn contribute to a purchase intention using E-Commerce (EC). A case study in the banking sector through a qualitative approach was conducted to verify the proposed relations, constructs, and measuring items.

Chapter 8

Eduardo Esteva-Armida, Instituto Tecnologico y de Estudios Superiores de Monterrey, Mexico
Alberto Rubio-Sanchez, University of the Incarnate Word, USA

This chapter tests the appropriateness of the Unified Theory of Acceptance and Use of Technology (UTAUT) model in the context of end user consumption by means of an online survey with 475 respondents (24% response rate). The chapter shows which factors have the greatest impact on the adoption process of VoIP technology in the US market in addition to the interactions of the main variables in the model (Performance Expectancy, Effort Expectancy, Social Influence, and Behavioral Intention to Adopt) and whether Trust can improve the predictive value of the UTAUT model to explain intention to adopt. Partial Least Squares (PLS) is used to evaluate the interactions of the main variables. The model includes four moderator variables (Gender, Age, Experience, and Voluntariness of Use). The results support most of the relationships identified in the original UTAUT model. More specifically, Performance Expectancy appears to have the strongest influence on the Intention of a consumer to adopt a new technology. The chapter provides information about whether the inclusion of Trust can generate good results for industry.

Technology is important to software development projects; however, virtual projects are more dependent on technology than traditional co-located projects due to communication and collaboration needs. Two research studies sought to determine whether seven technology-related risks pose a greater danger to virtual projects than traditional projects and to determine if technology-related risks have a high impact on project success. Results indicate that two technology-related risks exhibited a significantly greater impact on virtual IT projects: (1) inexperience with the company and its processes and (2) inadequate technical resources. Project managers need to be aware that traditional project risks can have a greater impact on virtual projects. Additionally, technology-related risks in the second study were found to have low levels of impact on project success. Results indicate, in cases where a majority of team members are experienced with the application, development technology, and project technology, the risk of technology-related issues seems to lessen.

Chapter 10

This chapter is built on two studies: Ishihara (2011) "A Forensic Authorship Classification in SMS Messages: A Likelihood Ratio-Based Approach Using N-Grams" and Ishihara (2012) "A Forensic Text Comparison in SMS Messages: A Likelihood Ratio Approach with Lexical Features." They are two of the first Likelihood Ratio (LR)-based forensic text comparison studies in forensic authorship analysis. The author attribution was modelled using N-grams in the former, whereas it was modelled using so-called lexical features in the latter. In the current study, the LRs obtained from these separate experiments are fused using a logistic regression fusion technique, and the author reports how much improvement in performance the fusion brings to the LR-based forensic text comparison system. The performance of the fused system is assessed based on the magnitude of the fused LRs using the log-likelihood-ratio cost (C_{llr}). The strength of the fused LRs is graphically presented in Tippett plots and compared with those of the original LRs. The chapter demonstrates that the fused system outperforms the original systems.

Preface

OUR DIGITAL NETWORKED WORLD: ISSUES, CHALLENGES, AND OPPORTUNITIES

Information defines us. It defines the age we live in, the societies we inhibit, the ways we conduct our lives, and ultimately, who we are as humans. Information is the output of our human intellectual endeavors. Since there are no limits to human intellectual capabilities, none can exist for information either. It is unmistakable that we are in the midst of a "digital revolution" with profound implications on the way we conduct our lives. This revolution is characterized by digital network pervasiveness and the resulting transformation of our daily lives in ways unimaginable less than a decade ago. New technologies make possible what was not possible before. We are more interconnected now than we have ever been in our history. The dizzying pace of advances in information technology that characterize this revolution and the extent to which these technologies have become "information appliances" have transformed our lives even more drastically than what we had envisioned. The digital ubiquity and the resulting interconnectedness have fundamentally redefined who we are and how we relate to one another and to the technology. Our world has been altered so drastically that we are no longer able to conduct our lives without the use of communication technologies such as our smartphones, social media, instant messaging, and chats. These technologies allow us to communicate and stay in touch more freely and effortlessly with our families and friends, to stay informed about current events that impact our lives and even shape these events, and to make more informed decisions, be it medical, financial, educational, or even emotional, but open us to underserved scrutiny and possible demonetization and retribution.

Perhaps the most sweeping aspect of this revolution can be found in the ways in which we relate, interact, and communicate not just with one another, including with those in businesses we transact with and government agencies representing us and also in the way we interact with the technology itself. Ultimately, it will redefine the way we perceive and identify ourselves as individuals and members of human society. By making available new options, technologies have led to a restructuring of the hierarchy of values by which we measure and assess the value of these interactions. The impact of this new and fluid value structure will be the driving force in our societal discourse for a long time to come. Technology has also redefined our relationships with businesses we interact with and governmental agencies representing us. We understand and hope that the governments are there to protect and fight for our rights while criminal hackers lurching in the myriad of technologies we use are intended to harm us. However, we also understand the issues and hiding in the shadows are not as clear-cut as we were once led to believe and are changing all the time. Although we are still clearly able to perceive and sometimes identify and thwart the bad guys intended on robbing us by stealing our personal identifies and other valuable information assets by means of hacking and other malicious intrusive and illegal intents whether they are hackers or spammers, or other criminal wrong doers, we are not so sure about who the good guys are and how to identify and deploy methods to thwart and punish the destructive and criminal behaviors of such groups. The government agencies created to protect us were once viewed and regarded as beacons of justice and proctor of our security and privacy. The extent of reach by the NSA in accessing, storing, eavesdropping, and mining our electronic communications have seriously eroded its "good guy" perception. The government is a prime example of this disambiguation of the perception we assign to it. Is the government a friend or a foe when it comes to protecting our privacy? The perception of the righteousness of our government's intentions in accessing, storing, mining, and analyzing our interactions with them or others has irrevocability changed negatively after Snowden's revelations. Given the complexities of the issues in understanding our relationships, including those between the people, their representative government and business entities, we are only at the threshold of what is promised to be by many experts. We are on the verge of the biggest societal transformation in the history of mankind traced directly to advances in the information technology. This transformation will most likely create new opportunities and many challenges we have yet to fathom.

On June 6, 2013, *The Guardian* and *Washington Post* simultaneously released PowerPoint slides revealing the existence of a top-secret mass-surveillance program called the PRISM. The revelations were made by the 29-year-old American whistleblower Edward Snowden. Although prior to Snowden's leak, it was widely believed that intelligence agencies were able to spy on communication systems, the extents of such capabilities revealed by Snowden were shocking. The 41-slide PowerPoint presentation provided by Snowden was classified by the National Security Agency (NSA) as "top secret with no distribution to foreign allies" (The Guardian, 2014) and was developed as part of a training program for intelligence operatives on the capabilities of PRISM. According to Snowden, the NSA and its British counterpart, the Government Communications Headquarters (GCHQ), were (are) using PRISM program to gain direct access to the servers of some of the world's biggest tech companies including tech giants like Apple, Google, Facebook, and Microsoft. Among the details that the PowerPoint presentation provided was the revelation that large tech companies had cooperated closely with these intelligence agencies to help them circumvent encryption and other privacy controls. *The Guardian* reported that using PRISM, "… these agencies are able to access information stored by major US technology companies, often without individual warrants, as well as mass-intercepting data from the fibre-optic cables which make up the backbone of global phone and Internet networks. The agencies have also worked to undermine the security standards upon which the Internet, commerce, and banking rely" (The Guardian, 2014). Snowden later revealed the existence of Boundless Informant, an NSA tool that provides the intelligence agency with "near real-time" spying statistical capabilities and Stellar Wind program to collect Internet metadata. It is expected that many more shocking revelations are yet to come. It is estimated that the NSA collected almost 3 billion pieces of intelligence on U.S. citizens in February 2013 alone, and it is able to track over 1 billion mobile calls daily. What Snowden disclosed had an immediate and far-reaching impact on not only the ongoing debate surrounding information security and privacy, but broader issues of our relationships with each other and with our government.

Since the events of September 11, 2001, the government has become more aggressively involved and open about the use of data mining and other profiling and data collection techniques, which are being deployed as a matter of national security. Although the government's use of these techniques is not new, as Snowden's revelations proved, they have become more prolific and invasive. These actions are fueling a heated debate on privacy. Security and Privacy of data has gained increased importance in this new age of information and terrorism. Because of the advances in technology and the lag of the legal/judicial system to amend laws, many organizations as well as the government have been able to collect and use personally identifiable data on individuals to their advantage. Some of this usage is known to the individual but much is collected unknown to the individual. The perceived use of this information is what has sparked many individuals to protest its very collection and use. The tragic events of September 11, 2001 have accelerated the governmental agencies' need for and use of personally identifiable information. These needs and uses are being justified in the name of protecting and promoting national, public, or individual security. For example, organizations and local, state, or federal agencies need to identify individuals faster and to make assessments and judgments about people more accurately and more reliably, in real or near-real time. They also need to authenticate the identities of individuals, check backgrounds and histories, and to verify their credentials and authorizations. In order to do this in a timely fashion, they need to access and sift through massive amounts of personal data quickly from many sources, both public and private, and across numerous jurisdictions, intercept communications and monitor electronic activities. Government agencies and organizations also need to share data and intelligence across different jurisdictions and domains. Data sharing, in particular, magnifies privacy violation risks and underlines the need for reliable Privacy-Preserving Data Mining techniques.

There is a pervasive belief in the American culture that individuals are entitled to a particular level of privacy. According to Justice Brandeis of the U.S. Supreme Court, the right to privacy is "the right to be left alone – the most comprehensive of rights, and the right most valued by civilized men" (Olmstead v. U.S., 1928). Westin (1967, p. 11) defined the right to privacy as "the right of the individuals… to determine for themselves when, how, and to what extent information about them is communicated to others." The level and the application may be debatable; however, individuals have a certain expectation of privacy, which they are reluctant to relinquish. "Privacy encompasses our right to self-determination and to define who we are. Although we live in a world of noisy self-confession, privacy allows us to keep certain facts to ourselves if we so choose. The right to privacy, it seems, is what makes us civilized" (Alderman & Kennedy, 1997, p. xiii).

Although this digital revolution has brought us closer and has made our lives easier and more productive, paradoxically, it has also made us more capable of harming one another and more vulnerable to be harmed by others. Our new vulnerabilities are the consequence of the evolving nature of our interconnectedness. Mason (1986) claims that unique challenges facing our modern societies are the result of the evolving nature of information itself. This evolving nature of information requires us to rethink the way we interact with one another. Mason argues that in this age of information, a new form of social contract is needed in order to deal with the potential threats to the information that defines us. Mason (1986) states, "Our moral imperative is clear. We must ensure that information technology, and the information it handles, are used to enhance the dignity of mankind. To achieve these goals, we must formulate a new social contract, one that insures everyone the right to fulfill his or her own human potential" (Mason, 1986, p. 26). This new social contract has profound implications for the way our society views information and the technologies that support them. For technology to enhance the "human dignity," it should assist humans in exercising and asserting their rights as individuals. Governments play an important role in not only setting the standards of what is acceptable but making sure that our society is protected from "wrong doers." What makes it hard for these agencies to regain the trust of those they are charged to protect is the prevailing notion that given this current climate of unbridled and unprecedented powers given to the governmental agencies like NSA, the agencies' powers can easily morph into a "big brother," watching you, creating the perception that the government is the "wrong doer" when it comes to protecting its citizens' freedom of expression and self-determination made possible by our constitution. This perception of the people that their governmental representatives are there to protect them can be easily eroded. This can prove very detrimental to these agencies, whose stated goal is protecting the citizens, since it is ultimately impossible to achieve this goal without the support of the citizens. Once this perception takes hold, which it has recently, it will be very difficult if not impossible to change. However, Americans are resilient and reasonable and understand the threats facing them may require new ways of fighting the adversary. What they are asking for are guaranties from these agencies that they understand and discriminate between what is right, ethical, legal, and permissible with what is necessary and vital to protecting our national security. The debate must go on.

LAYOUT OF THE BOOK

The authors present a new approach to Algorithm-Based Fault Tolerance (ABFT) for high performance computing systems. The Algorithm-Based Fault Tolerance approach transforms a system that does not tolerate a specific type of faults, called the fault-intolerant system, to a system that provides a specific level of fault tolerance, namely recovery. The ABFT techniques to detect errors rely on the comparison of parity values computed in two ways; the parallel processing of input parity values produce output parity values comparable with parity values regenerated from the original processed outputs can apply convolutional codes for the redundancy. This method is a new approach to concurrent error correction in fault-tolerant computing systems. Chapter 1 proposes a novel computing paradigm to provide fault tolerance for numerical algorithms. The authors also present, implement, and evaluate early detection in ABFT.

Investing in Information Technology (IT) security is a critical decision in the digital age. In most organizations, it is wise to allocate a significant amount of resources to IT infrastructure. However, it is difficult to determine how much to invest in IT as well as to quantify the maximum threshold, where the rate of return of this investment begins to diminish. The main research question is: How much and what financial resources should be allocated to IT security? Chapter 2 analyzes different practices and techniques used to determine the degree of investment in IT security and recommends some suitable methods for deciding how much should be invested in IT security.

Models transform the managerial inputs into useful information for managerial decision. The Project Evaluation and Review Technique (PERT) is the most widely used model for project management. However, it requires three estimates for the duration of each activity as its input. This uncertainty in the input requirement makes the Critical Path (CP) unstable, causing major difficulties for the manager. A linear programming formulation of the project network is proposed in chapter 3 for determining a CP, based on making one estimate for the duration of each activity. Upon finding the CP, Sensitivity Analysis (SA) of Data Perturbation (DP) is performed using the constraints of the dual problem. This largest DP set of uncertainties provides the manager with a tool to deal with the simultaneous, independent, or dependent changes of the input estimates that preserves the current CP. The application of DP results to enhance the traditional approach to PERT are presented. The proposed procedure is easy to understand, easy to implement, and provides useful information for the manager. A numerical example illustrates the process.

Authenticity means that the closeness of observation matters for acceptance of new knowledge. The social norm of authenticity can have positive effects of colleagues to appreciate "better" knowledge within opportunity structures for knowledge sharing. However, how ICT influences authenticity in knowledge sharing needs more attention in research on knowledge sharing through online networks. Chapter 4 reports and discusses recent finding of how ICT (here the interactive tool GoToMeeting™) facilitates authenticity.

Information privacy concerns are a dominant concern of the information age, a concern that results from tension between the correct use of personal information and the individual's desire for their information to be private. That tension has extended to the computer-mediated work environment as employees' awareness of the ways in which management can employ technologies to monitor their email and Internet interactions has increased. These concerns have the potential to negatively impact organisational productivity and employee morale. The aim of chapter 5 is to outline some of the key issues relating to workplace surveillance and provide a balanced perspective that identifies the emerging issues and subsequent privacy concerns from the employees' perspective as well as the rationale underlying managements' decision to employ monitoring technologies in the workplace. In doing so, it attempts to progress academic understanding of this issue and enhance practitioners' understanding of the factors that influence employees' technology-related privacy concerns.

Chapter 6 discusses information security challenges encountered during the wearIT@work project and selected legal aspects of wearable computing. Wearable computing will offer interesting opportunities to improve and reengineer work processes in organizations, but can introduce alignment problems as users in organizations may adopt the new technology before organizations are prepared. Further, alignment problems posed by the emerging trend "Bring Your Own Device" (BYOD) are discussed. In addition, needed supportive legal frameworks have not yet fully addressed the new wearable computing technology. Different alignment concepts for how such challenges can be managed are discussed in the chapter.

There are many collection and application sources of identity theft. The Internet is one of the vulnerable medias for identity theft and is used, especially, as an application source of identity theft. Chapter 7 has two objectives. As the first objective, it develops a conceptual framework to prevent/control identity theft of E-Commerce (EC) in conjunction with different sources of identity theft. From this framework and shedding light on the recent literature of sources of identity theft, the authors identify global laws, controls placed on organizations, publications to develop awareness, technical management, managerial policy, risk management tools, data management, and control over employees as potential measuring items to prevent identity theft in EC. All EC organizations are struggling to control identity theft. This chapter argues that control mechanisms of identity theft have both positive and negative impacts on EC. This chapter sets its second objective to explore the integrative effect of overall identity theft control mechanisms on consumer trust, the cost of products/services, and operational performance, all of which in turn contribute to a purchase intention using E-Commerce (EC). A case study in the banking sector through a qualitative approach was conducted to verify the proposed relations, constructs, and measuring items.

Chapter 8 tests the appropriateness of the Unified Theory of Acceptance and Use of Technology (UTAUT) model in the context of end user consumption by means of an online survey with 475 respondents (24% response rate). The chapter shows which factors have the greatest impact on the adoption process of VoIP technology in the US market in addition to the interactions of the main variables in the model (Performance Expectancy, Effort Expectancy, Social Influence, and Behavioral Intention to Adopt) and whether Trust can improve the predictive value of the UTAUT model to explain intention to adopt. Partial Least Squares (PLS) is used to evaluate the interactions of the main variables. The model includes four moderator variables (Gender, Age, Experience, and Voluntariness of Use). The results support most of the relationships identified in the original UTAUT model. More specifically, Performance Expectancy appears to have the strongest influence on the Intention of a consumer to adopt a new technology. The chapter provides information about whether the inclusion of Trust can generate good results for industry.

Technology is important to software development projects; however, virtual projects are more dependent on technology than traditional co-located projects due to communication and collaboration needs. Two research studies in chapter 9 sought to determine whether seven technology-related risks pose a greater danger to virtual projects than traditional projects and to determine if technology-related risks have a high impact on project success. Results indicate that two technology-related risks exhibited a significantly greater impact on virtual IT projects: (1) inexperience with the company and its processes and (2) inadequate technical resources. Project managers need to be aware that traditional project risks can have a greater impact on virtual projects. Additionally, technology-related risks in the second study were found to have low levels of impact on project success. Results indicate, in cases where a majority of team members are experienced with the application, development technology, and project technology, the risk of technology-related issues seems to lessen.

Chapter 10 is built on two studies: Ishihara (2011) "A Forensic Authorship Classification in SMS Messages: A Likelihood Ratio-Based Approach Using N-Grams" and Ishihara (2012) "A Forensic Text Comparison in SMS Messages: A Likelihood Ratio Approach with Lexical Features." They are two of the first Likelihood Ratio (LR)-based forensic text comparison studies in forensic authorship analysis. The author attribution was modelled using N-grams in the former, whereas it was modelled using so-called lexical features in the latter. In the current study, the LRs obtained from these separate experiments are fused using a logistic regression fusion technique, and the authors report how much improvement in performance the fusion brings to the LR-based forensic text comparison system. The performance of the fused system is assessed based on the magnitude of the fused LRs using the log-likelihood-ratio cost (C_{llr}). The strength of the fused LRs is graphically presented in Tippett plots and compared with those of the original LRs. The chapter demonstrates that the fused system outperforms the original systems.

Hamid Nemati
The University of North Carolina at Greensboro, USA

REFERENCES

Alderman, E., & Kennedy, C. (1997). *The right to privacy*. New York: Random House.

Ishihara, S. (2011). A forensic authorship classification in SMS messages: A likelihood ratio based approach using n-gram. In *Proceedings of the Australasian Language Technology Workshop 2011* (pp. 47-56). Academic Press.

Ishihara, S. (2012). Probabilistic evaluation of SMS messages as forensic evidence: Likelihood ration based approach with lexical features. *International Journal of Digital Crime and Forensics*, *4*(3), 47–57. doi:10.4018/jdcf.2012070104

Mason, R. O. (1986). Four ethical issues of the information age. *Management Information Systems Quarterly*, *10*(1), 4–12. doi:10.2307/248873

The Guardian. (2014). Retrieved February 21, 2014 from http://www.theguardian.com/world/the-nsa-files

U.S. Supreme court, Olmstead v. U.S., 277 U.S. 438 (1928).

Westin, A. (1967). *Privacy and freedom*. New York: Atheneum.

Chapter 1
A General Framework of Algorithm–Based Fault Tolerance Technique for Computing Systems

Hodjatollah Hamidi
K. N. Toosi University of Technology, Iran

ABSTRACT

The Algorithm-Based Fault Tolerance (ABFT) approach transforms a system that does not tolerate a specific type of faults, called the fault-intolerant system, to a system that provides a specific level of fault tolerance, namely recovery. The ABFT philosophy leads directly to a model from which error correction can be developed. By employing an ABFT scheme with effective convolutional code, the design allows high throughput as well as high fault coverage. The ABFT techniques that detect errors rely on the comparison of parity values computed in two ways. The parallel processing of input parity values produce output parity values comparable with parity values regenerated from the original processed outputs and can apply convolutional codes for the redundancy. This method is a new approach to concurrent error correction in fault-tolerant computing systems. This chapter proposes a novel computing paradigm to provide fault tolerance for numerical algorithms. The authors also present, implement, and evaluate early detection in ABFT.

DOI: 10.4018/978-1-4666-4856-2.ch001

INTRODUCTION

ABFT, proposed by Huang and Abraham (1984), is a fault tolerance scheme that uses Concurrent Error Detection (techniques at a functional level). System level applications of ABFT techniques have also been investigated (Acree, Ullah, Karia, Rahmeh, and Abraham, 1993; Banerjee, Rahmeh, Stunkel, Nair, Roy, and Abraham, 1990). These techniques assume a general fault model which allows any single module in the system to be faulty (Huang, and Abraham, 1984). ABFT is widely applicable and it has proved its cost-effectiveness especially when applied to array processor (Jou, and Abraham, 1986). Fault detection and diagnosis are integral parts of any fault tolerance scheme. There are two ways to detect faults:

1. By off-line checking.
2. By concurrent checking.

In an off-line checking scheme, the process is checked for its correctness while it is not performing any useful computation. This approach has the beneficial that the performance of the computer will be unaffected by the checking operation; however, this kind of checking can detect only permanent faults. Transient faults, which constitute 76-81% of faults in a Digital system (Jou, and Abraham, 1986), will not be detected by off-line checks. So that detects transient faults, concurrent error detection schemes such as duplication and comparisons have been suggested. It has been observed that ABFT techniques are very cost effective when applied to process elements. It may be noted, however, that the application of ABFT techniques is not limited to multi-process systems; they are also applicable to algorithms running on single process, probably with less efficiency. An algorithm executing on a multiple process system is specified as a sequence of operations performed on a set of processes in some discrete time steps.

CHARACTERISTICS OF ABFT

ABFT technique is distinctive by three characteristics:

1. Encoding the input sequence.
2. Plan again of the algorithm to act on the encoded input sequence.
3. Distribution of the redundant computational steps among the individual computational units in order to adventure maximum parallelism.

The input sequences are encoded in the form of error detecting or correcting codes. The modified algorithm operates on the encoded data and produces encoded data output, from which useful information can be recovered very easily. Obviously, the modified algorithm will take more time to operate on the encoded data when compared to the original algorithm; this time overhead must not be excessive. The task distribution among the processing elements should be done in such a way that any malfunction in a processing element will affect only a small portion of the data, which can be detected and corrected using the properties of the encoding. *Signal* processing has been the major application area of ABFT until now, even though the technique is applicable in other types of computations as well. Since the major computational requirements for many important real-time signals processing tasks can be formulated using a common set of matrix computations, it is important to have fault tolerance techniques for various matrix operations (Nair, and Abraham, 1990). Coding techniques based on ABFT have already been proposed for various computations such as matrix operations (Huang, and Abraham, 1984; Chen, and Dongarra, 2008; Ashouei, and Chatterjee, 2010), FFT (Jou, and Abraham, 1988; Biernat, 2010), QR factorization, and singular value decomposition (Salfner, Lenk, and Malek, 2010). Real number

Figure 1. General architecture of ABFT

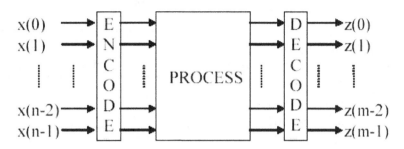

codes such as the Checksum (Huang, and Abraham, 1984) and Weighted Checksum codes (Jou, and Abraham,1986) have been proposed for fault-tolerant matrix operations such as matrix transposition, addition, multiplication and matrix-vector multiplication. Application of these techniques in processor arrays and multiprocessor systems has been investigated by various researchers (Banerjee, Rahmeh, Stunkel, Nair, Roy, and Abraham, 1990). Figure 1, (Moosavie Nia, and Mohammadi, 2007), shows the basic architecture of an ABFT system. Existing techniques use various coding schemes to provide information redundancy needed for error detection and correction. As a result this encoding/decoding must be considered as the overhead introduced by ABFT. The coding algorithm is closely related to the running process and is often defined by real number codes generally of the block types (Baylis, 1998). Systematic codes are of most interest because the fault detection scheme can be superimposed on the original process box with the least changes in the algorithm and architecture. In most previous ABFT applications, the process to be protected is often a linear system. In this chapter we assume a more common case consisting linear or nonlinear systems but still constrain ourselves to static systems.

Various methods such as checksum encoding, weighted checksum encoding and average checksum codes have been proposed for fault-tolerant matrix operations. These encoding schemes are especially suitable for computations in process

arrays (Hakkarinen, and Chen, 2010). The use of the checksum codes is limited due to the inflexibility of the encoding schemes and also due to potential numerical problems. Numerical errors may also be misconstrued as errors due to physical faults in the system. A generalization of the existing schemes has been suggested as a solution to these shortcomings (Hamidi, Vafaei, and Monadjemi, 2009; 2010;2011;2012).

We make the following contributions in this chapter: In section 2, we discuss error control coding, In section 3, we propose the architecture of ABFT, In section 4, we discuss the error correction system, In section 5, results and evaluations are presented and In section 6, discussion of the conclusions.

ERROR CONTROL CODING

A *fault* is any condition that causes a malfunction in a single process while performing operations. Some of the major causes which result in faults are: (1) manufacturing defects such as photolithography errors, deficiencies in process quality and improper designs; (2) wear out in the field due to electro migration, hot electron injection etc.; (3) environmental effects such as alpha particles and cosmic radiations (Veeravalli,2009; Choi, et al, 1996). The manifestations of these faults are called errors (Choi, Dongarra, and Walker, 1996). An *error* is any discrepancy between the expected result of an operation and the actual result of the operation. Since a process performs different types of operations, a fault in the process may result in errors in any of those operations. For example, if the process is performing some data computation, a fault in the process may produce a wrong value of the data. If the process is trying to read an address location, a fault may cause wrong address selection (addressing fault). We assume Byzantine type of faults (Ekici, Yildirim, and Poyraz, 2009). In order to detect the presence of a fault in a process, we resort to a technique called *data* value *checking* (Dongarra, and Whaley, 1995; Kumar, and Makur, 2010). Here, a fault is detected by detecting errors in the final data value generated by the process. One observes that the problem of detection of various faults such as addressing faults can be translated to the problem of detecting errors in the computed results (Rexford, and Jha, 1992; Elnozahy, Johnson, and Zwaenepoel, 1992). Therefore, all the faults are treated uniformly as those corrupting the final, computed result. On the other hand, if a particular fault does not necessarily produce any errors in the final data value computed by that process, we may disregard the presence of that fault. The computed result of a process may be checked by one or more other processes in the system. Processes which check the output of one or more processes are called *check, evaluating* processes or, in short, check, *processes*. We assume that any process in the system is capable of performing useful computations, check evaluation, or both. A *check* on the data element is any combination of hardware and software procedures performed on the data by processes which use the encoding of the data to generate a "pass" or "fail" output. All error correcting codes are based on the same basic principle: *redundancy* is added to information in order to correct any errors that may occur in the process of transmission or storage. In a basic (and practical) form, redundant bits are appended

Figure 2. A systematic block encoding for error correction

k Bits Data	(n-k) Bits Redundancy

to information bits to obtain a coded sequence or *code word*. For the purpose of illustration, a code word obtained by encoding with a *block code* is shown in Figure 2, (Morelos-Zaragoza, 2006). Such an encoding is said to be *systematic*. Systematic encoding means that the information bits always appear in the first (leftmost) k positions of a code word. The remaining (rightmost) $n - k$ bits in a code word are a function of the information bits, and provide redundancy that can be used for error correction and/or detection purposes. The set of all code sequences is called an *error correcting code*, and will henceforth be denoted by C (Morelos-Zaragoza, 2006).

The elements of the code are called *code words*. *Decoding* is an invertible process which transforms messages into code words, i.e. different messages are transformed into different code words. *Decoding* is performed in two consecutive steps: First, on the basis of a *decision rule*, the received word v is transformed into a decoded code word *c'* then according to the inverse of encoding, a u' message is assigned to the decoded code word c. The most frequently used decision rule chooses a code word *c'* which has the shortest Hamming distance to the received word *v*, i.e.

$$d(c', v) = \min_{c \in C} d(c, v) \qquad (1)$$

The minimum Hamming distance between the code words of a code is a very important parameter. It is called *code distance* and is denoted as $d_{\min}$. Thus, formally

$$d_{\min} = \min_{c \neq c', c', c \in C} d(c, c') \tag{2}$$

The aim of *error detection* is to decide whether the received word is a code word or not. If the number of errors within one received code word is not more than t and $d_{\min} > t$, then it is certain that no combination of errors results in another valid code word. This is very important because it would not be possible to detect errors on the receiving side if the received code was a false code word. Suppose that vectors $g_1, g_2 ... g_k$ form a base of the linear space C, i.e. which with these vectors an arbitrary c element of C can be generated as

$$c = \sum_{i=1}^{k} u_i g_i, i = 1, 2, 3, ..., K \tag{3}$$

Let us build a matrix G with size $k \times n$, the rows of which are $g_1, g_2 ... g_k$. Coding is done by $c = u \times G$ and the matrix G is called obviously as *generator matrix*. An (n, k) code C is called *systematic* if the first k bits of its code word correspond to the message. Generator matrix of a systematic code is unambiguous and according to the rules of matrix multiplication it is obviously of the following form:

$$G = (I_k, B) \tag{4}$$

where I_k is a unity matrix of size $k \times k$, B is a matrix of size $k \times (n-k)$. Structure of the code word belonging to the message u is as follows

$$c = (u_1, u_2 ... u_k, c_{k+1}, c_{k+2} ... c_n) \tag{5}$$

The segment of the first k coordinates of the code word is called the *message segment* and the segment of the last $n-k$ coordinates is called the *parity segment*. To select code words of C out of a set of 2^n binary vectors n bit long, an $H_{(n-k) \times n}$

binary matrix can be assigned to the linear code C. For this matrix

$$Hc^T = 0 \tag{6}$$

is true if and only if $\mathbf{c}$ is element of C. (T stands for the transposed matrix).

A matrix with such a characteristic is called a *parity-check matrix*. If the code is systematic then

$$H = (A, I_{n-k}) \tag{7}$$

where

$$A = -BT \tag{8}$$

so that

$$HG^T = 0 \tag{9}$$

Let $\mathbf{c}$ be the code word sent and $\mathbf{v}$ the word received. The difference of the two vectors is called the *error vector* (e). Notice that using (6)

$$Hv^T = H(c+e)^T = Hc^T + He^T = He^T \tag{10}$$

i.e. the value of Hv^T is dependent only on the error vector and is independent of the code word. The following quantity

$$s_{1 \times (n-k)} = e_{1 \times n} . H^T_{n \times (n-k)} \tag{11}$$

is called the *syndrome* of the error vector e. Syndromes of the code words are 0. Row vector eH^T corresponds to the column vector He^T.

ARCHITECTURE OF ABFT

To achieve fault detection and correction properties of convolutional code in a linear process with the minimum overhead computations (Moosavie

Figure 3. Our architecture of ABFT

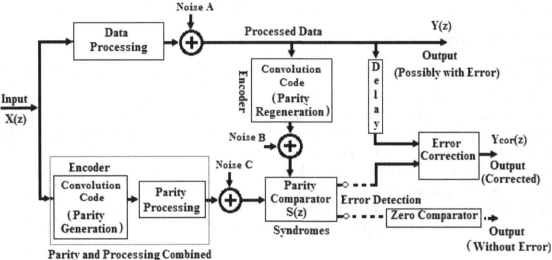

Nia, and Mohammadi, 2007; Turmon, Granat and Katz, 2000; Turmon, Granat, Katz and Lou, 2003), we propose the architecture in Figure 3. For error correction purposes, redundancy must be inserted in some form and, using the ABFT, convolutional parity codes will be employed. A systematic form of convolutional codes is especially profitable in the ABFT detection plan because no redundant transformations are needed to achieve the processed data after the detection operations. This Figure summarizes an ABFT technique employing a systematic convolutional code to define the parity values. The k is the basic block size of the input data, and n is block size of the output data, new data samples are accepted and (n - k) new parity values produced.

We have modeled faults in a linear process block with module noise A while the encoder and structured redundancy noises are modeled with modules B and C. Since these two last noises contribute in syndrome additively we can delete one of them without any degradation (Moosavie Nia, and Mohammadi, 2007). Convolutional codes are usually used over the transmission channels, through which both information and parity bits

are sent. The upper way, Figure 3, is the processed data flow which passes through the process block (data processing block) and then feeds the convolutional encoder (parity regeneration) to make parity values. On the other hand, the comparable parity values are generated efficiently and directly from the inputs (parity and processing combined, see Figure 3), without producing the original outputs. The difference in the comparable two parity values, which are computed in different ways, is called the syndrome; the syndrome sequence is a stream of zero or near zero values. The convolutional code's structure is designed to produce distinct syndromes for a large class of errors appearing in the processing outputs. Figure 3 employs convolutional code parity in detecting and correcting processing errors.

CLASS OF CONVOLUTIONALAL CODE: BINARY BURST-CORRECTING CONVOLUTIONALAL

We consider only systematic forms of convolutional codes because the normal operation of

Process block is not change and there is no need to decoding for obtaining true outputs. In addition Convolutional codes have good correcting characteristics because of memory in their encoding structure (Costello and Lin, 2004). A burst of length d is explained as a vector whose nonzero components are confined to d consecutive numeral situation, the first and last are nonzero (Morelos-Zaragoza, 2006), A burst apply to a group of errors which is characteristic of unforeseeable effects of errors in data computation. Costello et al. (2004) has shown that a sequence of error bits $e_{d+1}, e_{d+2}, ..., e_{d+a}$ is called a burst of length a concerning a guard space of length b if $e_{d+1} = e_{d+a} = 1$, and the b bits preceding e_{d+1} and the b bits following e_{d+a} are zero; and the a bits from e_{d+1} through e_{d+a} include no subsequence of b zero. Also, for any convolutional code of rate R that corrects all bursts of length a or less relative to a guard space of length b, $\frac{b}{a} \geq \frac{1+R}{1-R}$.

Binary burst-correcting convolutional codes at structure of the convolutional codes are appropriate and efficient in detecting and correcting errors from internal computing failures. Binary burst-correcting convolutional codes need guard bands (error-free regions) before and after bursts of errors, particularly if error correction is needed (Costello and Lin, 2004). One class of burst-correcting codes is the Berlekamp-Preparata-Massey (BPM) codes (Costello and Lin, 2004; Morelos-Zaragoza, 2006) that have many appropriate characteristic with regard to failure error-detecting. Their design properties vouch for detecting the onset of errors due to failures, regardless of any error-free region following the beginning of a burst of errors. Consider designing an $(n, k = n-1, m)$ systematic convolutional encoder to correct a phased burst error confined to a single block of n bits relative to a guard space of m error free blocks. One parity value is assigned for each input of $(n-1)$ values. Their constraint

length is $l = 2n-1$.to design such a code assure that each correctable error value $[E]_m = [e_0, e_1, ..., e_m]$ results in a distinct syndrome $[S]_m = [s_0, s_1, ..., s_m]$ .this infer that each error values whit $e_0 \neq 0$ and $e_d = 0, d = 1,2,...,m$ must produce a separate syndrome and that each of these syndromes must be separate from the syndrome caused by any error value with $e_0 = 0$ and a single block $e_d \neq 0, d = 1,2,...,m$. therefore, the first error block e_0 can be correctly decoded if first (m+1) blocks of e contain at most one non-zero block. An $(n, k = n-1, m)$ systematic code is depicted by the set of generator polynomials $g_1^{(n-1)}(D), g_2^{(n-1)}(D),..., g_{n-1}^{(n-1)}(D)$. The generator matrix of a systematic convolutional code, G, is a semi-finite matrix evolving m finite sub-matrixes as:

$$G = \begin{bmatrix} IP_0 & 0P_1 & 0P_2 & ... & 0P_m & & \\ & IP_0 & 0P_1 & ... & 0P_{m-1} & 0P_m & \\ & & IP_0 & ... & 0P_{m-2} & 0P_{m-1} & 0P_m \\ & & & \cdot & & \cdot & \\ & & & & \cdot & & \cdot \\ & & & & & \cdot & \\ \end{bmatrix}$$

$$(12)$$

Where I and 0 are identity and all zero $k \times k$ matrixes respectively (Viterbi et al., 1985) and P_i with $i = 0$ to m is a $k \times (n-k)$ matrix. The parity-check matrix, (13), is constructed from a basic binary matrix, labeled H_0, a $2n \times n$ binary matrix containing the skew-identity matrix in its top n rows, (13).

$$H_m = [H_0, H_1, ..., H_m] \qquad (13)$$

Where H_0 is an $n \times (m+1)$ matrix, (14):

$$H_0 = \begin{bmatrix} g_{1,0}^{(n-1)} & g_{1,1}^{(n-1)} & \cdots & g_{1,m}^{(n-1)} \\ \cdot & \cdot & & \cdot \\ \cdot & \cdot & & \cdot \\ \cdot & \cdot & & \cdot \\ g_{n-1,0}^{(n-1)} & g_{n-1,1}^{(n-1)} & & g_{n-1,m}^{(n-1)} \\ 1 & 0 & \cdots & 0 \end{bmatrix} \qquad (14)$$

For $0 < d \le$ m, we obtain H_d from H_{d-1} by shifting H_{d-1} one column to the right and deleting the column. In a mathematical form, this operation can be expressed as:

$$H_0 = \begin{bmatrix} 0 & 1 & 0 & \cdots & 0 \\ 0 & 0 & 1 & \cdots & 0 \\ \cdot & \cdot & \cdot & \cdot & \cdot \\ \cdot & \cdot & \cdot & \cdot & \cdot \\ \cdot & \cdot & \cdot & \cdot & \cdot \\ 0 & 0 & 0 & \cdots & 1 \\ 0 & 0 & 0 & \cdots & 0 \end{bmatrix} = H_{d-1}T \qquad (15)$$

Where T is an (m+1)×(m+1) shifting matrix. Another important parity check type of matrix is put together using H_0 and its d successive downward shifted versions (Berlekamp, 1962; Massey, 1965). However, all necessary information for forming the systematic parity check matrix H^T is contained in the basis matrix H_0. The lower triangular part of this matrix, (n-1) rows, (n-1) columns, hold binary values selected by a construction method to produce desirable detection and correction properties (Berlekamp, 1962). For systematic codes, the parity check matrix submatrices H_m in (13) have special forms that control how these equations are formed.

$$H_0^T = [P_0 | I_{n-k}], \; H_i^T = [P_i | 0_{n-k}] \; i = 1, 2, \ldots, L. \qquad (16)$$

Where I_{n-k} and 0_{n-k} are identity and all zero k ×k matrixes respectively and P_i is a (n-k)×k matrix. However, in an alternate view, the respective rows of H_0 contain the parity sub-matrices P_i needed in H^T, (13) and (16).

$$H_0 = \begin{bmatrix} P_0 & | & I_1 \\ P_1 & | & 0 \\ P_2 & | & 0 \\ \cdot & \cdot & \cdot \\ \cdot & \cdot & \cdot \\ \cdot & \cdot & \cdot \\ P_{L-1} & | & 0 \\ P_L & | & 0 \end{bmatrix} \qquad (17)$$

The n columns of H_0 are designed as an n dimensional subspace of a full (*2n*) dimension space comparable with the size of the row space. Using this notation, we can write the syndrome as

$$[S]_m = [E]_m \cdot [H^T]_m = e_0 H_0 + e_1 H_1 + \ldots + e_m H_m$$

$$= e_0 H_0 + e_1 H_0 T + \ldots + e_m H_0 T^m = \begin{bmatrix} s_i \\ s_{i+1} \\ \cdot \\ \cdot \\ \cdot \\ s_{i+n} \end{bmatrix} \qquad (18)$$

$[S]_m$ is a syndrome vector with (*l+1*) values, in this class of codes (n-k) equal 1. The design properties of this class of codes assure any contribution of errors in one observed vector, $[E]_m$, appearing in syndrome vector $[S]_m$ is linearly independent of syndromes caused by ensuing error vectors $[E]_{i+1}$, $[E]_{i+2}$,..., $[E]_{i+l}$ in adjacent observed vectors. At any time a single burst of errors is limited to set $[E]_m$, correction is possible by separating the error effects. These errors in $[E]_m$ are recognized with the top n items in $[S]_m$.

$$[E]_m = \begin{bmatrix} e_{i,1} \\ e_{i,2} \\ . \\ . \\ . \\ e_{i,n} \end{bmatrix} \qquad (19)$$

Then error values recognition

$$e_{i,n} = s_i, e_{i,n-1} = s_{i+1},..., e_{i,1} = s_{i+n+1} \qquad (20)$$

If there are nonzero error bursts in $[E]_{i+1}$, $[E]_{i+2}$, ..., $[E]_{i+l}$, their accumulate contribution is in a separate subspace never permitting the syndrome vector $[S]_m$ to be all zeros. The beginning of errors, even if they overwhelm the correcting capability of the code, can be detected. This distinction between correctable and only detectable error bursts is achieved by using an annihilating matrix, denoted F_0^T, which is $n \times 2n$ and has a defining property, $F_0^T H_0 = 0_n$. Hence, it is possible to check whether a syndrome vector $[S]_m$ represents correctable errors, $F_0^T \cdot [S]_m = 0$, then $[S]_m$ contain correctable model. For optimum burst error correcting code, $b/a = (1+R)/(1-R)$. For the preceding case with R = $(n-1)/n$ and $b = m.n = m.a$, this implies that $\dfrac{b}{a} = m = 2n-1$

H_0 is an $n \times 2n$ matrix.

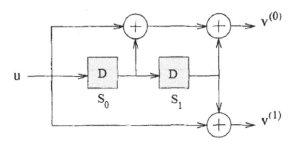

DECODING

There are several effective decoding algorithms for convolutional codes, but the most popular is the Viterbi algorithm, discovered by Andrew Viterbi in 1967. Viterbi decoders are now available on single integrated circuits (VLSI) from several manufacturers. Viterbi decoders are impractical for long constraint length codes because decoding complexity increases rapidly with constraint length. For long constraint length codes ($K > 9$), a second decoding algorithm called *sequential decoding* is often used. However, for linear block codes obtained from terminating convolutional codes and long information sequences, *maximum-likelihood decoder* (MLD) is simply too complex and inefficient to implement. An efficient solution to the decoding problem is a dynamic programming algorithm known as the *Viterbi algorithm*, also known as the *Viterbi decoder* (VD).

Example: Consider the convolutional encoder depicted in Figure 4, (Morelos-Zaragoza, 2006). For analysis and decoding purposes, this encoder is described in Table 1, (Morelos-Zaragoza, 2006).

ERROR CORRECTION SYSTEM

Error correction system, Figure 5, provides a more detailed view of some subassemblies in Figure 3,

Table 1. Input bits, state transitions and output bits

Initial State	Data	Final State	Outputs
$s_0[i] \, s_1[i]$	$u[i]$	$s_0[i+1] \, s_1[i+1]$	$v^{(0)}[i]v^{(1)}[i]$
00	0	00	00
00	1	10	11
01	0	00	11
01	1	10	00
10	0	01	10
10	1	11	01
11	0	01	01
11	1	11	10

in Figure 5. The processed data $\bar{d}_i$ can include errors $\bar{e}_i$ and the error correction system will subtract their estimates $\bar{e}'_i$ as indicated in the corrected data output of the error correction system. If one of the computed parity values, $\bar{p}_{u_i}$ or $\bar{p}_{l_i}$ in Figure 5, comes from a failed subsystem, the error correction system's inputs may be incorrect. Since the data are correct under the single failed subsystem assumption, the data contain no errors and the error correction system is operating correctly. The error correction system will observe the errors in the syndromes and properly estimate them as limited to other positions. Moreover, an excessive number of error estimates $\{ \bar{e}'_i \}$ could be deduct from correct data, yielding $\{ \bar{d}_i - \bar{e}'_i \}$ values at the Error Correction System's output, which the regeneration of parity values produces $\{ \bar{p}'_{u_i} \}$, as shown in Figure 5 at the final output.

$$\bar{p}'_{u_i} = \sum_{j=0}^{l} p_j (\bar{d}_{i-j} - \bar{e}'_{i-j}) \qquad (21)$$

Simultaneously, if the errors do not affect the parallel parity values $\{ \bar{p}_{l_i} \}$, its value is correct.

$$\bar{p}_{l_i} = \sum_{k=0}^{l} p_k \bar{d}_{i-k} \qquad (22)$$

The output checking syndromes $\{ \bar{s}'_i \}$ will become nonzero at the beginning of errors because of the burst-detecting nature of the code.

$$\bar{s}'_i = \bar{p}'_{u_i} - \bar{p}_{l_i} = \sum_{j=0}^{l} (-1) p_j \bar{e}_{i-j} \qquad (23)$$

Therefore, there are several indicators that will detect errors in the error correction system's input syndromes $\{ \bar{s}_i \}$. The checking syndromes $\{ \bar{s}'_i \}$ must indicate the beginning of errors, so the error correction system cannot subtract incorrect, even overwhelming errors from otherwise correct data without observation. The limited checking features inserted in and around the corrector will always detect its unsuitable behavior.

RESULTS

It is an easy matter to construct MATLAB to implement the convolutional codes. Thus, a series of simulations provide appraise of the probability of detection and failure. Several simulation schemes modeling the ABFT method for detecting numerical level errors were described in MATLAB, version 2010a, where the modeling errors were assumed Gaussian with zero means and statistically independent from symbol to symbol. Errors

Figure 5. Block diagram of the ABFT technique along with error correction system

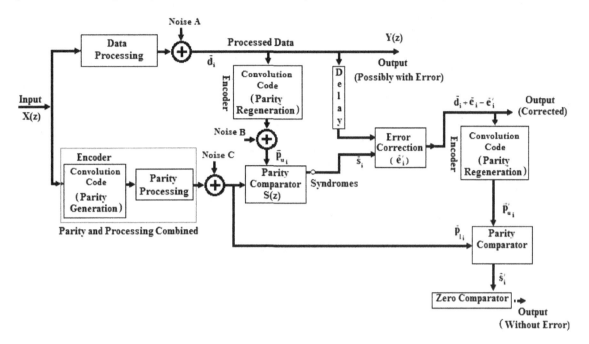

were allowed in the parity values computed by the combined data parity generator, Figure 3, and in the processed data symbols. Very researches were performed to verify the iterative decoding technique. The error modeling provides a strong set of conditions of failure effects and is completely general. A convolutional code with parameters (6, 5, 11) based on the Berlekamp-Preparata -Massey (BPM) class of binary burst-correcting convolutional codes (Costello and Lin, 2004) was employed. This code is capable of correcting any burst up to k bits long within a constraint length. The nonzero weights in parity generating matrix, which has one column because $(n - k) = 1$ are listed by the component index j with row $j = 0$ at the top: $j = 6, 10, 14, 18, 22, 30, 39, 47, 52, 54, 57, 59, 60, 64, 65, 66, 67$. In Figure 6 shows four syndrome sequences resulting from different processing error sample for a code that is used in above convolutional code. The code yields one syndrome value for each $k = 5$ input samples and employs a memory of 12 groups of samples, and two of the

sequences result from processing errors that create a ramp in the $k = 5$ input samples (Figure 6 (a)). One sequence results from an increasing ramp with respective values 1, 2, 3, 4, 5(Figure 6 (b)), while the other corresponds to a decreasing ramp with values 5, 4, 3, 2, 1 (Figure 6 (c)). The two other sequences are related to unity error values in a single position, one involving position 1 and the other concerned with adjacent position 2. It is clear that the syndrome sequences observed over the memory of the code are obviously different.

The matrices for the single-step were computed based on round-off variance at the processed output (data processing output) $v_u = 0.10$; round-off variance at parity processing output $v_d = 0.05$. The step variances, when the detection parameters exceed their thresholds, were taken as $\tau = 500$ and $\kappa = 500$ (step in variances due to failures). Large errors are detected by examining the magnitude of the respective syndromes and comparing against thresholds five times the standard deviation of

Figure 6. Syndrome values

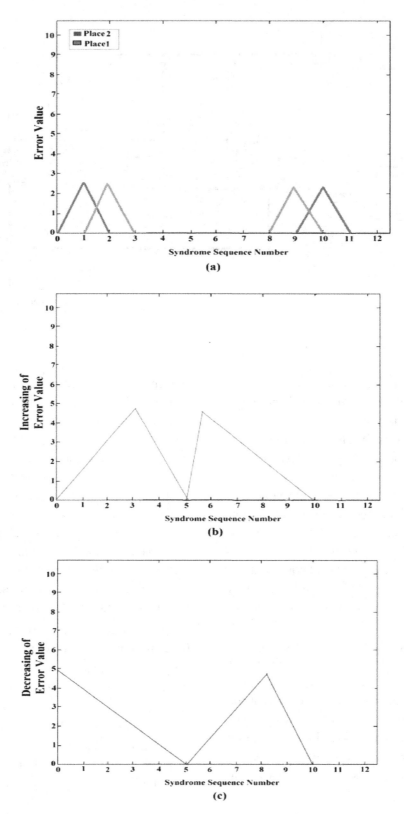

(a)

(b)

(c)

Figure 7. (a) Correction values for error in position 3, (b) Correction values for error in parity, (c) Correction values for errors due to ramp bursting

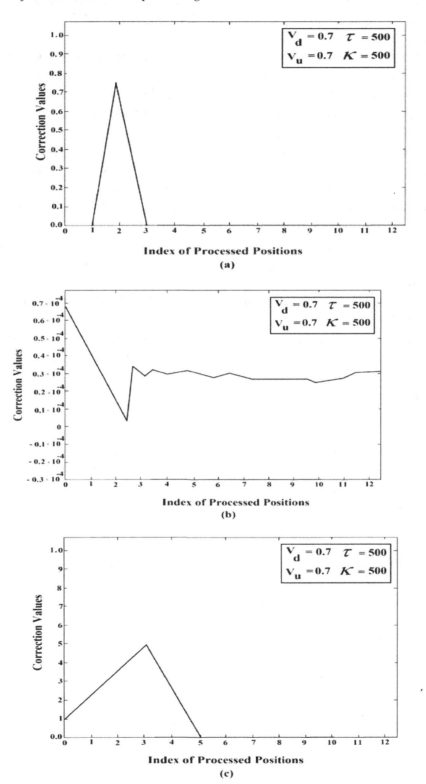

syndrome values when only low levels of round-off noise appear. Numerous examples were explored and the magnitude of the increases in τ and κ can be taken several orders of magnitude above the normal round-off variances v_u and v_d but yield the same correction levels, indicating good performance in the face of some uncertainty of the underlying noise statistics. The correction behaviors of various types of failures were tested starting with a single bit being in error at the processing output. When an error value was added to the processed output, the error correction block corrected it to within the variance of the round-off level, and Figure 7 (a) shows results associated with a unit error introduced in position 3. Figure 7 (a) depicts the correction value plotted on a linear scale. The abscissa indicates the symbol index position of the processed data, and the correction peak is in the proper place with virtually unit value (~0.998434...). Figure 7 (b) displays the feeble reaction to the error in the parity position at innovation index 1. In order to demonstrate the burst-correcting capability of the system, a series of consecutive errors were added to k=5 contiguous positions representing a block of processed outputs. The added values were a ramp starting with 1 and ending with 5 in the last position. Figure 7 (c) employs a linear scale to show the correction values for this ramp burst. The correction values match the ramp burst within four orders of magnitude, yet the corrections applied to the unaffected positions following the burst represent the corrector's attempt to track only round-off noise. A large number of samples randomly corrupted by round-off noise and large fault modeling errors were passed through a MatLab simulation of the corrector. A wide range of state noise variances was used and the measurement noise variance and step increases in both variances were tied to this one variance v_u.

ERROR CORRECTION AND MEAN SQUARE ERROR (MSE) PERFORMANCE

The decoding of finite-field convolution codes involves recursive algorithms. The finite size of the underlying encoder's state space limits the number of metrics that must be handled, even though the algorithm employs real number processing to recursively update the state metric's estimates at every stage. In contrast, real-number convolution codes have infinite state-space size, both theoretically and practically. Moreover, the presence of numerical round-off error is a second form of disruptive influence not present in decoding finite-field-based convolution codes. On the other hand, real convolution codes theory, which is predicated on a minimum mean-square error criterion, seems a natural choice for "decoding" (correcting) the outputs of a linear processing algorithm protected by real convolution codes. This chapter demonstrates how real convolution codes can be used for the correction of errors when the error-correcting capabilities are determined by a real convolution code. The protection designed for convolution encoder was implemented using computer software resources. The error detection is implemented restricted only in the encoder side. The error source corrupted the system by changing data bits of the code stream at random locations. The error rate is varies is a typical range from 10^{-4} to 10^{-1}. Since the error correction is not implemented in this chapter, the alternate form of error correction is repeat encoding for the corrupted blocks. The error correction performance is evaluated based on the Mean Square Error (MSE). Figure 8 shows the quality performance curves of the convolution encoder with and without error correction. The dash line and solid line curves present the reconstruction performance of input with and without repeat encoding request, respectively, versus error rate.

Figure 8. Quality performance curves with and without repeat encoding request

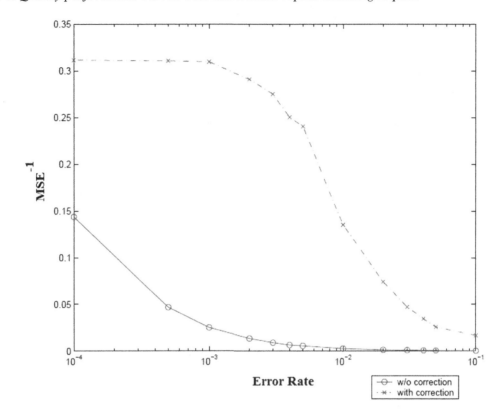

As a matter of fact, the fidelity is much improved when the error correction system is implemented.

SIMULATIONS AND EXPERIMENT RESULTS

Simulations are carried out on the set of 10,000 blocks. These blocks are generated by the random number generator that is shown in the code. Figure 9 plots the peak and the overall mean square error (MSE). An internal word length of 20 bits has been found to be adequate.

Figure 10 shows how the errors are reflected at the checker output (comparator). The top Figure shows a very small difference between the two parity values $\bar{p}_{u_i}$ and $\bar{p}_{l_i}$. The reason for the

nonzero differences is round off errors due to the finite answer of computing system. In the bottom Figure, the values of $| \bar{p}_{l_i} - \bar{p}_{u_i} |$ reflect errors occurred. If the error threshold is setup low enough, then most of the errors can be detected by the comparator; however, if we set the threshold too low, the comparator may pick up the round-off errors and consider those to be the errors due to the computer-induced errors. Thus, we need to find a good threshold, which separates the errors due to computer analysis limited and the computer-induced errors.

The simulation code randomly inserts a burst of errors in each block of input symbols, representing an encoded block. The choice of the burst is controlled by probability parameter ρ. Once an error situation is established in the simulation, n

Figure 9. Peak (a) and overall (b) mean square error vs. word length

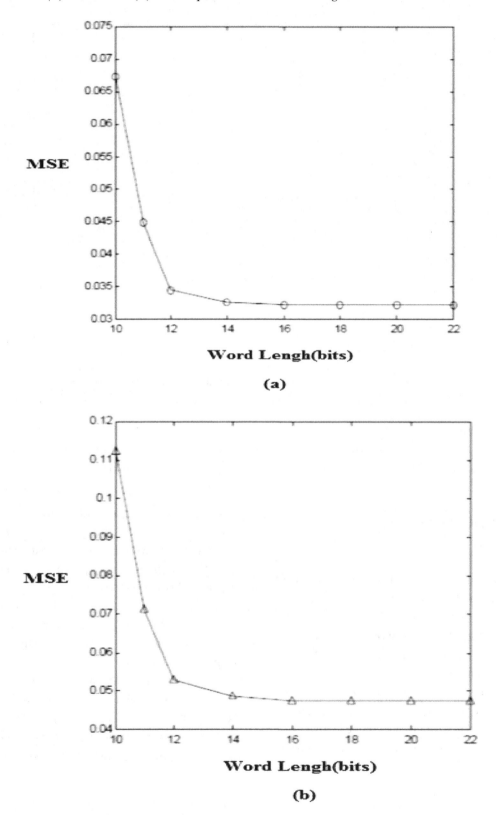

Figure 10. The responding to errors (computer-induced errors): (a) no errors (b) errors and the difference between the two parity values $\bar{p}_{u_i}$ and $\bar{p}_{l_i}$

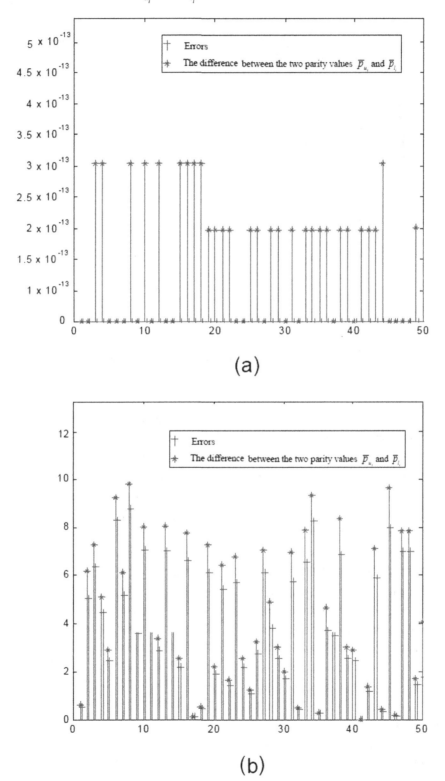

(a)

(b)

Figure 11. Detection and un-detection probabilities for two codes with R=3/4 and 6/7

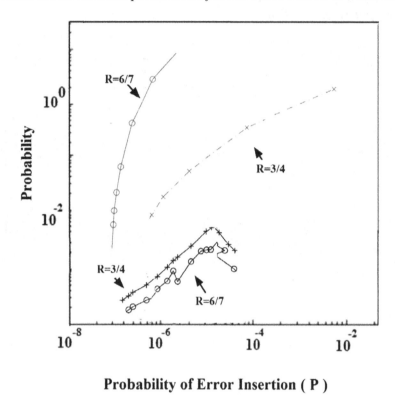

Probability of Error Insertion (P)

symbols representing a burst are determined using a uniform distribution and then are added to the n code symbols to model a burst. Many simulation steps are executed at various error rates ρ. For a high value of ρ, the error bursts are frequent enough that they may sometimes happen so close as to violate the protective band requirement for correction, leading to incorrect. A typical test used $n=6$ with $\rho=10^{-3}$ and employed 10^4 code word blocks. The experimental ratio of bursts introduced in one run of 10^4 is 0.000110, and the experimental conditional probability of correction is 0.969890, whereas that of failure was 0.030110. When the probability of a burst is lowered to $\rho=10^{-6}$, there are no failures for long runs. Moreover, statistically defined numerical errors are inserted randomly in the parity and data symbols. The inherent memory in the parity regeneration from data allows errors to produce large syndrome values beyond the first block in which they first appear. The simulation results are shown in Figure 11. Each estimation point employed 10^4 data blocks of k symbols, $k.\ 10^4$ symbols overall. Errors were inserted according to probability p, statistically independently for all positions. The probability of detection is the joint probability of detecting an error that is really present while the probability of un-detection is the joint probability of no detection when an error is there. The curves in Figure 11 for detection and un-detection probabilities are as the probability of error insertions p is varied, it is shown detection and miss probabilities for two codes with $R=3/4$ and $6/7$. The detection curves are separated because the rate at which errors occur in any blocking of data and parity symbols depends on n and the symbol error rate p. The two curves have respective block sizes of four and six. At high insertion rates p, there are on average more opportunities for un-detection which are masked by adjacent large errors that are detected in the same data block. Hence, the miss probabilities tend to decrease at high insertion rates.

CONCLUSION

In this chapter we present method for employ convolutional codes into systematic forms and evaluating them with a class of convolutional codes, which is based on burst-correcting codes, and bounds on the ABFT redundant computations are given. Convolutional codes can be used efficiently for detecting the errors in numerical processing systems. The processing system is protected through parity sequences specified by a high rate real convolutional code.

ACKNOWLEDGMENT

We are grateful to the comments from the Mrs Mahbobeh Meshkinfam that significantly improved the quality of our research.

REFERENCES

Acree, R. K., Ullah, N., Karia, A., Rahmeh, J. T., & Abraham, J. A. (1993). An object-oriented approach for implementing algorithm-based fault tolerance. In *Proceedings of the 12th Annual International Phoenix Computers and Communications Conference* (pp. 210-216). Academic Press.

Ashouei, M., & Chatterjee, A. (2009). Checksum-based probabilistic transient-error compensation for linear digital systems. *IEEE Transactions on Very Large Scale Integration Systems, 17*(10), 1447–1460. doi:10.1109/TVLSI.2008.2004587

Banerjee, P., Rahmeh, P. J. T., Stunkel, C. B., Nalr, V. S. S., Roy, K., & Abraham, J. A. (1990). Algorithm-based fault tolerance on a hypercube multiprocessor. *IEEE Transactions on Computers, 39*(9), 1132–1145. doi:10.1109/12.57055

Baylis, J. (1998). *Error-correcting codes: A mathematical introduction.* New York, NY: Chapman and Hall. doi:10.1007/978-1-4899-3276-1

Biernat, J. (2010). Fast fault-tolerant adders. *International Journal of Critical Computer-Based Systems, 1*(1-3), 117–127. doi:10.1504/IJCCBS.2010.031709

Chen, Z., & Dongarra, J. (2008). Algorithm-based fault tolerance for fail-stop failures. *IEEE Transactions on Parallel and Distributed Systems, 19*(12), 1628–1641. doi:10.1109/TPDS.2008.58

Choi, J., Dongarra, J. J., & Walker, D. W. (1996). PB-BLAS: A set of parallel block basic linear algebra subprograms. In *Proceedings of the Conference on Scalable High-Performance Computing* (pp. 534-541). Academic Press.

Costello, D., & Lin, S. (2004). *Error control coding fundamentals and applications* (2nd ed.). Upper Saddle River, NJ: Pearson Education.

Dongarra, J. J., & Whaley, R. C. (1995). *A user's guide to the BLACS v1.0* (Tech. Rep. No. CS-95-281). Knoxville, TN: University of Tennessee.

Ekici, S., Yildirim, S., & Poyraz, M. (2009). A transmission line fault locator based on Elman recurrent networks. *Applied Soft Computing, 9*(1), 341–347. doi:10.1016/j.asoc.2008.04.011

Elnozahy, E. N., Johnson, D. B., & Zwaenepoel, W. (1992). The performance of consistent checkpointing. In *Proceedings of the 11th Symposium on Reliable Distributed Systems* (pp. 39-47). Academic Press.

Hakkarinen, D., & Chen, Z. (2010). Algorithmic Cholesky factorization fault recovery. In *Proceedings of the 24th IEEE International Parallel and Distributed Processing Symposium.* Atlanta, GA: IEEE.

Hamidi, H., Vafaei, A., & Monadjemi, A. H. (2009). Algorithm based fault tolerant and checkpointing for high performance computing systems. *Journal of Applied Science, 9,* 3947–3956. doi:10.3923/ jas.2009.3947.3956

Hamidi, H., Vafaei, A., & Monadjemi, A. H. (2010). *A fault-tolerant approach for matrix functions in image processing.* Paper presented at the 6th Iranian Machine Vision and Image Processing Conference. Tehran, Iran.

Hamidi, H., Vafaei, A., & Monadjemi, A. H. (2011). A framework for ABFT techniques in the design of fault-tolerant computing systems. *EURASIP Journal on Advances in Signal Processing, 1,* 90. doi:10.1186/1687-6180-2011-90

Hamidi, H., Vafaei, A., & Monadjemi, A. H. (2012). Analysis and evaluation of a new algorithm based fault tolerance for computing systems. *International Journal of Grid and High Performance Computing, 4*(1), 37–51. doi:10.4018/ jghpc.2012010103

Hamidi, H., Vafaei, A., & Monadjemi, A. H. (2012). Analysis and design of an ABFT and parity-checking technique in high performance computing systems. *Journal of Circuits, Systems, and Computers*, *21*(3). doi:10.1142/S021812661250017X

Huang, K. H., & Abraham, J. A. (1984). Algorithm-based fault tolerance for matrix operations. *IEEE Transactions on Computers*, *33*, 518–528. doi:10.1109/TC.1984.1676475

Jou, J. Y., & Abraham, J. A. (1986). Fault-tolerant matrix arithmetic and signal processing on highly concurrent computing structures. *Proceedings of the IEEE, 74*(5), 732–741. doi:10.1109/PROC.1986.13535

Jou, J. Y., & Abraham, J. A. (1988). Fault-tolerant FFT networks. *IEEE Transactions on Computers*, *37*, 548–561. doi:10.1109/12.4606

Kumar, A. A., & Makur, A. (2010). Improved coding-theoretic and subspace-based decoding algorithms for a wider class of DCT and DST codes. *IEEE Transactions on Signal Processing*, *58*(2), 695–708. doi:10.1109/TSP.2009.2031727

Moosavie Nia, A., & Mohammadi, K. (2007). A generalized ABFT technique using a fault tolerant neural network. *Journal of Circuits, Systems, and Computers, 16*(3), 337–356. doi:10.1142/S0218126607003708

Morelos-Zaragoza, R. H. (2006). *The art of error correcting coding* (2nd ed.). New York, NY: John Wiley & Sons. doi:10.1002/0470035706

Nair, V. S. S., & Abraham, J. A. (1990). Real number codes for fault-tolerant matrix operations on process arrays. *IEEE Transactions on Computers*, 426–435. doi:10.1109/12.54836

Rexford, J., & Jha, N. K. (1992). Algorithm-based fault tolerance for floating-point operations in massively parallel systems. In *Proceedings of the International Symposium on Circuits and Systems* (pp. 649-652). Academic Press.

Salfner, F., Lenk, M., & Malek, M. (2010). A survey of online failure prediction methods. *ACM Computing Surveys*, *42*(3). doi:10.1145/1670679.1670680

Turmon, M., Granat, R., & Katz, D. (2000). Software-implemented fault detection for high-performance space applications. In *Proceedings of the IEEE International Conference on Dependable Systems and Networks* (pp. 107-116). IEEE.

Turmon, M., Granat, R., Katz, D., & Lou, J. (2003). Tests and tolerances for high-performance software-implemented fault detection. *IEEE Transactions on Computers, 52*(5), 579–591. doi:10.1109/ TC.2003.1197125

Veeravalli, V. S. (2009). Fault tolerance for arithmetic and logic unit. In *Proceedings of the IEEE Southeast Conference* (pp. 329-334). IEEE.

Viterbi, A. J., & Omura, J. K. (1985). *Principles of digital communication and coding* (2nd ed.). New York, NY: McGraw-Hill.

Chapter 2
Methods on Determining the Investment in IT Security

Amanda Eisenga
Florida Gulf Coast University, USA

Walter Rodriguez
Florida Gulf Coast University, USA

Travis Jones
Florida Gulf Coast University, USA

ABSTRACT

Setting aside capital to invest in Information Technology (IT) security is critical in the current digital age. In almost all large (or small) corporations, it is prudent to allocate a sufficient amount of resources to IT infrastructure. However, it is often difficult to determine at what level it is appropriate to invest in IT security in addition to the point at which the rate of return of this investment begins to diminish. This chapter examines methods to help determine the appropriate investment allocation to IT security in addition to how to apply these methods. It also looks at some of the assumptions and pitfalls of each.

INTRODUCTION

Investment in IT security is an important aspect in any business to help mitigate the risk of security breaches and challenges, which can be internal, such as an attack or a negligent employee, or ex-ternal, with the use of hackers. The average organizational cost of a data breach, in 2011, was $5.5 million (Olavsrud, 2012). The chart below notes the average cost per record of a security breach, from 2005 to 2011. According to the Ponemon Institute and Symantec, security breaches cost

DOI: 10.4018/978-1-4666-4856-2.ch002

Figure 1.

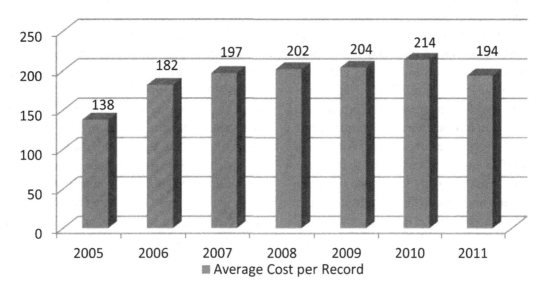

companies on average $214 per compromised record breach, in 2010. In 2011, the average per compromised record breach decreased to $194 (Olavsrud, 2012), but this is still a cost that can be largely avoided. Data breaches compromise any corporation's reputation and customer's satisfaction, as well as cost money. It is imperative that companies invest in some type of IT security, so they are protected from intruders, hackers, viruses and malwares, which could cause data breaches. Many types of security breaches are discussed below, with methods to examine how much to invest in IT security following. (see Figure 1)

TYPES OF SECURITY BREACHES

A data breach occurs when intruders gain access to the company's IT infrastructure. These intruders can gain access through easy passwords or employees divulging privileged information. This allows the intruder to create havoc. The intruder can add or delete information from the system, alter programs, or even create "time bombs". These time bombs are created with the use of a code and are scheduled to "explode" unexpectedly, creating a disaster.

Hackers are external and try to disrupt the system with attacks from without. An attack can be performed as a denial of service (DoS). A DoS attack occurs when the infrastructure device is disabled by flooding the servers with too many messages. This overwhelms the system, and every message appears to be an authentic interaction. A distributed denial of service (DDoS) occurs where an attack is initiated from multiple sources instead of a single source (Applegate, Austin, & Soule, 2009).

Viruses and malwares threaten a company's infrastructure. These are software programs that replicate and spread themselves throughout computers. The damage can be minor but also can incorporate and automate other attacks, such as a DoS attack.

A negligent employee can cause a risk to a company by exposing data and not taking the precautionary steps to avoid a security breach. In 2010 and 2011, the Ponemon Institute found that negligence caused 39 percent of the data breaches. Insiders in the organizations can pose a serious threat, especially with the increase in adopting the use of tablets smart phones, and cloud applications. With new technology, employees are able to access an organization's information anywhere and anytime, which leads to more opportunities for a security breach (Olavsrud, 2012). Negligence by an employee is an unintentional compromise of the sharing of information. An example of this is if an employee is speaking loudly about a new project or if an employee's work laptop is stolen. This exposes the company to risk. A negligent employee may not be receiving the right education tools to know how to protect the company. Even if the employee has received the right training, the employee may not be implementing the steps to protect his employer.

COST OF EXPOSURE TO A SECURITY BREACH

The costs of security breaches are comprised of loss of productivity, reputation, customer perception, and recovery of expenses. The combination of these costs can create a significant monetary loss for a company when an IT security breach occurs. The cost of a security breach often ranges from thousands of dollars to millions of dollars. Companies need to understand these costs to better be able to reduce and manage them.

The cost of loss of productivity is not easily determinable. Productivity loss will include how much service the company has lost and employees not being able to do their job properly, because the IT system is down. Loss of productivity, and therefore its cost, increases with how long the IT system is down. For example, suppose a company that is solely based online, and mainly makes its revenue during the winter holidays, has a security breach during the winter holidays. This security breach leaves the company's website server down for two to three days. This would not only cost the company a loss of productivity but the majority of the revenue it expected to earn for those days.

The overall cost of the loss of productivity will depend on the type of industry, the size of the company, and when the attack occurs. The example below illustrates the cost of loss of productivity for a small company with 2,500 employees, where the company incurred 60 hours of security related downtime for the year, with an average wage of $22 per hour for its employees. This cost is over $3 million, and this was a relatively small company, with a short IT security related downtime. It is clear that for a larger firm, the costs of loss of productivity would be much greater.

```
Example 1: Loss of Productivity
    2500 Employees
  × 60 hours of security related
       downtime this year
  × $22 average wage per hour
  = $3,300,000 loss of productivity
```

Recovery costs are more determinable than loss of productivity. An IT manager should be able to estimate how much it would costs for the system to start operating again depending on the type of attack. However, the cost of damage to a company's reputation is not determinable until after a security breach occurs. A company can estimate these costs but often cannot assert a valid monetary loss, until after the fact. The severity of the security breach will determine the monetary expense. A company's reputation is closely tied to its stock price. Once a security breach occurs and it is released to the press, a company's stock price would be expected to immediately decline. If the public feels that the security breach is major, the stock price of the company could decline significantly, leading to an increased cost to investors of the company. If a company is repeatedly attacked, the perception of the company will grossly deteriorate, and the probability that the company's stock will continue to decline is greater.

A security breach also affects customer perception. The company can lose customers after a breach in security. This will also create a monetary loss for the company. This cost could be extremely high depending on several factors, such as the type of company and the severity of the security breach. For example, if an online subscriber website has a security breach with its customers' credit cards, current customers may end their subscription, due to the perception that the customers feel their information with the company is not safe. This will also affect future customers. Customers who were interested subscribing to the website, but learn about the security breach, are much less likely to subscribe.

RISK

Risk is the likelihood that one is exposed to harm or a loss or the likelihood that harm or loss will occur. Every company is exposed to some type of risk. A fool proof IT security system does not exist and will never exist. An IT security system should be developed to mitigate the risk of an exposure to a detrimental security breach. Thus, it is important for a company to determine how much should be invested in an IT security system.

Company's managers should use risk management to determine the risks that the company is exposed to. The National Institute of Standard and Technology (NIST) created the standards for governmental agencies in the area of federal security (Stoneburner, Goguen, and Feringa, 2002). NIST provides nine steps in assessing risk. These nine steps to assessing risk include the following: (1) system characterization; (2) threat identification; (3) vulnerability identification; (4) control analysis; (5) likelihood determination; (6) impact analysis; (7) risk determination; (8) control recommendations; and (9) results documentation (Stoneburner,

Goguen, and Feringa, 2002). These nine steps are crucial in assessing a company's risk. This risk assessment can help determine what type of IT security system the company needs to develop and the investment in IT security. However, risk assessment does not determine the centralized question and the premise of this paper, which is how much should be invested in IT security. Investment in IT security and the different approaches to determine how much should be invested in IT security are discussed below.

INVESTMENT IN IT SECURITY

The most common approach to evaluate how much should be invested in IT security is Annual Loss Expectancy (ALE) (Gordon, and Loeb, 2006). Other techniques, which are worth evaluating, are the Return on Security Investment (ROSI), Net Present Value (NPV) and Internal Rate of Return (IRR), and the Balanced Scorecard Approach. Each one of these techniques will be discussed below evaluating the pros and cons of each approach.

ANNUAL LOSS EXPECTANCY

Annual Loss Expectancy is a quantitative method for performing risk analysis. The calculation of ALE is to provide the expected monetary loss for an asset due to risk. ALE is calculated by multiplying the single loss expectancy (SLE) by the annualized rate of occurrence (ARO) (Sonnenreich, Albanese, and Stout, 2006). In the context of investment in IT security, ALE is helpful in determining if a company will want to accept the risk of an IT attack or invest in IT security to prevent or reduce the ARO. The illustration, below, shows how ALE might work for IT security.

This method illustrates how much a security breach is expected to cost a company. ALE is an appropriate method, as long as the managers can accurately determine the SLE and ARO (Bistarelli, Fioravanti, and Peretti, 2006). However, it is hard to determine the precise accurate numbers for SLE and ARO. Illustration 1 is a simplistic illustration with precise information. This illustration most likely will not happen to a company, exactly as stated. Therefore, ALE lacks the precise information and may mislead managers to accept certain risks or believe that the security breach will be less costly than implementing a better IT security system. ARO is reduced by the strength of an IT security system. If a manager wants to reduce security risks, the manager must strengthen the IT security.

Illustration 1

The management of ABC Corporation expects that if the corporation suffers a DDoS attack, the loss expectancy would be $25,000. The IT manager believes that the rate of occurrence for this year is .45. The ALE for the current year would be $11,250. (*Note*: $25,000 [the SLE] multiplied by the .45 [the ARO] equals $11,250 [the ALE]).

RETURN ON SECURITY INVESTMENT

Return on Security Investment (ROSI) is a quantitative method (Sonnenreich, Albanese, and Stout, 2006). It is similar to the Annualized Loss Expectancy but takes into account the investment cost. A simple equation to calculate ROSI[1] is:

$$ROSI = \frac{\left(Risk\ Exposure * Risk\ Mitigated\right) - Investment\ Cost}{Investment\ Cost}$$

The multiplication of risk exposure essentially equates to the Annualized Loss Exposure. The risk exposure must be calculated to determine an appropriate monetary cost (Sonnenreich, Albanese, and Stout, 2006). To calculate the monetary cost, management must determine how many times per year the company is exposed to the risk in question. Management also needs to determine the monetary effect the risk has on the company. The monetary effect must then be multiplied by how many times a year the risk will occur.

Risk mitigated should be a percentage of how much risk is averted because of the investment in IT security. ROSI will show if the investment in the security is more advantageous than simply accepting the risk. ROSI results in a percentage, where if the percentage is greater than 100 percent, then the company should invest; if it is below 100 percent, then the company should not invest. Illustration 2 shows how ROSI might be applied to assess an investment in IT security.

This approach shows if the cost of security is an appropriate investment for the company. The majority of all ROSI calculated are calculated with estimated numbers; any company who uses this approach should keep this in mind. A company can build on past ROSIs to determine future ROSIs.

Illustration 2

ABC Corporation is deciding to invest in a virus security program. The virus security program is estimated to cost $40,000. The corporation expects to receive 5 viruses a year. Each virus costs the company $10,000. If the corporation invests in the virus security, it would be protected from 90 percent of the viruses. Given this information, the ROSI is 125 percent. ABC Corporation should invest in the IT security because the ROSI is greater than 100 percent. (*Note*: ROSI = (50,000 *.90) − 40,000 / 40,000 = .125)

NET PRESENT VALUE AND INTERNAL RATE OF RETURN

Net Present Value (NPV) can also be used to determine whether to invest in an IT security investment. NPV uses the discounted cash flows of the future benefits of the investment to determine the current value of a company's investment project. This approach helps analyze the time value of money for long-term projects. The NPV equation is as follows:

$$NPV = \sum_{t=0}^{n} \frac{CF_t}{(1+r)^t}$$

Cash flows generated by the project (either positive or negative) are denoted by *CF*. The cost of capital (also known as the discount rate) of the firm is represented by *r*. The subscript *t* represents the respective year that the cash flow occurs. The NPV needs to be greater than zero for the company to invest in the project. If the NPV is less than zero, then the company should not invest in the IT security project. If the NPV is exactly zero, the company does not benefit or lose anything from an investment in the project.[2] Illustration 3 gives an example of how a company might to NPV to analyze an IT security investment.[3] Illustration 4 is another example to further illustrate the concept.

The Internal Rate of Return (IRR) is similar in nature to NPV, because it uses the cash flows generated from the project. IRR is used to determine rate of return generated by the project. The IRR is the discount rate at which the NPV equals zero, and thus the present value of the cash outflows (costs) equals the present value of the cash inflows (benefits) of the project. Thus, if the IRR is greater than the cost of capital of the firm, the project has a positive NPV and provides a positive return to the firm. If the IRR of a project is, less than the firm's cost of capital, the project has a negative NPV and accepting the project would erode firm

value. Illustration 5 below presents how IRR can be used to assess whether to invest in IT security. The formula to compute IRR is:

$$NPV = 0 = \sum_{t=0}^{n} \frac{CF_t}{(1+IRR)^t}$$

Illustration 3

Using the example above, ABC Corporation is deciding to invest in a virus security program. The virus security program is estimated to cost $40,000 for a 3 year license. The corporation expects to receive 5 viruses a year at $10,000 each, or $50,000 cost per year. If the corporation invests in the virus security, it would be protected from 90 percent of the viruses, saving the company $45,000 per year (over 3 years) versus not having the virus program. If the discount rate is ABC Corporation's cost of capital of 15%, the NPV for this investment would be:

$$NPV = -\$40,000 + \frac{\$45,000}{(1+.15)^1} + \frac{\$45,000}{(1+.15)^2} + \frac{\$45,000}{(1+.15)^3} = \$62,745.13$$

ABC Corporation should invest in the virus program, because the NPV of doing so is greater than zero.

Illustration 4

XYZ Corporation is looking to purchase firewall protection. The cost of the firewall protection will be an upfront cost of $100,000. The discount rate is XYZ Corporation's cost of capital of 10%. The firm estimates that this firewall will save the company $50,000 a year for the next 3 years. The NPV of the firewall project is:

$$NPV = -\$100,000 + \frac{\$50,000}{(1+.10)^1} + \frac{\$50,000}{(1+.10)^2} + \frac{\$50,000}{(1+.10)^3} = \$24,342.60$$

Therefore, XYZ Corporation should invest in the firewall protection, because the NPV is greater than zero.

Illustration 5

Using the information from illustrations 3 and 4 above, the IRR is 98.00% for ABC Corporation's project and 23.38% for XYZ's project. Thus, if the cash flows are discounted at 98% and 23.38%, respectively, the sum of their present values equals zero, and the present value of the cost of the project is equal to the present value of its benefits.

$$ABC: NPV = -\$40,000 + \frac{\$45,000}{(1+IRR)^1} + \frac{\$45,000}{(1+IRR)^2} + \frac{\$45,000}{(1+IRR)^3} = \$0$$

$$XYZ: NPV = -\$100,000 + \frac{\$50,000}{(1+IRR)^1} + \frac{\$50,000}{(1+IRR)^2} + \frac{\$50,000}{(1+IRR)^3} = \$0$$

The IRR for both corporations exceeds their respective cost of capital of 15% and 10%, so these projects would be acceptable to each firm. If the IRR of a given project is less than the firm's cost of capital, then that project should not be pursued. IRR can help a firm determine whether or not to accept or reject a project, but IRR does not give the total dollar-value-added to the firm from the project.[4]

BALANCED SCORECARD APPROACH

The Balanced Scorecard, created by Dr. Robert Kaplan and Dr. David Norton, does not solely use financial measures. This approach highlights other nonfinancial objectives. These nonfinancial objectives need to be met for the organization to meet its financial objectives. The scorecard measures an organization's performance from four different perspectives. These four perspectives are financial, customer, internal processes, and employee learning and growth. The financial perspective should answer questions concerning shareholders, and external users determining the financial well-being of the firm. The customer perspective should answer the concerns that customers may have such as account information being hacked. It also should answer how the strategy is affecting the customer's perception and account information. Internal processes should evaluate how the company should operate in coordination with the strategy. Employee and learning growth should answer questions concerning the employees and the growth of the organization (Kaplan, and Norton, 1992). The balanced scorecard approach for investment in IT security should contain the four general perspectives when a security manager is using the balanced scorecard approach. Illustration 6 is an example of a balanced scorecard and providing some of the objectives is in each perspective.

Illustration 6: Example of a Balanced Scorecard

The security manager must evaluate each perspective to determine if the security investment is useful and pertains to the organization's strategy. For example, if an organization is looking to purchase a new virus protection software. The security manager will have to evaluate the security investment and each of the perspectives. The virus protection software must be measured to determine if the customers are protected from security risks. It also must be measured to determine if it reduces financial losses and if the software meets regulatory standards. (see Figure 2)

A well-designed scorecard can articulate a cause and effect scenario for the security manager. The balanced scorecard approach is most useful to help security managers persuade management, who often think in terms of a balanced scorecard, to invest in security technologies (Tallau, Gupta, and Sharman, 2010). The approach may lack economic data and could take time to develop. This approach is also limited to the fact

Figure 2.

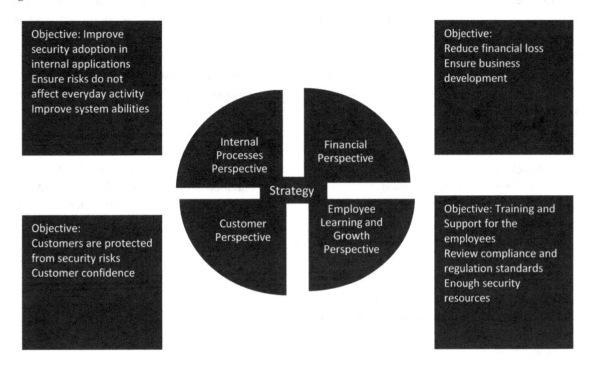

that some objectives are hypothesized. Therefore, management should not rely on the cause and effect relationships to be precise. Illustration 6 provides an example of how the balance scorecard approach might be used within a company.

Illustration 7: Balanced Scorecard Example

Accounting Specialists, a small accounting firm that has 48 employees and two are the IT personnel; is deciding to purchase firewall software or a hardware firewall. Accounting Specialists' employees spend 60 percent of their time in the office and 40 percent at their clients' offices. Accounting Specialists has 30 desktop and 20 laptop computers. The laptop computers are used primarily at their client's office and/or at home for the employees to finish work. Accounting Specialists has asked their IT employee to decide between the small business firewall software cost

2000 dollars and the hardware firewall cost 3000 dollars. Both software and hardware are designed to block unauthorized access to the company's computers.

Firewall software can be difficult to maintain and support, because each computer must have the software installed on (Froude, 2010). Software firewall lives on individual PCs and laptops, they intercept incoming request, are truly portable and reside on a PC or laptop to protect the computer (Froude, 2010).

Hardware firewalls are easier to maintain and administer, because the whole network is protected by the firewall (Froude, 2010). Hardware based firewalls does not affect the performance or speed of the individual desktop or laptops connected to the network (Froude, 2010). Employees will prefer this firewall compared to the software firewall.

Accounting Specialists' IT personnel decides to evaluate both firewalls by using the balanced scorecard. Upper management at Accounting

Specialists believes that the cost difference of the two firewalls is irrelevant. Therefore, the price difference will not affect the balanced scorecard evaluations.

This is the overall balanced scorecard for IT Security for Accounting Specialists. The firewall must meet these criteria in the respective perspectives to be deemed suitable.

- **Strategy:** To Protect the Company and its Clients' Records from Intrusion
- **Financial Perspective:** To reduce financial loss if an intrusion or attack occurs. Financial loss refers to the downtime it may take to repair the system after an intrusion and the disruption of work when the system will have to be inactive.
- **Customer Perspective:** To purchase a firewall that protects Account Specialists clients' records. The customers should feel confident and trust Account Specialists with their information.
- **Internal-Business Process Perspective:** Improve processes and ensure the firewall is working properly. Initiatives are to maintain the firewall by the IT staff.
- **Learning and Growth Perspective:** Detail the needs for the firewall to all the employees, only two employees at Accounts Specialists have a background in information technology. It is important that all the employees know why the firewall is a necessity.

Firewall Software Evaluation

Every computer will have to have its own firewall installed and maintained.

- **Financial Perspective Evaluation:** This firewall will protect the company from an intrusion.

- **Customer Perspective Evaluation:** The firewall provides accurate protection from an intrusion; therefore, the customer should be satisfied with the firewall.
- **Internal-Business Process Perspective Evaluation:** The firewall is manageable and the IT personnel know how to maintain the firewall.
- **Learning and Growth Perspective Evaluation:** The employees may not be satisfied with the firewall. The computers may become slow and not perform as well.
- **Conclusion:** The firewall software satisfies the first three perspectives. It however, lacks the fourth perspective because it may inhibit the employees' performance and productivity.

Firewall Hardware Evaluation

The office network will provide a firewall to protect all computers when logged on the office network.

- **Financial Perspective Evaluation:** This firewall will protect the company from an intrusion when the computers are logged on the office network.
- **Customer Perspective Evaluation:** The firewall may not provide accurate protection, because the firewall only provides protection when the computer is logged on the office network. Since, the employees travel and complete work at client's office the computer is at risk for an intrusion if it logs on to a network. The computers are not fully protected.
- **Internal-Business Process Perspective Evaluation:** The firewall is very easy to maintain and easy to administer.
- **Learning and Growth Perspective Evaluation:** The employees will not be affected by this firewall. The firewall will

not interrupt the computer's performance or speed.

- **Conclusion:** The firewall software satisfies the financial perspective, internal-business process perspective, and learning and growth perspective. It does not satisfy the customer perspective because if the computer is connected to another network other than the office network the computer and the information on the computer are at risk.

The IT personnel have decided to purchase the firewall software for all the computers. They believe that this firewall be most beneficial after conducting the balanced scorecard method. It was determined that the firewall hardware may not protect the customer's information, because the laptops may connect to unsecure networks. The IT personnel believe that they can maintain the firewall software and fix the issues the employees may have due to slower performance. The IT personnel believe that the computer's slower performance will be miniscule and will not disrupt the employees' productivity.

CHOOSING THE MODEL TO USE

The model that is best suited evaluate investments in IT security is a model that combines both financial and nonfinancial analysis. Calculations such as ALE, ROSI, NPV, and IRR are financial calculations. The Balanced Scorecard Approach is a nonfinancial calculation. The security manager needs to analyze the financial aspects of the IT security technology. For example, if the maximum protection virus software costs $200,000 and the security manager examines the budget and determines that the company can only afford virus software that costs $10,000, then the security manager should not purchase the maximum virus software. The security manager must constrain its IT security budget around how much the organiza-

tion can spend on IT protection. It is crucial for security managers to assess the division's finances and determine its budget constraints. The budget constraints determine the price range for the IT security protection. A manager must also complete an analysis that determines how effective the IT security technology will be. This analysis determines the risk avoided or the ARO, if the security manager is using the ALE method. [But the open question is: Does this mean that the actual rate of security breaches in a year is less than the annual rate of occurrence, ARO]. Risk avoided refers to the avoidance of a security breach. Once the risk avoidance is calculated, the manager should determine if the risk avoidance is at an appropriate level. An appropriate level is a predetermined level that the manager should have calculated by determining the costs associated with a security breach. This appropriate level is a range where the organization can accept a security breach.

For example, if the risk avoidance level for a new security technology is at 80 percent, the manager should then compare this avoidance to the appropriate avoidance[5], which is determined to be 10 percent. The manger should not implement the new security technology because its avoidance level is at 10 percent. For the manager to accept the new security technology the manager should invest in a new security technology that is at least 90 percent because appropriate avoidance level is 10 percent.

A security manger must also calculate a nonfinancial analysis. This nonfinancial analysis should determine how the employees would react to the security investment. For example, if a new security technology requires employees logging off the computers every time an employee leaves the computer, the employee may not log off the computer every time he or she leaves the computer. This will make the new security technology worthless and not useful for the organization. The security manager should conduct an analysis on how the new technology will affect the organization. The new security application should improve the system capabilities. The new security technology could actually slow down the system. It is important for the security manager to look at the nonfinancial impact of implementing a new security application to the organization's system. Sometimes inherently financial or seemingly beneficial programs affect the organization's system negatively.

The security manager at first should conduct a financial analysis such as ROSI with the budget constraints to determine if the new security application or technology is appropriate. Then the security manager should complete a balance scorecard approach to determine the benefits and if there are any negatives to implementing the new security into the organization's system. Once this analysis is completed, the security manager will be able to determine if the new security investment should be implemented. The exact threshold to determine if an organization should invest in a certain security program is dependent on the budget and the impact to the organization itself.

CONCLUSION

There are a multitude approaches that security managers can use to evaluate their organization's security technology. Many of these approaches use financial objectives to determine if it is valuable to invest in certain security applications. A security manager's foremost goal is to evaluate the financial benefits of the security technology. If there are no financial benefits or if the organization does not break-even on the technology, the organization should not invest in the technology. However, it is also the security manager's job to evaluate nonfinancial benefits of a potential investment. The majority of the popular approaches do not evaluate the nonfinancial benefits. A two-model approach is often best suited to determine the maximum threshold. It is appropriate to use the balanced scorecard approach with one of the financial calculations discussed above. The most common and appropriate financial calculation to use would be the Net Present Value (NPV) model. The NPV gives the most information by providing the current dollar benefit to the company of investing in the IT security in question. The two-model approach will measure both the financial and nonfinancial objectives of an organization. Depending on an organization's strategy, the security manager should use an approach that is quantitative and qualitative, insuring that both the financial and nonfinancial objectives of the organization will be met.

REFERENCES

Anderson, R. (2001). *Why information security is hard-an economic perspective.* Cambridge, UK: University of Cambridge Computer Laboratory. doi:10.1109/ACSAC.2001.991552

Applegate, L. M., Austin, R. D., & Soule, D. L. (2009). *Corporate information strategy and management: Texts and cases* (8th ed.). New York: McGraw-Hill Companies, Inc.

Baskerville, R. (1993). Information systems security design methods: Implications for information systems development. *ACM Computing Surveys.* doi:10.1145/162124.162127

Bistarelli, S., Fioravanti, F., & Peretti, P. (2006). *Defense trees for economic evaluation of security investments. Dipartimento di Scienze, Universita degli, Studi g. d'Annunzio.* D.O.I.

Bodin, L., Gordon, L. A., & Loeb, M. P. (2008). Information security and risk management. *Communications of the ACM, 51*(4), 64–68. doi:10.1145/1330311.1330325

Cavusoglu, H., Mishra, B., & Raghunathan, S. (2004). A model for evaluating IT security investments. *Communications of the ACM.* doi:10.1145/1005817.1005828

Froude, J. (2010). *How to choose a firewall.* Retrieved from http://www.inc.com/ss/how-choose-firewall#5

Garg, A. G., Curtis, J., & Halper, H. (2003). Quantifying the financial impact of of IT security breaches. *Information Management & Computer Security, 74*–84. doi:10.1108/09685220310468646

Gordon, L. A., & Loeb, M. P. (2006). Budgeting process for information security expenditures: Empirical evidence. *Communications of the ACM, 49*(1), 121–125. doi:10.1145/1107458.1107465

Hartman, J. C., & Schafrick, I. C. (2004). The relevant internal rate of return. *The Engineering Economist, 49*(2), 139–158. doi:10.1080/00137910490453419

Horngren, C. T., Datar, S. M., Foster, G., Rajan, M., & Ittner, C. (2009). *Cost accounting: A mangerial emphasis* (13th ed.). Upper Saddle River, NJ: Pearson Prentice Hall.

Kaplan, R.S., & Norton, D.P. (1992, January-February). The balanced scorecard-measures that drive performance. *HBR onPoint.*

Kaplan, R. S., & Norton, D. P. (1993, September-October). Putting the balanced scorecard to work. *Harvard Business Review.*

Mercuri, R. T. (2002). Analyzing security costs. *Communications of the ACM.* PMID:12238525

Olavsrud, T. (2012). Cost of data breaches declines. *CIO.* Retrieved from http://www.cio.com/article/702494/Cost_of_Data_Breaches_Declines?page=2&taxonomyId=3154

Ponemon Institute. LLC. (2010). *2009 annual study: Cost of a data breach understanding financial impact, customer turnover, and preventive solutions.* Ponemon Institute LLC. Retrieved from http://www.ponemon.org/local/upload/fckjail/generalcontent/18/file/US_Ponemon_CODB_09_012209_sec.pdf

Ponemon Institute. LLC. (2011). *2010 annual study: U.S. cost of a data breach compliance pressures, cyber attacks targeting sensitive data drive leading IT organizations to respond quickly and pay more.* Ponemon Institute LLC. Retrieved from http://www.symantec.com/content/en/us/about/media/pdfs/symantec_ponemon_data_breach_costs_report.pdf?om_ext_cid=biz_socmed_twitter_facebook_marketwire_linkedin_2011Mar_worldwide_costofdatabreach

Ross, S. (1995). Uses, abuses, and alternatives to the net-present-value rule. *Financial Management, 24*(3), 96–102. doi:10.2307/3665561

Ross, S., Westerfield, R., & Jordan, B. (2009). *Fundamentals of corporate finance* (9th ed.). New York: McGraw-Hill Irwin.

Sonnenreich, W., Albanese, J., & Stout, B. (2006). Return on security investment (ROSI)- A practical quantitative method. *Journal of Research and Practice in Information Technology.*

Stoneburner, G., Goguen, A., & Feringa, A. (2002). *NIST: National institute of standards and technology.* Retrieved November 10, 2011, from http://ibexsecurity.com/cissp/NIST%20Security%20Guides/sp800-30.pdf

Tallau, L. J., Gupta, M., & Sharman, R. (2010). Information security investment decisions: Evaluating the balanced scorecard method. *Int. J. Business Information Systems, 5*(1), 34–57. doi:10.1504/IJBIS.2010.029479

ENDNOTES

[1]   Adapted from Sonnenreich, Albanese, and Stout, Return on Security Investment- A Practical Quantitative Model

[2]   See Ross, et al., 2011 for more information on NPV and IRR.

[3]   See Ross, 1995, for how NPV is misused, in practice.

[4]   In certain situations, a project can have multiple IRRs, for more on this, see Hartman and Schafrick, 2004.

[5]   Appropriate avoidance is the percentage rate that an organization can accept security breaches.

Chapter 3
Critical Path Stability Region:
A Single-Time Estimate Approach

Hossein Arsham
The Johns Hopkins University, USA

Veena Adlakha
University of Baltimore, USA

ABSTRACT

Models transform the managerial inputs into useful information for managerial decision. The Project Evaluation and Review Technique (PERT) is the most widely used model for project management. However, it requires three estimates for the duration of each activity as its input. This uncertainty in the input requirement makes the Critical Path (CP) unstable, causing major difficulties for the manager. A linear programming formulation of the project network is proposed in this chapter for determining a CP based on making one estimate for the duration of each activity. Upon finding the CP, Sensitivity Analysis (SA) of Data Perturbation (DP) is performed using the constraints of the dual problem. This largest DP set of uncertainties provides the manager with a tool to deal with the simultaneous, independent, or dependent changes of the input estimates that preserves the current CP. The application of DP results to enhance the traditional approach to PERT is presented. The proposed procedure is easy to understand, easy to implement, and provides useful information for the manager. A numerical example illustrates the process.

DOI: 10.4018/978-1-4666-4856-2.ch003

1. INTRODUCTION

Project management is one of the fastest growing career fields in business education today. Most of the growth in this field is in the business sectors, where there are widespread reports about most projects being late, many over budget, and all too often do not satisfy design specifications. This paper is about business project management, although the principles apply to projects in any field. When proposing a new business system, the project manager will be confronted with many questions from top management, in particular "How much will it cost? And "When will it be done?" As many project managers know, these two questions are difficult to answer correctly.

A project involves getting a new, complex activity accomplished. Generally projects designed to accomplish something for the company undertaking them. Because projects involve new activities, they typically involve high levels of uncertainty and risk. It is very difficult to predict what problems are going to occur in business system development.

Projects are systems consisting of interrelated parts working together to accomplish project objectives. There are a number of important roles within business systems projects. Project managers have to balance technical understanding with the ability to motivate diverse groups of people (the project team) brought together on a temporary basis. Projects are collections of activities. If one activity is late, other activities are delayed. If an activity is ahead of schedule, workers tend to slow down to meet the original completion date. Business systems projects have many similarities to generic projects. They consist of activities, each with durations, predecessor relationships, and resource requirements. They involve high levels of uncertainty and often suffer from time and cost overruns, while rarely experiencing time

and cost underruns. However, business systems projects are different from generic projects in some aspects. While each project is unique, there are usually numerous replications of business systems project types. Most are served by a standard methodology, with the need to identify user requirements, followed by design of a system, production of the system, testing of the system, training and implementation, and, ultimately, maintenance of the system. These steps are not always in serial; there are often many loops back to prior stages.

Defining project success in itself is difficult. There are many views of what makes a project successful. Successful implementation has been found to require mastery of the technical aspects of systems, along with understanding key organizational and behavioral dynamics. There has been a great deal of research into business systems project failure. Failure can occur when design objectives are not met. The difference between successful and failed business systems projects often lies in planning and implementation. A great deal of research has been performed to identify factors that lead to project success. These factors include planning, user involvement, and good communication. Additional factors that are reported as important in business systems project success repeatedly include top management support and clear statement of project objectives.

Business systems project management can involve a wide variety of tasks. Typical business systems project types include maintenance work, conversion projects, and new systems implementation. Maintenance projects are by far the most common type of business systems project. They can arise from need to fix errors or to add enhancements to some system, or to involve major enhancements. Conversion projects involve changing an existing system. New systems development involves different management characteristics by type of system.

Business systems projects have high levels of uncertainty. The size of the project is usually not well understood until systems analysis has been completed. Most of the unexpected delay in these projects occurs during the latter stages of testing. Almost one third of the time used in typical projects is required for the planning phase, and coding typically consisted of one-sixth of the project. Coding is the most predictable portion of the project. The last half of the project is testing – one-quarter for component testing and one-quarter for system testing. The activity most difficult to predict was testing. Project managers currently use the critical path method (CPM) and/or project evaluation and review technique (PERT) in order to provide a planning and control structure for projects. CPM helps managers understand the relationships among project activities. Key personnel and other resources can be allocated to activities on the critical path. These activities can be closely monitored to avoid completion delays.

CPM identifies the sequence of activities that will have the longest completion time of the entire project. PERT extends CPM's scope to deal with uncertainties inherent in any project. Project activity network models ranked above all other quantitative decision making tools in terms of the percentage of business firms who used them. Although these techniques are widely used in practice and have provided economic benefit to their users, they are not problem-free. Problems derive from the nature of the underlying statistical assumptions, the potential for high computational expense, and from the assumption that factors determining activity duration are essentially probabilistic rather than determined by managerial action.

1.1 Critique of CPM/PERT

In this section examines the scope and limitations of CPM/PERT. The most widely used CPM/PERT algorithm is based on the following assumptions and procedure:

- **Activity Duration:** Rarely (if ever) known with certainty; the CPM asks the manager for three time estimates. Three time estimates are determined (by guesses, etc.) for each activity:
  - **a:** An optimistic completion time.
  - **m:** A most likely completion time (this is what we will use in this paper).
  - **b:** A pessimistic completion time.
- **Activity Approximations:**
  - An approximation for the *distribution* of an activity's completion time is a *BETA* distribution
  - An approximation for the *mean completion time* for an activity is a weighted average (1/6, 4/6, 1/6) of the three time estimates is $(a + 4m + b)/6$
  - An approximation for the *standard deviation* for the completion time for an activity is its range/6 or $(b - a)/6$
  - The *variance* of an activity's completion time is the square of the standard deviation $= [(b - a)/6]^2$
- **Project Assumptions:**
  1. The distribution of the project completion time is determined by the critical path using the mean activity completion times
  2. The activity completion times are *Independent*.
  3. There are enough activities (at least 30, to make sure) on the critical path so that the central limit can be used to determine the distribution, mean, variance and standard deviation of the project
- **Project Distribution:** Given the above assumptions, this means:
  - The project completion time distribution is *normal*.

- ◦ The *mean (expected) completion time*, μ, of the project is the sum of the expected completion times along the critical path.
- ◦ The *variance of the completion time*, σ², of the project is the sum of the variance in completion times along the critical path.
- ◦ The *standard deviation of the completion time*, σ, of the project is the square root of the variance of the completion time of the project.

The probability of completing by a certain date *t*, can now be found by finding the P(X < t) from a normal distribution with mean μ and standard deviation σ.

The critical path method requires three time estimates from the manager for each activity in the project. In a dialog with one of the authors, a manager said that *it is difficult enough to offer one estimate for the duration of one activity.* By asking for three estimates for each activity in the project, more uncertainty is introduced. *It makes sense to ask the manager for one good estimate.*

An alternative to the CPM/PERT is a stochastic activity network (Adlakha and Arsham, 1992). This approach assumes that the same project is to be performed repeatedly, and there is full knowledge of the time distribution function to be used in Monte-Carlo simulation experiments to approximate the expected CPM/PERT duration. This approach suffers from even more severe practical pitfalls, in addition to being computationally expensive.

The validity of the above assumptions has been a long-standing question (Kallo, 1996; Kamburowski, 1997; Keefer and Verdini, 1993; Kuklan, 1993). The solution based on inaccurate inputs result in the incorrect designation of the CPM/PERT, and the accuracy of the results decreases in relation to increased project complexity (Nakashima, 1999).

While Hasan and Gould (2001) support the sense-making activity of managers, more than half a century after the debut of CPM and PERT, they still are requiring complex user input. While modern decision support systems for project management are more sophisticated and comprehensive than CPM/PERT, they show insufficient progress in dealing with uncertainties (Trietsch and Baker, 2012). Czuchra (1999) presents recommendations on optimizing budget spending for software implementation and testing. Yaghoubi, Noori, Azaron and Tavakkoli-Moghaddam (2011) consider dynamic PERT networks where activity durations are unrealistically independent random variables with exponential distributions. Mouhoub, Benhocine, and Belouadah (2011) propose to reduce the number of dummy activities as much as possible, but the result is even more complex. Herrerı́as-Velasco· Herrerı́as-Pleguezuelo· and René van Dorp (2011), being aware of the difficulties with the interpretation of the parameters of the beta distribution, suggest an alternative to the PERT variance expression regarding the constant PERT variance assumption. Martín, García, Pérez, and Sánchez Granero (2012), propose a two-sided power and the generalized biparabolic distributions as an alternative to the mixture of the uniform and the beta distributions to the beta distribution in PERT methodology. Yakhchali (2012) expands the work of Nasution (1994) while addressing the problem of determining the degree of possible and necessary criticality of activities, as well as determining paths in networks that have fuzzy activity durations.

D'Aquila (1993) recommends simultaneous use of CPM/PERT. Mehrotra, Chai, and Pillutla (1996) suggest approximating the moments of the job completion. Banerjee and Paul (2008) use multivariate statistical tools analysis to measure the error in the classical PERT method of estimating mean project completion time when correlation is ignored. Premachandra (2001) yet provides approximations for the mean and the variance of activity based on "pessimistic", "optimistic" and "most likely" time estimates to get away from the beta distribution assumption.

Even ordinary sensitivity analysis is rarely performed in activity network projects, because the existing CPM/PERT algorithms do not contain enough information to perform the calculations necessary for this simplest form of Data Perturbation Analysis (DPA). To the best of our knowledge NETSOLVE is the only software available capable of dealing with ordinary sensitivity analysis for CPM (Jarvis and Shier, 1990; Phillips and Garcia-Diaz, 1990). The existing stochastic PERT software packages require a separate run for each scenario if any parameters are changed (Higgs, 1995; Lewis, 2007).

The probabilistic nature in both PERT models assumes random factors (e.g., bad luck, good luck) are present and does not allow for any managerially planned point of view to deal with uncertainty. In other words, much of the variability for activity duration may result from management decisions, rather than from random acts of nature.

1.2 An Alternative Computational Approach

This chapter discusses a non-statistical approach, referred to as Data Perturbation Analysis (DPA), to calculate a variety of activity duration uncertainties. DPA deals with a collection of managerial questions related to uncontrollable environmental factors in project estimation tasks. The underlying mathematics of the DPA is a linear program based formulation. This approach provides:

1. An assessment and analysis of the stability of the critical path(s) under uncertainty;
2. Monitoring of the admissible range of activity durations that preserve the current CP; and
3. Disclosure of the useful limits on simultaneous, dependent departures from the activity

duration estimates to determine maximum "crashing" of critical activity durations, the maximum "slippage" for non-critical activity durations; and the impacts of such departures on the entire project completion time.

These benefits allow the manager more leverage in allocating project resources. Knowing the stability of the critical path(s) under uncertainty allows the manager to perceive a range of timing changes before a new path of activities is critical. Monitoring the admissible range of activity durations that preserve the current CP aids in determining how resources should be applied among the activities to expedite the completion of the project and to smooth out workloads. Disclosure of information about departure times for critical and non-critical activities allows the manager to anticipate the consequences of slippage wherever it might occur in the project and to pre-determine back-up strategies.

This chapter develops a simplex-type solution algorithm to find the CP. The algorithm is easy to use and does not introduce any slack or surplus variables (as in the dual simplex method), or any artificial variables (Arsham, 1997a, 1997b); therefore it is computationally practical and stable to implement. A unified approach is presented to cover all aspects of the sensitivity analysis.

The remainder of this chapter is divided into five parts. First, based on one estimate for the duration of each activity, the CP is obtained by a linear program formulation and an efficient solution algorithm. This is followed by an illustrated numerical example. In the next section we discuss how the data manipulation leading to the CP provides the necessary information for the Data Perturbation Analysis (DPA) that provides the largest sensitivity region,. This is followed by the parametric analysis, which includes the ordinary sensitivity analysis and the so-called 100% rule. Then the tolerance analysis is developed and, as its by-products, we obtain the individual and symmetric tolerance analysis together with a discussion of some potential applications. The last section is devoted to concluding remarks. Throughout the paper the emphasis is on constructive procedures, proofs and a small numerical example since these lead directly to an efficient computer program for implementation. Furthermore, this algorithm facilitates PDA, including structural changes in the nominal project network.

2. LINEAR PROGRAM FORMULATION WITH A NEW SOLUTION TECHNIQUE

Suppose that in a given project activity network, there are m nodes, n arcs (i.e. activities) and an estimated duration, t_{ij}, associated with each arc (i, j) in the network. Without loss of generality, it is assumed that the activities durations are continuous. The beginning node of an arc corresponds to the start of the associated activity and the end node to its completion. To find the CP, define the binary variables X_{ij}, where $X_{ij} = 1$, if the activity (i, j) is on the CP, and $X_{ij} = 0$ otherwise. The length of the path is the sum of the durations of the activities on the path. Formally, the CP problem is to find the longest path from node 1 to node m, i.e.

$$\text{Maximize} \sum_{i=1}^{m} \sum_{j=1}^{m} t_{ij} X_{ij}$$

subject to:

$$\sum_{j=1}^{m} X_{1j} = 1 \tag{1}$$

$$-\sum_{j=1}^{m} X_{ij} + \sum_{k=1}^{m} X_{ki} = 0$$

for i ≠ 1 or m

$$\sum_{j=1}^{m} X_{jm} = 1,$$

where the sums are taken over existing arcs in the network, and all variable are non-negative. The first and the last constraints are imposed to start (node 1) and complete the project (node m) by critical activities, respectively; while the other constraints provide that if any node is arrived at by a critical activity, then it must be left by a critical activity. Note that the integrality conditions (i.e., $X_{ij}=0$ or 1) are changed to $X_{ij} \geq 0$ since it is known that the optimal solution to these types of LP problems satisfy these conditions. Note also that one of these m constraints is redundant; e.g. the first constraint is the sum of all other constraints.

The Critical Path Finder

The following notation is used in the new algorithm:

- **BVS:** Basic Variable Set
- **GJP:** Gauss-Jordan Pivoting
- **PR:** Pivot Row (Row to be assigned to the variable to come in BVS)
- **PC:** Pivot Column (Column associated with variable to come in BVS)
- **PE:** Pivot Element
- **OR:** Open Row. A row not yet assigned to a variable. Labeled (?).
- **(?):** Label for a row that is not yet assigned a variable (Open Row)
- **RHS:** Right Hand Side
- **C/R:** Column Ratio, RHS/PE
- **R/R:** Row Ratio, Last row/PR
- **OP:** Optimality Phase
- **FE:** Feasibility Phase

The algorithm consists of preliminaries for setting up the initialization followed by three main phases: Basic Variable Set Augmentation, Optimality, and Feasibility. The Basic Variable Set Augmentation Phase develops a basic variable set (BVS) which may or may not be feasible. Unlike simplex and dual simplex, this approach starts with an incomplete BVS initially, and then variables are brought into the basis one by one. This strategy pushes towards an optimal solution. Since some solutions generated may be infeasible, the next step, if needed, pulls the solution back to feasibility. The Optimality Phase satisfies the optimality condition, and the Feasibility Phase obtains a feasible and optimal basis. All phases use the Gauss-Jordan pivoting (GJP) transformation used in the standard simplex and dual simplex algorithms (Arsham, 2005). The proposed scheme is as follows:

Step 1. Set Up: The initial tableau may be empty, partially empty, or contain a full basic variable set (BVS).

Step 2. Push: Fill-up the BVS completely by pushing it toward the optimal vertex.

Step 3. Push Further: If the BVS is complete, but the optimality condition is not satisfied, then push further until this condition is satisfied; i.e., a primal simplex approach.

Step 4. Pull: If the BVS is complete, and the optimality condition is satisfied but infeasible, then pull back to the optimal vertex; i.e., a dual simplex approach.

Not all project networks must go through the Push Further and Pull sequence of steps, as shown in the numerical example. In essence, this approach generates a tableau containing all the information we need to perform all parts of DPA.

The large number of equality constraints, with zero value as their right-hand-side, raises concern for primal (pivotal) degeneracy that may cause pivotal cycling. In the proposed solution algorithm,

the BVS Augmentation Phase does not replace any BVs, and the Feasibility Phase uses the dual simplex rule, therefore, there is no pivotal degeneracy in these two phases. However, degeneracy (cycling) may occur in the Optimality Phase after the BVS Augmentation Phase and the Feasibility Phase are completed. This strategy reduces the possibility of any cycling. In the case of cycling in the Optimality Phase, this could be treated using the simple and effective anti-cycling rule for simplex method. Out of the many problems solved by this algorithm, no cycling was encountered.

It is common in applications of CPM/PERT to have side-constraints in the nominal model. Network-based approaches to problems with side constraints require an extensive revision of the original solution algorithms to handle even one side-constraint. Additional difficulties arise from multiple side-constraints. In the proposed algorithm, when the optimal solution without the side constraints does not satisfy some or all of the side constraints, the "most" violated constraint can be brought into the final tableau by performing the "catch-up" operation using the dual simplex rule. After doing so, the Feasibility Phase can be used to generate the updated final tableau. To ensure the integrality of the solution appropriate cutting planes can be introduced, if needed.

As part of PA, there is also interest in any structural changes to the nominal project network. There appear to be only a few references that deal with adding an arc to the network, and furthermore, updating the optimal solution requires solving a large number of sub-problems. The dual problem is used to determine whether the new arc changes the CP and if so, the new network is re-optimized. A distinction between basic and non-basic deleted arcs is made. If the deleted arc is a non-basic variable, then the solution remains unchanged. However, if the deleted arc is a basic variable, then the proposed algorithm replaces the deleted variable with a currently non-basic variable by using the optimality phase.

Set Up

Identify the largest t_{ij} value for the starting and finishing arcs. Subtract these largest values from the starting and finishing arcs activities respectively. Eliminate the first or the last constraint, whichever has the largest number of activities. Break any ties arbitrarily. Set up the initial simplex tableau without adding any artificial variables, and then start Phase I.

Phase I: Push Phase

1.0 Push Phase Termination Test
IF (?) Label exists, there are Open Rows.
THEN continue the BV Iteration.
OTHERWISE BVS is complete, start Push Further Phase (Step 2.0).

1.1 PE Selection
PC: Select the Largest t_{ij} and any ties as candidate column(s).
PR: Select OPEN ROWS as candidate rows.
PE: Select the candidate row and column with the smallest non-negative C/R. Arbitrarily break ties. If no non-negative C/R choose the C/R with the smallest absolute value. If the pivot element is zero, select the next best t_{ij}.

1.2 BVS Augmentation
1. Perform GJP.
2. Replace the (?) row label with the variable name.
3. Remove PC from the Tableau.
Continue Push Iteration (Loop back to 1.0)

Phase II: Push Further Phase

2.0 Push Further Termination Test
IF any t_{ij} is positive, THEN continue the OP Iteration,
OTHERWISE OP is complete, start Pull Phase Phase (Step 3.0).

2.1 PE Selection
PC: Select the Largest t_{ij} and any ties as candidate column(s).
PR: Select the candidate row and column with the largest positive C/R. Arbitrarily break ties.
If no positive C/R choose the C/R with the smallest absolute value. If the pivot element is zero, select the next best t_{ij}.

2.2 Push Further Iteration
1. Save PC outside the tableau.
2. Perform GJP.
3. Exchange PC and PR labels.
4. Replace the new PC with old PC with all elements multiplied by -1 except the PE.
Continue Push Further Iteration Loop back to 2.0.

Phase III: Pull Phase

3.0 Pull Phase Iteration Termination Test
IF RHS is non-negative,
THEN Tableau is Optimal. Interpret the results.
OTHERWISE continue Pull Phase Iteration (Step 3.1)

3.1 PE Selection
PR: row with the most negative RHS.
Tie Breaker arbitrary
PC: column with a negative element in the PR.
Tie Breaker: column with the smallest t_{ij}.
Further Tie Breaker arbitrary.

3.2 Pull Phase Transformation
1. Save PC outside the tableau.
2. Perform usual GJP.
3. Exchange PC and PR Labels.
4. Replace the new PC with old PC saved in (a).
Continue Pull Phase Iteration (Loop back to 3.0)

The final tableau generated by this algorithm contains all of the information needed to perform the DPA. There is also additional useful information in the final tableau; e.g., the absolute value of the last row in the final tableau provides the slack times for the non-critical activities. Such information is useful to project managers because it indicates how much flexibility exists in scheduling various activities without affecting succeeding activities. Clearly, the critical activities have slack time equal to zero. However, the reverse statement is not necessarily true; an activity can have slack-time equal to zero while being non-critical. This can happen whenever there are multiple critical paths. In this case the sensitivity analysis is not valid.

Theorem 1: The critical path is invariant under time reduction operations introduced in set-up phase.

Proof: The proof follows from the fact that multiplying the first and the last constraints by their maximum duration of starting and ending activities, respectively, and then subtracting from the objective function is equivalent to subtracting a constant from the objective function.

In real-life situations, it is common to have a few side-constraints or some structural changes, such as deletion or addition of an arc. The final tableau may be updated after incorporating the side-constraint or the structural changes and then apply the Pull Phase if needed. The violation of the total unimodularity does not affect the solution procedure. If the solution is not integral, then cutting planes may be introduced to ensure an integral optimal solution.

The proposed algorithm operates in the space of the original variables and has a geometric interpretation of its strategic process. The simplex method is a vertex-searching method. It starts at the origin that is far away from the optimal solution. It then moves along the intersection of the boundary hyper-planes of the constraints, hopping from one vertex to the neighboring vertex, until an optimal vertex is reached in two phases. It requires adding artificial variables since it lacks feasibility at the origin. In the first phase, starting at the origin, the simplex hops from one vertex to the next vertex to reach a feasible one. Upon reaching a feasible vertex; i.e., upon removal of all artificial variables from the basis, the simplex moves along the edge of the feasible region to reach an optimal vertex, improving the objective value in the process. Hence, the first phase of simplex method tries to reach feasibility, and the second phase of simplex method strives for optimality. The simplex works in the space of $n+(m-1)$ dimensions, leading to $m-1$ artificial variables, where m is the number of nodes and n is the number of arcs.

In contrast, the proposed algorithm strives to create a full basic variable set (BVS); i.e., the intersection of $m-1$ constraint hyper-planes that provides a vertex. The initialization phase provides the starting segment of a few intersecting hyper-planes and yields an initial BVS with some open rows. The algorithmic strategic process is to arrive at the feasible part of the boundary of the feasible region. In the Push Phase, the algorithm pushes towards an optimal vertex, unlike the simplex, which only strives for a feasible vertex. Occupying an open row means arriving on the face of the hyper-plane of that constraint. Any successive iteration in the Push Phase augments the BVS by including another hyper-plane in the current intersection. By restricting incoming variables to open rows only, this phase ensures movement in the space of intersection of hyper-planes selected in the initialization phase only until another hyper-plane is hit. Recall that no replacement of variables is done in this phase. By every algorithm's iteration the dimensionality of the working table is reduced until the BVS is filled, indicating a vertex. This phase is free from pivotal degeneracy. The selection of an incoming variable having the largest t_{ij}, pushes toward an optimal vertex. As a result, the next phase starts with a vertex.

At the end of the Push-Further phase the BVS is complete, indicating a vertex which is in the neighborhood of an optimal vertex. If feasible, this is an optimal solution. If this basic solution is not feasible, it indicates that the push has been excessive. Note that, in contrast to the first phase of the simplex, this infeasible vertex is on the other side of the optimal vertex. Like the dual simplex, now the Pull Phase moves from vertex to vertex to retrieve feasibility while maintaining optimality; it is free from pivotal degeneracy since it removes any negative; non- zero, RHS elements. The space of the algorithm is m-1 dimensions in the Push Phase and n dimensions in the Push Further and Pull Phases, m-1 being the number of constraints and n the number of arcs.

Theorem 2: The Push and Pull Phases are free from pivotal degeneracy that may cause cycling.

Proof: As it is known, whenever a RHS element is zero in any simplex tableau (except the final tableau), the subsequent iteration may be pivotal degenerate when applying the ordinary simplex method, which may cause cycling. In the Push phase, we do not replace any variables. Rather, we expand the basic variable set (BVS) by bringing in new variables to the open rows marked with "?". The Pull Phase uses the customary dual simplex rule to determine what variable goes out. This phase is also free from pivotal degeneracy since its aim is to replace any negative, non- zero RHS entries.

Theorem 3: The solution algorithm terminates successfully in a finite number of iterations.

Proof: The algorithm consists of the Set-up Phase to generate an initial tableau that contains some basic variables, followed by three phases. The Push Phase is a BVS augmentation process that develops a basic solution, which may or may not be feasible. The Push Further Phase aims to satisfy the optimality condition. If the BVS is not feasible, the Pull Phase is activated to obtain a feasible optimal solution. All phases use the usual GJP, but differ in the method used to select the pivot element. The Push Phase uses modified simplex column selection criteria to enter one variable at a time into an open row, rather than replacing a variable, while moving towards a vertex that is "close" to the optimal vertex. This strategy pushes toward an optimal solution, which may result in pushing too far into non-feasibility. The Pull Phase, if needed, pulls back to a feasible solution that is optimal.

The theoretical basis for the proposed algorithm rests largely upon the total unimodularity of the constraints coefficient matrix and it remains unimodal under the GJP operations. By the LP formulation, optimality is attained when all t_{ij}s in the last row of a tableau are non-positive and the algorithm terminates successfully. The current algorithm starts with some non-positive t_{ij}s. Removing the redundant constraint turns a column into a unit vector identifying a basic variable for the set-up phase.

Since we are adding (not replacing) variables to the BVS in the Initialization and Push Phases, deletion of basic columns is permissible. This reduces the complexity significantly and results in a smaller tableau. In the Pull Phase, if an RHS is negative, there exists at least one element of -1 in that row. If this were not the case, an inconsistent constraint would exist, which is impossible. In this phase, the reduced pivoting rule produces the same results as the usual pivoting with a smaller tableau. The proof follows from the well-known reduced pivoting rule in GJP.

The proposed algorithm converges successfully since the path through the Push, Push-Further and Pull Phases does not contain any loops. Therefore, it suffices to show that each phase of the algorithm terminates successfully. The Set-up Phase uses the structure of the problem to fill-up the BVS as much as possible without requiring GJP iterations.

The Push Phase constructs a complete BVS. The number of iterations is finite since the size of the BVS is finite. Push-Further Phase uses the usual simplex rule. At the end of this phase, a basic solution exists that may not be feasible. The Pull Phase terminates successfully by the well-known theory of dual simplex.

3. AN ILLUSTRATIVE NUMERICAL EXAMPLE

This section illustrates this new algorithm by walking through the project as shown in Figure 1. The LP formulation of this project network is:

Maximize $9X_{12} + 6X_{13} + 0X_{23} + 7X_{34} + 8X_{35} + 10X_{45} + 12X_{56}$

Subject to:

$X_{12} + X_{13} = 1,$

$X_{12} - X_{23} = 0,$

$X_{13} + X_{23} - X_{34} - X_{35} = 0,$

$X_{34} - X_{45} = 0,$

$X_{35} + X_{45} - X_{56} = 0,$

$X_{56} = 1,$ and all $X_{ij} \geq 0.$

Phase I: Set Up Phase

Subtract the largest duration of starting and ending activities (which are 9 and 12) from the starting and ending activity durations. Eliminate the first constraint. The reduced problem is

Maximize $-3X_{13} + 7X_{34} + 8X_{35} + 10X_{45}$

Subject to

$X_{12} - X_{23} = 0,$

$X_{13} + X_{23} - X_{34} - X_{35} = 0,$

$X_{34} - X_{45} = 0,$

$X_{35} + X_{45} - X_{56} = 0,$

$X_{56} = 1,$

Figure 1. An illustrative numerical example

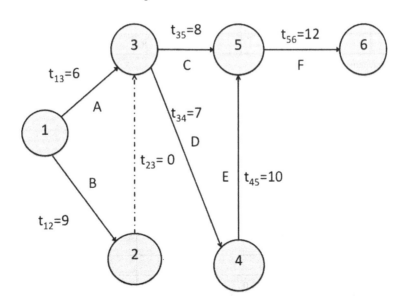

and all $X_{ij} \geq 0$.

Refer to Table 1 for the initial tableau, and Tables 2, 3, 4, 5, and 6 for the consequence tableaux.

End of Push Iteration

Phase II: Push Further

2.0 Push Further Iteration Termination Test
All t_{ij} are non-positive therefore end of OP Iteration

Table 1. Tentative initial simplex tableau

Node	Var	X_{12}	X_{13}	X_{23}	X_{34}	X_{35}	X_{45}	X_{56}	RHS
2	?	1		-1					0
3	?		1	1	-1	-1			0
4	?				1		-1		0
5	?					1	1	-1	0
6	?							1	1
	t_{ij}	0	-3	0	7	8	10	0	-21

Table 2. First tableau

Node	Var	X_{13}	X_{23}	X_{34}	X_{35}	X_{45}	X_{56}	RHS
2	X_{12}		-1					0
3	?	1	1	-1	-1			0
4	?			1		-1		0
5	?				1	[1]	-1	0
6	?						1	1
	t_{ij}	-3	0	7	8	10	0	-21

Note that the non-zero pivot element is enclosed by [ ].

Table 3. Second tableau

Node	Var	X_{13}	X_{23}	X_{34}	X_{35}	X_{56}	RHS
2	X_{12}		-1				0
3	?	1	1	-1	-1		0
4	?			1	1	-1	0
5	X_{45}				1	-1	0
6	?					[1]	1
	t_{ij}	-3	0	7	-2	10	-21

Table 4. Third tableau

Node	Var	X_{13}	X_{23}	X_{34}	X_{35}	RHS
2	X_{12}		-1			0
3	?	1	1	-1	-1	0
4	?			[1]	1	1
5	X_{45}				1	1
6	X_{56}					1
	t_{ij}	-3	0	7	-2	-31

Table 5. Fourth tableau

Node	Var	X_{13}	X_{23}	X_{35}	RHS
2	X_{12}	-1			0
3	?	1	[1]		1
4	X_{34}			1	1
5	X_{45}			1	1
6	X_{56}				1
	t_{ij}	-3	0	-9	-38

Table 6. The final tableau

Node	Var	X_{13}	X_{35}	RHS
2	X_{12}	1		1
3	X_{23}	1		1
4	X_{34}		1	1
5	X_{45}		1	1
6	X_{56}			1
	t_{ij}	-3	-9	-38

Phase III: Pull Phase

3.0 FE Iteration Termination Test
All RHS are non-negative
Therefore terminate FE Iteration
Tableau is optimal

Results are: $X_{12} = 1$, $X_{23} = 1$, $X_{34} = 1$, $X_{45} = 1$, $X_{56} = 1$ and all other $X_{ij} = 0$. That is, the CP path is $1 \rightarrow 2 \rightarrow 3 \rightarrow 4 \rightarrow 5 \rightarrow 6$ with a project completion time of 38 time units. The slack times for the two non-critical activities namely $(1 \rightarrow 3)$ and $(3 \rightarrow 5)$ are given as the absolute value of the last row in the final tableau that are 3 and 9, respectively. It is noteworthy that the proposed solution algorithm is more general than it appears. Specifically, having obtained the final tableau, it can handle revisions of the nominal project. Clearly, this capability would be useful in coping with the situation where some activities are deleted or some new activities are added to the nominal project. Rather than starting the algorithm again to find the CP, the current final tableau can be updated. Moreover, if one is interested in finding all critical paths, or counting (which is combinatorial) the number of CPs, the last row in the final tableau provides the necessary information. If any $t_{ij} = 0$, then there might be multiple critical paths. By bringing any X_{ij} with $t_{ij} = 0$ into the BVS, a new CP may be generated. Clearly, in such a case, the DPA results are valid for the current CP and may not withhold for the others.

4. DATA PERTURBATION ANALYSIS

Given the outcome of a linear program formulation and calculation for the set of project activities, a series of analyses can provide valuable information. These uncertainty ranges can be obtained by performing the following different types of Data Perturbation Analysis (DPA) depending on the nature of the uncertainty: perturbation analysis; tolerance analysis; individual symmetric tolerance analysis; symmetric tolerance analysis; parametric sensitivity analysis; and ordinary sensitivity analysis.

4.1 Construction of Perturbation Analysis Set

Simultaneous and independent changes in the estimated activity durations in either direction (over or under estimation) for each activity that will maintain the current CP. This provides the largest set of perturbations. Inclusion of all actual activity durations in this set preserves the current CP.

As we notice earlier, the LP formulation of this project network can be written as an LP, called the primal problem:

Maximize $9X_{12} + 6X_{13} + 0X_{23} + 7X_{34} + 8X_{35} + 10X_{45} + 12X_{56}$

Subject to:

$X_{12} + X_{13} = 1,$

$-X_{12} + X_{23} = 0,$

$-X_{13} - X_{23} + X_{34} + X_{35} = 0,$

$-X_{34} + X_{45} = 0,$

$-X_{35} - X_{45} + X_{56} = 0,$

$-X_{56} = -1,$

and all $X_{ij} \geq 0.$

The Dual Problem is:

Minimize U1 - U6

Subject to:

U1 – U2 ≥ 9 The Dual Constraint Related to Critical Activity $X_{12} = 1$

U1 – U3 ≥ 6 The Dual Constraint Related to Non-critical Activity $X_{13} = 1$

U2 – U3 ≥ 0 The Dual Constraint Related to Critical Activity, $X_{23} = 1$

U3 – U4 ≥ 7 The Dual Constraint Related to Critical Activity, $X_{34} = 1$

U3 – U5 ≥ 8 The Dual Constraint Related to Non-critical Activity $X_{35} = 1$

U4 – U5 ≥ 10 The Dual Constraint Related to Critical Activity $X_{45} = 1$

U5 – U6 ≥ 12 The Dual Constraint Related to Critical Activity $X_{56} = 1$

Uj's are unrestricted

The constraints of the dual formulation suggest that for any activity, the difference between finish and starting times exceeds the duration of the activity. The above constraints are related to seven X_{ij} as they appear in the objective function of the primal problem, respectively. Knowing the critical activities have zero slack time, the following constraints are binding:

$U1 - U2 = 9$

$U2 - U3 = 0$

$U3 - U4 = 7$

$U4 - U5 = 10$

$U5 - U6 = 12$

The parametric (i.e., perturbed) RHS of these constraints gives:

$U1 - U2 = 9 + T1$

$U2 - U3 = 0 + T3$

$U3 - U4 = 7 + T4$

$U4 - U5 = 10 + T6$

$U5 - U6 = 12 + T7$

Solving these parametric system of equations we obtain:

$U1 = U6 + T1 + T3 + T4 + T6 + T7 + 38$

$U2 = U6 + T3 + T4 + T6 + T7 + 29$

$U3 = U6 + T4 + T6 + T7 + 29$

$U4 = U6 + T6 + T7 + 22$

$U5 = U6 + T7 + 12$

Notice that the set of numbers in this solution are the shadow prices with optimal objective function value U1 - U6 = 38, as expected being the same as the primal optimal value.

For the larger projects this parametric solution can be obtained by using the JavaScript:

Solving Linear Parametric RHS: http://www.mirrorservice.org/sites/home.ubalt.edu/ntsbarsh/Business-stat/otherapplets/PaRHSSyEqu.htm

This solution must satisfy the constraints related to non-binding constraints. By plugging this solution in the dual inequalities for non-critical activities, we have:

$T1 + T3 \geq -3, T4 + T6 \geq -9$

The following proposition formalizes the shifting of parametric bon-binding constraint.

Proposition 1: For any given point $X^o = (X_1^o, X_2^o, ..., X_n^o)$ the parameter T value for any resource/production constraint is proportional to the (usual) distance between the point X^o and the hyper-plane of the constraint.

Proof: The proof follows from the fact that the distance from point $X^o = (X_1^o, X_2^o, ..., X_n^o)$ to any nonbinding hyper-plane, i.e. $a_1 X_1^o + a_2 X_2^o + ... + a_n X_n^o = b + T$ is Absolute value of $[a_1 X_1^o + a_2 X_2^o + ... + a_n X_n^o - b - T] / (a_1^2 + a_2^2 + ... + a_n^2)^{1/2}$ That reduces to: $T / (a_1^2 + a_2^2 + ... + a_n^2)^{1/2}$.

Therefore the parameter T value is proportional to the distance with the constant proportionality, that is $1/ (a_1^2 + a_2^2 + ... + a_n^2)^{1/2}$. This is independent of point X^o. In the above example X^o is the dual optimal vertex. This completes the proof.

Therefore, the sensitivity region for the two non-binding constraints are found by plugging in the shadow prices:

U1 – U3 ≥ 6 + T2, 38 - 29 ≥ 6 + T2, T2 ≤ 3

U3 – U5 ≥ 8 + T5, 29 -12 ≥ 8 + T5, T5 ≤ 9

Putting all together, i.e., the union of all sensitivity regions, we obtain the largest sensitivity region for the duration of all activities:

S = { Tj, j=1, 2, 3, 4, 5, 6, 7 | T1 ≥ -9, T2 ≥ -6, T3 = 0, T4 ≥ -7, T5 ≥ -8, T6 ≥ -10,

T7 ≥ -12, T1 + T3 ≥ -3, T2 ≤ 3, T4 + T6 ≥ -9, T5 ≤ 9}

Notice that *Data Perturbation set S* in convex and non-empty since it contains the origin, i.e. when all Tj = 0. Perturbation is said to be CP preserving, if the perturbed model has the same CP as the nominal project. Clearly, the DPA are concerned with CP preserving as outlined in the Introduction. *This set could be used to check whether a given numerical perturbed activity durations has any impact on the current CP.*

The following presents different types of popular sensitivity analysis for non-degenerate problems. For treatment of degeneracy see Lin and Wen (2003), Arsham (2007), Lin (2010), and Lin (2011)

4.2 Parametric and Ordinary Sensitivity Analysis

Parametric analysis is of particular interest whenever there are some kinds of dependency among the activity durations. This dependency is very common in project activity networks. This analysis can be considered as simultaneous changes in a *given* direction. Define a perturbation vector **P** specifying a perturbed direction of the activity durations. Introducing a scalar parameter a ≥ 0, it is required to find out how far the direction of P can be moved while still maintaining the current CP.

In our numerical example let us assume the activity duration times [9, 6, 0, 7, 8, 10, 12] are perturbed along the dependent vector **P** = (0, 0, -1, 3, 1, -2, -1). To find scalar parameter a, substitute for vector a **P** = (0, 0, -a, 3a, a, -2a, -a) in the critical region

S = { Tj, j=1, 2, 3, 4, 5, 6, 7 | T1 ≥ -9, T2 ≥ -6, T3 = 0, T4 ≥ -7, T5 ≥ -8, T6 ≥ -10, T7 ≥ -12, T1 + T3 ≥ -3, T2 ≤ 3, T4 + T6 ≥ -9, T5 ≤ 9}

Now all terms are converted in terms of parameter a. The smallest positive value for a in 3.

Therefore the current CP remains critical for any perturbation aP, where 0 ≤ a ≤ 3.

4.3 Ordinary Sensitivity Analysis

In this sub-section interest is in finding the range for *any particular* activity duration, holding all other activity durations unchanged. Clearly, the ordinary sensitivity is a special case of parametric analysis where it is required to find the extent of the move in positive and negative directions of any one of the axes in the n-parametric space t_{ij}. Here, **P** is a unit row vector or is negative depending on whether an upper or a lower limit is required. The ordinary sensitivity analysis is summarized in Table 7. Alternatively, to find the allowable uncertainty T_i for any particular activity duration time i, set all other T = 0 in perturbation set S. The results are summarized in Table 7.

Table 7. One change at a time sensitivity limits

	Lower Limit	Upper Limit
T1	-3	M
T2	-6	3
T3	0	0
T4	-7	M
T5	-8	9
T6	-9	M
T7	-12	M

The above analysis deals with one duration-uncertainty at-a-time analysis. Suppose we want to find the simultaneous allowable changes all activity durations, in such a case one may apply what is known as the 100% rule.

4.4 The 100% Rule

The 100% rule states that simultaneous increase (decrease) changes is allowed as long as the sum of the percentages of the change divided by the corresponding maximum increase (decrease) allowable change in the range of ordinary sensitivity analysis for each coefficient does not exceed 100%.

Therefore, base on this rule, the CP will be preserved if

$$T2 / 3 + T5 / 9 \leq 1,$$

where the two denominators are the allowable increases from the sensitivity analysis for t_{13} and t_{35} respectively. That is, as long as this inequality holds, the current CP remains unchanged. Clearly, this condition is *sufficient* but not necessary. Similarly, the application of the 100% rule for decreasing some activity duration provides:

$$T1 / (-3) + T2 / (-6) + T4 / (-7) + T5 / (-8) + T6 / (-9) + T7 / (-12) \leq 1,$$

with a similar interpretation.

As mentioned earlier the Data Perturbation Set, S, is useful to check for any numerically known values of durations if current CP remains critical. However the algebra becomes messy if one tries to find, for example, what is the largest percentage change for all activities to maintain the current CP? Arsham (1990) provides detailed treatments of this and other useful sensitivity analyses with numerical examples including the followings.

4.5 Tolerance Analysis

Simultaneous and independent changes expressed as the maximum allowable *percentage* of the estimated activity duration in either direction (over or under estimation) for *each* activity that will maintain the current CP. Such an analysis is useful whenever the uncertainties in the estimated activity durations can be expressed as some percentages of their estimated values. Here, the lower and upper uncertainty limits to maintain the current CP, i.e. error in both directions: over and under estimation for all activities must be found. Let B denotes the matrix in the body of the final tableau, then matrix A denotes the row-wise augmented matrix B, constructed by pending an identity matrix **I** of order k as its last k rows where k is the number of non-critical activities in the final tableau. That is, $\mathbf{A} = [\mathbf{B} \mid \mathbf{I}]^T$, where the superscript T means transpose. Denote $\tau_j = C.A_j$ where A_j is the absolute value of the jth column of A, in the body of the final tableau, and T is the estimated activity duration time vector. From now on, the critical and non-critical activities must be differentiated.

a. Tolerance Limits for Critical Activities

For any critical activity duration, i.e., for any t_{sk}, the upper tolerance limit is unbounded. However, the lower tolerance limit for t'_{sk} is:

$$t_{sk}^- = \max \{t_{sk} [(\text{lower sensitivity limit})_j / \tau_j], \text{ and the lower limit from the sensitivity analysis}\},$$

where the max is over all j such that the (t'_{sk} row and the jth column) element of A is positive.

In the numerical example, the augmented matrix A is shown in Table 8 and C = (9, 0, 7, 10, 12, 6, 8). The element of matrix $\tau = C.A$, are $\tau_1 = 15$ and $\tau_2 = 25$.

Table 8. Matrix A as a tool for tolerance analysis

		t'_{13}	t'_{35}
A =	t'_{12}	1	0
	t'_{23}	1	0
	t'_{34}	0	1
	t'_{45}	0	1
	t'_{56}	0	0
	t'_{13}	1	0
	t'_{35}	0	1

For example, the lower tolerance limit for the activity duration t'_{12} can be found as follows:

$$t'_{12}{}^- = \max \{9(-3)/15, 9(-9)/25, -3\} = -9/5$$

b. Tolerance Limits for Non-Critical Activities

For any non-critical activity duration, i.e., for any t'_{sk}, the lower tolerance limit is the ordinary sensitivity limit, and its upper limit for t'_{sk} is:

$$t'_{sk}{}^+ = \min \{t_{sk} [(T_n{}^*)_j / - \tau_j], \text{ and the upper limit}$$
from the sensitivity analysis},

where the min is over all j such that the (t'_{sk} row and the jth column) element of A is positive. For example, the upper tolerance limit for the activity duration t_{13} is:

$$t'_{13}{}^+ = \min\{6 (-3) / -15, 6(-9)/-25, 3\} = 6/5.$$

The tolerance limits of all activity duration for the numerical example are shown in Table 9.

The symmetric tolerance limits reflect the maximum allowable equal percentage error in both directions (over and under estimations) that hold simultaneously over all activity durations. Clearly, the symmetric tolerance range is a subset of the tolerance range. From Table 3, it is clear that the symmetric tolerance limit for the numerical example is 20%.

4.6 Application to Enhance the Traditional PERT Approach

The modeler asks the manager to express the duration of uncertainty for each activity by a percent change in either direction. Clearly, there might be different percentage for different activities, thus many scenarios, however, suppose the uncertainty is at most 20% in either direction for all activities. This makes sense to have equal uncertainty since larger durations will have larger uncertainty range. In this case; by setting lower and upper limits of individual symmetric tolerance analysis (ISA) as the largest lower bound for optimistic and the smallest upper bound for pessimistic estimates respectively. The data shown in Table 10 pertain to the network of Figure 1.

Table 9. Tolerance limits for all durations

	Lower Limit	Upper Limit
t'_{12}	-9/5 (20%)	M
t'_{13}	-6 (100%)	6/5 (20%)
t'_{23}	0	0
t'_{34}	-63/25 (36%)	M
t'_{35}	-8 (100%)	72/25 (36%)
t'_{45}	-18/5 (36%)	M
t'_{56}	-12 (100%)	M

Table 10. Data for Figure 1

Notation	Activity	Optimistic Time a	Most Likely Time m	Pessimistic Time b	$t_e = (a+4m+b)/6$
1→3	A	4.8	6	7.2	6
1→2	B	7.2	9	10.8	9
2→3	Dummy Activity				
3→4	D	5.6	7	8.4	7
3→5	C	6.4	8	9.6	8
4→5	E	8	10	12	10
5→6	F	9.6	12	14.4	12

The optimistic time (a) is the amount of time that an activity will take if everything goes well. The probability that the activity will take less than this amount of time is 0.01.

The pessimistic time (b) is the amount of time that an activity will take if everything goes poorly. The probability that the activity will exceed this duration is 0.01.

The most likely time (m) is the time that the estimator thinks an activity will probably take. The activity could be performed many times under the same conditions (no learning), this is the time that would occur most often.

Suppose the optimistic time, most likely time, and pessimistic time for each activity are acceptable to the members of the project team. Note that since the pessimistic time and the optimistic time are symmetrical with regard to the most likely time, the mean completion time ET is equal to the most likely time for each activity.

Note that in an AOA convention, a node represents both the end of an activity and the start of another. It is sometimes useful to present the network in Activity-on-node (AON) convention

to distinguish between the early finish time for the predecessor and the early start time for successor. Another advantage of an AON convention is that it does not need dummy activities. Figure 2 presents the network of Figure 1 in AON convention.

The following steps are required in developing and solving a network:

1. Identify each activity to be done in the project.
2. Determine the sequence of activities and construct a network reflecting the prece-

Figure 2. Network in Activity-on-node (AON) convention

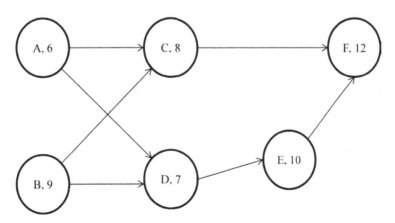

Table 11. Calculation of Figure 2 network

Activity	Time	ES	EF	LS	LF	Slack
A	6	0	6	3	9	3
B	9	0	9	0	9	0
C	8	9	17	18	26	9
D	7	9	16	9	16	0
E	10	16	26	16	26	0
F	12	26	38	26	38	0

dence relationships. The network consists of nodes and arrows. In a CPM network, nodes represent activities and arrows denote precedence relationships only.

3. Four values are calculated for each activity:
   - **Earliest Start, ES:** earliest time an activity can start based on completion of all predecessor activities
   - **Latest Start, LS:** latest time an activity can start and still achieve its latest finish time
   - **Earliest Finish, EF:** earliest time an activity can be completed given that it starts at its earliest start time
   - **Latest Finish, LF:** latest time an activity can be completed if its successor activities are to begin by a set time and/or if the project is to be completed by a set time.

Forward and backward passes are needed for the calculation of early start, early finish, late start, and late finish times for activities. This information in turn can be used to identify the critical path, slack times and project completion time.

The slack time for each activity is defined as either LS - ES or LF - EF. The slack time is the amount of time by which the start of a given event may be delayed without delaying the completion of the project. The critical path is the longest sequence of connected activities through the network and is defined as the path with zero slack time.

The management significance of the critical path is that it constrains the completion date of the project since it is the longest path of activity times from the start to the end of the network. As a result, activities on the critical path should be intensively managed to avoid slippage. Other activities, not on the critical path, can be allowed to slip somewhat, up to their amount of slack, without affecting the project completion date. Table 11 provides the ES, EF, LS, LF and slack for all activities for the network in Figure 2.

Note that there are four paths with total length of time as indicated below:

1. A→C→F, total time = 26
2. A→D→E→F, total time = 35
3. B→C→F, total time = 29
4. B→D→ E→F, total time = 38

The critical path is B→D→ E→F, the longest path and the project completion time is 38. Note that EF and LF are equal for activities on the critical path providing slacks for all activities as 0. So you cannot delay these activities.

Table 12. Ranges for the Ordinary Sensitivity Analysis (OSA), Tolerance Analysis (TA), Individual Symmetric Tolerance Analysis (IST), and Symmetric Tolerance Analysis (STA) with Critical Activities in Bold

	Crash Durations				Duration	Slippage Durations			
	SA	TA	IST	STA		STA	IST	TA	SA
t_{12}	**6**	**7.2**	**7.2**	**7.2**	**9**	**10.8**	**10.8**	**M**	**M**
t_{13}	0	0	4.8	4.8	6	7.2	7.2	7.2	9
t_{23}	**0**	**0**	**0**	**0**	**0**	**0**	**0**	**0**	**0**
t_{34}	**0**	**4.48**	**4.48**	**5.6**	**7**	**8.4**	**9.52**	**M**	**M**
t_{35}	0	0	5.12	6.4	8	9.6	10.88	10.88	17
t_{45}	**1**	**6.4**	**6.4**	**8**	**10**	**12**	**13.6**	**M**	**M**
t_{56}	**0**	**0**	**0**	**9.6**	**12**	**14.4**	**24**	**M**	**M**

4.7 Further Application of the DPA Results for the Managers

Table 12 summarizes some parts of our findings from analysis applied to the numerical example, using the sensitivity region:

$S = \{$ Tj, j=1, 2, 3, 4, 5, 6, 7 | T1 $\geq$ -9, T2 $\geq$ -6, T3 = 0, T4 $\geq$ -7, T5 $\geq$ -8, T6 $\geq$ -10, T7 $\geq$ -12, T1 + T3 $\geq$ -3, T2 $\leq$ 3, T4 + T6 $\geq$ -9, T5 $\leq$ 9$\}$

As always, care must be taken when rounding the DPA limits. Clearly the upper limit and lower limit must be rounded down and up, respectively.

Since project managers are concerned with the stability of the CP under uncertainty of the estimated durations, the output information from our various DPA should be of interest to project managers. As long as the actual activity durations remain within these intervals, the current CP remains critical. Some specific implications from these results for the project manager are that they provide means for discussion and analysis by the project team members as to how to consider modifying the project prior to its implementation. The results given in Table 7 help the project manager to assess, analyze, monitor, and manage all phases of a project; i.e. planning, scheduling,

and controlling. When the issues caused by the inherent uncertainty in any project are considered, there are other benefits to be gained by using the proposed DPA approach; e.g., it provides various ranges of uncertainty with the lower limits as the maximum "crashing" for critical activity durations and the upper limits as the maximum "slippage" for non-critical activity durations and their impacts on the entire project completion time. These results could be helpful in some large projects, e.g., if certain activities could be moved into certain intervals or be divisible into smaller sub-activities and "tucked in" at several locations.

The proposed approach can also provide a rich modeling environment for strategic management of complex projects using Monte-Carlo simulation experiments. In this treatment, a priori duration distribution function may be selected for each activity with the support range produced by the tolerance analysis. Clearly, in the case of complete lack of knowledge uniform distribution function could be used.

Throughout the DPA it has been assumed that duration of all activities are continuous. Clearly, whenever some activity durations are required to be discrete, then this admissibility condition must be added to all parts of DPA. The discussion of DPA did not include other important managerial issues, such as time-cost-performance tradeoff, including penalty for delay, reward for timely completion of the entire project; resource allocation; leveling; and constrained resource scheduling; and the human side of project management. The proposed model should serve as an aid to management judgment; therefore the project manager's experience must be incorporated in the proposed prescriptive model.

Winston (2003) stated correctly that: "The assumption that the critical path found by the critical path method will always be the critical path for the project network may not be justified. For example if activity A = 1→ 3 with duration 6 days was significantly delayed and activity B = 1 → 2 with duration 9 days was completed ahead of schedule, then the critical path might be different." The main managerial question is: How much delay and how much ahead of schedule? Unfortunately, the answer is not generally given. However, this needed information is obtained using the DPA results given in Table 6 as follows: Using the TA upper limit = 7.2 and the lower limit = 7.2 for these two activities duration, respectively, the answer is a delay of at least 1.2 days (7.2 - 6 = 1.2) for A, and a crash of at least 1.8 days (9 - 7.2 = 1.8) for B. Since we are dealing with two activities only, a better result can be obtained by using a parametric analysis along vector P = {-9a, 6b, 0, 0, 0, 0, 0}. Plugging into set S, we get a = 1/3, b = 1/2. Therefore a better answer is a delay of at least 3 days (i.e., t_{13} = 6 + 3 = 9) for A, and ahead of time of at most 3 days (i.e., t_{12} = 9 – 3 = 6) for B.

5. CONCLUSION

As long as the actual activity durations remain within intervals introduced in this paper the current critical path (CP) remains critical. By using the Data Perturbation Analysis (DPA) approach, project managers are provided means for negotiation and analysis by the project team members to how to consider modifying the project prior to its implementation. Moreover, the project manager

is able to assess, analyze, monitor, and manage various types of uncertainties in all phases of a project; i.e. planning, scheduling, and controlling.

When the issues caused by the inherent uncertainty in any project are considered, there are other benefits to be gained by using the proposed DPA approach. It provides various ranges of uncertainty with the lower limits as the maximum "crashing" for critical activity durations and the upper limits as the maximum "slippage" for non-critical activity durations, and their impacts on the entire project completion time. These results could be helpful in some large projects where certain activities could be moved into certain intervals or be divisible into smaller sub-activities and "tucked in" at several locations.

The proposed approach can also provide a rich modeling environment for strategic management of complex projects using Monte-Carlo simulation experiments. In this treatment, a priori duration distribution function may be selected for each activity with the support domain produced by the tolerance analysis. In the case of complete lack of knowledge a uniform distribution function may be used. Therefore the DPA report to the manager can enhance any other method of project management.

When the three-point estimate PERT is used, then the lower and upper limits of individual symmetric tolerance analysis can serve as the largest lower bound for optimistic and the smallest upper bound for pessimistic estimates, respectively. This may relieve the project managers from guessing. Throughout the DPA, it has been assumed that the durations of all activities are continuous. As a result, whenever some activity durations are required to be discrete, then this admissibility condition to all parts of DPA must be added.

The DPA approach may be further extended by consideration of important managerial issues, such as time-cost-performance tradeoff, including penalty for delay, reward for timely completion of the entire project, resource allocation, leveling and constrained resource scheduling, and the human side of project management. Clearly, the proposed model in this paper should serve as an aid to, rather than substitute for, management judgment. Therefore, the project manager's experience must be incorporated in the proposed prescriptive model. The proposed approach has the advantage of being computationally practical, easy for a project manager to understand, and provides useful practical information.

ACKNOWLEDGMENT

We are most appreciative to reviewers for their comments and useful suggestions on an earlier version.

REFERENCES

Adlakha, V., & Arsham, H. (1992). A simulation technique for estimation in perturbed stochastic activity networks. *Simulation, 58*(2), 258–267. doi:10.1177/003754979205800406

Arsham, H. (1990). Perturbation analysis of general LP models: A unified approach to sensitivity, parametric, tolerance, and more-for-less analysis. *Mathematical and Computer Modelling, 13*(8), 79–102. doi:10.1016/0895-7177(90)90073-V

Arsham, H. (1997a). Initialization of the simplex algorithm: An artificial-free approach. *SIAM Review, 39*(5), 736–744. doi:10.1137/S0036144596304722

Arsham, H. (1997b). Affine geometric method for linear programs. *Journal of Scientific Computing, 12*(3), 289–303. doi:10.1023/A:1025601511684

Arsham, H. (2005). A computer implementation of the push-and-pull algorithm and its computational comparison with LP simplex method. *Applied Mathematics and Computation, 170*(1), 36–63. doi:10.1016/j.amc.2004.10.078

Arsham, H. (2007). Construction of the largest sensitivity region for general linear programs. *Applied Mathematics and Computation, 189*(2), 1435–1447. doi:10.1016/j.amc.2006.12.020

Banerjee, A., & Paul, A. (2008). On path correlation and PERT bias. *European Journal of Operational Research, 189*(3), 1208–1216. doi:10.1016/j.ejor.2007.01.061

Cassone, D. (2010). A process to build new product development cycle time predictive models combining fuzzy set theory and probability theory. *International Journal of Applied Decision Sciences, 3*(2), 168–183. doi:10.1504/IJADS.2010.034838

Czuchra, W. (1999). Optimizing budget spendings for software implementation and testing. *Computers & Operations Research, 26*(7), 731–747. doi:10.1016/S0305-0548(98)00086-0

D'Aquila, N. (1993). Facilitating in-service programs through PERT/CPM: Simultaneous use of these tools can assist nurses in organizing workshops. *Nursing Management, 24*(2), 92–98. PMID:8265089

Gido, J., & Clements, J. (2011). *Successful project management with Microsoft*. New York, NY: South-Western College Pub.

Hasan, H., & Gould, E. (2001). Support for the sense-making activity of managers. *Decision Support Systems, 1*(31), 71–86. doi:10.1016/S0167-9236(00)00120-2

Herrerı'as-Velasco, J., Herrerı'as-Pleguezuelo, R., & René van Dorp, J. (2011). Revisiting the PERT mean and variance. *European Journal of Operational Research, 210*(2), 448–451. doi:10.1016/j.ejor.2010.08.014

Higgs, S. (1995). Software roundup: Project management for windows. *Byte, 20*, 185–186.

Hoffer, J., Valacich, J., & George, J. (2011). *Essentials of systems analysis and design*. Englewood Cliffs, NJ: Prentice Hall.

Jarvis, J., & Shier, D. (1990). Netsolve: Interactive software for network optimization. *Operations Research Letters, 9*(3), 275–282. doi:10.1016/0167-6377(90)90073-E

Kallo, G. (1996). The reliability of critical path method (CPM) techniques in the analysis and evaluation of delay claims. *Coastal Engineering, 38*(1), 35–39.

Kamburowski, J. (1997). New validations of PERT times. *Omega, 25*(3), 323–328. doi:10.1016/S0305-0483(97)00002-9

Keefer, D., & Verdini, W. (1993). Better estimation of PERT activity time parameters. *Management Science, 39*(6), 1086–1091. doi:10.1287/mnsc.39.9.1086

Keramati, A., Dardick, G., Mojir, N., & Banan, B. (2009). Application of latent moderated structuring (LMS) to rank the effects of intervening variables on the IT and firm performance relationship. *International Journal of Applied Decision Sciences*, 2(2), 167–188. doi:10.1504/IJADS.2009.026551

Kerzner, H. (2009). *Project management: A systems approach to planning, scheduling, and controlling*. New York, NY: Wiley.

Kuklan, H. (1993). Effective project management: An expanded network approach. *Journal of Systems Management*, 44(1), 12–16.

Lewis, J. (2007). *Mastering project management: Applying advanced concepts to systems thinking, control & evaluation, resource allocation*. New York: McGraw-Hill.

Lin, C.-J. (2010). Computing shadow prices/costs of degenerate LP problems with reduced simplex tables. *Expert Systems with Applications*, 37(8), 5848–5855. doi:10.1016/j.eswa.2010.02.021

Lin, C.-J. (2011). A labeling algorithm for the sensitivity ranges of the assignment problem. *Applied Mathematical Modelling*, 35(10), 4852–4864. doi:10.1016/j.apm.2011.03.045

Lin, C.-J., & Wen, U.-P. (2003). Sensitivity analysis of the optimal assignment. *European Journal of Operational Research*, 149(1), 35–46. doi:10.1016/S0377-2217(02)00439-3

Martín, M., García, C., Pérez, J., & Sánchez Granero, M. (2012). An alternative for robust estimation in project management. *European Journal of Operational Research*, 220(2), 443–451. doi:10.1016/j.ejor.2012.01.058

Mehrotra, K., Chai, J., & Pillutla, S. (1996). A study of approximating the moments of the job completion time in PERT networks. *Journal of Operations Management*, 14(3), 277–289. doi:10.1016/0272-6963(96)00002-2

Meredith, J., & Mantel, S. Jr. (2008). *Project management: A managerial approach*. New York, NY: Wiley.

Mouhoub, N., Benhocine, A., & Belouadah, H. (2011). A new method for constructing a minimal PERT network. *Applied Mathematical Modelling*, 35(9), 4575–4588. doi:10.1016/j.apm.2011.03.031

Nasution, S. (1994). Fuzzy critical path method. *IEEE Transactions on Systems, Man, and Cybernetics*, 24(1), 48–51. doi:10.1109/21.259685

Nicholas, J., & Steyn, H. (2008). *Project management for business, engineering, and technology*. New York, NY: Butterworth-Heinemann.

Phillips, D., & Garcia-Diaz, A. (1990). *Fundamental of network analysis*. Englewood Cliffs, NJ: Prentice-Hall.

Pirdashti, M., Mohammadi, M., Rahimpour, F., & Kennedy, D. (2008). An AHP-Delphi multicriteria location planning model with application to whey protein production facility decisions. *International Journal of Applied Decision Sciences*, 1(2), 245–259. doi:10.1504/IJADS.2008.020326

Premachandra, I. (2001). An approximation of the activity duration distribution in PERT. *Computers & Operations Research*, 28(5), 443–452. doi:10.1016/S0305-0548(99)00129-X

Satzinger, J., Jackson, J., & Burd, S. (2011). *Systems analysis and design in a changing world*. New York, NY: Course Technology.

Shipley, M., & Olson, D. (2008). Interval-valued evidence sets from simulated product competitiveness: A Bulgarian winery decision. *International Journal of Applied Decision Sciences*, 1(4), 397–417. doi:10.1504/IJADS.2008.022977

Trietsch, D., & Baker, K. (2012). PERT 21: Fitting PERT/CPM for use in the 21st century. *International Journal of Project Management*, 30(4), 490–502. doi:10.1016/j.ijproman.2011.09.004

Valacich, J., George, J., & Hoffer, J. (2001). *Essentials of systems analysis and design*. Englewood Cliffs, NJ: Prentice Hall.

Winston, W. (2003). *Operations research: Applications and algorithms*. Boston, MA: PWS-KENT Pub. Co.

Wu, S., & Wu, M. (1994). *Systems analysis and design*. New York: West Publishing Company.

Yaghoubi, S., Noori, S., Azaron, A., & Tavakkoli-Moghaddam, R. (2011). Resource allocation in dynamic PERT networks with finite capacity. *European Journal of Operational Research*, *215*(3), 670–678.

Yakhchali, S. (2012). A path enumeration approach for the analysis of critical activities in fuzzy networks. *Information Sciences*, *204*, 23–35. doi:10.1016/j.ins.2012.01.025

Chapter 4
Authenticity in Online Knowledge Sharing:
Experiences from Networks of Competence Meetings

Inge Hermanrud
Hedmark University College, Norway

ABSTRACT

Authenticity means that the closeness of observation matters for acceptance of new knowledge. The social norm of authenticity can have positive effects of colleagues to appreciate "better" knowledge within opportunity structures for knowledge sharing. However, how ICTs influence authenticity in knowledge sharing needs more attention in research on knowledge sharing through online networks. This chapter discusses recent findings of how ICTs (here the interactive tool GoToMeeting™) facilitate authenticity.

INTRODUCTION

Information and communication technology has, due to the weight given to communication and information in knowledge work, been closely associated with the development of knowledge management initiatives and in the commercial arena knowledge management have a strong IT focus (Hayes, 2011). Much of the literature and practice on knowledge management assumes that knowledge can be codified and stored. Sambamurthy and Subramani (2005) is an example of this

DOI: 10.4018/978-1-4666-4856-2.ch004

assumption, when they suggest that knowledge management involves:

developing searchable document repositories to support the digital capture, storage, retrieval, and distribution of an organization's explicit documented knowledge.(p. 2)

The assumption that knowledge can be transferred by the use of ICT has attracted criticism from process and practice based researchers. Brown (1998) maintains that reliance on IT (internet) as a means for transferring knowledge is insufficient. In particular, it is regarded as more difficult if the sharing takes place across domains of knowledge. Abstractions recorded and shared on the Internet must, according to Brown, be considered as inseparable from historical and social locations of practice. When there is no history of working together, Zack (1999) argues that integrative applications are unsuitable. Instead, he recommends the use of interactive applications (chat, videoconferencing) that support collaboration, of which GoToMeeting™ ™ in this study is an example. While the apprentices in Lave and Wenger (1991)'s community of practice can observe the genuine know-how of the master first-hand with considerable accuracy with the ability to observe (face-to-face) a certain level of detail, this article illustrate how a collaborative tool, GoToMeeting™ ™, facilitates the observation of detail.

CASE DISCRIPTION

The Inspection Authority (herein referred to as the Authority) discussed is a large distributed health and safety inspection authority in a Nordic country. The main task of the authority is to supervise that the work environment in the country are according to the statutory requirements. The employees are based at several locations and they are given a high degree of individual autonomy. The employees in this organization often work alone at small district offices or from home offices. The inspectors have over the years developed individual inspection practices, which has made it difficult to promote sharing and learning in the organization. Different districts have different industries, which has also influenced inspection practices and created variations in competences among the distributed inspectors.

The authority is challenged by rapid changes within the domain it is responsible for, such as changes regarding how clients behave and new insights from research – all of which might change the use of the legislation it is overseeing that has to be complied with by its clients. The region 1 unit, one out of seven in the authority, has around 50 employees and out of these around 40 are inspectors. The budget is approximately 40 million kroner (equal to US$6.6 million). The networks' mission is to ensure organizational learning in the authority on the topic area they are set up for. The organizational culture among the inspectors can be described as a very independent work culture, where the inspectors are used to working alone or in pairs and making their own decisions; often working with their clients more than with colleagues. Even though they often work alone, and have few colleagues at the office, a sense of identity with a group and identity with the organization have been developed by telephone calls to colleagues conducting similar tasks or experts at the core of the organization (the directorate, see Figure 1, The organizational chart).

The Inspectors conduct inspections of use and storing of chemicals, installed ventilation facilities as well as measure taken to prevent accidents at work. Usually they are at their office or home office when communicating with each other in the competence network meetings. This case focuses on the ability of GoToMeet-

Figure 1. The organizational chart of the inspection authority

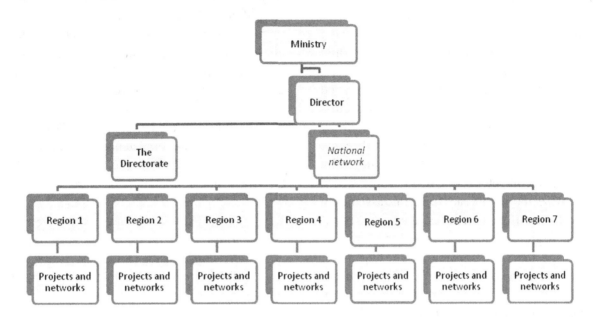

ing™ to promote knowledge sharing by the representation of inspection practice online. A context were knowledge about chemistry or engineering, experiences and the legislation has to be integrated. The IT infrastructure consists of many applications, newer and very old software. Sometimes the same information has to be reported into several systems.

Organizational Structure and Management Responsibilities

The organization has a long history that goes back more than 100 years. The authority's mission is to encourage its clients to work systematically towards compliance with the laws and regulations. The organization has gone through substantial changes in the last seven years. The core of the organization, the directorate, has had its number of employees reduced, and responsibilities have been handed over to the seven regions in the authority. An organizational chart is presented in Figure 1.

The conduction of inspections by this authority is meant to take place in projects and organizational learning in the networks. The purpose of the national networks is to ensure knowledge sharing and learning across the regions. These network is set up with coordinators from the regional networks. In Mintzberg's (1983) terminology the organization has reduced its techno-structure and moved towards more flexible forms of organizing using more project work and networking, much in line with the current trend in organizational design. The organization specific argument for this design is that the inspectors are individually very knowledgeable, but very independent; they need to collaborate more in projects and networks to meet the challenges of the organization. The networks have so far been more a less permanent assignment to a specific competence network for the individual. Projects on the other hand runs from one to three years.

The mode of learning that has dominated the organization until now comprises an apprentice conducting inspections with a senior inspector. In other words, face-to-face-based learning– where the apprentice observes the senior inspector conducting inspections. While this organization used to have experts at its core, the expert knowledge now has to be developed in the regions – among dispersed inspectors in the intra-organizational networks set up by management. They are now supposed to become experts collectively. This is to be achieved by setting up competence networks of inspectors. The inspectors within each region are assigned to one of four different networks, more or less based on their professional orientation or interest.

Inspectors work from regional headquarters, from one of the different local offices, or from home offices distributed all over their region. The distance between the different members in this region can be as much as 1,300 km, and, owing to the limited budget, they may only see each other face-to-face twice a year for two days. In addition, the inspectors are often on the move as they perform their tasks. The members in the network have different professional backgrounds, ranging from engineering, degrees in social science to lawyers; some with lengthier professional education, like lawyers, to others with work experience from relevant industries. The organization employs a total of 500 inspectors, of whom approximately 40 work in region 1. The 40 inspectors in this region are assigned to one out of four different competence networks. Each network is set up with a coordinator, but this assigned person has no formal authority or formal sanctions towards the network members. Each coordinator for each region is represented in national networks. The management responsibility in this context is to support the networks so that they develop the necessary for knowledge and expertise to be able to conduct their tasks.

External consultants have suggested that the authority should set up competence networks

in where the inspectors could develop their individual and collective competencies by reflecting upon experiences and practices, and give input to the organization. The Authority implemented competence network structures in 2005. The experiences in this case were collected in 2009 and 2010. GoToMeeting™ have since 2006 been the selected collaborative IT for the teams as well as the competence networks in the organization. At the time the alternative tools for synchronic communication were:

1. Ordinary phone conferences (without screen sharing)
2. Video-conferencing (studio)
3. GoToMeeting™ (teleconferencing, screen sharing and chat).

The competence networks have used the GoToMeeting™ tool. Since there were no videoconferencing studio facilities available at every district office and since many of the Inspectors work from home-offices, videoconference has rarely been used. Since many of the participants would have to travel anyhow. The selected tool GoToMeeting™, we can argue, had also an advantage since participants in the networks of competence did not need to learn an extra tool. It was already in use.

THE ROLE OF AUTHENTICITY IN KNOWLEDGE SHARING

Authenticity means that the closeness of observation matters for acceptance of new knowledge. The social norm of authenticity can have positively effects of colleagues to appreciate 'better' knowledge within opportunity structures for knowledge sharing. However, how ICT influence authenticity in knowledge sharing needs more attention in research on knowledge sharing through online communities (von Krogh, 2011).

Opportunity structures refer to the benefits of sharing knowledge in the community and occurrences for doing so. Narrow opportunity structures imply that knowledge sharing benefits can only be realized through a limited number of relationships with colleagues, sharing very specific knowledge at very specific times and places. On the other hand, broader opportunity structures involve more relationships that share broader and more explicit types of knowledge in several virtual and physical places. Opportunity structures do not mean that colleagues should have full knowledge of each other, which is impossible from a practice based view of knowledge. Yet, given that interests and knowledge are intimately connected, and as it takes time to identify sharing possibilities – because colleagues often have different knowledge interests –cues about when, where and how knowledge sharing can take place, help to coordinate the differing interests of knowledge (von Krogh, 2011).

The introduction of ICT for knowledge sharing can, from this perspective, aid new opportunities for sharing broader explicit types of knowledge, but the development of new cues for handling various interests in knowledge might be needed to facilitate the sharing of tacit knowledge. However, collectively meaningful cues take long time to evolve and learn. From the perspective of opportunity structures, an online meeting can facilitate a new arena for knowledge sharing, a broad opportunity structure, but it is not clear whether individuals will coordinate the knowledge sharing of tacit knowledge, as an example there might be limitations on how much the experienced are willing and able to share and what they are capable of doing.

However, when interests in knowledge are diverse, it is also possible that the social norm "authenticity" could have an impact on the community or network as a resource for knowledge sharing. Authenticity means that the closeness

of observation matters for acceptance of new knowledge. The social norm of authenticity can have helpful effects of colleagues to appreciate 'better' knowledge within opportunity structures.

Varieties of Groups, Networks, Communities and IT

Communities of practice have existed since individual craftsmen got together to share issues, ideas and solutions. Today technology acts as an enabler linking dispersed individuals in terms of time and place, and facilitates their interaction. Brown and Duguid (2000:143) describe a continuum of networks from communities of practice defined as: "*relatively tight-knit groups of people who know each other and work together directly... typically face to face communities that continually negotiate with, communicate with, and coordinate with each other directly in the course of their work*" to electronic networks of practice consisting of weak ties where individuals may never get to know each other or meet face-to-face. A relatively new aspect of this phenomenon is the managerial ambition to integrate geographically spread units into one integrated unit using ICT and networks aiming to develop communication, collaboration and learning horizontally in the organization (Newell et al., 2009), which this case is an example of (see Table 1).

The competence networks in this case are somewhat controlled by management since one manager (sometimes) participates in the meetings and the networks are evaluated by the organization. On the other hand the assigned coordinator of each network can't force anyone to contribute. While the participants in the competence networks perceive face-to-face interaction as the best setting for sharing practices, sharing using technology is seen as a good alternative due to long travel distances. The

Table 1. Varieties of groups and networks from Wasko and Teigland (2006, p139), except last column right, which describes key features of the competence networks in this case

Macrostructural property	Work Groups	Virtual Team	Communities of Practice	Electronic Networks of Practice	Competence Networks
Control	Formal control, not voluntary	Formal control, not voluntary	No formal control, voluntary	No formal control, voluntary	Some formal control e.g., managerial participation, evaluations, but not possible to force anyone to contribute
Communication channel	Face to face	Text-based computer mediated (e-mail, intranet, can benefit from interactions face-to-face or on video)	Face to face	Text-based computer mediated (like blogs, bulletin boards and e-mail lists)	Screen sharing and telephone conferencing e.g. text, picture and voice-based, computer mediated, and occasionally face-to-face
Network size	Small	Small	Small	Large	Small, potentially large
Access	Restricted, assigned by a formal control	Restricted, assigned by a formal control	Restricted, locally bounded, limited to co-location	Open	Restricted, assigned by formal control, distributed participants
Participation	Jointly determined, specific task outcomes	Jointly determined, specific task outcomes	Jointly determined	Individual determined	Jointly and individual determined, a few times with some specific task outcomes

tool GoToMeeting™, is a highly rated (Lipschutz, 2007) web-based tool that allows everyone in a group meeting to share whatever is on each participant's computer. The tool contains features such as screen sharing, sharing of keyboard and mouse controls, web-chat, and phone conferencing, and the tool is also integrated with e-mail and the Outlook calendar to efficiently book meetings (see http://www. GoToMeeting™ .com). While you can share everything you have on your computer and have a telephone meeting, the contenders do not see each other. When the networks are given tasks from the organization, such as answering hearings, these activities resemble a virtual team (see Table 1), and the strengths of GoToMeeting™ perceived in this activities are the ability

to talk, read and write together simultaneously. The network size of the competence networks is small, since they are staffed with eight to14 members, but as they are linked to other networks in other regions by the national network, experiences could potentially be shared among hundreds of people (see Figure 1).

Participation in communities of practice is regarded as jointly determined, since individuals generally approach specific others for help. In electronic networks of practice, participation is individually determined; knowledge seekers have no control over who responds to their questions or the quality of the responses. In turn, knowledge contributors have no guarantee that seekers will understand the answer provided or be willing to reciprocate the favor. The compe-

Table 2. Wenger's communities evolution model. (A modified table of Dotiska (2006) p259.)

Stages	Main Functions	IT Enabling Technologies
1	Connect, plan, commit	E-mail, e-conferencing (see, hear, text chat, present and share information in a collaborative manner), listservers, online forums, internet, corporate intranets
2	Form framework, create context	As above, plus remote login facilities, file transfer, information repositories
3	Operate, collaborate, grow, improve, mature	As above, plus online directories, analytical and decision-making tools, intelligent agents, e-surveying, and feedback facilities also portals
4	Sustain, renew, maintain, wind-down	
5	Shut down	Knowledge repositories may remain for use by future communities

tence networks can, since they are not fully developed communities, therefore be described as a mixed participation context – both jointly and individual determined, and also sometimes with specific task outcomes (like answering hearing).. Access and participation is restricted and structured by management, since the inspectors are assigned to a specific competence network, but ultimately the participation is dependent on mutual engagement. All in all the competence networks offers a mixed context.

Evolution of communities and ICT needs

An ICT perspective on communities of practice relates to how people use ICT to organize the social world to be able to learn. It is about how ICT enables the establishment and maintenance of ongoing relationships between people who have the potential to help each other. A tool is not a community of practice in itself, but it might enable you to share experience and learn from others. Organizations use ICT to accommodate knowledge work and learning. But the impact of ICT on sharing and learning is influenced by human agency, the physical properties of a particular ICT and the context that it is used in (Newell et al., 2009). To develop communities of practice there is a need in the early stages to share information about individual competen-

cies –sharing experiences to develop a sense of shared meaning, identity and knowledge. In later stages the ICT can facilitate ongoing collaboration and the storing of experiences relevant for the community. A more detailed description of the needs in different stages is presented in Table 2.

The role of management in this approach, according to Wenger (2004, 2005) is to coach managers, fund activities and supply the network with technology, facilitating arenas where people can talk about their work and their practices. One the other hand, heavy reliance on ICT may be a burden on the community members, especially when they are not used to interacting with technology. Lack of competence, lack of self-confidence, and or resistance to technology may reduce members' participation in the community (Dubè, Bourhis & Jacob, 2006).

Mature communities of practice are often regarded as skillful at putting all kinds of tools to good use, regardless of their designer's intention (Wenger, White, & Smith, 2009). Wenger et al. (2009) describe several strategies for communities in their effort to build community ICT structure. Strategies ranged from setting up a unique platform for the community or using existing internal and or external tools. This case describes groups who build on and are using what the organization offers. The ICT in use in the competence networks comprise e-mail, intranet and the GoToMeeting™ tool. Web 2.0 applications in terms of wikis, blogs and other social networking features are not a part of any of the official applications in use so far, and freeware is forbidden due to virus problems and the potential leaking of sensitive information.

CASE DESCRIPTION

The main objective of this case is to explore the experience in a distributed organization, a public inspectorate, using the GoToMeeting™ tool to facilitate knowledge sharing activities. In this organization, which is often the case with older organizations, old and newer ICT tools and systems co-exist, but not all of them are used daily or by everybody. I can list as examples intranet, internet, e-mail, GoToMeeting™, as well as old and newer systems related to task handling, registration and time-management. The GoToMeeting™ tool was introduced in the organization at the same time as the competence networks were established, and has become an important tool in the inspectors' daily tasks in project work and is the main channel for the networks, which meet once a month online, but only once or twice a year face-to-face. Five to 10 participants participating in the GoToMeeting™ meetings and the duration of the meeting are from one up to two hours. GoToMeeting™ can be labelled as an audio-conferencing tool with web-based conference services, where active and reflexive listening (like rephrasing participants' statements) is needed for smooth and effective communication (Munkvold & Akselsen, 2003). Screen sharing and the use of text, illustrations or pictures have further positive effects in this respect. The activities in an average meeting in the competence networks are described in Table 3.

ePhorte: A task handling system, that includes a powerful search engine that makes it possible for the Inspectors to search by case number and in free text.

Vyr: The Authority records the reported damage to a business and occupational injury into a register called Vyr. The Authority and the competence networks use Vyr to analyze the registered data to monitor the situation within different branches. Figure 2 Shows examples of how GoToMeeting™ looks like on screen.

The two snapshots are examples of text in e-mail (snapshot 1) and word document (snapshot 2) shared on GoToMeeting™. They just open their personal e-mail and share the content. On snapshot 2, right hand side, note that the participants also can see who is logged on. The picture on text page is an example or what is shared and discussed on GoToMeeting™.

In the conversation and storytelling regarding this picture they focused on the work processes related to this job, the problem of dust in work processes and experiences regarding risk preventing efforts. This is then reflected on and made sense of. The picture illustrates how polluted air is taken out of the production hall through a point extraction, put on the machine were the dust is produced. The picture illustrate a solution to a more general problem situation for the inspectors. They often struggle to find effective solutions to fulfill the requirement of the legislation and in a cost-efficient way for the inspected work place, i.e. finding solutions that can work for both parts. When they talk about these pictures, the presenter address attention towards certain eras of the picture to illustrate how the problem were solved, or show the problem to get help in solving the problem.

So what is going on at face-to-face meetings taking place once or twice a year? Then they often visit a business as a group and discuss what they experienced there. Or they invite an

Table 3. Examples of activities' taking place in an average meeting in the competence networks

Activity	ICT in Use
Log on sequence The individual logs on the web- and teleconferencing (phone). All the necessary information regarding how and when to log on is provided by Outlook.	Outlook e- mail and calendar, Web and teleconferencing (phone)
Initial small talk ... About the weather or similar, sometimes about rumours about what is going on in the organization are shared (3-4 minutes). Among does who are online.	Phone
Who are here? Coordinator asks who is present or not, like " are you there Hans"? "I can see you are logged on Elin!". "Svein is sick". All of the participants say something in turn, like "yes I am here". "Here, but I have to leave this meeting early, due to..."	Phone / web
Coordinator introduces the agenda for the meeting Word document presented (also send by e-mail before the meeting)	Screen sharing
Change of screen control Coordinator let the presenter (network participant or external expert) of the day control the screen	Screen sharing
SHARING PART 1 **Experiences shared** Power point presentations are taking place. Conversations are triggered by the help of stories, documents and pictures.	Screen sharing: Documents and pictures from PC and or ePhorte or Vyr (see below after table)
SHARING PART 2 **Discussion, questions raised and answered** Sharing of experience, opinions and ideas. Construction of meaning. What does the new information mean?	Teleconferencing. Sometimes participants during the meeting search the world wide web or intranet for answers to questions
Evaluation of the meeting Everyone are "forced" to say something. Comments are very short like: "it was okay", " I have nothing to say", " interesting topic", "well organized meeting", " two hours without a break is too long", "remember to turn of the microphone when you are not talking - your noises disturb the others", " it is so sad that only a few took part in the discussion"	Phone

external expert lecturer or practitioner, or both, who talks about a topic.

GOTOMEETING™ FACILITATING LEARNING ACTIVITES ACROSS BOUNDARIES

An ICT perspective on communities or networks of practice implies that we describe them by their ICT use. In the following I describe and discuss the competence networks through three different narratives. The experience is told

through three inspectors, two senior members of staff, Tor and Stein, and one newcomer, Nils.

GoToMeeting™ Facilitate Sharing of Tor's "Workbench"

Tor has worked for 20 years in the authority, within different issues but mainly within engineering. He has also worked part-time as a lecturer at a university. He regarded himself as very open-minded towards ICT. From the early days he has worked from his home office, where his boss has let him try out the new technol-

Figure 2. Snapshots 1 and 2

ogy. Tor is an early adopter of ICT. Today he has a fully equipped office at home, the same technology as at the office. He sees many opportunities for ICT-based sharing of knowledge related to his work, and he has used it on several projects. Additionally, he has been an assigned mentor and a union man online. He is assigned to a competence network for technical expertise.

Tor likes to do PowerPoint presentations when using the GoToMeeting™ tool, and he also likes to pick up files from his PC or intranet and present them as the discussion moves on. His intentions behind this are threefold:

1. To enrich the discussion with cases presented orally, accompanied by the use of pictures and documents.
2. To help others to view and exploit the possibilities that the GoToMeeting™ tool contains.
3. To help others to look up and put together relevant information from different systems that they have: intranet, Vyr and ePhorte.

When using the GoToMeeting™ tool Tor can access rich illustrations regarding content and processes on inspected enterprises, while he is elaborating on a given topic. To illustrate his work he uses his own "work bench" – his computer with access to everything he needs stored on it or available online. He shares the legislation he uses, how he interprets it, how he writes letters to inspected businesses and their answers. He does this by presenting documents from the task-handling register, cases he has previously worked with. He picks out an accident – a file describing what happened at the site, pictures of it and the letters he wrote and how the business responded to it. He moves around between different applications to underline and illustrate his key points, as well as showing the others how to use the GoToMeeting™ tool. He stresses the importance of taking and attaching pictures to the case before putting it into the archive, useful for task handling and for later sharing online on GoToMeeting™ in the competence network setting. This informs us that work activities and learning activities are dependent on each other. Taking pictures in the work context provides the means for later online knowledge sharing and learning. Several times Tor has gone through accidents, sometimes the whole process, and at other times only what happened. Tor regards the tool to be very efficient:

If the legislation is changing, pictures on screen can easily create a mutual understanding of the new legislation. Like when I present machines and equipment that are in line with the new rules. (Tor, senior member of staff)

In his view they are not ready for video-conferencing, but may be in the future if the organization becomes more specialized and the need for communication and interaction internally within the organization increases.

Tor's story tells us that GoToMeeting™ can be a very useful tool for enhancing sharing conversations. It has the ability to gather people and their artifacts (documents and pictures) and participants have conversations about the artifacts. For this purpose GoToMeeting™ is more efficient than face-to-face meetings. Since the participants in GoToMeeting™ meetings, compared to face-to-face meeting, have more easy access to documents. The result of the activity is justifications, mutual understanding of the practice of the others and more collective practice. In other words processes and outcome promoting a community. However the sharing of documents and their conversations depends upon how open they are, and that differ. Some are more reluctant to disclose too much about what they actually do, as they are afraid to lose some of their flexibility when 'in-action', since new routines increasing the standardizing can then be forced upon them.

Tor address a problem when using the Go-ToMeeting™ tool. The problem is the emergent 'multitasking' during the GoToMeeting™ meetings in the competence network. The engage-

ment in the discussions varies from participant to participant. Not everybody is interested in every issue all the time. They do not work with the issue discussed, or they have other opinions. Since nobody sees the individual, some are tempted to do other things while being logged on to the conference. This might not be true all the time, but the impression of 'lack of engagement' among some can turn into vicious circle of 'reduced engagement' in the network. Hindering the participants in creating a community. To reduce this problem coordinator are asked to involve everybody at the meetings, by addressing each and everyone directly.

GoToMeeting™ Enables Stein to Share His Practice, Which are Traceable in Documents

Stein is an experienced member of staff with more than 10 years' experience working with the authority. Previously, he worked for more than 10 years as a teacher. He is assigned to a competence network for technical expertise. He works from a regional office and has taken a university course about ICT use in the distributed environment, which addressed how to work together while not physically being together. At the course he learnt the importance of ensuring that everybody is heard and addressed during a GoToMeeting™ meeting. He speaks very highly of the GoToMeeting™ tool for sharing of experiences. He puts it this way:

We are discussing something. I say, yes, but I have something on my PC, just give me the screen and I'll look up, and so I find it, and I find statements, pictures or any other orders given before. So screen sharing is very useful. It is flexible. (Stein, senior member of staff)

Stein regards it as too cumbersome to meet face-to-face too often. Instead, he points out that by using the GoToMeeting™ tool they share the documents needed if he runs into a similar case. He puts his point this way:

We can't share by referring to what we remember, we need to find the case, our sharing must be traceable. (Stein, senior member of staff)

In bureaucracies, such as this authority, action is taken on the basis of and recorded in written rules (Weber, 1971). This is also true regarding sharing and learning as pointed out by Stein. Sharing and learning starts with recorded cases and the written rules in use. This implies that the sharing of documents is necessary to inform people about what legislation they use and how they use it when sharing experience and their knowledge.

The use of documents is a necessary resource for learning activities in a bureaucratically organizational context. To achieve 'equal handling', documents are needed to understand the practice of others, and works as the window into it and contribute to shared meaning and and community.

GoToMeeting™ Enables Nils to Discuss and Learn from Practice across the Organizational Boundary

Nils has worked for three years in the authority, from a regional office, and mainly with industries. This is his first job after finishing college. Around half of his tasks are related to chemistry – the area the competence network he is assigned to is set up for. He thinks the meetings in his competence network have improved lately, since they are now are discussing more and more professional issues – recent developments in research and the experiences of colleagues and other practitioners. For Nils, GoToMeeting™ is the best they have so far:

'GoToMeeting™ is the best we have, you can invite external experts and practioners – to develop a dialog between our authority, researchers and our businesses. (Nils, newcomer)

This use of GoToMeeting™ reveals networking outside of and across the boundaries of the organization. Bringing different people together using GoToMeeting™ is possible. Everyone have access to a phone and to the world wide web, that is all that is needed.

When people with different backgrounds, but who are engaged in similar work start to have discussions, there is an extra 'spin- off' effect according to Nils. Practioners and researchers start to share and discover solutions together. This is best achieved face-to-face, but is also possible using GoToMeeting™ . Like Tor, Nils stresses the role of pictures and documents in sharing and learning using GoToMeeting™ . The sharing of pictures can be of well-placed ventilation facilities in a welding shop and why it is well placed. Sharing documents can be very useful because they give many ideas about what to look for when conducting inspections, according to Nils. Nils also argues for storing PowerPoint presentations presented at the network meetings on intranet for later use. As he puts it:

When you need ideas and names of people to contact about a special issue, then the PowerPoint presentations can be very useful. (Nils, newcomer)

Nils reveals an insight to us here. Useful informal contacts across the organizational boundaries are not only made up of people you know, but also names stored on your computer or intranet, accessible when needed in your work. These names and contact information contributes to access to a larger Network of Practice for the individual.

Even though GoToMeeting™ has several strengths there are also limitations according to Nils. One dilemma exists between time and cost-efficient knowledge sharing and relation building. Nils puts it this way:

Face-to-face meetings are important, when you are using the phone, not seeing each other, then you don't get to know each other. (Nils, newcomer)

Not getting to know each other means that the social network, the ties, might not develop as strongly as they could have. GoToMeeting™ seems not to be a sufficient tool to develop the stronger ties and the mutual recognition that defines a fully developed community of practice. Since face-to-face meetings take time and travel costs are high over long distances, they need to find other ways to develop their relations, and, in particular, develop the "know-who" - the experts among them within particular areas. One way is to select a richer media when sharing (like videoconferencing or more face-to-face interactions) or engage others (in particular people you don't know) in your project.

DISCUSSION AND CONCLUSION

In this case GoToMeeting™ enables the sharing of work practices across distances well through its ability to gather the inspectors, their documents and their pictures. Through presenting accounts, documents and pictures inspectors are able to represent and reflect upon their work practices. GoToMeeting™ is regarded by Tor, Nils and Stein (three engaged and dedicated network members) as a very useful tool for sharing and learning. GoToMeeting™ enables efficient sharing and learning activities across distances. Tor's sharing of ICT skills seems also to be a best practice, of which the organization could look into for developing the use of Go-ToMeeting™ for sharing and learning further.

The narratives highlight that collaborative IT can enhance 'sharing conversations'- when collaborating and when representing work practice. The narratives highlight that collaborative IT can enhance 'sharing conversations'- when collaborating and when representing practice in documents or pictures.

Closeness to actual work practice is also accomplished by the use of actual documents, stories and pictures, which supports the sharing of more tacit types of knowledge related to inspection and discretion within the technical, positivist and natural science networks of competence (accident and occupational hygiene). The sharing of letters and orders makes it possible for others to some extend to observe how other conduct their writing of orders, which fact they collect and how they write up their use of the legislation. We could say that inspection knowledge and knowing is contained in writing practice which can be shared through GoToMeeting™ . This is an important role of ICT in a practice based perspective (Ardichvili, 2006), that facilitate sharing of practice that other participants can enact in their work.

The narrative of Nils also tells us that the Powerpoint presentations information that facilitate contact to a broader network of prac-

Table 4. Two types of Knowing facilitated by GoToMeeting™

ICT Facilitate	Activity	Knowing
Easy access to pictures and documents	Sharing pictures and documents	Knowing work practice (Knowing how the legislation are used in practice)
Easy storing of documents being presented at GoToMeeting™	Storing Powerpoint presentations	Knowing where to contact a broader network of practice

tice across the organizational boundary. These findings are accounts of two types of knowing shared through GoToMeeting™ as presented in Table 4.

On the other hand, pictures and documents useful when sharing knowledge are more or less stored "by chance" by the individual on PC or intranet, and not very access able for everyone. For some, often the case for experienced veteran employees, it is too difficult to import documents from the systems and into PowerPoint presentations for sharing at GoToMeeting™ . On *Wenger's community evolution model* these networks have not moved more than to stage 2. By the use of GoToMeeting™ they are able to connect, plan and commit (stage 1) and they are also able to form and create context (stage 2) by sharing documents and pictures. But it is harder to grow and mature further.

On problem is that it is hard to get to know each other on GoToMeeting™ . Participants who are not that interested or out- spoken and who do not engage themselves in discussions online, are not well known among the rest of the network participants. GoToMeeting™ facilitates sharing of documents, but don't sufficiently support the development of social relations. One reason might be the strong individualistic culture as well as the face-to-face learning mode among the inspectors in this organization. To develop the social relations there is a need for more face-to-face interactions.

My conclusion is that the ICT in use, GoToMeeting™, enables the sharing of work practices across distances through its ability to gather together the inspectors, their documents, and their pictures – the objects and artifacts to which they attach meaning in their practice. By presenting accounts, documents, and pictures the inspectors are able to represent and reflect upon their work practices GoToMeeting™ is regarded by Tor (accident network), Stein (accident network) and Nils (occupational hygiene) - three engaged and dedicated network members - as a very useful tool for sharing and learning GoToMeeting™ enables efficient sharing and learning activities across distances.

This article contributes to our understanding of how the use of this collaborative ICT might ensure authenticity in knowledge sharing (von Krogh, 2011). While the apprentices in Lave and Wenger (1991)'s community of practice can observe the genuine know-how of the master first-hand with considerable accuracy with the ability to observe (face-to-face) a certain level of detail, Stein's story illustrates how this collaborative tool, GoToMeeting™, facilitates the observation of detail regarding how the Inspector uses collected data and the legislation when writing up a case. Subsequently, when inspection practice is 'traceable' in documents (real cases) and the story is told by the case handler, this increases the reliability of what is shared. It may also increase the validity of the shared knowledge, when it reviles writing practice. If it does, whoever listens to the shared knowledge in real cases can extended the practice to their own cases.

REFERENCES

Ardichvili, A. A. (2006). Russian orthodoxy worldview and adult learning in the workplace. *Advances in Developing Human Resources, 8*(3), 373–381. doi:10.1177/1523422306288430

Brown, J. S., & Duguid, P. (1998). Organizing knowledge. *California Management Review, 40*(3), 90–111. doi:10.2307/41165945

Brown, J. S., & Duguid, P. (2000). *The social life of information*. Boston, MA: Harvard Business School Press.

Dotsika, F. (2006). An IT perspective on supporting communities of practice. In E. Coakes, & S. Clarke (Eds.), *Encyclopedia of communities of practice in information and knowledge management* (pp. 257–263). Hershey, PA: Idea Group. doi:10.4018/978-1-59140-556-6.ch045

Dubé, L., Bourhis, A., & Réal Jacob, R. (2006). Towards a typology of virtual communities of practice. *Interdisciplinary Journal of Information, Knowledge, and Management, 1.*

Hayes, N. (2011). Information technology and the possibilities for knowledge sharing. In *Handbook of organizational learning and knowledge management*. Chichester, UK: John Wiley & Sons.

Lave, J., & Wenger, E. (1991). *Situated learning: Legitimate peripheral participation*. Cambridge, UK: Cambridge University Press. doi:10.1017/CBO9780511815355

Lipschutz, R. P. (2007). *GoToMeeting™ 3.0 review*. Retrieved September 13, 2010 from http://www.pcmag.com/article2/0,2817,2154128,00.asp

Mintzberg, H. (1983). *Structure in fives: Designing effective organizations*. Engelwood Cliffs, NJ: Prentice Hall.

Munkvold, B. E., & Akselsen, S. E. (2003). *Implementing collaboration technologies in industry: Case examples and lessons learned*. London: Springer. doi:10.1007/978-1-4471-0073-7

Newell, S., Robertson, M., Scarborough, H., & Swan, J. (2009). *Managing knowledge work and innovation*. Basingstoke, UK: Palgrave Macmillan.

Sambamurthy, V., & Sumbramani, M. (2005). Special issue on information technologies and knowledge management. *MIS Quartely, 29*(1), 1–7.

von Krogh, G. (2011). Knowledge sharing in organizations: The role of communities. In *Handbook of organizational learning and knowledge management*. Chichester, UK: John Wiley & Sons.

Wasko, M., & Teigland, R. (2006). Distinguishing work groups, virtual teams, and electronic networks of practice. In E. Coakes, & S. Clarke (Eds.), *Encyclopedia of communities of practice in information and knowledge management* (pp. 138–140). Hershey, PA: Idea Group. doi:10.4018/978-1-59140-556-6.ch027

Weber, M. (1971). *Makt og byråkrati: Essays om politikk og klasse, samfunn*. Oslo: Gyldendal.

Wenger, E. (1998). *Communities of practice: Learning, meaning and identity*. New York: Cambridge University Press. doi:10.1017/CBO9780511803932

Wenger, E. (2003). Communities of practice and social learning systems. In *Knowing in organizations: A practice-based apporach*. New York: M.E. Sharpe.

Wenger, E. (2004). Knowledge management as a doughnut: Shaping your knowledge strategy through communities of practice. *Ivey Business Journal, 1*, 1–8.

Wenger, E. (2005). *Technology for communities*. CEFRIO. Retrieved September 19, 2010 from http://technologyforcommunities.com/CEFRIO_Book_Chapter_v_5.2.pdf

Wenger, E., McDermott, R., & Snyder, W. M. (2002). *Cultivation communities of practice*. Cambridge, MA: Harvard Business School Press.

Wenger, E., White, N., & Smith, J. D. (2009). Digital habitats: Stewarding technology for communities. Portland, OR: CPsquare Publishing.

Zack, M. (1999). Managing codified knowledge. *Sloan Management Review*, *40*(4), 45–58.

Chapter 5
Information Privacy Concerns and Workplace Surveillance:
A Case of Differing Perspectives

Regina Connolly
Dublin City University, Ireland

ABSTRACT

Consumers' privacy concerns have escalated in parallel with our increasing dependence on technology and its pervasiveness into social and work environments. Many of these concerns emanate from the paradox that is the willingness of consumers to provide personal information in order to achieve a specific outcome, whilst equally harbouring the contradictory desire for such personal information to be treated as private. Although examinations of information privacy have tended to focus on the transaction environment, the computer-mediated work environment has emerged as a new and significant area of concern due to increased awareness of the ways in which technologies are now being used to monitor employee email, Internet interactions, and work productivity. Such surveillance concerns are likely to negatively impact employee morale and consequent productivity. However, little attention has been paid to this issue to date. This chapter examines a number of emerging issues concerning technology-enabled workplace surveillance and considers whether the privacy concerns of employees can be successfully balanced against managements' justification for the employment of such technologies in the workplace. In doing so, it provides a balanced perspective that will be of assistance to academics and practitioners alike in dealing with this emerging and contentious issue.

DOI: 10.4018/978-1-4666-4856-2.ch005

INTRODUCTION

Despite the fact that privacy has been studied across a wide range of disciplines, it has been described as a concept that is 'in disarray' (Solove 2006: 477) due to the fact that there is no consensus regarding how it should be defined or conceptualized (Margulis 2003). One consequence of this is that our understanding of privacy concerns remains fragmented as, being defined by the field and focus of each researcher, the concepts that are examined and the ways in which they are validated remain inconsistent and therefore are of limited generalizability. As Solove (2006: 479) notes, 'privacy seems to be about everything and therefore is about nothing'.

Undoubtedly, information privacy (as opposed to physical privacy) is a multidimensional concept (Xu et al., 2011) and many overlapping concepts such as secrecy and anonymity have been linked to it, consequently adding to the confusion that surrounds the construct. However, progress is being made in this regard. For example, whilst some information systems studies have equated information privacy with control, more recent work (Dinev & Hart 2006) has shown that while control influences privacy concerns, it does not in itself equate to privacy. Thus, Dinev et al., (2013) assert that there is a need to integrate the different perspectives acquired from different fields in order to build a more rigorous, empirically testable framework of privacy and its closely associated correlates, which have often been confused with or built into definitions of privacy.

The imperative for greater clarity stems from the fact that information privacy is an issue of increasing concern to many stakeholders, including consumers, employers, privacy activists, researchers and policy makers. To a great extent, these concerns relate directly to the exponential growth of Internet-based technologies. Whilst the benefits bestowed by such technologies is undisputed, it is an undeniable fact that they have generated considerable concern regarding the way in which they can be used to collate and use information on individuals without their prior permission. For example, the recent surge of pervasive technologies into the workplace environment has generated privacy concerns amongst employees. The pervasive computing environment is characterised by the seamless integration of technologies into society, and it is this transparent nature that has fuelled many of these privacy concerns with employees becoming increasingly aware of the ways in which management can employ such technologies to monitor their email and computer interactions in the workplace. However, as profit-driven organisations aim to manage their business in an efficient and productive manner, it is perhaps unrealistic to expect that such organisations would not avail of the obvious empowering benefits that these communication-monitoring technologies afford them. Furthermore, it can be argued that they may in fact have legitimate reasons to monitor employee actions in the first place.

A number of questions surround the issue of workplace surveillance in particular those relating to the ethical nature of managements' ability to monitor employees' computer interactions. The aim of this paper therefore is to outline some of the major issues relating to workplace surveillance, to identify the emerging issues and subsequent privacy concerns from the employee's perspective, as well as the motivation behind managements' decision to employ monitoring technologies in the workplace. As such, this paper explores the ethical impact of monitoring in the computer-mediated work environment, addressing whether management's ability to monitor employee actions in workplace represents good business practice or constitutes an invasion of privacy.

INFORMATION PRIVACY

As noted, privacy is a complex construct and one that remains beset by conceptual and operational confusion. It is an ambiguous concept in the sense that it is difficult to either define or understand as for every definition of privacy sourced from the literature, a counter example can be easily produced (Introna, 1996). This conceptual confusion has been exacerbated by the multiplicity of perspectives that have been applied to examinations of the construct, resulting in a highly fragmented set of concepts, definitions and relationships. For example, privacy is often examined as a psychological state, a form of power, an inherent right or an aspect of freedom (Parker, 1974; Acquisti, 2002; Rust, Kannan, & Peng, 2002). Many overlapping concepts such as confidentiality, anonymity, secrecy and ethics have added to the confusion that surrounds the construct (Margulis, 2003). In an attempt to reduce this confusion, Clarke (1999) identifies four dimensions of privacy: privacy of a person, personal behaviour privacy, personal communication privacy, and personal data privacy. However, as the majority of communications today are digitised and stored, Bélanger and Crossler (2011) contend that personal communication privacy and data privacy can be merged into the construct of information privacy.

The distinction between information privacy as opposed to physical privacy is easily identifiable. The latter concerns physical access to an individual and the individual's surroundings and private space, whilst the former concerns access to individually identifiable personal information (Smith, Dinev, & Xu, 2011). In terms of historical development, attention was initially paid to the concept of physical privacy, but more recently with the increasing pervasiveness of communication technologies, the concept of information privacy has acquired greater significance. As far back as 1986, Mason predicted that four major concerns would result from the increased use of information and communication technologies - privacy, accuracy, property and accessibility. This prediction has proved to be correct and particularly so in relation to concerns regarding information privacy. Examinations of information privacy are based on the assumption that the ultimate target of review is information as opposed to physical privacy. Because information privacy is part of general privacy research, many of the early privacy concepts have been applied to information privacy, although it is also true that information-specific privacy concepts exist. For example, Smith, Milberg, and Burke (1996) propose four dimensions of information privacy: collection, unauthorized secondary use, improper access, and errors.

Central to our understanding of the privacy construct is the issue of control, specifically the individual's need to have control over their personal information. Control has been defined as *"the power of directing command, the power of restraining"* (Oxford, 1996, p. 291) and is consistently proposed in the literature as a key factor in relation to understanding individual privacy concerns. The concept of privacy as control can be traced back to Westin's (1967) and Altman's (1975) general privacy theories. Altman described general privacy as the selective control of access to the self (1975, p. 24). This emphasis on control was subsequently developed by Altman (1975), Culnan (1993), and Smith *et al.* (1996). However, Dinev & Hart (2006) have shown that while control influences privacy concerns, it does not in itself equate to privacy. Consequently, definitions of 'privacy as control' have evolved into privacy as *'ability* to control,' a distinction that has been emphasised by Smith *et al.* (2011).

Personal control is important as it relates to the interest of individuals to control or significantly influence the handling of personal data (Clarke, 1988). Practitioner reports confirm the importance that individuals attribute to being able to control their personal information particularly in relation to the use of Internet-based systems. For example a 1999 Louis Harris poll indicated that 70% of online users felt uncomfortable disclosing personal information, while a 2003 Harris poll of 1010 adults also found that 69% of those surveyed described their ability to control the collection of personal information as being 'exceptionally important.' Similarly, a Pew Internet survey showed that 85% of adults considered it to be very important that they should be able to control access to their personal information (Madden, Fox, Smith, & Vitak, 2007). Statistics like these indicate the increasing concern of individuals regarding the violation of their privacy and their desire to be able to control their personal information. Moreover, information privacy concerns have been shown to influence consumer attitudes such as their willingness to use online transaction environments (Bélanger, Hiller, & Smith, 2002; Pavlou, Liang, & Xue, 2007) and a greater reluctance to provide personal information to websites (Dinev & Hart, 2006)

Interestingly, while individuals' sensitivity to control of private information is an issue of increasing concern, the truth regarding the extent of control over that personal information is often misunderstood, particularly amongst the Internet-using public. This is confirmed by a 2005 study by the Annenberg Public Policy Centre which discovered that 47% of the 1500 adults surveyed falsely believed they were able to control personal information distributed about them online simply because they had the right to view data collated by the on-line vendor, while a further 50% falsely believed they could

control the depth of information contained on them by having the ability to edit information as and when they saw fit (Turow *et al.,* 2005). The value of such practitioner reports lies in the acknowledgement that individuals yearn to become empowered decision makers relating to the level of control they maintain over their sensitive information, thus providing a basis for future research from a rigour and relevance perspective.

This issue of control and privacy may not always be as clear-cut as it at first seems however. In fact, it can be argued that not every loss or gain or control necessarily constitutes a loss or gain of privacy (Parker, 1974). For example, a user of an Internet-based technology who voluntarily provides personal information in the course of their interaction may not necessarily view this as a loss of control and consequently a loss of privacy. Even if the knowledge that each of their computer-based interactions leaves behind a detailed trail of information regarding who they are, their behaviour and habits and other potentially sensitive information about themselves – it may not necessarily constitute a lack of control or loss of privacy in their eyes. Once again it becomes apparent that the definition and scope of privacy is dependent upon the situation or event in question as well as attitudes and perceptions of those involved.

There is a general consensus that the advent of the information age has made the art of communication significantly easier. However, as previously noted, the influx and increased adoption of technology has also made it significantly easier for third parties to intercept and collate communications by others (Ghosh, 1998). In fact, the adoption of the Internet for both business and recreational purposes simply fuels the privacy debate as the potential for individuals to gain unauthorised access to electronic networks poses as a significant threat

(Laudon & Laudon, 2002). The increasing pervasiveness of technologies into our working lives has opened up a spectrum of unregulated behaviour whereby previously accepted distinctions regarding correct and immoral behaviour are no longer always clear (Turban, Leidner, McClean, & Wetherbe, 2006). Researchers such as Safire (2002) note how extreme pervasive surveillance tends to result in a 'creepy feeling' among those being monitored despite the fact that they may have done nothing wrong to merit such scrutiny. In some cases individuals may be conscious that they are being monitored, they are just not sure of the extent and detail of that monitoring. Neither are they aware of how that collated information is being used by the monitoring body. As such it is clear that there are two distinct issues relating to surveillance – one relating to the actual act of monitoring or surveillance itself, the second relating to how the collated information can be used.

While it is clear that the exponential growth of Internet-based technologies has changed the scope and indeed the capabilities of such practices it is important to note that many of these monitoring techniques have a long established presence in the offline world also. One of the earliest known examples relates to an observation unit known as the Panopticon, which was designed to house prison inmates in the 18th century. The unit was designed to allow an observer to observe undetected so that prison inmates were seamlessly individualised, were made constantly visible, were always seen but could never see themselves (Foucault, 1977). In this way they were a constant source of information, but subsequently unable to communicate in the existing relationship. The basic principles of this observation system played on the fundamental vulnerability of human nature, turning visibility into a trap and ensuring that a covert presence held the power.

Examples of modern day computer-mediated surveillance techniques rely heavily on these basic principles. Clarke (1988) coined the term dataveillance to describe the systematic monitoring of the actions or communications of individuals. Modern technologies provide the opportunity for constant observation and continuous data collection ensuring that surveillance is employed through an individual not over them. In fact, the monitoring of employees' computer-related interactions has previously been described as an 'electronic whip' used unfairly by management (Tavani, 2004). In this way employees are now facing an electronic form of panopticism whereby they can be observed by an electronic supervisor who never leaves the office (Wen *et al.,* 2007).

SURVEILLANCE: AN EMPLOYEE PERSPECTIVE

Technology has enabled an invasion of employee privacy on a hitherto unimagined scale. For example, a 2005 study carried out by AMA found that as many as 55% of US firms not only retain, but also review an employee's email messages, a figure which has risen 8% since 2001. Managements' ability to monitor employee actions also stretches to use of the Internet within the workplace. AMA (2005) further revealed that 76% of organisations monitor an employee's Internet usage, 65% of which are blocking access to particular websites highlighting Web surfing as a primary concern for many organisations. It is now estimated that as many as 80% of organisations monitor employee activities in the workplace – a figure which has doubled since 1997 (AMA, 2001; D'Urso, 2006). While the speed and productivity benefits of email are immense from an organisational perspective, the placing of stringent controls by management on the use of email systems may also jeopardise an employee's privacy.

Moreover, this monitoring is not limited to email surveillance. In a drive to reduce costs and improve efficiency, companies are employing an increasing array of tracking and monitoring technology to allow them to view what their employees are doing at all times. Companies such as StealthGenie specialise in monitoring employees' mobile phones, Inland Empire requires its employees to carry scanning devices that show how quickly they are moving boxes and the outcomes of such tracking is subject to performance reviews, whilst employees at the Unified Grocers warehouse in the US wear headsets which tell them what to do and how much time they have to do it. Such tracking is used extensively in call centres with companies such as Paychez tracking the duration of phone calls and time between phone calls at their call centre. However, tracking has also pervaded the health service delivery industry with nurses at Mills-Peninsula Health services hospital in California having to wear tracking devices so that the hospital can see where they are at all times. Such metrics may show increased productivity, but they come at a cost to employees. For example, micromanagement control systems increase employee stress and break the psychological trust contract between employee and employer. As Connolly (2013) (in Semuels; 2013) notes, the technology is being used to satisfy the needs of the employer, but is being leveraged against the employee. Thus the playing field is being tilted in favour of the industry against the employee with employees having little say on how the tracking data are used. The information can be used to justify pay cuts, to pay people piecemeal or to fire people outrights. In short, it provides employers with an increasing array of data to use to justify changes in the workplace. Workplace privacy is becoming highly comprised by technology as the knowledge power dynamic in the workplace shifts in favour of the employer.

Despite the fact that management are entitled to monitor employee behaviour primarily for 'business-related reasons' a study carried out by McParland and Connolly (2009) found that only 45% of employees surveyed knew their actions could be monitored by management while in the workplace. From this, only 22% believed that their actions were monitored on a regular – such as daily or weekly – basis. Interestingly however a significant number of respondents indicated a strong degree of privacy concerns in relation to managements' ability to monitor their email interactions in the workplace, despite the fact that many were unsure of whether or not such activities actually occurred. For example, 35% were concerned that employers could log into and record their personal emails, 42% were concerned that they could access their emails without their knowledge and 45% were concerned with how management would or could use information obtained from their personal emails. Employees indicated a stronger level of concern regarding the monitoring of personal emails they receive (32%) as opposed to those they send themselves from their work email account (12%) confirming the notion that control is an important aspect in relation to privacy issues.

The concept and art of surveillance is based on the notion that one is 'under watch' or being observed in some way. However based on the fundamental principles of the 'Hawthorne Effect' it is reasonable to assume that if one is aware they are under observation they may alter their actions according. For example, McParland and Connolly (2009) found that 84% of employees surveyed were careful about the type of information they would send in an email while in the workplace with only 32% sending a personal email if they thought their employer could not see them. Furthermore 57% sent emails from their own personal (yahoo, gmail) account in order to prevent management from tracking their behaviour with only 54% of the overall sample accepting managements' right to monitor staff email interactions in the workplace.

While it is apparent that employees often alter or modify their behaviour in response to management monitoring activities, it is important to note that the use of such techniques may result in other more worrying outcomes. For example, many workers experience high degrees of stress because their activities and interactions can be monitored by employers (Tavani, 2004). Once again based on the fundamental principles of panopticism the question can be raised as to whether it is the presence of the 'invisible supervisor' that generates or in part fuels this distress. Ironically however, it is the computer-based information worker whose work is dependent upon the use of computer systems that is often the one most subjected to this form of monitoring. In a study carried out by McParland and Connolly (2009) it was found that many individuals felt extremely uncomfortable being under watch by management expressing explicit concerns, questioning how the information collated is used and in some instances even translating it into a failing performance or lack of ability on their behalf. This obvious negative impact that such surveillance techniques have on employee morale is a serious issue and one which must be addressed. In fact, the use of electronic surveillance in the workplace has been compared to that of a work environment tantamount to an 'electronic sweatshop' in some instances (Tavani, 2004).

Workplace surveillance clearly raises many ethical and social issues. However in order to adequately address many of these issues we must first consider the motivations behind managements decision to employ monitoring technologies in the first place.

SURVEILLANCE: A MANAGEMENT PERSPECTIVE

While many reports emphasis the risks faced by the employee, it is reasonable to assume that in some instances management may have legitimate reasons to monitor their employee's actions. For example, profit driven organisations aim to manage their business in an efficient and productive manner and as such it may be unreasonable to expect that such companies would not avail of methods or employ technologies to ensure that their employees are completing the job they are being paid to do. Furthermore and perhaps more notably, organisations continually face the risk of adverse publicity resulting from offensive or explicit material circulating within the company and as such many employ monitoring technologies to protect themselves from costly litigation claims (Laudon & Laudon, 2001). The Internet has increased the possible threat of hostile work environment claims by providing access to inappropriate jokes or images that can be transmitted internally or externally at the click of a button (Lane, 2003). In fact, a study carried out in 2000 concluded that 70% of the traffic on pornographic Websites occurs during office hours, with ComScore networks reporting 37% of such visits actually taking place in the office environment (Alder, Noel, & Ambrose, 2006).

Moreover, the risks to organisations stretch also to the abuse of the email system, with virtually all the respondents in an AMA (2003) survey reporting some sort of disruption resulting from employee's email use. For example, 33% of the respondents experienced a computer virus, 34% reporting business interruptions and

38% of which had a computer system disabled for some time as the result of a bogus email. In a similar vein, Jackson, Dawson, and Wilson (2001) conducted a study to investigate the cost management endure as a result of such email interruption. The study indicated that it took the average employee between 1 and 44 seconds to respond to a new email when the icon or pop up box appeared on their screen. 70% of these mails were reacted to within 6 seconds of them appearing and a further 15% were reacted to within a 2 minute time period. Overall the study found that it took on average 64 seconds for an employee to return to a productive state of work for every one new mail sent. Other practitioner reports also identify the potential cost of email usage with as many as 76% reporting a loss of business time due to email problems, 24% of which estimating a significant two day loss of company time (AMA, 2003). These statistics are not so surprising given the amount of time the average employee spends online. The survey further reported that the average employee spends 25% of his or her working day solely on their emails, with a further 90% admitting to sending and receiving personal mails during company time.

Whilst the need to improve productivity is a common rationale for employee monitoring, other motivations such as minimising theft and preventing workplace litigation can be considered equally justifiable in the eyes of management seeking to protect the interests of the organisation. The former motivation is particularly understandable as research shows that employees stole over 15 billion dollars in inventory from their employers in the year 2001 alone (Lane, 2003). In addition, the seamless integration of technology into the workplace has increased the threat of internal attacks with Lane (2003) noting the ease at which sensitive corporate data and trade secrets can be downloaded, transmitted, copied or posted onto a Web

page by an aggrieved employee. Internal attacks typically target specific exploitable information, causing significant amounts of damage to an organisation (IBM, 2006). Management need to ensure that their employees use their working time productively and are therefore benefiting the organisation as a whole (Nord, McCubbins, & Horn Nord, 2006). It is apparent however, that tensions will remain constant between both parties unless some form of harmony or balance between the interests of both the employer and employee is achieved.

In order to balance this conflict of interests however it is vital that clearly defined rules and disciplinary offences are implemented into the workplace (Craver, 2006). The need for structure becomes all the more apparent when one considers the differing views and tolerance levels certain managers may hold (Selmi, 2006). For example, if an employee is hired to work, then technically they should refrain from sending personal emails or shopping online during working hours. However, as a general rule, most management will overlook these misdemeanours as good practice or in order to boost worker morale. The situation becomes more serious however when the abuse of Internet privileges threatens to affect the company itself, be it through loss of profits or adverse publicity for the company. Furthermore, the problem increases as boundaries in the modern workplace begin to blur and confusion between formal and informal working conditions arise (Evans, 2007). For example by allowing an employee to take a company laptop into the privacy of their own home, management could be sending out a message that the computer can be used for personal use which may lead to the employee storing personal data on management's property. Legally, the employer would have claims over all of the data stored on the computer and could use it to discipline or even terminate an employee. In fact, it is this apparent lack of natural limit in regards what is acceptable or indeed unacceptable relating to workplace privacy which makes the task of defining appropriate principles all the more difficult to comprehend (Godfrey, 2001).

ORGANIZATIONAL JUSTICE AND WORKPLACE SURVEILLANCE

The recent surge in the use of communication monitoring technologies within the computer-mediated work environment has further brought the issues of justice and fairness centre stage in the literature. In fact, justice and fairness are often cited as key drivers in managing the ethical and privacy concerns of employees who are subjected to monitoring practices within the computer-mediated work environment (Stanton, 2000a, 2000b; Zweig & Webster, 2002). Organisational justice is an overarching term used to describe individuals' perceptions of what is fair and just within the workplace. For researchers such as Stanton (2000b) justice theories thus provide researchers with a solid framework to help predict the perceived fairness of specific organisational procedures, outcomes and actions.

Justice perceptions for the main are separated into three specific forms notably (1) procedural justice, (2) distributive justice, and (3) interactional justice. The first of these antecedents, procedural justice centres around an individuals' perception that the organisational decision-making process will produce fair and just outcomes (Barrett-Howard & Tyler, 1986; Stanton, 2000b; Hauenstein, McGonigle, & Flinder, 2001). In this way, procedural justice act as a critical factor for understanding the relations between the supervisors' social power and the employees' subsequent reactions to it whereby they perceive positive outcomes in a more favourable light (Mossholder, Bennett,

Kemery, & Wesolowski, 1998). Distributive justice refers to the distribution of outcomes, measuring the extent to which employees feel recognised and therefore appropriately rewarded for their efforts within the workplace (Stanton, 2000b; Cohen-Charash & Spector, 2001; Hauenstein *et al.*, 2001). In this way management are required to treat employees who are similar in respect to a certain outcome in the same manner, as opposed to basing decisions on arbitrary characteristics (Daft, 2000). According to Cohen-Charash and Spector (2001) if a distributive injustice is perceived, it will affect an employee's emotions, cognitions and their overall behaviour. The final facet of organisational justice, interactional justice stems from the interpersonal communications of the workplace, examining the quality of the interpersonal treatment employees experience at the hands of the company power- holders (Bies & Moag, 1986; Cohen-Charash & Spector, 2001). More specifically it examines the extent to which employees' believe they have been treated with dignity, sincerity and respect during the distribution of outcomes as well as the process undertaken to achieve them by company decision-makers (Stanton, 2000b; Helne, 2005). Consequently if an employee perceives interpersonal injustice they are more likely to act negatively towards their direct supervisor as opposed to the organisation or the injustice in question (Cohen-Charash & Spector, 2001).

Organisational justice theories have been linked to research on performance monitoring – specifically electronic performance monitoring (EPM) in the literature (Stanton & Barnes-Farrell, 1991; Stanton, 2000a, 2000b). EPM differs from traditional (non-electronic) forms of monitoring in that it can be carried out on a continuous, large scale basis recording multiple dimensions of a single workers performance (Stanton, 2000a). The ubiquitous nature of these monitoring technologies contributes to the employees' ethical concerns relating to loss of personal privacy in the workplace.

Trust and risk perceptions also play an important role in the issue of workplace surveillance. For example studies on trust – in particular relating to trust in leaders - are becoming increasingly prominent in the literature. Mayer, Davis, and Schoorman (1995) for example developed a model that suggested that integrity, benevolence and ability were major factors that had the potential to affect an individual's perception of trustworthiness in a leader. Similarly, a study carried out by Robinson and Rousseau (1994) found that as many as 55% of respondents reported a reduced level of trust in an employer as a result of management violating a psychological contract with them. The seamless integration of communication-monitoring technologies into the workplace can influence an employee's perception of the risks they face working in the computer-mediated environment. Therefore, it is conceivable that an employees' attitude towards the technology will act as an important determinant in the implementation process of communication-monitoring technologies into the workplace.

Furthermore it is apparent that risk perceptions can affect how an individual makes specific decisions, subsequently influencing their behaviour. In fact studies show that when an employee is aware they are under surveillance, they modify their behaviour accordingly. For example, a recent study carried out by SHRM in 2005 found that as many as 75% of employees display a certain degree of caution in relation to what they write in emails due to possible monitoring by the organisation. Similarly, the study showed that 47% are equally cautious in relation to telephone conversations while in the workplace environment. Studies show however that the degree of risk perceived by an individual can be reduced if trust exists in

a particular situation (So & Sculli, 2002). In this way the significance of trust within studies on risk perception cannot be understated. In fact, an individuals' need to trust often relates directly to the risks involved in a given situation and consequently the pervasive nature of communication-monitoring practices within the computer-mediated organisation hold risks that are unique to that context (Mayer *et al.,* 1995). In order for trust to be engendered however, employees must feel confident that the boundaries between what is acceptable and unacceptable in relation to information monitoring are clearly and openly stated. Those companies that are successful at building that trust and managing the uncertainty associated with communication monitoring practices will benefit from increased employee confidence.

It is becoming increasingly apparent that there is a significant disparity between management and employee perspectives on the issue of workplace surveillance. The uncertainty and lack of control related to the use of these communication monitoring technologies in the workplace reflects the significant asymmetry that exists in terms of what they mean to management versus the employee. While it is apparent that technology has created better, faster and cheaper ways for individuals to satisfy their own needs, the capability to leverage this technology is far higher for companies than for the employee. Because unequal forces, leading to asymmetric information availability, tilt the playing field significantly in favour of industry, such technologies do not create market benefit to all parties in an equitable manner (Prakhaber, 2000). As such one of the major tasks facing the computer-mediated organisation is that of identifying the factors to improve employees' attitudes and behavioural reactions towards surveillance in the workplace. There is a distinct need for clear measures to be implemented, that govern the effective and fair use of communication technologies in the workplace allowing management to monitor their staff in a reasonable and rational manner. Management should consider the ethical and social impacts that surveillance techniques may have within the workplace and employ specific policies which may both minimise the negative implications associated with the use of such technology as well as helping to improve employee receptiveness overall.

WORKPLACE SURVEILLANCE ETHICS

Organisations looking for ways in which to balance this conflict of interest between management and employees are focusing towards the use of workplace policies, many of which are framed on established or predefined codes of ethics. For example, Marx and Sherizen (1991) argue that employees should be made aware in advance of any monitoring practices conducted in the workplace before it actually occurs. In this way the individual can electively decide whether or not he or she wishes to work for that particular organisation. Furthermore the authors suggest that the employee should have the right to both view information collated on them and challenge inaccurate information before it can be used against them. This idea of 'transparency' in relation to surveillance methods is commonly supported by privacy advocates however it can be argued that it goes against fundamental principles of the act of surveillance. Similarly we can once again note the impact of the 'Hawthorne Effect' in that individuals will alter their behaviour if they believe they are being observed in some way. In this way management need to have clearly defined sanctions in place within the organisation informing employees of the depth and detail of monitoring practices in the

company whilst deterring them from abusing workplace systems.

Other ethical strategies focus solely on how management use the information collated on employees in the workplace. Again we can note that the scope of surveillance is generally divided into two main components - one relating to the actual act of monitoring or surveillance itself, the second relating to how the collated information can be used. In some cases it is reasonable to assume that employees may not fear the act of surveillance but more so how the information could be used and whether or not employers will make subsequent judgments about them (Introna, 2001). For example, McParland and Connolly (2009) found that 33% of employees they surveyed were concerned that their employers would react negatively to their use of personal email in the workplace however 24% still thought it was reasonable to use work email to chat freely with their friends and colleagues. Once again the lines regarding what are acceptable or indeed unacceptable forms of behaviour begin to blur.

In order to alleviate much of this confusion other researchers such as Turban, King, Lee, Liang, and Turban (2010) apply the basic ethical principles to information collected in an online environment. It is apparent however that these basic ethical principles can also be applied to the use of communication-monitoring technologies in the workplace environment thus providing a solid framework to guide management in their efforts to monitor employees in a fair and effective manner. The basic principles include the following;

- **Notice or Awareness:** Employees should be made aware of the extent and detail of monitoring techniques, prior to the collection or use of personal information.

- **Choice or Consent:** Employees should be made aware of how the collated information can be used and consent must be granted by the employee by signing a workplace policy or notification which outlines the companies monitoring practices.
- **Access or Participation:** Employees should be able to access certain information on them and challenge the validity of the data.
- **Integration or Security:** Employees should be assured that their personal information is kept secure within the organisation and cannot be used in a way which was not intended.
- **Enforcement or Redress:** Employees must be made aware of organisational sanctions set in place such that a misuse of workplace systems will be detected and punished by management. Otherwise there is no deterrent or indeed enforceability to protect privacy.

Effective workplace policies need to protect the interests of all parties involved, ergo a code needs to be developed that protects the interests of both the employee and the employer. Little progress can be made in this area however unless the current privacy legislation is addressed.

THE ROLE OF PRIVACY LEGISLATION

Privacy legislation differs considerably between Europe and the United States. While both Europe and the United States define privacy in a similar way, it is the fundamental objective of their information privacy laws that signifies the major difference between the two. For example, in Europe privacy protection is considerably stronger than in the United States as it focuses on controlling and regulating managements' collection and use of employee data. While the European Directive is based on the Fair Information Doctrine of the United States it extends the level of control an individual can exercise over their own personal information (Laudon & Traver, 2010). In this way European law lends itself more to the protection of data – and therefore the individual – compared to the United States which focuses more on the use and collection of data. Any country that is a member state of the European Union [EU] must comply with the legislation that is passed by any one of its major institutions as well as any national laws or regulations set in place. Furthermore, under the Directive 95/46/EC and Article 29 WP55 all monitoring in the organisation must pass a number of specified criteria before being implemented into the workplace.

Under current EU legislation, the employer must prove that electronic observation is a necessary course of action for a specific purpose before engaging in it. In this way, management are encouraged to consider traditional and less intrusive measures of observation before resorting to electronic means (Directive 95/46/EC). For the purpose of Internet or indeed email surveillance, it is likely that some form of electronic monitoring would be enlisted, however in such instances the employer by law can only keep the data in question no longer than necessary for the specific monitoring action. In a similar vein, the second principal of finality denotes that any data collected, must be used for an explicit purpose and therefore cannot be processed or used for any other purpose than initially intended (Directive 95/46/EC).

Under EU law, management must also be clear and open regarding the surveillance practices of the organisation and are therefore obliged to provide employees with information regarding organisational monitoring policies.

In this way employees are advised of improper procedures and disciplinary offences that justify the scope of invasive monitoring techniques (Directive 95/46/EC). Furthermore details of the surveillance measures undertaken are also provided so as the employee will know who is monitoring them, how they are being monitored as well as when these actions are taking place. This principal of transparency also provides individuals with access rights to personal data processed or collated by management, allowing them to request its rectification or deletion where appropriate (Directive 95/46/EC).

The fourth criterion, legitimacy is similar to that of necessity in so far as data can only be obtained for a justifiable purpose and must not contravene an employee's fundamental or inherent right to privacy. Under this element of the legislation however, data of a very sensitive nature can be deemed too personal to collect and collection therefore must be specifically authorised by a national law in extreme circumstances (Directive 95/46/EC). Organisations must also comply with the notion of proportionality, using the most non-intrusive or least excessive action in order to obtain the desired information. For example the monitoring of emails should if possible focus on the general information such as the time and transmission as opposed to the content if the situation permits. If however viewing of the email content is deemed necessary then the law presides that the privacy of those outside of the organisation should also be taken into account and that reasonable efforts be made to inform the outside world of any monitoring practices (Directive 95/46/EC).

Any data that is collated on an employee must only be retained for as long as is necessary under this European law and data that is no longer needed should then be deleted. Management should specify a particular retention period based on their business needs so as employees are constantly aware of the ongoing process

(Directive 95/46/EC). Furthermore, provisions should be set in place to ensure that any data that is held by the employer will remain secure and safe from any form of intrusion or disturbance. The employer is also required to protect the technological medium from the threat of virus as a further means of protecting the personal data (Directive 95/46/EC).

It is apparent that the central concept of the European Directive relates to the processing and flow of information (Elgesem, 1999). As a result researchers such as Evans (2007) note how the existence of these European laws that favour the employee are consequently putting considerable pressure on the United States to adopt similar laws. In fact, it has been previously suggested that the various proposals and directives – or at least the relevant aspects of them - should be combined into one robust comprehensive model (Tavani, 2004). While such a model combining the interests of both the organisation and the employee would appear to be a sensible solution however for Wang, Lee and Wang (1998) it poses 'one of the most challenging public policy issues of the information age.'

FUTURE RESEARCH DIRECTIONS

Although there is evidence that workplace tracking and surveillance is increasing, the lines regarding what are correct and moral forms of behaviour continually blur thus limiting our overall understanding of the main issues involved as well as the ways in which to target them. In fact, the use of Internet-based technologies in the workplace presents businesses and employees with opportunities to engage in behaviours for which comprehensive understandings or rules have not yet been established.

As such it is imperative that future research aims to alleviate this confusion by addressing these issues from both a rigorous and relevant perspective. The themes identified in this paper have implications for future academic work in the area of workplace surveillance In order to examine and understand the factors that inhibit and amplify workplace surveillance issues future researchers must begin by exploring these issues directly with those that face them. There is significant scope for a large-scale detailed study to be conducted that addresses some if not all of these issues from both an employee and employer perspective. A study conducted in such a manner could not only identify the frequent concerns that exist in response to workplace surveillance techniques but could further explore what technologies IS departments employ to monitor activities and perhaps more importantly why. Only then can we try to establish some form of balance or harmony between both parties in the computer-mediated workplace environment.

Further research into the main issues of workplace surveillance will be of great significance and interest to practitioners also. Employees are the lifeblood of any organisation and only by understanding the behavioural outcomes of such individuals can we begin to understand the factors that predict the perceptions, attitudes and beliefs that are generated through the implementation of communication monitoring techniques in the workplace. Consequently future research into some of these major issues will have significant and important consequences for the businesses that employ these growing and developing technologies.

electronic monitoring in the computer-mediated work environment. This paper explored the ethical impact of monitoring in the computer-mediated work environment, addressing whether managements ability to monitor employee actions in workplace represents good business practice or constitutes an invasion of privacy. While it is apparent that management may have legitimate reasons to monitor employees' actions in the workplace, the privacy rights of the employee cannot be ignored. In this way it is paramount that some form of harmony or balance between the interests of the employer and the employee is achieved.

Whilst much colloquial discussion of workplace surveillance exists, empirical studies on this issue are in short supply. A greater awareness of increased surveillance and the corresponding acuteness of information privacy concerns point to the need for research on this issue. It is apparent that European laws favour the rights of the employee however within the literature no hierarchy of privacy or ethical concerns on the part of employers and employees has yet been identified. Moreover as far as it is possible to ascertain, the factors influencing employers and IS managers in their decisions to electively employ surveillance technologies have not been explored. Consequently, our understanding of these issues and the ways in which employee privacy concerns could be diminished, thus positively impacting productivity and morale, provide a fruitful avenue for future privacy research.

CONCLUSION

Technology-enabled surveillance and tracking of employees in increasing both in terms of pervasiveness and sophistication. The primary objective of this paper was to address the issue of

ACKNOWLEDGMENT

The author would like to acknowledge Cliona McParland for her contribution to the research on which this work is based.

REFERENCES

Acquisti, A. (2002). *Protecting privacy with economic: Economic incentives for preventive technologies in ubiquitous computing environment.* Paper presented at the Workshop on Socially-informed Design of Privacy-enhancing Solutions in Ubiquitous Computing. New York, NY.

Alder, G. S., Noel, T. W., & Ambrose, M. L. (2006). Clarifying the effects of internet monitoring on job attitudes: The mediating role of employee trust. *Information & Management, 43*(7), 894–903. doi:10.1016/j.im.2006.08.008

Altman, I. (1975). *The environment and social behaviour: Privacy, personal space, territory, and crowding.* Monterey, CA: Brooks/Cole.

AMA Survey. (2001). *Workplace monitoring and surveillance.* Retrieved from http://www.amanet.org/research/pdfs/ems_short2001.pdf

AMA Survey. (2003). *Email rules, policies and practices survey.* Retrieved from http://www.amanet.org/research/pdfs/email_policies_practices.pdf

AMA Survey. (2005). *Electronic monitoring and surveillance survey.* Retrieved from http://www.amanet.org/research/pdfs/ems_summary05.pdf

Barrett-Howard, E., & Tyler, T. R. (1986). Procedural justice as a criterion in allocation decisions. *Journal of Personality and Social Psychology, 50*(2), 296–304. doi:10.1037/0022-3514.50.2.296

Bélanger, F., & Crossler, R. E. (2011). Privacy in the digital age: A review of information privacy research in information systems. *Management Information Systems Quarterly, 35*(4), 1017–1041.

Bélanger, F., Hiller, J. S., & Smith, W. J. (2002). Trustworthiness in electronic commerce: The role of privacy, security, and site attributes. *The Journal of Strategic Information Systems, 11*(3-4), 245–270. doi:10.1016/S0963-8687(02)00018-5

Bies, R. J., & Moag, J. F. (1986). Interactional justice: Communication criteria of fairness. In R. J. Lewicki, B. H. Sheppard, & M. H. Bazerman (Eds.), *Research on negotiations in organisations* (Vol. 1, pp. 43–55). Greenwich, CT: JAI Press.

Clarke, R. (1999). Internet privacy concerns confirm the case for intervention. *Communications of the ACM, 42*(2), 60–67. doi:10.1145/293411.293475

Clarke, R. A. (1988). Information technology and dataveillance. *Communications of the ACM, 31*(5), 498–512. doi:10.1145/42411.42413

Cohen-Charash, Y., & Spector, P. E. (2001). The role of justice in organizations: A meta-analysis. *Organizational Behavior and Human Decision Processes, 86*(2), 278–321. doi:10.1006/obhd.2001.2958

Craver, C. B. (2006). Privacy issues affecting employers, employees and labour organizations. *Louisiana Law Review, 66*, 1057–1078.

Culnan, M. J. (1993). How did they get my name? An exploratory investigation of consumer attitudes toward secondary information use. *Management Information Systems Quarterly, 17*(3), 341–364. doi:10.2307/249775

D'Urso, S. C. (2006). Who's watching us at work? Toward a structural-perceptual model of electronic monitoring and surveillance in organisations. *Communication Theory, 16*, 281–303. doi:10.1111/j.1468-2885.2006.00271.x

Daft, R. L. (2000). *Management* (5th ed.). Hinsdale, IL: The Dryden Press.

Dinev, T., & Hart, P. (2006). An extended privacy calculus model for e-commerce transactions. *Information Systems Research*, *17*(1), 61–80. doi:10.1287/isre.1060.0080

Dinev, T., Xu, H., Smith, J. H., & Hart, P. (2013). Information privacy and correlates: An empirical attempt to bridge and distinguish privacy-related concepts. *European Journal of Information Systems*, *22*, 295–316. doi:10.1057/ejis.2012.23

Elgesem, D. (1999). The structure of rights in directive 95/46/EC on the protection of individuals with regard to the processing of personal data and the free movement of such data. *Ethics and Information Technology*, *1*(4), 283–293. doi:10.1023/A:1010076422893

European Union. (2002). *Directive 95/46/EC: Article 29 WP55*. Retrieved from http://ec.europa.eu/justice_home/fsj/privacy/docs/wpdocs/2002/wpss_en.pdf

Evans, L. (2007). Monitoring technology in the American workplace: Would adopting English privacy standards better balance employee privacy and productivity? *California Law Review*, *95*, 1115–1149.

Foucault, M. (1977). *Discipline and punish: The birth of the prison*. London, UK: Penguin Books.

Ghosh, A. P. (1998). *E-commerce security – Weak links, best defences*. Hoboken, NJ: John Wiley & Sons.

Godfrey, B. (2001). Electronic work monitoring: An ethical model. In *Selected papers from the second Australian institute conference on computer ethics* (pp. 18-21). Academic Press.

Harris Interactive. (2003). *Poll*. Retrieved from http://www.harrisinteractive.com/harris_poll/index.asp?PID=365

Hauenstein, N. M. A., McGonigle, T., & Flinder, S. W. (2001). A meta-analysis of the relationship between procedural justice and distributive justice: Implications for justice research. *Employee Responsibilities and Rights Journal*, *13*(1), 39–56. doi:10.1023/A:1014482124497

Helne, C. A. (2005). Predicting workplace deviance from the interaction between organizational justice and personality. *Journal of Managerial Issues*, *17*(2), 247–263.

IBM. (2006). *Stopping insider attacks: How organizations can protect their sensitive information*. Retrieved from http://www-935.ibm.com/services/us/imc/pdf/gsw00316-usen-00-insider-threats-wp.pdf

Introna, L. D. (1996). Privacy and the computer: Why we need privacy in the information society. *Metaphilosophy*, *28*(3), 259–275. doi:10.1111/1467-9973.00055

Introna, L. D. (2001). Workplace surveillance, privacy and distributive justice. In R. A. Spinello, & H. T. Tavani (Eds.), *Readings in cyberethics* (pp. 519–532). Sudbury, MA: Jones and Barlett.

Jackson, T., Dawson, R., & Wilson, D. (2001). *The cost of email interruption* (Item No. 2134/495). Loughborough, UK: Loughborough University Institutional Repository. Retrieved from http://km.lboro.ac.uk/iii/pdf/JOSIT%202001.pdf

Lane, F. S. (2003). *The naked employee: How technology is compromising workplace privacy*. New York, NY: AMACOM.

Laudon, K. C., & Laudon, J. P. (2001). *Essentials of management information systems: Organisation and technology in the networked enterprise* (4th ed.). Upper Saddle River, NJ: Prentice Hall.

Laudon, K. C., & Laudon, J. P. (2002). *Management information systems: Managing the digital firm* (7th ed.). Upper Saddle River, NJ: Prentice Hall.

Laudon, K. C., & Traver, C. G. (2010). *E-commerce 2010 – Business technology society* (6th ed.). Upper Saddle River, NJ: Prentice Hall.

Louis Harris and Associates. (1999). *Poll*. Retrieved from http://www.natlconsumersleague.org/FNLSUM1.PDF

Madden, M., Fox, S., Smith, A., & Vitak, J. (2007). *Digital footprints: Online identity management and search in the age of transparency*. Retrieved July 29, 2012, from http://pewresearch.org/pubs/663/digital-footprints

Margulis, S. T. (2003). On the status and contribution of Westin's and Altman's theories of privacy. *The Journal of Social Issues, 59*(2), 411–429. doi:10.1111/1540-4560.00071

Marx, G., & Sherizen, S. (1991). Monitoring on the job: How to protect privacy as well as property. In T. Forester (Ed.), *Computers in the human context: Information technology, productivity, and people* (pp. 397–406). Cambridge, MA: MIT Press.

Mason, R. (1986). Four ethical issues of the information age. *Management Information Systems Quarterly, 10*(1), 4–12. doi:10.2307/248873

Mayer, R. C., Davis, J. D., & Schoorman, F. D. (1995). An integrative model of organisational trust. *Academy of Management Review, 20*(3), 709–734.

McParland, C., & Connolly, R. (2009). *The role of dataveillance in the organsiation: Some emerging trends*. Paper presented at the Irish Academy of Management Conference. Galway, UK.

Mossholder, K. W., Bennett, N., Kemery, E. R., & Wesolowski, M. A. (1998). Relationships between bases of power and work reactions: The mediational role of procedural justice. *Journal of Management, 24*(4), 533–552. doi:10.1016/S0149-2063(99)80072-5

Nord, G. D., McCubbins, T. F., & Horn Nord, J. (2006). Email monitoring in the workplace: Privacy, legislation, and surveillance software. *Communications of the ACM, 49*(8), 73–77.

Parker, R. B. (1974). A definition of privacy. *Rutgers Law Review, 27*(1), 275.

Pavlou, P. A., Liang, H., & Xue, Y. (2007). Understanding and mitigating uncertainty in online exchange relationships: A principal–agent perspective. *Management Information Systems Quarterly, 31*(1), 105–136.

Prakhaber, P. R. (2000). Who owns the online consumer? *Journal of Consumer Marketing, 17*(2), 158–171. doi:10.1108/07363760010317213

Robinson, S. L., & Rousseau, D. M. (1994). Violating the psychological contract: Not the exception but the norm. *Journal of Organizational Behavior, 15*(3), 245–259. doi:10.1002/job.4030150306

Rust, R. T., Kannan, P. K., & Peng, N. (2002). The customer economics of internet privacy. *Journal of the Academy of Marketing Science, 30*(4), 455–464. doi:10.1177/009207002236917

Safire, W. (2002). The great unwatched. *The New York Times*. Retrieved from http://query.nytimes.com/gst/fullpage.html?res=9A03E7DB1E3FF93BA25751C0A9649C8B63

Selmi, M. (2006). Privacy for the working class: Public work and private lives. *Louisiana Law Review, 66*, 1035–1056.

Semuels, A. (2013, April 8). Monitoring up-ends balance of power at workplace some say. *Los Angeles Times*. Retrieved from http://www.latimes.com/business/money/la-fi-mo-monitoring-upends-balance-of-power-at-workplace-20130408,0,7425573.story

SHRM. (2005). *Workplace privacy – Poll findings: A study by the society for human resource management and careerjournal.com*. Retrieved from http://www.shrm.org/Research/Survey-Findings/Documents/Workplace%20Privacy%20Poll%20Findings%20-%20A%20Study%20by%20SHRM%20and%20CareerJournal.com.pdf

Smith, H. J., Dinev, T., & Xu, H. (2011). Information privacy research: An interdisciplinary review. *Management Information Systems Quarterly, 35*(4), 989–1015.

Smith, H. J., Milberg, J. S., & Burke, J. S. (1996). Information privacy: Measuring individuals' concerns about organizational practices. *Management Information Systems Quarterly, 20*(2), 167–196. doi:10.2307/249477

So, M. W. C., & Sculli, D. (2002). The role of trust, quality, value and risk in conducting e-business. *Industrial Management & Data Systems, 102*(9), 503–512. doi:10.1108/02635570210450181

Solove, D. J. (2006). A taxonomy of privacy. *University of Pennsylvania Law Review, 154*(3), 477–564. doi:10.2307/40041279

Stanton, J. M. (2000a). Reactions to employee performance monitoring: Framework, review, and research directions. *Human Performance, 13*(1), 85–113. doi:10.1207/S15327043HUP1301_4

Stanton, J. M. (2000b). Traditional and electronic monitoring from an organizational justice perspective. *Journal of Business and Psychology, 15*(1), 129–147. doi:10.1023/A:1007775020214

Stanton, J. M., & Barnes-Farrell, J. L. (1996). Effects of electronic performance-monitoring on personal control, satisfaction and performance. *The Journal of Applied Psychology, 81*, 738–745. doi:10.1037/0021-9010.81.6.738

Tavani, H. T. (2004). *Ethics and technology: Ethical issues in an age of information and communication technology*. Chichester, UK: John Wiley & Sons.

Turban, E., King, D., Lee, J., Liang, T. P., & Turban, D. (2010). *Electronic commerce 2010: A managerial perspective* (6th ed.). Upper Saddle River, NJ: Pearson.

Turban, E., Leidner, D., McClean, E., & Wetherbe, J. (2006). *Information technology for management – Transforming organisations in the digital economy* (5th ed.). New York, NY: John Wiley & Sons.

Turow, J., Feldman, L., & Metlzer, K. (2005). *Open to exploitation: American shoppers online and offline*. Philadelphia, PA: Annenberg Public Policy Centre, University of Pennsylvania.

Wang, H., Lee, M. K. O., & Wang, C. (1998). Consumer privacy concerns about internet marketing. *Communications of the ACM, 41*(3), 63–70. doi:10.1145/272287.272299

Wen, H. J., Schwieger, D., & Gershuny, P. (2007). Internet usage monitoring in the workplace: Its legal challenges and implementation strategies. *Information Systems Management, 24*, 185–196. doi:10.1080/10580530701221072

Xu, H., Dinev, T., Smith, J. H., & Hart, P. (2011). Information privacy concerns: Linking individual perceptions with institutional privacy assurances. *Journal of the Association for Information Systems*, *12*(12), 798–824.

Zweig, D., & Webster, J. (2002). Where is the line between benign and invasive? An examination of psychological barriers to the acceptance of awareness monitoring system. *Journal of Organizational Behavior*, *23*(5), 605–633. doi:10.1002/job.157

Chapter 6
Wearable Computing:
Security Challenges, BYOD, Privacy, and Legal Aspects

John Lindström
Luleå University of Technology, Sweden

Claas Hanken
Nemetschek Bausoftware GmbH, Germany

ABSTRACT

Wearable computing is gaining more and more interest as new "wearables," intended for both work and leisure, are introduced. This trend brings benefits and challenges; for instance, the potential to improve work processes and issues related to IT management and privacy. The introduction and use of wearable computing provides opportunities to improve and reengineer work processes in organizations but can at the same time introduce alignment problems, as users in organizations may adopt the new technology before organizations are prepared. Further, alignment problems posed by the emerging trend, "Bring Your Own Device" (BYOD), are discussed. In addition, as in the cloud computing area, needed and necessary supportive legal frameworks have not yet fully addressed the new wearable computing technology. In the light of recent developments regarding global intelligence gathering, security and privacy concerns must be given careful consideration. Different alignment concepts for managing security challenges and legal aspects related to wearable computing, such as cultivation, care, hospitality, and care with hospitality, are discussed in the chapter.

DOI: 10.4018/978-1-4666-4856-2.ch006

INTRODUCTION

This chapter, which is to a large extent based on experiences gained during the wearIT@work[1] project, addresses how organizations can approach security challenges and legal aspects while introducing wearable computing in their organizations. If no well considered approach is used, relying on for instance ad hoc principles, there is a risk that instead of rendering business value, the introduction and use of wearable computing can cause the opposite by usage and user behaviour not aligned with the organization's set of rules and beliefs (Davis, 2002; Lindström, 2009). Looking to the future, there is a need for organizations to find ways to improve work productivity, quality and safety. To reengineer work processes in areas where process innovation has been hard without the proper (wearable) supportive tools, there is a need for new and better technology supporting improved performance and productivity (Davis, 2002; Stanford, 2002a; Pasher, Popper, Raz, & Lawo, 2010). Many lines of work do not allow workers to use a computer, e.g., a laptop or tablet, in the workplace due to the nature of their work, for instance where free or clean hands are required. For those groups, there is a large potential in using wearable computers and systems. Further, the emerging trend "bring your own device" (BYOD), mainly involving laptops, tablets, smart phones and other portable (wireless) devices, adds additional challenges for organizations to handle (Olivier, 2012; Miller, Voas & Hurlburt, 2012), while at the same time having potential to improve productivity and support business value creation.

The *wearable computing* paradigm has evolved around three factors: smaller, more powerful computers, greater personal mobility and increasing personalization of devices. Closely related to each other are *ubiquitous computing*, which is introduced by Weiser (1991), and *pervasive computing,* which refers to the vision where computers are integrated in the environment and the usage is completely transparent to the user. Wearable computing may thus fall under the category of pervasive computing. Lyytinen and Yoo (2002) argue that pervasive computing services require more effort regarding design and maintenance compared to ubiquitous ones, making the availability and usefulness of pervasive computing services limited. However, we think that the recent advances within context awareness-, localization-, and cloud services make this previous gap small today. Wearable computing is also introduced by the wearIT@work project[2] as follows:

Wearable mobile computing can empower professionals to higher levels of productivity by providing more seamless and effective forms of access to knowledge at the point of work, collaboration and communication. The new technology of wearable mobile computing will meet the need of many individual professionals for acting more flexibly, effectively and efficiently in the increasingly complicated and challenging European work environment. It can be used to enhance jobs in industry and services to make them both more rewarding and effective and re-elevate the role of the professional at work...

As wearable computers and systems for different business mature, they can be used in a lot of work areas where there is at present very little or no IT-support. Wearable computers will most likely be used more and more, not only at work but also during leisure time. This is due to the fact that wearables, being very small, integrated into clothing and able to interact intelligently with the surrounding environment as well as detect other computing devices (Lyytinen & Yoo, 2002), will be brought almost everywhere.

This exposure to a variety of unsecure or hostile network environments will require a higher level of information security to protect personal integrity and privacy, confidential information and communications. At the same time, the legal frameworks need to adapt to the use of wearables, as they put new requirements on the protection of personal integrity and privacy as well as information security. However, one of the problems with legal frameworks and IT is that the pace of development of IT is so fast that the adaption and development of the legal frameworks is almost always a couple of years or more behind, often forcing the frameworks to be very general.

Related Work

Security issues for wearable and pervasive computing have been evolving during the last two decades as the technologies have matured and come into professional use. Dagon, Martin, and Starner (2004) warn early of viruses as well as theft-of-service and denial-of-service attacks, and Stanford (2002b) adds that use within the healthcare sector requires a balance between usability and privacy, and that there is a need to develop security guidelines regarding, for instance, security administration, network security, data security and strong user authentication, and that a layered approach for wireless security can be a good idea. Mann, Nolan, and Wellman (2003) highlight the risk for social surveillance if privacy is not safeguarded. In addition, looking at fundamental challenges to secure pervasive computing, Thomas and Sandhu (2004) mean that there is a need to integrate a socio-technical perspective and that the classical perimeter security breaks down, requiring support for dynamic trust relationships. Further, they add a need for balance in between non-intrusiveness and security

strength, support for context awareness and increased mobility, dynamism and adaptability, as well as resource-constrained operations due to limited computing power.

In the recent security research for wearable and pervasive computing, Stajano (2010) states that the main security problems are, particularly in relation to location data and use of RFID tags, authentication, device pairing, achieving balance between security and usability, and understanding people. Further, Guelzim and Obaidat (2011) mean that security classics such as perimeter security and access control are still in focus, but that more effort is needed regarding hardening of pervasive networks and privacy of users. Mohammad and Munir (2009) posit that new security mechanisms are required by pervasive computing, as the traditional mechanisms are not able to cope with the new challenges and become barriers rather than enablers. They divide security challenges into the three areas: network-, device-, and user security, highlighting differences, compared to traditional security, in for instance authentication, privacy, defence against malicious code, access control and information protection. They posit that this partly depends on the inherent limited computing resources, heterogeneous hardware and software platforms, and exposure to hostile network environments.

Some distinguishable trends in the above are while being usable, wearable computing needs to: uphold network security and data security, be able to run virus and attack protection, as well as safeguard the integrity and privacy of users. This requires strong authentication in combination with additional security mechanisms. As many wearables are aware of context and localization, this capability can be used to extend and enhance existing security mechanisms and to develop new ones. Some examples of context-based security can be found in the work by

Mostéfaoui, Chae,J., Kim, and Chung (2004), addressing how to secure transactions and make the security level more adaptive, and by Brézillon and Mostéfaoui (2004a, 2004b), who define "security context" and discuss context-based security policies. As context awareness can be used to extend existing security mechanisms, one novel idea introduced in the paper is authorization by proximity enabling transfer of authorization from one party to another party. Allowing a controlled transfer of authorization from one individual to another can improve work processes and better enable teamwork.

Olivier (2012) posits that the term BYOD can be misleading, giving the impression that employees only use their personal devices, e.g. tablets or smart phones, to access corporate networks and applications, whereas employees often use the corporate equipment (of latest consumer-type style) for personal use outside of the corporate environment to take photos or surf on the web. According to Olivier (2012), many employers claim to have a policy in place to manage BYOD issues, while less than half of employees seem aware of the existence of such a policy. Further, security risks are communicated to the employees by employers, albeit not on a regular basis. Olivier (2012) proposes that for BYOD to render business value, first of all a BYOD strategy is required and that it is implemented in a policy or policies which is/are kept updated. An interesting perspective on BYOD is given by Miller, Voas and Hurlburt (2012), who assert that BYOD is supplanted by the term "bring your own technology" (BYOT), which includes both hardware and software. According to them, this poses both security and privacy concerns where, mainly for the employer, security may be jeopardized, while the employee may stand to lose more in terms of privacy. The main security concerns, according to Miller, Voas and Hurlburt (2012), arise when

an employee's personal device is connected to the employer's network, thereby exposing the network to the risk of malware migrating into the network and further, that sensitive information "is likely to make its way onto the personal device" (p.54) and thus no longer be under control. One problem with many personal devices is that it is less likely that the employer's security policy is enforced when such devices are used, and thus the security level may be insufficient. Alas, with usage of cloud computing storage, many personal devices are configured to automatically store photos, documents and contacts in the cloud. Regarding this matter, Miller, Voas and Hurlburt (2012) suggest the use of a clear barrier and partitioning between personal and employer data/information. Elaborate partitioning is required, but is it really possible to implement and is it feasible to prevent leakage of sensitive employer information?

In legal publications, wearable computing and associated fields of technology are mentioned nearly exclusively in the context of future privacy problems ending up in recommendations for updates of the relevant privacy laws. Barfield (2006) deals with issues of privacy that are impacted when an individual's image is recorded by a video-based wearable computer, analyzed using facial recognition software, and uploaded to the Internet. Pitkänen and Niemelä (2007) cover privacy and data protection in emerging radio frequency identification (RFID) applications. Spiekermann and Langheinrich (2008) look forward to privacy research based on realistic prototypes. As part of the wearIT@ work project, Oechsner and Wimmer (2007) delivered a legal-expert opinion on wearable computers and regulations concerning working conditions. Our chapter summarizes a number of selected important EU legal aspects regarding the use and lifecycle of wearable computers.

Questions Addressed and Organization of Chapter

The introduction of wearable computing for large-scale professional use appears to be a next logical step in many industries to improve performance and productivity. This will not only introduce new technology but also have impact on work processes, interaction between people, as well as other societal and legal aspects. The intersection between the areas of wearable computing, information security and legal frameworks is an interesting field of study.

The main question addressed by this chapter is how organizations can approach security challenges and legal aspects while introducing wearable computing in their organizations. Also addressed are aspects of information security and the European Union's legal framework that are of special interest for wearable computing, considering the experience gained from the wearIT@work project. Additionally, the chapter highlights additional selected EU legal issues concerning wearables, emerging BYOD issues, as well as indicating the need for new security mechanisms due to new requirements discovered. The findings are analyzed from the viewpoint of strategic alignment of IT, to suggest how new requirements from wearables can be managed in organizations in a proactive rather than reactive manner.

Following this introduction are sections on alignment theory and methodology. These are followed by sections on security challenges, novel ideas on security and selected legal aspects. Lastly, an analysis and conclusions are presented.

TOWARDS ALIGNING THE USE OF WEARABLE COMPUTERS WITH SECURITY AND LEGAL ASPECTS

Users of wearable computers must, like any user of general IT resources in an organization, use the IT resources as they are intended to be used to achieve the desired outcome, i.e., business value. Davis (2002, p. 68) means that *"organizations and individuals may make unanticipated responses as they adapt to new technology,"* which leads to the creation of new structures to promote or restrict its use. Further, Davis (2002, p. 68) adds that it is *"useful to anticipate both desirable and undesirable responses and consequences."* There are different possibilities for an organization to achieve the desired alignment of usage and behaviour, and, commonly awareness training, policies and user guidelines are used. Addressed in this paper are security and legal aspects, which are aspects that must be observed throughout the whole lifecycle and use of the wearable computers to ensure that their use does cause the opposite of the desired outcome, e.g. leakage of sensitive information and/or broken laws causing bad will, loss of trustworthiness, and possibly also fines or penalties. Thus, the way in which this alignment of usage and behaviour is achieved is an important consideration for any organization.

Looking back on alignment of IT resources, Sauer, Yetton, Benjamin, Ciborra, Coombs, Craig *et al.* (1997) state that the management of IT focused during the 1970s and 80s on technical activities. During recent years, however, corporations have become more and more aware of the potential business value of IT; subsequently, interest in IT management has increased. Sauer *et al.* (1997) also state that, since the mid-1980s two particular approaches to managing IT have become popular: strategic planning and organizing to achieve strategic alignment. Strategic planning of IT has to do with ensuring that IT plans match the strategic plans of an organization and are consistent with the priorities of the core activities and initiatives (Ward, Griffiths, & Whitmore, 1990). Organizing to achieve strategic alignment is about setting an organization (by structural separation of the IT function) so that IT mirrors the management of an organization in that IT is strategically, structurally and managerially aligned with organizational strategy, structures and management processes (Sauer *et al.*, 1997; Henderson & Venkatraman, 1992).

Alignment is further about how to achieve synergy between strategy, organization, processes, technology and people in order to sustain the quality of interdependence and thus achieve competitive advantage (Hsaio & Ormerod, 1998). Aligning business strategy with IS/IT strategy is an issue for organizations and is a key concern of senior management. However, alignment may be a moderating variable between the usage and organizational performance (Chan, Huff, Barclay, & Copeland, 1997). Alignment assists an organization by positioning the IT-strategy in a closer relation to the business strategy (Sauer *et al.*, 1997; Henderson & Venkatraman, 1992). The outcome of this relationship is improved IT effectiveness and higher profitability (Porter, 1987; Luftman, 1996; Levy, Powell, & Yetton, 2001; Cragg, King, & Hussin, 2002; Avison, Jones, Powell, & Wilson, 2004). In the research on alignment, three trajectories are defined: the return on IT-investment, the way that IT can provide direction and flexibility to react on new opportunities, and the social dimension of information alignment.

Ciborra (1997) discusses drifting technology due to problems in managing it, and calls the learning process whereby users and managers understand how to use technology in the work processes "drift."

Further, Ciborra (2002), criticizing the management agenda of today's business, states that firms today are too narrow in their perspective on managerial issues. Ciborra thinks that too much focus is placed on what can be controlled (heterogeneous resources), trying to control with a narrow management information system mindset, and not on the fact that IS/IT crosses organizational borders. Ciborra (1997) thinks that this misalignment can be addressed by using "cultivation," which is about destabilizing the current strategy and creating imbalance with the current technology. This creates a tension that will stimulate learning while at the same time forcing users to give feedback on the technology used and how it affects their work situation.

Ciborra (1998) further states that the phenomenon "technology drifting" can be confronted by doing either as management science suggests and *"build an ideal world of 'how things should be'"* (p. 13) or try to operate in the messy reality towards the idealized model and reflect upon what is observed. Ciborra (1998) argues that if the latter course is taken, phenomenon as "care" and "hospitality" can be encountered and used in addition to "cultivation." "Care" is about familiarity, intimacy and continuous commitment from an initial requirement analysis all the way until training of users. A particular form of care is "understanding," and understanding, for instance, a system *"means becoming so intimately familiar with it that it disappears from the cone of our alert attention, and becomes taken for granted, encapsulated into the routines of our daily absorbed coping... and so "aligned" with the execution of our daily tasks that they disappear and become part of the world"* (p. 13). This, according to Ciborra (1998), offers a new approach to understanding strategic alignment. "Hospitality" is about when technology is in motion in organizations and is ambiguous. Acceptance needs to cope with the ambiguity, and then become hospitality. Ciborra (1998) also states that hospitality is unstable and quickly can turn into hostility instead, but if used correctly together with caring ("care with hospitality"), absorbed coping, intimacy, etc. can make technologies be integrated in the work flows and be understood. Ciborra's four concepts "cultivation," "care," "hospitality," and "care with hospitality" for how to deal with alignment problems pertaining to wearable computing will be used as an analytic grid when analyzing the results.

METHODOLOGY

This chapter is based on the findings from a survey and conceptual ideas formed during the wearIT@work project as well as a literature review. The survey was based on the wearIT@work project's requirement specifications, which were developed using an iterative process driven by four User Centred Design (UCD) teams. The UCD teams followed the ISO 13407 standard, having 3 innovation cycles (Boronowsky, Herzog, Knackfuss, & Lawo, 2005). These UCD teams entailed groups with generalists as well as specialists working with 4 domains spanning rescue services (mainly a fire brigade in a large city), automotive production (passenger cars), healthcare (general care at hospitals) and airplane maintenance (large passenger airplanes). The requirement specification work was supported by the Volere[3] requirement specification technique. *Volere*, Italian for want or wish, is a requirements technique developed to give a common language to people with different skill sets to find and discover requirements as well as to connect the requirements to solutions. Both hardware[4] and software[5] platform requirements,

related to the 4 domains mentioned above, were thoroughly engineered[6].

The security-related requirements were filtered out from the final requirement specifications, and a survey with a questionnaire for self-completion (Brace, 2004) was sent out via e-mail to the UCD team leaders and the hardware and software architects. The purpose of the survey was to find and confirm the most relevant and important security requirements. In total, there were 7 respondents, who had been part of creating the requirements. The total number of possible respondents was 14. However, it was decided to target only those 7 holding the key roles in the project, i.e., technical manager, hardware architect, software architect and the 4 UCD team leaders. Survey was chosen as the methodology because the existing requirement specifications were available and provided a suitable basis for a questionnaire, and the respondents were distributed throughout Europe. The respondents were all very busy and had tight schedules, and, instead of using interviews, a survey was used so that the respondents could answer the questions at their leisure and not have to respond immediately during, for instance, a phone interview. It was also possible to ask additional complementary questions after the survey, if needed. All 7 targeted respondents answered, which gave a response rate of 100%, and non-response bias problems can be eliminated. This corroborated the findings, i.e., that the requirements were relevant and also initiated the prioritization of the requirements. Miles and Huberman (1994) suggest that getting feedback from the informants to test or confirm findings is "*one of the most logical sources of corroboration...*" Construct validity (Yin, 2003) was addressed by using well designed questions derived from the requirement specifications, questions which were sent to 7 respondents, all of whom answered. The data collection process was simple, consistent and stable over time. The survey can be repeated with the same respondents and all documentation is available, ensuring reliability (Yin, 2003; Miles & Huberman, 1994).

Following the survey, as the data had been analyzed using a matrix (Miles & Huberman, 1994) to visualize the different requirement and the prioritization order, the results were categorized as general or UCD pilot-specific and summarized into two reports. These reports were reviewed, to ensure that the results made sense and satisfied the requirement of internal validity (Yin, 2003), by all respondents as well as about 15 more members from the wearIT@ work project. Later, the findings were used with a different categorization of the requirements in project deliverables[7], which were reviewed by the EU Commission reviewers. The following areas of security were used for categorization of the security requirements in the project deliverables: *authentication, authorization, non-repudiation, privacy, logging, warning messages* as well as *confidentiality, integrity and availability*.

The conceptual ideas regarding security were found using structured and unstructured brainstorming meetings during the wearIT@ work project. These ideas were not added to the requirement specifications, but noted and further developed. Three of these novel ideas are described later.

Further, the legal part of this chapter is based on a literature review and analysis of prior research results from the wearIT@work project. In both Sweden and Germany, literature reviews were conducted focusing on EU-level Directives and Council decision regarding privacy, data security/protection and wearables.

We searched periodically during a period of almost two years, from early-2007 to late-2009, by doing meta searches in journal databases (Ebsco, ebrary, JSTOR General Science, SAGE Journals, ScienceDirect (Elsevier), SCOPUS (Elsevier) and Web of Science (ISI)), and key word searches in Google Scholar and Google. EU legal databases were searched using English, Swedish and German for retrieval (assuming that the greater part of the database content has been translated into English and other major languages used in EU member states). The following search strings were used: privacy, information security, IT security, data security, data protection, ubiquitous, pervasive and wearable. The search results were summarized and analyzed, and the EU legal sources used are found in the Appendix.

The survey covered only one project, which makes it harder to generalize from the findings, but as the survey covered four User Centred Design (UCD) teams working on pilots in four different contexts the conclusions are to a certain extent transferable between different contexts. Since the wearIT@work project was during the years 2004-2009 the largest research and development project in its field, with a budget of approximately 23.7 million euros and about 40 partners participating (whereof many of the IT industry's largest corporations and research groups from a number of well known universities), it can be seen as unique and revelatory (Yin, 2003) both in terms of size/volume and due to the fact that no similar projects have yet been conducted.

Regarding the literature review, the conclusions from the study pertaining to the legal framework are fairly general and could be used by almost any organization where this matter is of importance. Overall, the results are conceptual and thus adaptable to specific needs and requirements that may be posed.

SECURITY CHALLENGES FOR WEARABLE COMPUTING

The four most important security challenges encountered during the wearIT@work survey are highlighted below. The challenges are both current and emerging ones, and point in the same direction as the research done by Thomas and Sandhu (2004), Mohammad and Munir (2009), Stajano (2010), and Guelzim and Obaidat (2011).

Protecting Sensitive Information

If integrated in clothing, a wearable is harder to lose or forget somewhere compared to a laptop, tablet or advanced mobile phone. Nevertheless, if sensitive information, like files or login credentials, is stored inside a wearable[8] it should be protected by storing it on a hard drive using file encryption (Mohammad & Munir, 2009). This is due to the fact that a wearable might get lost anyway: the owner may accidentally forget or lose the garment embedding the wearable device.

Authentication

A user of wearables might not be able to type in a password, etc. on a keyboard, and thus there is a need for stable and mature biometric authentication solutions that are easily integrated into clothing. This need will most likely grow in the future, making wearables easier to use and operate. For instance, having authentication tokens embedded in clothes, facilitating authentication by proximity, is an interesting possibility increasing usability and decreasing the intrusiveness for the user (Bardram, Kjaer,

& Pedersen, M 2003; Ebringer *et al.*, 2000; Ferreira & Dahab, 2000; Thomas & Sandhu, 2004).

Unsecure Networks and Hostile Environments

Using wearables and laptops outside of controlled wireless networks require higher security for communications regarding encryption, information integrity (Stajano, 2010; Guelzim & Obaidat, 2011) and, in some cases, non-repudiation (i.e., making sure that a party in a dispute cannot refute the validity of a statement). If using ad-hoc networks or unreliable access points, there are a number of well-known security problems (Nichols & Lekkas, 2002; Pangboonyanon, 2004) and attacks (Komninos, Vergados, & Dogligeris, 2006) regarding both the information sent as well as availability of the network access. Unfortunately, encryption and integrity checks require some processing power (Mohammad & Munir, 2009), which can set limitations on the strength of encryption algorithms and encryption key lengths used for wearables.

Body Area Network Security

Another challenge for wearables is the *body area network* (Knospe & Pohl, 2004) which comprises the wearable computer, all attached devices and sensors, etc. The body area network is open to a number of security threats (Verbauwhede, Hodjat, Hwang, & Lai, 2005; Friedewald, Vildjiounaite, Punie, & Wright, 2007) if sensitive information stored is at risk. Further, also privacy and safety issues can arise if the wearer is identified and/or the electronic identity stolen. An example is if thieves know where a wearer is, based on the capability to electronically track the wearer's location, the thieves can pay a visit to the wearer's house or apartment while shopping elsewhere.

NOVEL IDEAS ON SECURITY

Three novel ideas on security that were conceptualized during the wearIT@work project are outlined below. Examples are given to better illustrate the ideas and contexts in which application is possible. Regarding the earlier mentioned research on fundamental and new challenges for pervasive and wearable computing, our chapter extends that research and adds novel ideas for security mechanisms and concepts.

Authorization by Proximity: New Way to Authorize by Using Context Information

Previously, Ferriera and Dahab (2000), Bardram *et al.* (2003), and Thomas and Sandhu's (2004) have used context awareness in modelling or realizing authentication by proximity. Here we take a further step, using context information also for authorization by proximity, as new ways of using computers will appear when wearables are introduced to substitute paper-based work or laptops and tablets. An example where wearable computing could enable process innovation is in hospitals, where much work is still paper-based and inherently repetitive and resource demanding. This leads to an outcome with high costs, less time with patients for doctors and nurses, risk for errors when subsequently typing new notes into patient files, or typing out prescriptions from handwritten notes. There is also a need to store all the paperwork, and it is also inefficient sending paperwork around inside a hospital or between hospitals. At the ward round in hospitals, doctors and nurses may want to do things that require personal login to a variety of information systems, due to reasons of traceability/logging, accountability (digital signing), etc. This makes it hard to use only a group laptop[9] or a few tablets used by ward-round members not directly in contact with patients.

If all the doctors and nurses who participate in ward rounds could be online using wearable computers, it would add another dimension of *usability and possible context awareness.* This would require novel ways of operating the computer and inputting information. Sensors on for instance arms, legs and feet, as well as voice control, may be used to operate the computer without a keyboard as well as delegating the authority to input information to a doctor or nurse close by.

This introduces a need for novel and more advanced authorization mechanisms, where also the surrounding context (Sbodio & Thronicke, 2006) needs to be taken into account. An example is the ward round scenario in a hospital where a doctor visiting a patient wants to order an x-ray for the patient, and the doctor asks a nurse or doctor participating in the ward round to order it on her/his behalf using her/his *personal* wearable computer. Another example scenario is related to airplane maintenance: a specialized worker conducting maintenance inside a wing replaces some mechanical parts, and can delegate to one of his/her co-workers to digitally track the part number of the mechanical parts being replaced using the wearable.

This can be referred to as *authorization by proximity*, which is a mechanism that allows the controlled *transfer of authorization privileges from an authorizing party to the party (normally unauthorized) performing some task that requires authorization.*

For authorization by proximity to be useful, it needs to be combined with the traditional user authorization within information systems (or applications). Each information system needs to declare a list of tasks where authorization by proximity can be used and a list of parties who are allowed to transfer and receive authorization by proximity. Context awareness will provide the information system with the information needed to detect, at run-time, if and how authorization by proximity is possible. Such information should comprise information on task and surrounding parties. It is necessary to maintain the traceability (and accountability) of tasks or actions where authorization by proximity has been used. This can be enabled by logging information on both the user who transferred authorization and the user who received it (for example, the log can store the *task conducted by 'username "a" + username "b"'* where "a" is the authorizing person and "b" is the person authorized by proximity). If any actions or tasks require a digital signature to be completed, this must be done with the authorizing person's personal encryption key (preferably[10] at/in the wearable, or perhaps in a smart card, if used, where the personal key resides).

Below is an example to better illustrate *authorization by proximity* where *dynamic context information is used to connect the authorizing party with the conducting party*:

The initial lead doctor needs to set up a ward round context at the start of the ward round using all participants RFID tags (or using a screen on the wall to select from lists of employees). Preselecting an initial person who is authorized to order x-rays or prescriptions, etc. streamlines the process. Assumed is that the patients are identified using an RFID tag. Further assumed is also that the medical staff when logging in to their personal wearable, using for instance biometric authentication, also open up their personal credential store (smart card or similar) where, among other things, their personal digital encryption keys are stored. As the ward team may need to access encrypted information, group keys for wards could be used to protect the files with patient information. The group keys need to be distributed among the users. One option is to use static groups of users; typically those often involved in specific ward rounds, and securely store the needed group keys in their credential

stores. Another option is to distribute the group keys when needed in a context (group keys are securely kept during the duration of the context). The first option using fixed groups of users is less dynamic than the second option, where groups of users are set up by the context at run-time.

The following are possible context types to be used for linking the ward round context to the doctors/nurses and the patients, as well as the patient to the doctor:

- **Ward round context** [ward name; date, start, stop; *patient RFID, lead doctor RFID,* list of doctors, list of nurses, '*person authorized by lead doctor' RFID,...*]
- **Personal context** [name, *RFID,* type of profession (doctor, nurse, etc), level of authentication,...]
- **Patient context** [name, *patient RFID,* sign in date, name of doctor, *doctor RFID,...*]

After having created the initial ward round context, the context can change depending on which patient is in focus and the lead doctor may change to be the one identified by the patient context. The person authorized by the lead doctor may, of course, also change during the course of the ward round depending on skill set or if someone has to leave the ward round. Thus, the contexts are dynamic and can change during the course of the ward round.

The authentication level in the personal context can give single sign-on to the hospital's information systems, where all orders for treatment, prescriptions, etc. can be stored and processed. The patient's electronic file can be updated during the ward round, eliminating today's paper-based systems where the electronic patient file needs to be processed by a nurse after the ward round ends. For traceability reasons, changes in the ward round context can be logged automatically, as well as that all tasks conducted are logged in information systems as described earlier (for accountability reasons if authorization by proximity is used). If anything needs to be signed, like the electronic patient file, the lead doctor can do it in his/her personal wearable – and thus a hash, etc. of the patient file needs to be sent to the doctor's wearable (or smart card if used) to be signed with the personal key. Then, the resulting signature needs to be returned and stored in the information system's database. If any user interaction is needed from the lead doctor when signing, it can be displayed on the bedside screen and handled by either using gestures or by using the voice to keep the hands clean and free.

Pairing Mechanism for Wearables: To Use Devices on Other Wearables

Another novel idea to increase interoperability between wearables that appeared during the wearIT@work requirement engineering study is *the ability for a wearable "A" to use devices attached to wearable "B,"* by having an authentication mechanism similar to the pairing mechanism in Bluetooth (2009) where both parties need to be authenticated (mutually). The necessity for device pairing has also been recognized by Stajano (2010). This would probably require a security policy that allows or denies access to devices from other wearables (or a set of wearables), as well as to types of devices on other wearables (or a set of wearables). *This could also have impact on how to manage a local information security policy together with the organizational information security policy,* as the user may need to be able to decide which wearables (and perhaps also types of devices) to allow or deny access from and to. Thus, the organizational information security policy may

state if pairing with devices on other wearables is allowed at all and how (and if there are pre-defined sets of wearables and types of devices to allow/deny), and then distribute the rest of the allow/deny decisions to the user and local information security policy. Allowing distributed decisions by the users seems necessary for professionals to be able to perform their tasks quickly using their professional judgment regarding the possible security risks invoked by pairing.

Typically, a user is tied into work processes with other users, such as a doctor with a nurse or a group of workers doing maintenance. In a wearable scenario this entails the coupling of wearable devices as well, which raises the need for a security policy that treats working groups and their devices as a kind of a pool of services where all must trust each other.

Intelligent Policy Management: To Handle External Security Challenges

The world surrounding the user today unfortunately requires the users of wearables and common computers to protect themselves from hackers, viruses, malicious code and spyware, etc. (Dagon *et al.*, 2004; Mohammad & Munir, 2009). This is usually managed by having a baseline (the minimum requirement level) of security software. However, the baseline might differ depending on context and where a computer is used. Mostéfaoui *et al.* (2004) and Brézillon and Mostefaoui (2004a and b) have earlier created a foundation for the idea of using context information to achieve context-aware security adaptation and policies. Below, we continue further in that direction.

Having an advanced *dynamic information security policy* that is context-dependent and dynamically changes the level of the baseline depending on the surrounding environment would be suitable for almost all computers, particularly wearables, due to the limited system resources. To realize such dynamics, *a more intelligent policy management is needed to only put the needed (optimized) security-related load on wearable system resources.* However, a similar result may be achieved by using a number of predefined security zones (or static contexts) which are set either when initiating the computer, when recognizing which network is used, or manually set. Mohammad and Munir (2009) have an interesting idea, possible to apply here, suggesting use of both reactive and proactive risk management. Further, they state that it is important to have a convenient and flexible way to manage and define dynamic security policies.

An additional problem arising in today's business world is the heterogeneity of wearable devices introduced, as well as that an increasing number of employees want to use their own devices in professional work tasks. This puts an additional burden on the enforcement and upholding of security policies.

As wearables' properties can differ substantially, an important consideration is how to approach wearables in relation to viruses, malware and local firewalls. Whether the wearable has enough system resources and capacity to run, for instance, software as anti-virus, anti-malware and local firewall must also be taken into account. Another view is to look at ordinary wearables as embedded or encapsulated systems[11] that are fairly well protected and not in need of these extra measures, as the attack patterns are different compared to powerful wearables which resemble mini PCs, tablets or advanced smart phones.

Looking from the first view, using wearables which most likely will have close access to the *wearers' personal and biometric information*, an integrity/privacy problem may arise if spyware starts to try to collect information from a wearable. There are no simple means to protect wearable computers from viruses and other malware. There is a considerable negative impact of traditional anti-virus and anti-malware software on system performance. Light-weight firewalls can prevent unauthorized traffic, but also require system resources to run. Another way to protect system integrity is to allow only files that are signed by trusted parties to be executed or stored. Thus, there is a need to decide, depending on a wearable's properties, if it needs a baseline of minimum extra protection, where the minimum level depends on the use and context, or if the wearable is to be considered as embedded or encapsulated.

Further, storing information using device or file encryption, strong authentication, secure communications, ensured integrity or digital signatures might also need to be considered as part of a baseline as well as other security services required by the context.

As the above-mentioned security software consume system resources they need to be tested and properly customized/configured for wearables; otherwise, the wearable might be unable to perform adequately. Another option is to have some or most of these as server-side functions, relieving burden from the wearable.

For many types of wearables, the current performance problems will undoubtedly be eliminated within the foreseeable future as the development of hardware- and software technology progresses. It is probable that many future wearable devices will be able to run local security software if needed.

SELECTED LEGAL ASPECTS ON SECURITY FOR WEARABLE COMPUTING

Five selected legal aspects of wearable computing are highlighted below. These legal aspects are deemed as necessary to consider before and during the whole lifecycle of wearables.

Protection of Personal Data

The right to privacy and data protection is a fundamental right contained in Article 8 of the Charter of Fundamental Rights of the European Union[12]. Although open-handed distribution of personal data (for instance, by means of social-networking software, weblogs and discount cards) continues to gain broad popularity, the majority of European citizens regard personal privacy as an important issue.

The Charter and data protection laws in the EU Member States determine that personal data may be processed only for specified purposes and on the basis of informed consent, or some other legitimate basis determined by law. The purpose of informed consent is to empower the individual to make a voluntary informed decision based on knowledge of the purpose, alternatives, risks and benefits.

Wearable computers, using near-field communication like RFID, make it easier to track persons and gather other personal data and therefore pose a high threat to privacy. Small and embedded computers can be powerful surveillance tools; instead of one Big Brother there are a large number of stealthy Small Brothers (Roßnagel, 2002). Setting up RFID control gates or checkpoints to track personal information for undetermined future use is unlawful in all EU member states. Passing on personal data has to be a deliberate act. Gate systems should at least implement some form of visualization and approval on a computer terminal.

The EU Commission has presented a Recommendation on the implementation of privacy and data protection principles in applications supported by RFID on 12.5.2009 – C(2009) 3200 final. The Commission recognizes the potential of RFID to be both ubiquitous and practically invisible and therefore sees the need to include privacy and information security features already in the design process (security and privacy-by-design). Member States have to make sure that industry, in collaboration with relevant civil society stakeholders, develops a framework for privacy and data protection impact assessments.

The Commission affirms that the rights and obligations laid down in the Data Protection Directive (95/46/EC) and in the Directive on Privacy and Electronic Communications (2002/58/EC) are fully applicable to the use of RFID applications that process personal data.

- When processing, storing or transferring personal data, the confidentiality and integrity of the data must be secured. Healthcare with professional secrecy may process sensitive personal data if in interest for public health and social protection (Directive 95/46/EC).
- The use of certificates is encouraged and certificate service providers must protect the personal information used for issuing certificates. Harmonizing the equivalence of handwritten and electronic signatures is not completed all over the EU Member States (Directive 1999/93/EC).
- Wearable devices are most likely to conform to the Directive 1995/5/EC; however, Article 3.3 depends on the EU Commission's decision as to whether certain "apparatus" belongs to this category or not.
- Council resolution of 28th Jan. 2002 on the area of network and information security promotes use of best practice and standards to ensure better security for solutions within eGovernment and eProcurement by using, for instance, electronic signatures and strong authentication in the exchange of information with regard to information security.

As mentioned earlier, wearables will most likely handle the wearer's biometric data in the body area network. The phrase "when processing, storing or transferring personal data, the confidentiality and integrity of the data must be secured" covers this issue on a high level, but for IT and information security policy-makers more guidance regarding adequate levels of encryption algorithms, minimum key lengths and protection of the keys would be helpful. The Directive 1995/5/EC and Article 3.3 (dependent on decision by the EU Commission for categories of apparatus) would add some further level of detail for "smaller devices" (apparatus) like mobile phones, etc. where also wearable computers fit in. Paragraph "c," "it incorporates safeguards to ensure that the personal data and privacy of the user and of the subscriber are protected", would add further guidance. The problem is to decide the level at which "protected" is met. Some Member States like Sweden have for certain public-sector services like healthcare developed a national IT strategy where these issues are addressed to some extent, but do not give much more specific information than on the EU level. Even though it may be hard to keep up to date, a general EU- or national public recommendation for what "protected" comprises would add guidance for many industries and organizations.

Current legislation generally takes for granted that computer systems are equipped with large displays and keyboards. Laws are somewhat biased towards existing technical solutions (Pikänen & Niemälä, 2007). Thus, there is a need for interpretation if existing privacy protection laws do not cover a subject in detail.

Take, for example, a jacket with GPS capability determining and transmitting positional data: will it be sufficient to accept the fact that this garment continuously reports about the wearer's whereabouts just by making a purchase contract? What kind of user interface does the jacket need to comply with privacy laws? At least it has to have an on/off switch to make sure it can be worn anywhere.

Some wearables (for instance, devices that are used for electronic ticketing in public transport) require special protective measures. How can one make sure that information will not be intercepted over long distances with directional aerials? The user needs to be guided on how to shield the device from unauthorized retrieval attempts or how to deactivate the device. Passive RFID tags cannot be switched off like, e.g., mobile phones.

To preserve privacy, wearable computers holding private data should be designed using secure authentication and public key infrastructure as a means to user-determined access rights restriction.

Looking at patient care and geriatric nursing as a field of application, some legal particularities can be observed (National Institutes of Health, 1979). Patients can find themselves in an exceptional situation and may be no longer competent to take an informed decision (yet, normally, there is someone who can do it for them). In some cases the physician must even consult a representative. Exceeding the defined field of wearable computers in medical technology there can even be computers that are embedded in and directly connected to the human body, which poses new problems, like altered perception, which are not discussed in this chapter.

Data Security

Data security means the preservation of the confidentiality, integrity and availability of data. To a great extent, obligations in this field verge on the requirements for the protection of personal data.

Applications that affect individuals by processing, for example, biometric identification data or health-related data, are especially critical with regard to information security and privacy and therefore require specific attention (European Commission, C (2009) 3200 final). Mitrakas (2006) further contends that efforts have to be taken to show to what extent the existing legal framework can be applied to new security threats in the field of emerging technologies and applications.

When using, for instance, augmented reality for conceptual work, companies have to make sure that transmitted data cannot be read by a third party. Therefore, they need to implement encryption methods and provide practical work instructions.

Product Safety

Wearable computers must comply with European product safety standards and can only be distributed when labelled with the letters CE. The CE label is a proof of conformity that allows manufacturers and exporters to circulate products freely within all EU Members States. It indicates that the manufacturer has satisfied all assessment procedures specified by law for its product to be sold on the European market.

An example is workwear equipped with sensors and alarms (e.g., for firemen or pilots), which must undergo appropriate testing before professional use.

Regulations Concerning Working Conditions

In some cases, regulations concerning working conditions affect the usage of wearable computers. For instance, in Germany or Austria, wearables allowing employee tracking may only be used if an agreement between workers' committee and management ("Betriebsvereinbarung") has been concluded (for Austria: "Rechtliche Stellungnahme WearIT@work" by Oechsner and Wimmer (2007).

Disposal

Wearable computers may contain hazardous electronic waste substances and are therefore classified as hazardous household waste. Waste Electrical and Electronic Equipment (WEEE) is not to be disposed of in regular garbage (unsorted waste).

The Waste Electrical and Electronic Equipment Directive (2002/96/EC), together with the RoHS Directive (Restriction of the use of certain hazardous substances – 2002/95/EC), sets collection, recycling and recovery targets for all types of electrical goods. WEEE is to be marked with the EEE Symbol (a crossed-out trashcan). The rules for returning products depend on the country where the product is bought.

ANALYSIS

In the analysis, the results will be looked at from a view of strategic alignment of IT. Ciborra's concepts "cultivation," "care," "hospitality," and "care with hospitality" are used as an analytic grid to find different options for what can and needs to be done to deal with the potential alignment problems caused by the introduction of wearables. However, one must bear in mind that, instead of current technology, mainly emerging or future technology and legal aspects are addressed in this context.

An alignment problem is how to handle emerging and future technologies that will emerge gradually over time. If the technology and the surrounding legal framework are already in line with the existing alignment and do not radically change the organization, the work processes and the users' daily work, all is just fine. Then, it is a matter of adjustments. However, if the technology and legal framework may allow for large or radical changes, then the impact on the alignment may be greater or even problematic. This is due to the fact that it takes time for the updates and adjustments needed, even in smaller organizations. The future challenges from technology like wearable computing and the related legal frameworks need to be analyzed and addressed in security services and controls (policies, etc.) at an early stage to better

Table 1. Alignment concept applied to the aggregated results

	Security Challenges	Novel Ideas on Security	Legal Aspects
Cultivation (is about destabilizing the current strategy and creating imbalance with the current technology, causing a tension that will stimulate learning at the same time forcing users to give feedback on the technology used and how it affects their work situation)	Would need quick feedback loops on security matters from the technology as well as the impact on users' work situation to work. "Cultivation" is deemed to induce high risk. Is the concept possible to use?	The novel ideas would preferably be used firstly in a test environment before introduced in work processes. If just introduced without further preparations, it would most likely induce high risk. Is the concept possible to use?	Would require users to be aware of the legal framework (if not already addressed in the alignment). "Cultivation" is deemed to induce medium risk. Resembles common practice in many organizations.
Care (is about familiarity, intimacy and continuous commitment from an initial requirement analysis all the way until training of users. A particular form of care is "understanding")	Would probably work well as starts from the initial requirement analysis and there is time to reach understanding and make smaller adjustments to the alignment if the introductory process is not too quick. "Care" is deemed to induce low risk. Concept seems usable.	Would probably work well as "care" allows for a process with time to adjust the alignment. "Care" is deemed to induce low risk. Concept seems usable, however not suitable for quick introductions.	Would allow legal aspects to slowly (if the introductory process is not very short) be understood and taken up, not disrupting the alignment. "Care" is deemed to induce low risk. Concept seems usable.
Hospitality (is about when technology is in motion in organizations and is ambiguous. Acceptance needs to cope with the ambiguity, and then become hospitality)	As the security challenges imply that technology is in motion and likely also ambiguous, using "hospitality" probably requires profound planning and preparations to reach acceptance and not instead hostility. "Hospitality" is deemed to induce medium risk. Concept seems usable if used together with careful planning.	The novel ideas may cause quite a lot of ambiguity and it is questionable if "hospitality" alone is able to get to acceptance without a lot of hostility. "Hospitality" is deemed to induce high risk. Concept may be usable.	May cause problems if the ambiguity is large, but with careful planning and preparations acceptance can be reached without causing too much hostility. "Hospitality" is deemed to induce medium risk. Concept seems usable, however requires planning and preparations.
Care with hospitality (hospitality used correctly together with caring can lead to absorbed coping, intimacy etc. and can make technologies be integrated in the work flows and be understood)	Would probably work well if the introductory process is not very short. "Care with hospitality" is deemed to induce low risk. Concept seems very usable.	Would probably work well if the ambiguity is not too large and the introductory process is not very short. "Care with hospitality" is deemed to induce medium risk. Concept seems very usable.	Would probably work well if the introductory process is not very short and implications from legal aspects too disrupting requiring major changes regarding organizational aspects as well. "Care with hospitality" is deemed to induce low risk. Concept seems very usable.

support work processes while keeping the security level intact. This requires the work with alignment to be proactive, so as to avoid being overrun by new technology with great impact. However, it is of course always possible to postpone or adapt very slowly to use of the new technology and, hence, be able to keep the alignment intact. Looking at improved IT effectiveness and higher profitability

as outcomes from alignment efforts, those results indicate that (if possible) it might be good practice to act proactively regarding alignment.

Ciborra's concepts are used on the aggregated results from this paper, i.e., security challenges, novel ideas on security, and legal aspects to discuss what can be done regarding the alignment problem. Moreover, we assess the *risk level* which the concept might induce if used in an organization to handle alignment problems. The risk assessment is used in the evaluation whether the concept is usable or not. The risk levels shown in Table 1 are used in the matrix: low, medium, high.

Looking at the Table 1, using the "cultivation" concept seems a bit extreme and also introduces medium to high risk. Thus, the concept could be used, but the organization should be aware of the risk level and evaluate other concepts before applying this one. Both "care" and "hospitality" seem usable; however, "care" is deemed to introduce lower risk and be slightly more applicable over all the aggregated results. Thus, if the choice is between "care" and "hospitality," we suggest "care." "Care with hospitality" is assessed to outrank the other concepts both regarding risk level and usability, and is therefore suggested as the best concept (of the ones used in this chapter) when addressing alignment problems pertaining to emerging- and future technology like wearable computing as well as related legal aspects.

In addition, regarding the emerging BYOD trend, the duality of BYOD (Olivier, 2012) combined with the additional security and privacy concerns (Miller, Voas & Hurlburt, 2012) adds extra alignment problems. However, in order to create business value, the "care with hospitality" concept looks promising as a means of addressing BYOD, although this concept requires employee attentiveness towards employer security policy and risk assessment, as well as employer thoroughness regarding security and privacy matters.

CONCLUSION

Wearables, in the form of, e.g. smart phones, glasses or embedded in clothes, with an ability to use sensors and other equipment attached to a body network, have been introduced on the market and are gradually starting to be used by an increasing number of private and professional users. More and novel forms of wearables, as well as potential new ways to use them for leisure or in professional tasks and processes, are foreseen. However, to be able to tap the full potential from wearable computing, usability must be balanced towards security (Stajano, 2010) and what is allowed according the surrounding legal frameworks. To achieve usability requires an understanding of people (Thomas & Sandhu, 2004), i.e., how users act and interact in between and with different systems. Thus, it is critical to design and set up the security so that it enhances and supports usability – not the other way around. If not supportive, users will find ways to circumvent "the perceived security hinders" creating a non-aligned behaviour (Lindström, Samuelsson, Harnesk, & Hägerfors, 2008). This may upset persons/roles assigned to enforce security policies and ensure there are adequate security controls in order to do so, but circumvention is in many cases the reality.

This chapter has addressed alignment problems while introducing emerging and future technologies (including the BYOD trends), information security challenges and novel ideas encountered during the wearIT@work project, as well as selected legal aspects for wearable computing.

There are different ways to deal with emerging and future technologies that are introduced into organizations. The introduction can give rise to alignment problems technology-wise, as well as cause or introduce security and legal problems. The analysis made shows that Ciborra's concept "care with hospitality" is most usable and is recommended for use when addressing such alignment problems.

Security challenges concerning wearables have been highlighted, showing that wearables will raise new requirements on many security services in general, and that there must be a balance between usability and security. This depends on a need to adapt to increased mobility while at the same time upholding an adequate level of security, most likely also including dynamic context information to better support new work processes and better integrate into existing IT-infrastructures. Further, the BYOD trend can assist in business value creation if it is backed by employee attentiveness and employer thoroughness regarding the arising risks as well as security and privacy concerns. Another aspect to factor into the security and privacy concerns is the global surveillance of traffic over networks and potential access to data in cloud services. As wearables can provide access to users' personal/biometric data and sensitive communications, and since the security level on wearables does not always provide adequate protection, security and privacy aspects should be considered thoroughly, at least for professional use. In addition, to avoid unpleasant surprises later in life, individual users must be aware of what personal/biometric information is shared with (and in between) providers of cloud services or "apps" for private use. Examples of such cloud services or apps are those that concern personal identifiable data, physical exercise data, medical and health queries/history, etc., and can be linked to, for instance, future work or insurance applications – unless such sharing has not been prohibited.

Three novel ideas on security have been outlined. *Authorization by proximity* using dynamic context information can be used to increase usability by enabling controlled transfer of authorization from one party to another party. *A wearable pairing mechanism* to use devices on other wearables, and a *more intelligent management of dynamic information security policies* to only put the optimized security related load on wearables' system resources can be used to increase the wearables' range of use and find an adequate security level depending on the surrounding context. The last idea includes having, if needed, a *dynamic security baseline for wearables* to maintain the integrity and confidentiality of the body area network as

well as the privacy of the wearers' personal and biometric information. Recent developments in behavioural biometric solutions for continuous authentication may within a few years have a large impact on the security mechanisms and concepts of today, further improving the usability aspect as well as the level of security itself.

The study of the EU legal framework pertaining to security for wearables shows that legal texts are on a very general level. In terms of privacy and protection of personal data, the current EU legal framework needs interpretation if existing laws do not cover a subject. Data security, which is closely related to the privacy and protection of personal data, requires sensitive data communicated to be encrypted and (professional) users need to be instructed. Wearables, like other electrical equipment or apparatus, require CE labels and are also in some EU member states regulated as to how they may be used at work. Wearables are further classified as electrical waste and need to be marked with the EEE symbol and disposed accordingly.

Organizations need to address wearables and wearable devices in their information security policies to set up an adequate level of security and also comply with the legal frameworks, since wearables add new challenges to the ordinary ones (Mohammad & Munir, 2009; Guelzim & Obaidat, 2011). Wearables will also be used in new ways and in novel and sometimes more hostile environments compared to ordinary computers. In general and depending on context, wearables should thus probably require a higher security level than ordinary computers if used for the same purposes. Thus, acting in a proactive way early will alleviate future alignment problems. Changing from a reactive nature to a proactive nature is recommended to avoid problems, since there will be problems if work processes are affected and changed. In addition, currently, many corporations and organizations face wishes from employees to use their private devices (wearable and mobile) also for professional use at work. This, in combination with the large heterogeneity pertaining to already professionally used wearable and mobile devices, poses a difficult task for those responsible for compliance with security policies and legal frameworks.

Support from general EU or national public recommendations regarding what "protected" means security-wise would add guidance for many industries and organizations. The term privacy should, in light of the recent exposure of global surveillance tools and programs, be debated and discussed on a broad scale so that users of wearables know what to expect and what information they should never allow to be stored, processed, communicated or shared. A complete harmonization of the use of electronic certificates within the EU Member States would be a good start to increase the security level for authentication, communications and digital signatures based on certificates; but then, there is also a further need to align this with states outside of the EU. Thus, for widespread uptake and use of wearable computing (ranging from local software and apps running on the wearable to use of global cloud services) it is necessary to facilitate essential changes and preconditions on many levels, i.e. from policy/ regulatory level to technical level – and do it in a coordinated manner to avoid unnecessary fragmentation.

FUTURE WORK

It would be interesting to investigate the impact from wearables' security challenges on future information security policies within certain industry domains.

ACKNOWLEDGMENT

The majority of the security requirements were collected by wearIT@work project members during the initial phase of the project. A special thanks to Prof. Michael Lawo at TZI, University of Bremen, Dr. Marco Luca Sbodio at HP Italy Innovation Centre, Dr. Wolfgang Thronicke at ATOS for their valuable input. Parts of the results in this text were published at the 4th International Forum on Applied Wearable Computing, Tel Aviv, Israel, 2007. This work was partly funded under grant 004216 by the integrated European Commission project wearIT@work – Empowering the mobile worker by wearable computing. More information on the wearIT@work project is available at: http:// www.wearitatwork.com.

REFERENCES

Avison, D., Jones, J., Powell, P., & Wilson, D. (2004). Using and validating the strategic alignment model. *The Journal of Strategic Information Systems*, *13*, 223–246. doi:10.1016/j.jsis.2004.08.002

Bardram, J. E., Kjaer, R. E., & Pedersen, M. Ö. (2003). Context-aware user authentication – Supporting proximity-based login. In *Proceedings of the Ubiquitous Computing 5th International Conference*. Seattle, WA: Academic Press.

Barfield, W. (2006). *Information privacy as a function of facial recognition technology and wearable computers* (Legal Series Paper 1739). Berkeley, CA: Berkeley Electronic Press. Retrieved from http://law.bepress.com/expresso/eps/1739

Bluetooth. (2009). *Security*. Retrieved April 4, 2012, from http://www.bluetooth.com/Pages/Simple-Secure-Everywhere.aspx

Boronowsky, M., Herzog, O., Knackfuss, P., & Lawo, M. (2005). wearIT@work – Empowering the mobile worker by wearable computing – The first results. In *Proceedings of the AMI@work Forum Day*, (pp. 38-45). Munich, Germany: AMI@work.

Brézillon, P., & Mostéfaoui, G. K. (2004a). Context-based security policies: A new modeling approach. In *Proceedings of Second IEEE International Conference of Pervasive Computing and Communications*. Orlando, FL: IEEE.

Brézillon, P., & Mostéfaoui, G. K. (2004b). Modelling context-based security policies with contextual graphs. In *Proceedings of Second IEEE International Conference of Pervasive Computing and Communications*. Orlando, FL: IEEE.

Chan, Y., Huff, S., Barclay, D., & Copeland, D. (1997). Business strategy orientation. *Information Systems Research*, *8*(2), 125–150. doi:10.1287/isre.8.2.125

Ciborra, C. U. (1996). Introduction: What does groupware mean for the organization hosting it? In C. U. Ciborra (Ed.), *Groupware & teamwork*. Chichester, UK: John Wiley & Sons.

Ciborra, C. U. (1997). De Profundis? Deconstructing the concept of strategic alignment. *Scandinavian Journal of Information Systems*, *9*(1), 67–82.

Ciborra, C. U. (1998). Crisis and foundations: An inquiry into the nature and limits of models and methods in the information systems discipline. *Scandinavian Journal of Information Systems*, *7*(1), 5–16.

Ciborra, C. U. (2002). *The labyrinths of information: Challenging the wisdom of systems*. Oxford, UK: Oxford University Press.

Cragg, P. B., King, M., & Hussin, H. (2002). IT alignment and firm performance in small manufacturing firms. *The Journal of Strategic Information Systems*, *11*, 109–132. doi:10.1016/S0963-8687(02)00007-0

Dagon, D., Martin, T., & Starner, T. (2004). Mobile phones as computing devices: The viruses are coming! *Pervasive Computing*, *3*(4), 11–15. doi:10.1109/MPRV.2004.21

Davis, G. B. (2002). Anytime/anyplace computing and the future of knowledge work. *Communications of the ACM*, *45*(12), 67–73. doi:10.1145/585597.585617

Ferreira, L. C., & Dahab, R. (2000). Beyond parasitic authentication. In *Proceedings of the Workshop de Segurança em Informática – Simpósio Brasileiro de Computadores Tolerantes a Falhas*. Curitiba, Brasil: Academic Press.

Friedewald, M., Vildjiounaite, E., Punie, Y., & Wright, D. (2007). Privacy, identity and security in ambient intelligence: A scenario analysis. *Telematics and Informatics*, *24*, 15–29. doi:10.1016/j.tele.2005.12.005

Guelzim, T., & Obaidat, M. S. (2011). Pervasive network security. In M. S. Obaidat, M. Denko, & I. Woungang (Eds.), *Pervasive computing and networking* (pp. 159–172). Chichester, UK: John Wiley & Sons. doi:10.1002/9781119970422.ch10

Henderson, J. C., & Venkatraman, N. (1992). Strategic alignment: A model for organizational transformation through information technology. In T. A. Kochan, & M. Ussem (Eds.), *Transforming organizations*. New York, NY: Oxford University Press.

Hsaio, R., & Ormerod, R. (1998). A new perspective on the dynamics of IT-enabled strategic change. *Information Systems Journal, 8*(1), 21–52. doi:10.1046/j.1365-2575.1998.00003.x

Knospe, H., & Pohl, H. (2004). RFID security. *Information Security Technical Report, 9*(4), 39–50. doi:10.1016/S1363-4127(05)70039-X

Komninos, N., Vergados, D., & Dogligeris, C. (2006). Layered security design for mobile ad hoc networks. *Computers & Security, 25*(2), 121–130. doi:10.1016/j.cose.2005.09.005

Levy, M., Powell, P., & Yetton, P. (2001). SMEs: Aligning IS and the strategic context. *Journal of Information Technology, 16*(3), 133–144. doi:10.1080/02683960110063672

Lindström, J. (2009). *Models, methodologies and challenges within information security for senior managements*. (Doctoral thesis). Luleå University of Technology, Luleå, Sweden.

Lindström, J., Samuelsson, S., Harnesk, D., & Hägerfors, A. (2008). The need for improved alignment between actability, strategic planning of IS and information security. In *Proceedings of the 13th International ITA Workshop*, Krakow, Poland (pp. 14-27). ITA.

Luftman, J. N. (1996). *Competing in the information age: Strategic alignment in practice*. New York, NY: Oxford University Press.

Lyytinen, K., & Yoo, Y. (2002). Issues and challenges in ubiquitous computing. *Communications of the ACM, 45*(12), 63–65.

Mann, S., Nolan, J., & Wellman, B. (2003). Sousveillance: Inventing and using wearable computing devices for data collection in surveillance environments. *Surveillance & Society, 1*(3), 331–355.

Miles, M., & Huberman, M. (1994). *An expanded sourcebook – Qualitative data analysis* (2nd ed.). Thousand Oaks, CA: Sage.

Miller, K. W., Voas, J., & Hurlburt, G. F. (2012). BYOD: Security and privacy considerations. *IT Professional, 14*(5), 53–55. doi:10.1109/MITP.2012.93

Mitrakas, A. (2006). Information security and law in Europe: Risks checked? *Information & Communications Technology Law, 15*(1), 33–53. doi:10.1080/13600830600557984

Mohammad, L. A., & Munir, K. (2009). Security issues in pervasive computing. In V. Godara (Ed.), *Risk assessment and management in pervasive computing: Operation, legal, ethical, and financial perspectives* (pp. 196–217). Hershey, PA: IGI Global.

Mostéfaoui, G. K., Chae, J., Kim, J., & Chung, M. (2004). Context-based security management for heterogenous networks using MAUT and simple heuristics. In *Proceeding of the Workshop on State-of-the-Art in Scientific Computing*. Lyngby, Denmark: Academic Press.

National Institutes of Health. (1979). Microprocessor-based intelligent machines in patient care. In *Proceeding of the Consensus Development Conference Statement*. Bethesda, MD: Academic Press.

Nichols, R. K., & Lekkas, P. C. (2002). *Wireless security: Models, threats, and solutions*. New York, NY: McGraw-Hill.

Oechsner, S., & Wimmer, F. (2007). *Rechtliche stellungnahme zum thema wearIT@work*. Linz, Austria: wearIT@work.

Olivier, R. (2012). Why the BYOD boom is changing how we think about business it. *Engineering and Technology*, *7*(10), 28.

Pangboonyanon, V. (2004). *Network-layer security in AODV networks*. Bremen, Germany: University of Bremen.

Pasher, E., Popper, Z., Raz, H., & Lawo, M. (2010). WearIT@work: A wearable computing solution for knowledge-based development. *International Journal of Knowledge-Based Development*, *1*(4), 346–360. doi:10.1504/IJKBD.2010.038043

Pikänen, O., & Niemelä, M. (2007). Privacy and data protection in emerging RFID-applications. In *Proceedings of the European RFID Forum*. Brussels, Belgium: RFID.

Porter, M. E. (1987). From competitive advantage to corporate strategy. *Harvard Business Review*, *12*, 15–31. PMID:17183795

Roßnagel, A. (2002). Freiheit im cyberspace. *Informatik-Spektrum*, *25*(1), 33–35. doi:10.1007/s002870100204

Sauer, C., Yetton, P. W., Benjamin, R., Ciborra, C. U., Coombs, R., & Craig, J. …Zmud, R. W. (1997). Steps to the future: Fresh thinking on the management of IT-based or organizational transformation. San Francisco, CA: Jossey-Bass.

Saxena, N., Ekberg, J., Kostiainen, K., & Asokan, N. (2006). Secure device pairing based on a visual channel. In *Proceedings of the IEEE Symposium on Security and Privacy* (pp. 306-313). IEEE.

Sbodio, M. L., & Thronicke, W. (2006). Context processing within an open, component-oriented, software framework. In *Proceedings of the 3rd International Forum on Applied Wearable Computing*. Bremen, Germany: Academic Press.

Spiekermann, S., & Langheinrich, M. (2008). An update on privacy in ubiquitous computing. *Personal and Ubiquitous Computing*, *13*(6), 389–390. doi:10.1007/s00779-008-0210-7

Stajano, F. (2010). Security issues in ubiquitous computing. In H. Nakashima, H. Aghajan, & J. C. Augusto (Eds.), *Handbook of ambient intelligence and smart environments, Part III* (pp. 281–314). New York, NY: Springer. doi:10.1007/978-0-387-93808-0_11

Stanford, V. (2002a). Pervasive health care applications face tough security challenges. *Pervasive Computing*, *1*(2), 8–12. doi:10.1109/MPRV.2002.1012332

Stanford, V. (2002b). Wearable computing goes live in industry. *Pervasive Computing*, *1*(4), 14–19. doi:10.1109/MPRV.2002.1158274

Thomas, R. K., & Sandhu, R. (2004). Models, protocols, and architectures for secure pervasive computing: Challenges and research directions. In *Proceedings of the Second IEEE Annual Conference on Pervasive Computing and Communications Workshop*, (pp. 164-168). IEEE.

Verbauwhede, I., Hodjat, A., Hwang, D., & Lai, B.-C. (2005). Security for ambient intelligent systems. In W. Weber, J. M. Rabaey, & E. Aarts (Eds.), *Ambient intelligence*. Berlin, Germany: Springer-Verlag. doi:10.1007/3-540-27139-2_10

Ward, J., Griffiths, P., & Whitmore, P. (1990). *Strategic planning for information systems*. New York, NY: John Wiley & Sons.

Weiser, M. (1991). The computer for the 21st century. *Scientific American*, *265*(3), 94–104. doi:10.1038/scientificamerican0991-94

Yin, R. (2003). *Case study research: Design and methods* (3rd ed.). Thousand Oaks, CA: Sage.

ENDNOTES

[1] To date, the wearIT@work project has been the largest EU-funded integrated project within wearable computing. The aim of the project has been to develop future wearable computing platforms and also to grow knowledge on organizational and societal aspects from the introduction of wearable computing to professionals at work. The wearIT@work project had four demonstrators comprising the following areas: healthcare/hospital, aircraft maintenance, car manufacturing and emergency response. For more information on the wearIT@work project, please see http://www.wearitatwork.com

[2] wearIT@work project: Annex I – Description of Work, p6.

[3] Overview of Volere requirements techniques - http://www.volere.co.uk/

[4] Deliverable D07 – Showcase platform architectural design and specification – A technical document.

[5] Deliverable D06N – Show case framework architectural design and specification.

[6] Deliverable D09N – A European industrial mobile computing platform including sector specific aspects – Requirements.

[7] Deliverable D29 – Design and specification of wearIT@work computing system, and Deliverable D48 – Design and specification of wearIT@work computing system.

[8] Regarding USBs – there are USBs with file encryption available on the market. Thus, these should be considered instead of using regular ones without encryption.

[9] Today, most hospitals use workstations to do the majority of the work, but introducing laptops (which is a step on way towards wearables) during ward rounds is a reality at many hospitals trying to reduce paperwork and speed up processes.

[10] There are also server-based digital signing solutions, which may be considered for digital signing.

[11] To change or affect these, one needs to have the physical wearable device in possession or proximity, as it is not possible to do this remotely.

[12] www.europarl.europa.eu/charter/

APPENDIX

- Charter of Fundamental Rights of the European Union; www.europarl.europa.eu/charter/
- Directive 1995/5/EC of 9th of March 1999 "on radio equipment and telecommunications terminal equipment and the mutual recognition of their conformity"
- Directive 1995/46/EC of 24th of Oct 1995 "Protection of individuals with regard to the processing of personal data and the free movement of such data"
- Council of 28-Jan-1981 "Protection of individuals with regard to Automatic Processing of Personal Data"
- Directive 1999/93/EC 13th of Dec 1999 "On a Community Framework for Electronic Signing"
- Directive 2002/19/EC of 7th of March 2002 "Access Directive"
- Directive 2002/20/EC of 7th of March 2002 "Authorization Directive"
- Directive 2002/21/EC of 7th of March 2002 "Framework Directive"
- Directive 2002/22/EC of 7th of March 2002 "Universal Service Directive"
- Directive 2002/58/EC of 12th of July 2002 "Privacy and Electronic Communications"
- Directive 2002/95/EC of 27th January 2003 "Restriction of the use of certain hazardous substances in electrical and electronic equipment"
- Directive 2002/96/EC of 27th January 2003 "Waste Electrical and Electronic Equipment (WEEE)
- Council resolution of 28th of Jan 2002 on the area of network and information security
- Information Security and Law in Europe vol. 15, No 1, March 2006
- Directive 2006/24/EC of 15th of March 2006 "Retention of data generated or processed in connection with the provision of publicly available electronic communications services or of public communications networks and amending Directive 2002/58/EC "Recommendation on the implementation of privacy and data protection principles in applications supported by RFID" of 12.5.2009 – C(2009) 3200 final.

Chapter 7
Control Mechanism of Identity Theft and Its Integrative Impact on Consumers' Purchase Intention in E-Commerce

Mahmud A. Shareef
Carleton University, Canada

Vinod Kumar
Carleton University, Canada

Uma Kumar
Carleton University, Canada

ABSTRACT

There are many collection and application sources of identity theft. The Internet is one of the vulnerable medias for identity theft and is used, especially, as an application source of identity theft. This current chapter has twofold objectives. As the first objective, it develops a conceptual framework to prevent/ control identity theft of E-Commerce (EC) in conjunction with different sources if identity theft. From this framework and shedding light on the recent literature of sources of identity theft, the authors identify global laws, controls placed on organizations, publications to develop awareness, technical management, managerial policy, risk management tools, data management, and control over employees are the potential measuring items to prevent identity theft in EC. All EC organizations are struggling to control identity theft. This chapter argues that control mechanism of identity theft has both positive and negative impact on EC. This chapter sets its second objective to explore the integrative effect of overall identity theft control mechanism on consumer trust, the cost of products/services, and operational performance, all of which in turn contribute to a purchase intention using E-Commerce (EC). A case study in banking sector through a qualitative approach was conducted to verify the proposed relations, constructs, and measuring items.

DOI: 10.4018/978-1-4666-4856-2.ch007

BACKGROUND

Proliferation of online transaction throughout the world has made supply chain management, business-to-business (B2B), Electronic-commerce (EC), and Electronic-government operations feasible and more citizen-centric; eventually, it also has created many sources of substantial crimes (Acoca, 2008). Among many types of cyber crimes, identity theft is one of the major devastating types of crime which sometimes challenges the enormous success of online transactions. Though the major source of identity theft is not EC transactions (Collins, 2003; Newman, 2004); identity theft plays a significantly negative role in purchase intention for the consumers of EC. Identity theft is a new type of crime, facilitated through established and traditional crimes such as forgery, robbery, stealing, counterfeiting, check and credit card fraud, computer fraud, impersonation, and pick pocketing (Barker et al., 2008; Mediati, 2010). With the passage of the Identity Theft Assumption and Deterrence Act.1 in 1998, the United States declared identity theft a crime. Identity theft is defined as the illegal and unauthorized acquisition of personal identity in order to engage in unlawful acts (Seminole County Sheriff's Office, 2003; Sorbel, 2003; Hutchins, 2007). California Department of Motor Vehicles (2002) described personal identifying information as a person's name, address, telephone number, driver's license number, social security number, place of employment, employee identification number, mother's maiden name, demand deposit account number, savings or checking account number, or credit card number. Identity theft may be broadly defined as the unlawful acquisition and/or use of any aspect of an individual's personal information for the commission of some form of criminal activity (Hoar, 2001; LoPucki, 2001; Slosarik, 2002; Federal Trade Commission, 2007, Anderson et al., 2008). Identity theft occurs when thieves use the personal or financial information of a person (the victim) to create a fake identity. This fake identity is used to obtain money from the victim or an institution, credit, goods, services, privilege, any type of opportunity, or property to commit a felony or misdemeanor, or to hide personal identity. Several researchers agreed that identity theft is one of the potential risks for the proliferation of EC (Goel and Shawky, 2009; Miller and Tucker, 2009; Roberds and Schreft, 2009)

According to a report published by Privacy & American Business Survey (2003), 33.4 million Americans have been victims of identity theft since 1990. More than 13 million Americans have become victims of identity theft since January 2001. Consumer are losing $1.5 billion annually since January 2001. 34 percent of those surveyed report that someone obtained their credit card information, forged a credit card in their name, and used it to make purchases. 12 percent say that someone stole or obtained improperly a paper or computer record with their personal information on it and used that to forge their identity. 11 percent report that someone stole their wallet or purse and used their identity. 10 percent say that someone opened charge accounts in stores in their name and made purchases on these accounts. 7 percent report that someone opened a bank account in their name or forged checks and obtained money from their account. Another 7 percent say that someone stole their mail and used the information obtained to steal their identity. 5 percent say that when they lost their wallet or purse someone used their identity. 4 percent report that someone obtained information from a public record that they used to steal their identity. 3 percent say that someone created a false ID to get their government benefits or payments. 16 percent say that a friend, relative, or co-worker stole their identity. The seven million victims, which the survey identified in 2002, represent an 81 percent rise over the numbers of victims in 2001. This is a partial picture of identity theft.

Identity theft is the fastest growing crime in America (Nakasumi, 2003; Hoofnagle, 2007). According to Gartner Research and Harris Interactive, approximately 7 million people became victims from August 2002–July 2003. This was a 79 percent increase from the previous year (Gartner Group, 2003). A national survey conducted by the U.S. Federal Trade Commission (FTC) (2008) revealed that 4.7 percent of the American adults surveyed reported having been a victim of identity theft that involved the use of their personal information within the previous five years. Furthermore, results from the same survey estimate that nearly 3.25 million Americans had their personal information fraudulently used within the 12 months prior to September 2007. The FTC (2008) reports that identity theft is the prime cause of the consumer complaints it receives; almost 32 percent of all those received in 2007. Such complaints numbered 258,427. According to the Identity Fraud Survey Report of Javelin Strategy and Research (2006, 2010), in the USA the total amount of fraud in one year rose from $53.2 billion in 2003 and $54.4 billion in 2005 to $56.6 billion in 2006. The mean fraud amount per fraud victim rose from $5,249 in 2003 and $5,885 in 2005 to $6,383 in 2006.

Different plausible measures to prevent/control identity theft are advocated in recent literature, newspapers, and government policies. This current research addresses the issues of identity theft; source, type, and preventive measuring tools; and the effect on consumers' purchase intention in business-to-customer (B2C) EC. There are many collection and application sources of identity theft. The Internet is one of the vulnerable medias for identity theft and is used, especially, as an application source

of identity theft. Recently, the proliferation of identity theft is presenting a strong challenge to the root of EC. The Internet is a global medium, especially as used for EC. Thus, the Internet is the source of many new legal and social issues facing the global community. The availability of personal data on the Internet, due to the rapid increase in commercial activity in the medium, has caused an increase in identity theft. The availability of personal information is a particular problem because digital information is easier and less expensive than non-digital data to access, manipulate, and store, especially from disparate, geographically distant locations. According to Forester Research, online shopping is the fastest growing area of Internet use. Further research indicates that 30 percent of all current Internet users already have purchased goods online and the total number of Internet users is increasing every day. It is estimated that 75 percent of the billions in online sales every year are made by strictly EC retailers that do not have physical stores. This is the story that everyone talks about. The hidden story is that losses due to identity fraud in the year 2003 are expected to be in excess of $2.3 billion. With fraud losses of 10 percent it is extremely difficult, if not impossible, to show a profit. For their own survival, E-merchants must recognize the threat and implement cost effective measures to prevent this identity fraud (Fichtman, 2001). As Miller et al. (2011) identified the impact of identity theft on firm's reputation, "...... the loss of customer data can have substantial negative consequences for firms. The costs can stem from litigation or fines, or from negative publicity that harms the firm's reputation and erodes customer loyalty).

Stormy and difficult to control development of EC transactions, massive competition, and the unknown operational conditions accompanying these transactions can create different types of crimes and E-businesses are rushing to put in use new and untried solutions. A number of factors associated with the special characteristics of the Internet increase the risk of identity theft, especially as the application source using the Internet. These include anonymity, speed, absence of physical presence or verification, possibility of many transactions within a short time, less control, global set-up, lack of opportunity to verify credit card or signature, lack of universal laws, and almost zero identification (Copes et al., 2010).

Several researchers have addressed the issues of general identity theft and suggested guidelines to prevent identity theft (Fichtman, 2001; Davis, 2003; Newman, 2004; Van Dyke, 2007; Arango and Taylor, 2009; Katzan, 2010). They have also identified the problems of EC regarding identity theft and plausible solutions. However, these articles did not comprehensively address identity theft types, sources, and prevention in an objective manner and did not provide type and source based preventative measuring tools. These articles also are lacking in identifying the plausible impact of identity theft on the trust of consumers, the cost of products/services, and operational performance, which in turn contribute to the intention to purchase through EC. In this perspective, this research has set two research objectives. These are:

- What are the possible techniques to prevent/control identity theft for different sources of identity theft, in general, and specifically to EC?
- What is the integrative impact of control mechanism of identity theft on consumers' trust, product/service cost, and the operational performance of EC?

The main aim of this paper is to identify the sources of identity theft and measuring tools to prevent/control identity theft in general. Then it attempts to develop a solution matrix signifying the relation of the sources and preventive tools of identity theft, and it identifies the prevention tools with possible sources of identity theft specific to the functional characteristics of EC. After using expert opinion of the fraud management authorities of financial institutions through a case study in banking sector, this study shows the relation of sources of identity theft with prevention tools for EC.

All EC organizations are struggling to control identity theft. This study argues that control mechanism of identity theft has both positive and negative impact on EC. In this context, it develops a model to postulate the integrative ultimate impact of the proposed control mechanism of identity theft of EC on the price of products/services, operational performance, and consumers' perception of trust in EC; all of these, in turn, affect the intention to purchase in EC. This research focuses on a new dimension in this field and will contribute to conceptualizing some tools to solve identity theft in conjunction with sources and reduce the impact on the intention to purchase in EC. In the following section, we review literature dealing with identity theft, criminology, and EC. Source-specific preventive tools of identity theft are identified in this section. In the next section, a matrix of measure to prevent/control identity theft is developed. Then the research methodology for the rest of this study is discussed. The next section identifies the sources and protection tools of identity theft for EC and discusses the implications of these protection tools on operational performance, the price of products/services, and trust in EC, which in turn affects the purchase intention. Propositions and proposed models are presented in this section. Finally, conclusions and future research guidelines in this context are presented.

IDENTITY THEFT AND DIFFERENT SOURCES

Different authors have identified sources of identity theft in different ways. Classifying identity theft sources is difficult, as it involves a wide variety of crimes and related problems. However, the identified motives for identity theft can be used to define the general concept. Research indicates that there are three dominant motives for identity theft depending on the application source. These are financial, informational, and criminal (Davis, 2003; Morris II, 2004; Newman, 2004; Douglass, 2009; Duncan, 2009). Data sources vary in quality and often provide conflicting or different estimates, especially concerning the extent and cost of identity theft. Identity theft has two basic sources. The first one is collection sources, or the sources from which identity theft offenders illegally collect the identity of others. The second one is the application source, or the sources where one tries to use these illegally collected identities to gain unlawful objectives. Depending on this argument, this research has identified and classified the followings into these two source groups.

Collection Sources (CS)

Following is the summary of collection sources of identity theft based on the literature review (Jackson, 1994; Mandebilt, 2001; Udo, 2001; Davis, 2003; Lacoste & Tremblay, 2003; Newman, 2004):

- **Office database (OD):** There are several types of government offices, like customs and revenue agency, ministry of transportation, birth registration, election commission, social security administration, etc., that preserve client/citizen and also employee information. This is one of the major sources of identity theft. FTC victimization reports (2003, 2004) identify government office databases as one of the commonly used sources of identity theft. Generally, some employees are the source of this illegal data collection (Lacoste & Tremblay, 2003; Newman, 2004). Similar to government offices, business offices also preserve personal information of customers and their own employees. Some employees pull out personal identity information about employees and customers from company databases, either paper documents or electronic (Fichtman, 2001; Collins, 2003). A research on 1,037 identity victims indicated that as much as 70 percent of all identity thefts are committed in the workplace by employees or by people impersonating employees (Collins and Hoffman, 2002).

- **Dumpster diving (garbage) (DD):** One of the more basic and versatile methods includes what is termed "dumpster diving" (Lease & Burke, 2000; Fichtman, 2001; Hoar, 2001; Mandelbilt, 2001; Slosarik, 2002; Perl, 2003; U.S. Department of Justice, 2004). This form of identity theft involves simply rummaging through a potential victim's garbage to find some piece of information that can serve as a key to access the victim's personal information. Any and every piece of personal information may make it easier for the thief to conduct criminal acts (Slosarik, 2002). In addition, in the 1988 the U.S. Supreme Court ruled in the case of Greenwood v. California, 486 U.S. 35 that any garbage left out for collection is no longer private property. This ruling may have increased opportunities for identity thieves.

- **Business transactions (Workplace) (BT):** A more devastating form of identity theft involves corporate employee access to sensitive information during business transactions. Recent research of 1,037 cases indicated that as much as 70 percent of all identity thefts are committed in the workplace by employees or by people impersonating employees (Collins & Hoffman, 2002). These employees, often contract or temporary workers, obtain employment for the sole purpose of personal or business identity thefts (Collins, 2003; Morris II, 2004).

- **Stolen/Lost documents (ST):** Stolen and lost documents, like parts, wallets, and cardholders are traditional sources of identity theft (Fichtman, 2001; Morris II, 2004). Victims might loose their identity information due to their own mistakes or identity thieves picking their pockets. Then someone who finds these lost identity documents or the thieves who steal can use this information.

- **Reply to spam mail (SM):** Spam mail is becoming a potential source of the increase of identity theft. People commonly receive email messages that pose as legitimate sources requesting personal information. However, in many cases, the recipient of such an email unknowingly discloses vast amounts of information directly into the hands of the criminal (Buba, 2000).

- **Hacking from Internet and fake websites (HI):** Web services run on the Internet, which is an inherently insecure environment (Ratnasingam, 2002). The web service architecture is open, mostly uncontrolled, and unmonitored. All the web-browsing systems have some degree of loop faults. As a result, hackers can easily intercept Internet web information. The U.S. Department of Justice (USDOJ) notes that in recent years, the Internet has become an increasingly attractive source of information for the potential identity thief (2004). Theft of this kind usually results from unauthorized interception of or changes to computer systems handling Internet domain names and associated addresses (Farmer, 2000; Pilawski, 2001). All kinds of personal or business information stored in the Internet, either collected directly from the Internet users' information or brick and mortar customer information documented electronically, are the targets of hackers (Udo, 2001). Hackers are also involved in the cloning of a legitimate EC website. The identity thieves create fake websites that are identical to the sites of original businesses. By mimicking legitimate banking businesses, the hackers collect credit card numbers, social security numbers, and other information from the customers who interact on these websites (Collins, 2003). The International Chamber of Commerce (ICC) uncovered a global Internet banking scam involving about $ 3.9 billion (ICC Commercial Crime Services, 2001). A related form of identity theft is referred to by Slosarik (2002) and Buba (2000) as data mining. This activity is one kind of hacking and it involves using computer technology to access data banks of sensitive personal, organizational, or governmental information (Hatch, 2001).

- **Mail box (MB):** Another common method of identity theft is removing delivered mail from mailboxes and stealing a consumer's identity right from a credit card bill or bank statement. Bank and credit card statements are common and convenient sources of identity theft. Identity thieves collect these statements from mailboxes and can use this information, especially on the Internet, very easily (Fichtman, 2001). The postal inspection service recently uncovered a ring, posing as a flyer delivery service, that would steal consumers' mail from their mailboxes (Fichtman, 2001, Mandebilt, 2001). Mandebilt (2001) notes that identity thieves often file a change of address form through the U.S. Postal Service without the victim being aware of this act.

- **Shoulder surfing (SS):** Shoulder surfing is described as the act of observing a victim in public places and gaining information during the transaction of a legitimate activity, sometimes simply by looking directly over the victim's shoulder (U.S. Dept. of Justice, 2004; Slosarik, 2002). For instance, the identity thief may watch the numbers the victim types while using an ATM or punching a credit card **in** any transaction.
- **Internet chatting sites (CS):** On some Internet chat sites a third person can easily share user information (McCarty, 2003).

Application Source (AS)

Following is a summary of application sources of identity theft based on the literature review (Mativat, & Tremblay, 1997; Udo, 2001; Davis, 2003; Lacoste & Tremblay, 2003; Newman, 2004; Hartmann-Wendels et al., 2009):

1. **Financial purpose (FP):** Perl (2003) notes that the application source of financial identity theft is based on an illegal acquisition of financial means through the abuse of a victim's personal information. This may include:

   ○ **Use of a credit card:** After collecting others' credit card information, identity thieves use it generally on the Internet, ATM machine, and retail stores for different purposes including borrowing money, purchasing goods and services, etc. A major source of this application is the Internet (Fichtman, 2001; Morris II, 2004; Newman, 2004; Sullivan, 2008). Depending on the definition of identity theft, the most common type of identity theft is credit card fraud of various kinds and there is evidence that the incidences of credit card fraud on the Internet (and by telephone) have increased because of the opportunities provided by the Internet. Federal Trade Commission Survey (2003) revealed that 67 percent of identity theft victims — more than 6.5 million victims in the year 2002 — report that existing credit card accounts were misused.

   ○ **Apply for a new credit card/loan:** With other persons' information, thieves can apply for a new credit card or several types of loan, and then conduct financial crimes. Some credit issuing companies overlook what should be an obvious red flag and grant credit cards or loans (Fichtman, 2001; Sullivan, 2010).

   ○ **Use of a debit card:** Getting other persons' debit card or information, thieves use it to withdraw money from an ATM. A Federal Trade Commission Survey in 2003 revealed that 19 percent of identity theft victims reported the misuse of checking or savings accounts.

- ○ **False bank account:** Sometimes thieves open a temporary bank account using other persons' information and collect a huge loan using that account.

2. **Non-financial purpose (NFP):** Identity thieves also collect information to use illegally for non-financial purposes. The offender may use the victim's information to open fraudulent utility accounts, including basic utilities and telecommunications accounts. The Federal Trade Commission Survey in 2003 revealed that 15 percent of all victims — almost 1.5 million people in 2002 — reported that their personal information was misused in non-financial ways to obtain government documents, for example, tax forms.

3. **Criminal purpose (CP):** Criminal records identity theft occurs when offenders use the victim's personal information to hide their own personal identity. Several criminal facts lie behind this intention, including avoiding legal sanctions, involvement in terrorism, and getting passports and visas through false information (Perl, 2003).

MEASURING TOOLS TO PREVENT/CONTROL IDENTITY THEFT

Identity theft is not likely to be clearly understood from a general standpoint, i.e., from one general theory, due to its multi-faceted character. Though identity theft is not an old topic, it has drawn the attention of the international authorities, governments of different countries, and state governments. Business organizations concerned with this topic are ones that deal with EC; financial organizations including banks and credit issuing companies; insurance companies; law enforcement organizations; software companies; web browser providers; and academicians. Consequently, several insufficient and scattered measures to prevent/control identity theft have been proposed using different approaches (Fichtman, 2001; Davis, 2003; Fergerson, 2003; Foley, 2003; Morris II, 2004; Newman, 2004; Sproule and Archer, 2010). These proposals do not provide any comprehensive solution and, although the identity theft problem is expanding like an epidemic, preventive strategies are still not well developed and consistent. From a general perspective, measures to prevent/control identity theft are basically two types. First, preventive (P) or proactive measures, or the measures which should be adopted to prevent identity theft from the source of collection. Second, action (A) or reactive measures, or the measures which should be adopted to stop identity theft at the source of application. Again, the measures to prevent/control identity theft can be adopted and applied from two sources: First, external, to be applied by global agreement and institution, governments, and personal; and second, internal, to be applied by the organization itself.

External

1. **Global law (MGL):** Though this measure to prevent/control identity theft starts working at the outset of application sources, it also helps to reduce the collection sources of identity theft. Therefore, it is both a preventive and an action measure. This measure is especially important for Internet operations, such as EC, since it also bears global characteristics. This measuring strategy to prevent/control identity theft lies in strengthening international regimes to allow for the development of effective and consistent laws and uniform law enforcement. The international com-

munity must create truly global agreements regarding cyber crime that will specifically target identity theft. In addition, the international community should create an international body to enforce laws on cyber identity theft and to work through the kinks of international cooperation (Davis, 2003). The lack of uniform global laws on identity theft crime, combined with discordant attitudes among countries towards this issue, results in a varying degree of enforcement and punishment. Uniformity is important and essential to detecting, investigating, and prosecuting identity thieves, especially professional, gang/group, and survivalist identity thieves. This construct assumes that creation of uniform, consistent, and globally approved laws by some international bodies approved by the United Nations, and the effective enforcement and application to detect, investigate, and prosecute identity thieves, in turn, will deter identity theft more effectively. It will protect consumers by making it clear to the international public that identity thieves cannot escape prosecution simply by being in a foreign nation (Davis, 2003). This will help to protect identity theft internationally from all the collection sources and application sources.

2. **Control of organizations (MCO):** This is a preventive type of measure that will act to protect the collection source of identity theft. According to the proposals of the London meeting draft (2000) and the European Union data protection directive (1998), government should enforce more strict laws and regulations on organizations to make them bound to protect customers' security and privacy. The ideal treaty on identity theft must also create laws that will work in conjunction with industry

self-regulation (Davis, 2003). However, the strategies and roles of government intervention in business practices — whether by criminal justice agencies or other government agencies — are highly complex and necessitate serious research on their own. This construct proposes that government of any country should create, adopt, and implement systematic, uniform, and appropriate rules and regulations in conjunction with industry laws and traditional state laws to force organizations — either government, private, or public — to protect employee and customer security and privacy and preserve their information safely. This will help to protect and control identity theft from all collection sources. However, its main application is on organizations countrywide to preserve all organizational information either regarding employees, customers, or business process information. This means that it will be especially effective in protecting identity theft from collection sources such as office databases (OD), business transactions (Workplace) (BT), and hacking from the Internet/fake websites (HI).

3. **Controlled bank/credit card statement (MCS):** This is also a preventive type measure and will act to protect the collection source. Bank and credit issuing companies should be careful to protect customers' credit card and bank information. They might print only four digits instead of printing the full number of the card in the statement. Credit companies must adhere to policies that both prevent identity theft crimes and allow victims to more easily gain the information and protection they need to restore their credit records and prevent future breaches of their accounts (Morris II, 2004). This construct assumes that if the financial organizations are more

careful to provide vulnerable identity information in the customers' financial statements, and adopt some strategic techniques, it will have ancillary functions to protect identity theft especially from dumpster diving (Garbage) (DD) and mail box (MB) collection sources.

4. **Publications to develop awareness (MPA):** This is a completely preventive type measure and will act to protect the collection source. Different publications are essential to develop awareness among the public to proactively defend occurrences of identity theft. Maintaining one's own security and privacy is partly the responsibility of everyone (Udo, 2001). Everyone should be aware of identity theft and address the problem at the outset of the collection source. They should be especially careful before throwing any type of personal statement in the garbage, replying to spam mail, and using a credit or debit card in public places. Government and different non-profit organizations might develop and publish different public awareness statements and reports to create public consciousness about sources of identity theft and personal protection mechanisms, which can significantly decrease risk of identity theft. This technique is especially effective in collection sources such as dumpster diving (Garbage) (DD), stolen/lost documents (ST), replies to spam mail (SM), mail box (MB), shoulder surfing (SS), and some Internet chat sites (CS) to protect identity theft. This will also help the public to be more prompt in informing the respective authorities immediately after any documents of identity have been stolen/lost and to be more careful not to exchange any identity information with criminals, and thus it will help to protect all application sources.

5. **Child protection (MCP):** This is also a preventive type measure and will act to protect the collection source. Sometimes, children dispense personal information about their parents through the Internet. Therefore, parents should be careful to handle this situation. They will need to be more strict and careful in giving vulnerable information to children and will need to monitor children's computer activity. This will help to prevent identity theft from reply to spam mail (SM) and hacking from the Internet/fake websites (HI) collection sources.

Internal

1. **Risk management tool (MRM):** This type of measure to prevent/control identity theft specifies that business organizations should apply enough screening techniques to process any customer orders, so that any discrepancy or abnormality can be verified immediately. This is an action or reactive based measure and will work in the application source. This is basically an intelligent strategic technique that implies some general quos to identify any inconsistent order pattern. This technique will follow the past history of a consumer and, at the same time, match it with the present order. For instance, if the same credit card number is being used 10 times within three minutes, that would significantly elevate the risk of any of those 10 transactions and the order should be examined more carefully (Fichtman, 2001). This measure is especially important for web-based operations. It requires that documents containing personal or business identities be cross-shredded before disposing and be red flagged to identify potentially bogus credit card, bank, retail account or other applications. In addition, proper training

for employees is key to recognizing bogus applications (Collins, 2003). However, the inefficient side of this measure is that it might negatively affect company performance (Fichtman, 2001). This technique is very useful and effective to protect identity theft from the application sources such as financial purposes (FP), non-financial purposes (NFP), and criminal purposes (CP).

2. **Technical management (MTM):** This is a versatile measuring technique to prevent/control identity theft that is both preventive and action and is used to protect both the collection and application sources. This popular technique includes use of different software to protect both information stealing and illegal use. Numerous types of software with several limitations have developed and are being developed continuously to protect identity theft, like encryption, digital signature, authentication, address verification system, and so on (Fichtman, 2001; Udo, 2001; Morris II, 2004). This technology based technique will help organizations to protect their employee/customer databases, local business networks, and customer transactional information; it will also help individuals to protect their information while interacting on the Internet. This will particularly help to protect identity theft from collection sources such as office database (OD), business transactions (Workplace) (BT), reply to spam mail (SM), hacking from the Internet/fake websites (HI), some Internet chatting sites (CS), and from all application sources such as financial purpose (FP), non-financial purpose (NFP), and criminal purpose (CP).

3. **Managerial policy (MMP):** Management should develop, deploy, and publish explicit policy regarding protection of the security and privacy of their employees and customers. It means that all organizations should develop and publish their own rules, regulations, and information processing, handling, and preserving policies; and they should implement these policies effectively and efficiently to encourage and ensure that employees adhere to these rules, regulations, policies. This is a preventive measure and can act both in the collection and application sources. Managerial policy will also include developing and emphasizing ethical company cultures and reinforcing and rewarding employees who promote honesty in the workplace (Collins, 2001). This will particularly help to protect identity theft from the collection sources such as office database (OD) and business transaction (Workplace) (BT).

4. **Data Management (MDM):** This strategy demonstrates the safe preservation of personal data of employees and customers by organizations, either government or private. At present there are many technical and methodological instruments that can assist organizations in managing and preserving any sort of business information safely, and protect and prevent unauthorized interception of organizational data (Slattery, 2002; Collins, 2003; Newman, 2004). This technique implies that by creating and implementing safe data management techniques, an organization can protect identity theft from collection sources such as office databases (OD), business transactions (Workplace) (BT), and hacking from the Internet/fake websites (HI).

5. **Control over employees (MCE):** Previous researchers (Collins, 2003; Newman, 2004) reveal that an employee is one of the prime sources of personal information

Table 1. Matrix of source and measure to prevent/control identity theft

Source of Identity Theft		Measure to Prevent/Control Identity Theft									
		External					Internal				
Collection Source		*MGL*	*MCO*	MCS	*MPA*	MCP	*MTM*	*MMP*	*MRM*	*MDM*	*MCE*
	OD	x	x				x	x		x	x
	DD	x		x	x						
	BT	x	x				x	x		x	x
	ST	x			x						
	SM	x			x	x	x				
	HI	x	x				x	x		x	x
	MB	x		x	x						
	SS	x			x						
	CS	x			x		x				
Application Source	*FP*	x			x		x		x		
	NFP	x			x		x		x		
	CP	x			x		x		x		

disclosure. Therefore, the key issue in preventing identity theft in the distribution phase lies within the periphery of employee control (Collins & Hoffman, 2002). Employees, who look after customers' personal information must be screened through specific organizational protocols (Collins & Hoffman, 2002; Collins, 2003; Newman, 2004). This is a very important identity protection technique and the effectiveness of this technique lies mostly on the shoulders of organizations. This identity theft protection technique assumes that organizations should control their employees in accessing and processing vulnerable information and databases of both employees and customers. All employees should be closely monitored while handling vulnerable information that might hamper employees and customers' informational security and privacy. This will particularly help to protect identity theft from the collection sources like, office database (OD) and business transaction (Workplace) (BT).

IDENTITY THEFT SOURCE-CONTROLLING TOOLS RELATIONS

The previous discussion about sources and measures to prevent/control identity theft sheds light on their plausible relations. Different sources of identity theft characterized by their inherent properties of occurrence, whether collection or application, suit one or more specific measuring strategies. Therefore, based on the previous definition, description, and demonstration of types, sources, and preventive/controlling measures of identity theft grounded on literature review, we propose a matrix, given in Table 1, to depict a conjoint relationship of different measures to prevent/control identity theft with sources.

RESEARCH METHODOLOGY

Since identifying and preventing identity theft is a very new topic in information technology, especially for online transactions, no comprehensive empirical studies have so far been conducted in this context. Therefore, this study needs some explanations about the methodologies followed. As mentioned earlier, the specific objective of this paper is to develop a matrix of the general relations of preventing tools of identity theft with possible sources from literature review. Then, based on the matrix, this research is engaged in identifying the specific relation of prevention tools with sources of identity theft for EC and verifying these relations through a case study in the banking sector following a qualitative approach. Finally, it attempts to evaluate the impacts of these prevention tools of identity theft on the functions of EC. To accomplish these objectives, this study conceptualizes a model based on literature review and validates that based on the case study in the financial sector. In this connection, this study conducted interviews with a semi-structured questionnaire among six practitioners who are expert in online fraud management in financial institutions. We have selected EC as our field of interest and banking sector as our case study, because, from our literature review, it is obvious that online transactions are more vulnerable to identity theft than offline transactions and it is even more vulnerable in financial sector. Therefore, the virtual environment of B2C EC of banking sector is a significant field of study to verify the impact of these prevention tools on trust, performance, and price, all of which, in turn, affect consumers' purchase behavior.

This study, at this stage, does not address customers' opinion about trust, operational performance, and price of products or services due to application of preventing tools of identity theft. This is a major problem of this specific study. We are trying to grasp the effect of those prevention tools of identity theft on trust, operational performance, and the price of products or services, which ultimately affect the purchase intention of customers. So, in that sense, customers would be the better option as the respondents of any empirical study in this context. However, we did not do that because we realize that at this premature stage of the application of different prevention tools for identity theft in company security functions of EC, customers cannot predict or evaluate the direct effect of these prevention tools on trust, operational performance, and price of products or services. Rather, persons at the company management level can detect the sources and possible tools of identity theft and perceive the fundamental effects of these prevention tools on operational performance, price, and any possible effect on consumers' trust. We also recognized that financial institutions are the most sensitive organizations in relation to identity theft. Therefore, we conducted a case study through a qualitative approach and selected six personnel who are expert on online identity theft management in different financial institutions in Canada. Flick (1998) and Neuman (1997) defined the importance of case study through focus groups for exploratory research. Based on literature review, we prepared a semi-structured questionnaire to obtain the following information:

1. Possible sources of identity theft specific to EC.
2. Prevention tools of identity theft specific to these sources of EC.
3. The effect of these sources on operational performance, price, and consumers' trust.

Then, based on the questionnaire prepared through literature review on identity theft, we conducted the case study through interviews among six top management authorities who are responsible for identity theft management in their respective financial institutions and asked them to verify, edit, modify, and finalize all relations mentioned earlier. They also pre-tested the structure, constructs, and respective measurement items that are presented in Appendix A.

In this study, we randomly selected from the list of the banking institutions six leading financial institutions (banks) who are conducting their banking all over Canada. Then the authors contacted top authorities of the respected banks through telephone seeking interviews with someone in the bank who is primarily responsible for developing identity theft management policy of that bank in conjunction with existing regulations of Canadian financial institutions. All the banks authorities who are contacted gave appointment to the first author of this research. We then conducted interviews with the top management authority of each bank who is primarily responsible for developing policy regarding identity theft management. All the interviewees are top level managers in their respective financial institutions. The interviews based on the semi-structured questionnaire were lasted for two hours in average.

Discussion and Propositions

As we discussed, there are several types of identity theft. Accordingly, different types of measures to prevent/control identity theft are advocated by scholarly articles, which we comprehend in the above table to focus the relation of different sources with plausible techniques or strategies to prevent/control identity theft. Therefore, by using this matrix table, we can identify the plausible controlling/preventive techniques to prevent identity theft, which are distinctive to any specific type of source of identity theft. Depending on the industry, organization, and business pattern, different sources of identity theft are common or frequent. To prevent/control that source of identity theft, we do not need to use all the measuring techniques. Using this matrix table, it is possible to allocate resources to only the related measures to prevent/control that specific source of identity theft. From literature reviewed here and the opinions of the researchers based on plausibility and major measures, which have an impact in preventing/controlling any specific source of identity theft, are identified in the matrix table and marked by an "x".

Now our next step is to identify the sources and corresponding prevention/controlling techniques of identity theft specific to trust formation and ultimately purchase intention in EC. Let us consider identity theft in EC transaction. Among the type of sources presented in the previous section, some items reflect only a direct connection with web-based transactions. Some might occur both in offline and online transactions with a similar possibility, i.e., avoiding online transactions cannot reduce the scope of that source; and some occur only in offline media, i.e., physical presence. Identity theft can occur through the Internet in several ways, as we have already described in collection and application sources. As an application source, the Internet is the best and easiest media for identity thieves. This is due to some inherent properties of the Internet, like anonymity, speed, frequency of ordering, and intangibility. The vast majority of EC transactions are paid for by credit card. For instance, in EC, payment by credit card happens without the physical presence of the credit card and signature verification, and merchants cannot see consumers. So this is a chance for identity thieves to collect others' personal identity and to use it without difficulty. The Internet is an anonymous environment where one does not necessarily know with whom he/she is doing business. An infinite number of monikers and e-mail addresses can be used to mask individuals. In this information age, technology is invading private space, and controversies about spam, cookies, and the click stream are a few of the present threats experienced by online information technology users.

However, while dealing with privacy, security, trust, and purchase intention of consumers in EC, E-retailers are only interested and thus restricted in those sources of identity theft that can be avoided partially (without exposure to another vulnerable identity theft source) or completely by giving up web based purchase. In other words, now we are identifying the sources and causes of identity theft that trigger fear of losing privacy and security, which in turn affect trust and purchase intention of customers in EC, and cause them to resist going further with the EC transaction (Brown & Muchira, 2004; Gauzente, 2004; Zhou & Zhang, 2007). We argue that we are interested in only those collection sources of identity theft, which are solely or at least mostly responsible for losing trust in EC and related to EC transactions. Again, we argue that, though the Internet is the most convenient media of application sources of identity theft, application sources of identity theft are not viable factors of losing trust and purchase intention in EC. Though the Internet as a general media of information technology is responsible for this, it is not EC, and avoiding EC by consumers will not reduce the occurrence of application sources of identity theft. However, we argue if application sources of identity theft can be controlled and protected, identity thieves will also significantly loose their interest and enthusiasm to work in the collection sources of identity theft. Protection of application sources of identity theft might have an indirect effect on protection of collection sources of identity theft. Therefore, we will concentrate both on collection and application sources of identity theft and will pick up only those sources of identity theft that are solely responsible for consumers' trust and purchase concern in EC.

Based on the matrix table presented in Table 1 and current scholarly articles on privacy, security, trust, and purchase intention of EC (Fichtman, 2001; Udo, 2001; Collins, 2003; Davis, 2003, Shareef *et al.,* 2008), the plausible collection sources of identity theft related to EC transactions, which reflect negative impact on consumers perception of trust and intention to purchase in EC, are office databases, business transactions, and hacking from the Internet. Application sources are financial purposes (FP), non-financial purposes (IP), and criminal purposes (CP). Though office database and business transaction sources and all application sources are related to both online and offline transaction, the Internet is more vulnerable (Udo, 2001). Therefore, using the matrix table presented in Table 1, we can argue that the corresponding measures to protect/control identity theft specific for EC are *global laws, control of organizations, technical management, managerial policy, publications to develop awareness, risk management tools, data management, and control over employees*. The interviewee group identified the sources and possible prevention tools. They asserted that all the collection and application sources mentioned here are significant in identity theft management; however, hacking from the Internet as the collection source is the most vulnerable. However, our literature review is somewhat contradictory to this finding, which identifies company employees as the major source of identity theft. The interviewee group evaluated and modified the prevention tools of identity theft. They confirmed that all the eight tools might have an impact in controlling identity theft; however, they unanimously assumed global laws and public awareness have a very minor effect on preventing online identity theft. Application of uniform global laws is very difficult and its country specific implication is not obvious. And public awareness is a spontaneous issue that has always some positive aspects; however, experience shows that thefts are more active than public awareness. Therefore, we

Figure 1. Source-prevention model for EC

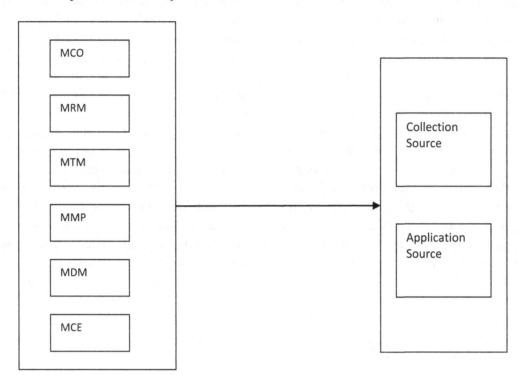

have rejected those two prevention tools for EC. The interviewee group redefined the constructs and their measuring items. This is included in Appendix A.

Therefore, depending on the matrix table presented in Table 1 and drawing inferences from the above arguments of the interviewee group, we propose the following propositions to protect the collection and application sources of identity theft in EC. Based on the propositions, *Source-Prevention Model for EC* is presented in Figure 1.

Pr$_1$: Global law (MGL) measuring technique of identity theft can control/prevent collection and application sources of identity theft.

Pr$_2$: Control of organizations (MCO) measuring technique of identity theft can control/prevent collection and application sources of identity theft.

Pr$_3$: Technical management (MTM) measuring technique of identity theft can control/prevent collection and application sources of identity theft.

Pr$_4$: Managerial policy (MMP) measuring technique of identity theft can control/prevent collection and application sources of identity theft.

Pr$_5$: Data Management (MDM) measuring technique of identity theft can control/prevent collection and application sources of identity theft.

Pr$_6$: Control over employees (MCE) measuring technique of identity theft can control/prevent collection and application sources of identity theft.

Now, at the final stage, the interviewee group examined the ultimate plausible impact of these proposed protection mechanism techniques of identity theft specific to EC on the cost of products/services and operational performance, and also on consumers' perception of trust in EC. In relation to the proposed protection mechanism techniques of identity theft, these related three constructs are very important. Managers of B2C EC are always interested in the purchase intention of customers in EC (Shareef *et al.,* 2008), and it is strongly believed that the cost of products/services, operational performance, and consumers trust in websites significantly affect purchase intention in EC (Yoo *et al.,* 2001; Devaraj *et al.,* 2002; Janda *et. al.,* 2002; Loiacono *et al.,* 2002; Zhang *et al.,* 2002; Cai *et al., 2003;* Santos, 2003; Wolfinbarger *et al.,* 2003; Parasuraman *et al.,* 2005; Bauer *et al.,* 2006; *Collier et al.,* 2006; Fassnacht *et al,* 2006; Kim *et al.,* 2006; Sebastianelli *et al.,* 2006).

Operational Performance and Cost of Product/Service

Based on our literature review (Collins, 2000; Fichtman, 2001; Udo, 2001; Collins & Hoffman, 2002; Davis, 2003; Morris II, 2004; Newman, 2004; Cavoukian, 2009; Fung, 2008; Sun, 2010) it is argued that, the use of measures like control of organizations, technical management, managerial policy, risk management tools, data management, and control over employees face the complicated task of balancing the competing needs of protecting consumers and encouraging EC growth. This is due in part to the differing values placed on consumer protection and privacy in various parts of the world and in part to the laws regulating EC in order to protect consumers that necessarily add costs to EC in a variety of ways. For instance, changes to security measures that enhance personal privacy increase transactional costs for EC and can lead to reductions in productivity. Implementation of these different identity theft controlling/preventing techniques can increase

the processing time of customers' orders/queries. It might slow the whole processing of EC (Newman, 2004). Customers also might face complexity in placing orders and take a longer time to order. Therefore, these identity theft controlling/preventing techniques might decrease the operational performance of EC (Collins, 2003; Newman, 2004). The interviewee group affirmed those identifications. They revealed that implication of these prevention tools can result in more complexity and be more time consuming in order placing and retrieving. However, at the same time, they also argued that E-retailers are engaged continuously with a lot of processing time to solve different identity theft problems. When identity theft problems will be solved significantly in EC, E-retailers can save processing time that has previously been devoted to solve different identity theft problems. Therefore, it is argued that, though at the stage of implementing these identity theft controlling/preventing techniques, EC operational performance might be decreased severely, when the identity theft problem is solved, ultimately the operational performance of EC will be improved. However, they unanimously asserted that overall operational performance will be somewhat decreased. This study conceptualizes operational performance of EC as the complexity and time required to process orders from the management side and complexity and time required to place orders from the customer side.

The interviewee group remarked that the same thing might affect the cost of products/services. Due to implementation of the proposed identity theft controlling/prevention techniques in EC, E-retailers might have to incur more operational cost that will, in turn, affect the cost of products/services (Udo, 2001). However, at the same time, EC bears the huge cost of compensating customers' losses due to identity theft (Gartner Group, 2003; Federal Deposit

Insurance Corporation, 2004). When identity theft problems will be solved significantly in EC, E-retailers can save a great deal of money, which has previously been devoted to solving different identity theft problems. However, five interviewees out of six affirmed that the implementation of these identity theft controlling/preventing techniques might somewhat increase the cost of products/services of EC. The rest interviewee was still not sure about the effect of identity theft controlling/preventing techniques on cost of products/services of EC.

Trust

Trust is the perception of confidence in the Internet's reliability, legitimacy, and integrity (Hair *et al.,* 1995; Be'langer *et al.,* 2002; Ranganathan *et al.,* 2002; Torkzadeh *et al.,* 2002; Brown *et al.,* 2004; Hu et al., 2010)). Trust is a significant driving force in the online environment, because a customer has few tangible and verifiable cues regarding the service-provider's capabilities and intentions (Urban *et al.,* 2000). Referring Kim (2008) and Awad and Ragowsky (2008) Shareef et al. (2013) identified through empirical study that, "Consumers interact with different B2C EC websites like eBay, Amazon, Wal-Mart, Best Buy, Future Shop to get product information and finally develop buying behavior. In this aspect, perceived trustworthiness on the website has potential causal effect on forming buying behavior in the virtual medium". Trust can be viewed as a generalized expectance held by a customer that the website where he/she is intending to interact is reliable (Rotter, 1967). Trusting becomes the crucial strategy for dealing with uncertain and uncontrollable information, statements, policies, and action (Sztompka, 1999). A Cheskin Research/Sapient report (1999) identified six building blocks of trustworthiness: seals of approval, brand, navigation, fulfillment, presentation, and tech-

nology. The study conducted in a developing country (Shareef et al., 2008) discloses that perceived site security, perceived operational security, perceived trust disposition attitude, and perceived local environmental security are the main antecedents of perceived trust. Staples and Ratnasingham (1998) identified trust in online from two perspectives: cognition based and affect based. Jarvenpaa et al. (2000) revealed that trust formation is related to perceived size, perceived reputation, attitude, and risk perception. They also suggested that these factors ultimately lead to willingness to buy. Reviewing Gefen's framework (2002), it is also found that trust is related to familiarity and disposition to trust, which affect purchase behavior. Lee et al. (2000) view comprehensive information, shared value, and communication as antecedents of trust that affect customers' revisit to a website. Bélanger et al. (2002) found that pleasure, privacy, security, and web features are related matters to perceived trustworthiness of a website. Warkentin et al. (2002) extensively discussed the impact of trust in online system adoption, and consequently proposed that institutional-based trust, characteristics-based trust, and process-based trust – which all together captures the essence of perceived security, privacy, and less uncertainty in EC – will lead to the adoption intention of EC. Easton (1965) first defined and delineated the types of trust in the organization as being specific and diffuse. Specific support explains satisfaction with organizational output and the overall performance of authorities. Diffuse support controls the consumers' attitude toward regime-level managerial objects, regardless of performance. Specific support encapsulates the economic value of the exchange between consumers and the organization, whereas diffuse support encapsulates the intrinsic value. Like Warkentin et al. (2002), Parent et al. (2005) also explained and identified through an empirical study the impacts of three components of trust – namely institutional-based trust, characteristics-based trust, and process-based trust – on EC performance. Thomas (1998) outlined the three means by which trust is produced. The first, characteristics-based, is produced through expectations associated with the demographic characteristics of a person. In the light of theory of planned behavior, this component is related to behavioral intention. Secondly, institutions may create trust either directly through adoption of professional standards or measures of security, or indirectly through the observance or administration of laws and regulations. This component is related to making sense of organizational performance, online policies, and credibility beliefs. If actors of EC do not feel institutional trust, according to the institutional theory, they might not diffuse the institutional norms of EC. Third, process-based trust results from expectations of the overall process. This component of trust is directly related to identity theft concern. Process-based trust also has a technological aspect. Since EC is predominantly governed by ICT, perceived security and privacy in ICT will lead to perceived trust in the process of EC. Nye and Zelikow (1997) classified these causal factors as social-cultural, economic, or political. From the marketing aspect, if a customer does not have trust in the institution and process, he/she might not embrace that organization for interaction.

Security and privacy, which in turn lead to trust formation in EC, are severely affected by identity theft. Although, there are so many causes for consumers of EC to be concerned about security and privacy, identity theft is one of the prime sources. This argument can get its strength from the fatal picture of identity theft occurrences as depicted in introduction section of this research. Public lack of confidence in EC due to security and privacy concerns is the number one reason web users are not purchasing over the web and it poses a serious impediment to full-scale EC (Lardner, 1999; Gupta et al., 2010). Consumer reluctance to the use of EC is partly due to the fact that the barrier to shopping on the Internet is relatively high (Boswald *et al.,* 1999). Many factors negatively affect consumers' perception of security, privacy, and ultimately trust in EC and make them reluctant to transact with EC. Among these factors, identity theft is the most significant one (Fichtman, 2001). Related issues of identity theft with security and privacy are the abuse of consumers' financial information during an EC transaction mostly by credit card and also abuse of their non-financial personal identity information — mostly address, telephone number, name, and date of birth by identity thieves. A study by Forrester Research revealed that two-thirds of the potential customers are worried about protecting personal information during interactions with E-retailers (Branscum, 2000). The focus group also affirmed that many consumers have concern over potential interception and hacking of personal information they disclose during purchase. These security factors and privacy concern are potential indicators for trust formation in EC as the authentication of web transaction, protection of disposed information, and perfection and guarantee of the web statements (Bellman *et al.,* 1999; Schaupp *et al.,* 2005).

Every customer attempts to evaluate trustworthiness of a website before committing to a business transaction. The construct of perceived trust, in this research, captures the level of trust a customer places in EC in the expectation that the website will act in the customers' best interest without exposing them to the vulnerability of financial and informational security caused by identity theft. All the six interviewees who are highly involved in identity theft management with their respective financial institutions unanimously revealed that — due to effective design, implementation, and functionalization

Figure 2. Identity theft-purchase intention model for EC

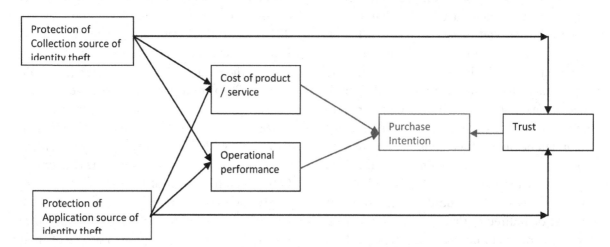

of preventing tools to alleviate identity theft — customers perceive higher financial security, informational security, and privacy in online transaction and express a high level of trust in EC. Trust is one of the most important driving forces for making a purchase decision in EC (May *et al.,* 2002). Therefore, effective implementation of different proposed identity theft controlling/preventing techniques enhance trust in EC, which in turn will positively influence customers' purchase intention in EC (Davis, 2003; Brown & Muchira, 2004). Depending on the above arguments, this current study proposes:

Pr₇: Protection of identity theft in EC decreases operational performance.

Pr₈: Protection of identity theft in EC increases cost of products/services.

Pr₉: Protection of identity theft in EC increases consumers trust.

Pr₁₀: Price of product/service has an impact on customers' purchase intention.

Pr₁₁: Operational performance has an impact on customers' purchase intention.

Pr₁₂: Trust of customers will lead to purchase intention.

Five members of the interviewee group also revealed that the combined effects of operational performance, cost of products/services, and trust on purchase intention is positive. Only one member was suspicious of the outcome of the effects of operational performance, cost of products/services of EC, and trust on purchase intention, although he admitted that they are managing identity theft in their financial institution in such a way that ultimately the aforementioned effects will be forced to be positive. It means that the ultimate effect of the above mentioned prevention/controlling tools of identity theft decrease operational performance, increase price of product/service, and increase consumers' trust on EC, which comprehensively affects purchase behavior and finally increase consumers' purchase intention in EC. The interviewee group also identified the measuring items of operational performance, price of products/services, and trust, which are presented in Appendix A. Depending on the above propositions, the identity theft-purchase intention model for EC is presented in Figure 2.

The above three propositions Pr_{10}, Pr_{11}, and Pr_{12} are well established in different EC literature (Yoo *et al.,* 2001; Devaraj *et al.,* 2002; Janda *et al.,* 2002; Loiacono *et al.,* 2002; Zhang *et al.,* 2002; Balasubramanian *et al.,* 2003; Cai *et al.,* 2003; Santos, 2003; Wolfinbarger *et al.,* 2003; Parasuraman *et al.,* 2005; Bauer *et al.,* 2006; Collier *et al.,* 2006; Fassnacht *et al,* 2006; Kim *et al.,* 2006; Sebastianelli *et al.,* 2006, Shareef *et al.,* 2008*).* Therefore, in this research paper, we are not attempting to identify those mentioned three relations.

CONCLUSION AND FUTURE RESEARCH DIRECTION

This research article set its objective to conceptualize sources of identity theft and measuring techniques and to develop a source-related measuring matrix to prevent/control identity theft. Then the relations of sources and possible prevention tools of identity theft in EC identified through literature review were verified and edited by a group of policy makers of identity theft management in Canadian financial sector. Finally, through a case study following a qualitative approach in financial sector based on a semi structured questionnaire, the interviewee group identified the relation of those preventing tools with operational performance, price of products/services, and trust in EC and the combined effect on purchase intention. They also edited the constructs and measuring items. Based on these findings, two models, *Source-Prevention Model for EC* and *Identity Theft-Purchase Intention Model for EC* have been developed. Practitioners asserted that office databases, business transactions, and hacking from the Internet/fake websites are three major collection sources of identity theft for the virtual environment. However, they pursue that hacking from the Internet/fake website is the most sensible cause in this aspect. This finding is somewhat contradictory to findings of several reports which argue that company employees are the major source of identity theft. One reason for this contradiction might be in

the fact that higher management authorities do not like to show mistrust of their employees. All the three application sources are identified as vulnerable for the online environment. The interviewee group was primarily confident of protection tools that they had used, such as internal techniques and any punishment measurements employed by their own government. They do not rely on external techniques like global laws and public awareness. The reason is obvious. Global laws are still an imaginary issue and hackers' promptness mostly surpass public awareness. The interviewee group affirmed that implementation of different protection tools has a negative impact on operational performance and the price of products/services. They revealed that transacting in EC is more complex and time-consuming due to the application of several protection tools of identity theft. At the same time, the overall price of products/services might be somewhat increased. However, the potential benefits of implementing these tools lie in the significant increase of consumers' trust in EC. Shareef et al (2013) revealed from extensive empirical study that, "Consumers will develop their trust and form their buying behavior for a particular website based only how retailers can fulfill their needs through the website, buying process, pricing, product availability, product delivery, and product quality and how they ensure consumers security needs for personal and financial data which they disclose during purchase". This finding acknowledges that trust has substantial positive impact on consumers purchase decision. As a result, finally, the combined effect of these three aspects on purchase intention is positive. Due to the implementation of several prevention tools in EC operation to alleviate identity theft, ultimately the consumers purchase intentions increase. This finding has potential implication for EC and ICT. Now all kinds of business organizations are very keen to develop their supply chain management and B2C EC through the application of Internet which is a vulnerable source of identity theft (Miller et al., 2011). This study has provided empirical evidence that although application of different controlling mechanisms of identity theft may have adverse effect individually on some driving forces of business proliferation and consumers' acceptance, integrative impact of controlling mechanism of identity theft is obviously positive. This revelation can provide wide encouragement to practitioners in developing ICT related business where consumers trust leading to adoption is important.

Identity theft is expanding like an epidemic disease and its devastating power is destroying and destabilizing the future sustainability of different industries and organizations, such as EC, and at the same time exploiting innocent customers who are the driving force of the market economy and contribute to world economic growth. Identity theft is one of the major fatal problems of the 21st century and the global information technology is at a vulnerable state. World leaders, economists, and law enforcing bodies are searching for probable measures of identity theft. However, for the E-retailers and financial institutions, this is not merely a social problem; rather it is distracting their potential customers from them and affecting their very existence. Therefore, enabling identity theft prevent/control matrix in conjunction with sources and conceptualizing relations regarding the effect of proposed measuring items of EC with cost of product/service, operational performance, and customers' perception of trust leading to purchase intention in EC are significant advancements and contribute to identity theft issues, especially relating to EC. We expect that the Matrix of Sources and Measure to Prevent/Control Identity Theft, Source-Prevention Model, and Identity Theft-Purchase Intention Model for EC will serve as the conceptual theory of further empirical study in this field.

REFERENCES

Acoca, B. (2008). Online identity theft. *The OECD Observer. Organisation for Economic Co-Operation and Development*, (268): 12–13.

Alba, J., Lynch, J., Weitz, B., Janiszweski, C., Lutz, R., Sawyer, A., & Wood, S. (1997). Interactive home shopping: Consumer, retailer, and manufacturer incentives to participate in electronic marketplaces. *Journal of Marketing*, *61*(3), 38–53. doi:10.2307/1251788

Anderson, K. B., Durbin, E., & Salinger, M. A. (2008). Identity theft. *The Journal of Economic Perspectives*, *22*(2), 171–192. doi:10.1257/jep.22.2.171

Arango, C., & Taylor, V. (2009). *The role of convenience and risk in consumers' means of payment (Discussion Papers 09-8)*. Ottawa, Canada: Bank of Canada.

Awad, N. F., & Ragowsky, A. (2008). Establishing trust in electronic commerce through online word of mouth: An examination across genders. *Journal of Management Information Systems*, *24*(4), 101–121. doi:10.2753/MIS0742-1222240404

Balasubramanian, S., Konana, P., & Menon, N. M. (2003). Customer, satisfaction in virtual environments: A study of online investing. *Management Science*, *7*, 871–889. doi:10.1287/mnsc.49.7.871.16385

Barker, K. J., D'Amato, J., & Sheridon, P. (2008). Credit card fraud: Awareness and prevention. *Journal of Financial Crime*, *15*(4), 398–410. doi:10.1108/13590790810907236

Bauer, H. H., Falk, T., & Hammerschmidt, M. (2006). eTransQual: A transaction process-based approach for capturing service quality in online shopping. *Journal of Business Research*, *59*, 866–875. doi:10.1016/j.jbusres.2006.01.021

Bélanger, F., Hiller, J., & Smith, W. (2002). Trustworthiness in electronic commerce: The role of privacy, security, and site attributes. *The Journal of Strategic Information Systems*, *11*, 245–270. doi:10.1016/S0963-8687(02)00018-5

Bellman, S., Lohse, G., & Eric, J. (1999). Predictors of online buying behavior. *Communications of the ACM*, *42*(12), 32–38. doi:10.1145/322796.322805

Boswald, M., Hagin, C., & Markwiz, W. (1999, June). Methods and standards for privacy and authentication in communications networks: An overview. *International Journal of Electronics and Communications*, 234.

Branscum, D. (2000). Guarding online privacy. *Newsweek*, *135*(23), 77-78.

Brown, M., & Muchira, R. (2004). Investigating the relationship between internet privacy concerns and online purchase behavior. *Journal of Electronic Commerce Research*, *5*(1), 62–70.

Buba, N. M. (2000). Waging war against identity theft: Should the United States borrow from the European Union's battalion? *Suffolk Transnational Law Review*, *23*, 633.

Cai, S., & Jun, M. (2003). Internet users' perceptions of online service quality: A comparison of online buyers and information searches. *Managing Service Quality*, *13*(6), 504–519. doi:10.1108/09604520310506568

California Department of Motor Vehicles. (2002). Retrieved from http://dmv.ca.gov/pubs/vctop/appndxa /civil/civ1798_92.htm

Cavoukian, A. (2009). *Privacy in the clouds*. Toronto: Information and Privacy Commission of Ontario.

Collier, J. E., & Bienstock, C. C. (2006). Measuring service quality in e-retailing. *Journal of Service Research*, *8*(3), 260–275. doi:10.1177/1094670505278867

Collins, J. M. (2001). *Preventing identity theft in the workplace using the four-factor model to secure people, processes, proprietary information, and property (virtual and actual)*. Paper presented at the Academy of Criminal Justice Sciences 38th Annual Meeting. Washington, DC.

Collins, J. M. (2003). Business identity theft: The latest twist. *Journal of Forensic Accounting, 1524*(5586), 303–306.

Collins, J. M., & Hoffman, S. K. (2002). *Identity theft: Perpetrator (n = 1,037) profiles and practices: Case study conducted in preparation for grant funding*. Washington, DC: National Institute of Justice, U. S. Department of Justice, Office of Justice Programs.

Copes, H., Kerley, K. R., Huff, R., & Kane, J. (2010). Differentiating identity theft: An exploratory study of victims using a national victimization survey. *Journal of Criminal Justice, 38*(5), 1045–1052. doi:10.1016/j.jcrimjus.2010.07.007

Davis, E. S. (2003). A world wide problem on the world wide web: International responses to transnational identity theft via the internet. *Journal of Law and Policy, 12*, 201–227.

Devaraj, S., Fan, M., & Kohli, R. (2002). Antecedents of B2C channel satisfaction and preference: Validating e-commerce metrics. *Information Systems Research, 13*(3), 316–333. doi:10.1287/isre.13.3.316.77

Douglass, D. B. (2009). An examination of the fraud liability shift in consumer card-based payment systems. *Economic Perspectives, 33*(1), 43–49.

Duncan, B.D. (2009). An examination of the fraud liability shift in consumer card-based payment systems. *Econ Perspect*, (Q I), 43-49.

European Union Data Protection Directive. (n.d.). Retrieved from http://europa.eu.int/ISPO/legal/en/dataprot/dataprot. html

Farmer, M. (2000). *Agency lists top 10 security threats*. CNET News. Retrieved from http://news.cnet.com

Fassnacht, M., & Koese, I. (2006). Quality of electronic services: Conceptualizing and testing a hierarchical model. *Journal of Service Research, 9*(1), 19–37. doi:10.1177/1094670506289531

Federal Deposit Insurance Corporation. (2004). Retrieved from www.fdic.gov/consumers/consumer/idtheftstudy/ identity theft.pdf

Federal Trade Commission. (2007). *Consumer fraud and identity theft complaint data: January-December 2006*. Washington, DC: Federal Trade Commission.

Fergerson, J. (2003, June 3). *Five tools you can use to prevent fraud*. Retrieved from http://retail-industry.about.com/library/uc/02/uc_fraud1.htm

Fichtman, P. (2001). Preventing credit card fraud and identity theft: A primer for online merchants. *Information Systems Security, 10*(5).

Flick, U. (1998). *An introduction to qualitative research*. London: Sage Publications.

Foley, L. (2003). *Enhancing law enforcement–Identity theft communication*. Identity Theft Resource Center. Retrieved from http://www.idtheftcenter.org

Fung, T. K. F. (2008). Banking with a personalized touch: Examining the impact of website customization on commitment. *Journal of Electronic Commerce Research, 9*(4), 296–309.

Gartner Group. (2003, June 2). *Gartner says identity theft is up nearly 80 percent*. Retrieved from http://www3.gartner.com/5_about/press_releases/pr21july2003a.jsp

Gauzente, C. (2004). Web merchants' privacy and security statements: how reassuring are they for consumers? A two-sided approach. *Journal of Electronic Commerce Research*, *5*(3), 181–198.

Goel, S., & Shawky, H. A. (2009). Estimating the market impact of security breach announcements on firm values. *Information & Management*, *46*(7), 404–410. doi:10.1016/j.im.2009.06.005

Gupta, B., Iyer, L. S., & Weisskirch, R. S. (2010). Facilitating global e-commerce: A comparison of consumers' willingness to disclose personal information online in the U.S., & in India. *Journal of Electronic Commerce Research*, *11*(1), 41–52.

Gupta, M., Chaturvedi, A. R., Mehta, S., & Valeri, L. (2000). The experimental analysis of information security management issues for online financial services. In *Proceedings of the Twenty First International Conference on Information Systems*, (pp. 667-675). Brisbane, Australia: Academic Press.

Hair, J. F. Jr, Anderson, R. E., Tatham, R. L., & Black, W. C. (1995). *Multivariate data analysis with readings*. Upper Saddle River, NJ: Prentice Hall.

Hartmann-Wendels, T., Mählmann, T., & Versen, T. (2009). Determinants of banks' risk exposure to new account fraud – Evidence from Germany. *Journal of Banking & Finance*, *33*, 347–357. doi:10.1016/j.jbankfin.2008.08.005

Hatch, M. (2001). The privatization of big brother: Protecting sensitive personal information from commercial interests in the 21st century. *William Mitchell Law Review*, *27*(3), 1457–1502.

Hoar, S. B. (2001). Identity theft: The crime of the new millennium. *Oregon Law Review*, *80*, 1423.

Hoofnagle, C. J. (2007). Identity theft: Making the known unknowns known. *Harvard Journal of Law & Technology*, 21.

Horton, R. L. (1976). The structure of perceived risk. *Journal of the Academy of Marketing Science*, *4*, 694–706. doi:10.1007/BF02729830

Hu, X., Wu, G., Wu, Y., & Zhang, H. (2010). The effects of web assurance seals on consumers' initial trust in an online vendor: A functional perspective. *Decision Support Systems*, *48*, 407–418. doi:10.1016/j.dss.2009.10.004

Hutchins, J. P. (Ed.). (2007). *Data breach disclosure laws - State by state*. Washington, DC: American Bar Association.

International Chamber of Commerce (ICC). (2003, August 8). *Crime services CSS foils multibillion internet banking fraud*. Retrieved from http://www.iccwbo.org/ccs/news_archives/2001/fraud.asp

Jackson, J. (1994). Fraud masters: Professional credit card offenders and crime. *Criminal Justice Review*, *19*(1), 24–55. doi:10.1177/073401689401900103

Janda, S., Trocchia, P. J., & Gwinner, K. P. (2002). Consumer perceptions of internet retail service quality. *International Journal of Service Industry Management*, *13*(5), 412–431. doi:10.1108/09564230210447913

Javelin Strategy and Research. (2006). *Identity fraud survey report*. Retrieved from http://www.javelinstrategy.com/reports/2006IdentityFraudSurveyReport.html

Javelin Strategy and Research. (2010). *The 2010 identity fraud survey report*. Javelin Strategy & Research.

Katzan, H. Jr. (2010). Identity analytics and belief structures. *Journal of Business & Economics Research*, *8*(6), 31–40.

Kim, D. J. (2008). Self-perception-based versus transference-based trust determinants in computer mediated transactions: A cross-cultural comparison study. *Journal of Management Information Systems*, *24*(4), 13–45. doi:10.2753/MIS0742-1222240401

Kim, M., Kim, J.-H., & Lennon, S. J. (2006). Online service attributes available on apparel retail web site: an E-S-QUAL approach. *Managing Service Quality*, *16*(1), 51–77. doi:10.1108/09604520610639964

Lacoste, J., & Tremblay, P. (2003). Crime innovation: A script analysis of patterns in check forgery. *Crime Prevention Studies*, *16*, 171–198.

Lardner, J. (1999). I know what you did last summer and fall. *U.S. News & World Report*, *126*(15), 55.

Lease, M. L., & Burke, T. W. (2000). Identity theft: A fast growing crime. *FBI Law Enforcement Bulletin*, *69*(8), 8.

Loiacono, E. T., Watson, R. T., & Goodhue, D. L. (2002). WEBQUAL: A measure of website quality. In K. Evans, & L. Scheer (Eds.), *Marketing educators' conference: Marketing theory and applications* (Vol. 13, pp. 432–437). Academic Press.

London Conference. (2000). *Declining & referring jurisdiction in international litigation*. International Law Association.

LoPucki, L. M. (2001). Human identification theory and the identity theft problem. *Texas Law Review*, *80*(1), 89–135.

Mandebilt, B. D. (2001). Identity theft: A new security challenge. *Security*, *38*(8), 21–24.

Mativat, F., & Tremblay, P. (1997). Counterfeiting credit cards: Displacement effects, suitable offenders, and crime wave patterns. *The British Journal of Criminology*, *37*(2), 165–183. doi:10.1093/oxfordjournals.bjc.a014153

May, W. C. S., & Sculli, D. (2002). The role of trust, value and risk in conducting e-business. *Industrial Management & Data Systems*, *102*(9), 503–512. doi:10.1108/02635570210450181

McCarty, B. (2003). Automated identity theft. IEEE Computer Society, 89-92.

Mediati, N. (2010). Do identity-theft protection services work? *PCWorld*, *28*(10), 41–43.

Miller, A. R., & Tucker, C. (2009). Privacy protection and technology adoption: The case of electronic medical records. *Management Science*, *55*(7), 1077–1093. doi:10.1287/mnsc.1090.1014

Miller, A. R., & Tucker, C. E. (2011). Encryption and the loss of patient data. *Journal of Policy Analysis and Management*, *30*(3), 534–556. doi:10.1002/pam.20590 PMID:21774164

Morris, R. G., II. (2004). *The development of an identity theft offender typology: A theoretical approach*. Retrieved from http://www.shsu.edu/~edu_elc/journal/research%20online/re2004/Robert.pdf

Nakasumi, M. (2003). Credit risk management system on e-commerce: Case based reasoning approach. In *Proceedings of the 5th International Conference on Electronic Commerce*, (pp. 438-449). Pittsburgh, PA: ACM.

Neuman, W. L. (1997). *Social research methods – Qualitative and quantitative approaches* (3rd ed.). Boston: Allyn and Bacon.

Newman, G. R. (2004). *Identity theft, problem-oriented guides for police (Problem-Specific Guides Series, No. 25)*. Washington, DC: U.S. Department of Justice. doi:10.1037/e379342004-001

Parasuraman, A., Zeithaml, V. A., & Malhotra, A. (2005). E-S-QUAL a multiple-item scale for assessing electronic service quality. *Journal of Service Research*, *7*(3), 213–233. doi:10.1177/1094670504271156

Patterson, P. G., Johnson, L. W., & Spreng, R. A. (1997). Modeling the determinants of customer satisfaction for business to business professional services. *Academy of Marketing Science Journal*, *25*(1), 4–17. doi:10.1007/BF02894505

Perl, M. W. (2003). It's not always about the money: Why the state identity theft laws fail to adequately address criminal record identity theft. *The Journal of Criminal Law & Criminology*, *94*(1), 169–208. doi:10.2307/3491307

Privacy & American Business Survey. (n.d.). Retrieved from http://www.pandab.org/id_theftpr.html

Ranganathan, C., & Ganapathy, S. (2002). Key dimensions of business to consumer web sites. *Information & Management*, *39*, 457–465. doi:10.1016/S0378-7206(01)00112-4

Ratnasingam, P. (2002). The importance of technology trust in web service security. *Information Management & Computer Security*, *10*(5), 255–260. doi:10.1108/09685220210447514

Roberds, W., & Schreft, S. L. (2009). Data breaches and identity theft. *Journal of Monetary Economics*, *56*(7), 918–929. doi:10.1016/j.jmoneco.2009.09.003

Rotter, J. B. (1967). A new scale for the measurement of interpersonal trust. *The American Psychologist*, *26*, 443–452. doi:10.1037/h0031464

Santos, J. (2003). E-service quality: A model of virtual service quality dimensions. *Managing Service Quality*, *13*(3), 233–246. doi:10.1108/09604520310476490

Schaupp, L. C., & Bélanger, F. (2005). A conjoint analysis of online consumer satisfaction. *Journal of Electronic Commerce Research*, *6*(2), 95–111.

Sebastianelli, R., Tamimi, N., & Rajan, M. (2006). *Perceived quality of internet retailers: Does shopping frequency and product type make a difference?* Siena, Italy: EABR & ETLC.

Shareef, M. A., Archer, N., Fong, W., Rahman, M., & Mann, I. J. (2013). Online buying behavior and perceived trustworthiness. *British Journal of Applied Science & Technology*, *3*(4), 662–683.

Shareef, M. A., Kumar, U., & Kumar, V. (2008). Role of different electronic- commerce (EC) quality factors on purchase decision: A developing country perspective. *Journal of Electronic Commerce Research*, *9*(2), 92–113.

Slattery, J. (2002). *The problem of business identity theft.* CBS 2. Retrieved from http://www.cbsnewyork.com/investigates/local_story_297105022.html

Slosarik, K. (2002). Identity theft: An overview of the problem. *The Justice Professional*, *15*(4), 329–343. doi:10.1080/0888431022000070458

Sorbel, J. (2003). *Identity theft and e-commerce web security: A primer for small to medium sized businesses.* GIAC Security Essentials Certification (GSEC), Sans Institute, Practical, Version 1.4b, Option 1.

Sproule, S., & Archer, N. (2010). Measuring identity theft and identity fraud. *Int J Bus Govern Ethics*, *5*(1-2), 51–63. doi:10.1504/IJBGE.2010.029555

Sullivan, R. J. (2008). Can smart cards reduce payments fraud and identity theft? *Econ Rev Fed Reserv Bank Kans City*, *93*(3), 35–62.

Sullivan, R. J. (2010). The changing nature of U.S. card payment fraud: Industry and public policy options. *Econ Rev Fed Reserv Bank Kans City*, *95*(2), 101–133.

Sun, H. (2010). Transferring attributes of e-commerce systems into business benefits: A relationship quality perspective. *Journal of Electronic Commerce Research*, *11*(2), 92–109.

Sztompka, P. (1999). *Trust: A sociological theory.* Cambridge, UK: Cambridge University Press.

Torkzadeh, G., & Dhillon, G. (2002). Measuring factors that influence the success of internet commerce. *Information Systems Research*, *13*(2), 187–204. doi:10.1287/isre.13.2.187.87

Udo, G. J. (2001). Privacy and security concerns as major barriers for e-commerce: A survey study. *Information Management & Computer Security, 9*(4), 165–174. doi:10.1108/EUM0000000005808

Urban, G. L., Sultan, F., & Qualls, W. J. (2000). Placing trust at the center of your internet strategy. *Sloan Management Review, 42*(1), 39–48.

U.S. Department of Justice (USDOJ). (2004, March 24). *Identity theft and fraud.* Retrieved from http://www.usdoj.gov/fraud/idtheft.html

U.S. Supreme Court case of Greenwood v. California, 486 U.S. 35, (1988).

Van Dyke, J. (2007). *Reading behind the lines: How identity fraud really happens.* Javelin Strategy & Research.

Wolfinbarger, M., & Gilly, M. C. (2003). eTailQ: Dimensionalizing, measuring, and predicting etail quality. *Journal of Retailing, 79*(3), 183–198. doi:10.1016/S0022-4359(03)00034-4

Yoo, B., & Donthu, N. (2001). Developing a scale to measure the perceived quality of an internet shopping site (sitequal). *Quarterly Journal of Electronic Commerce, 2*(1), 31–46.

Zhang, P., & von Dran, G. (2002). User expectations and rankings of quality factors in different web site domains. *International Journal of Electronic Commerce, 6*(2), 9–33.

Zhou, L., Dai, L., & Zhang, D. (2007). Online shopping acceptance model -- A critical survey of consumer factors in online shopping. *Journal of Electronic Commerce Research, 8*(1), 41–62.

APPENDIX

Table 2. Collection sources of identity theft for EC. (Question 1)

Sector	Question: To what extent do you think...	Answer					
		Always	Most of the time	Sometimes	Mostly Not	Never	N/A
Office database	...Employees have unauthorized access to employee information databases?						
	...Employees have unauthorized access to customer information data bases?						
	...Employees have the scope to steal information from employee information databases?						
	...Employees have the scope to steal information from customer information databases?						
	...Employees have the scope to use information of employee information databases without your consent?						
	...Employees have the scope to use information of customer information databases without your consent?						
Business Transaction	...Employees have the scope to steal information during customer transaction?						
	...Employees have the scope to use information of customer transaction without your consent?						
	...Employees have the scope to intercept or hide some part of information of customer transaction?						
	...Employees have the scope to manipulate or change credit card or debit card information during customer transaction?						
	...Employees have the scope to preserve customer transaction information for their personal interest without your consent?						

continued on following page

Table 2. Continued

Sector	Question: To what extent do you think...	Answer					
		Always	Most of the time	Sometimes	Mostly Not	Never	N/A
Hacking from the Internet /Fake website	...Internet Hackers can find some access in your web information system?						
	...Internet Hackers can steal information from your web information system?						
	...Internet Hackers have the scope to intercept, hide, or manipulate some part of information of your web information system?						
	...Internet Hackers have the scope to change customers' billing addresses from your web information system						
	...Internet Hackers have the scope to create a fake website identical to your website?						
	...Internet Hackers have the scope to operate a fake website identical to your website?						

Table 3. Application sources of identity theft for EC. (Question 2)

Sector	Question: To what extent you think…	Answer					
		Always	Most of the time	Sometimes	Mostly Not	Never	N/A
Financial Purpose	…Customers have scopes to use others credit cards to purchase product/service from your organization?						
	…Customers have scopes to use others credit cards to borrow money from your organization?						
	…Customers have scopes to use others debit cards to purchase product/service from your organization?						
	…Customers have scopes to use others debit cards to borrow money from your organization?						
	…Customers have scopes to use others information to get a new credit card from your organization?						
	…Customers have scopes to use others information to get a new debit card from your organization?						
	…Customers have scopes to use others information to get a loan from your organization?						
	…Customers have scopes to use others information to open a new account in your organization?						
Non-financial Purpose	…Customers have scopes to use others identity information to interact with your organization?						
	…Customers have scopes to use others identity information to do any transaction in your organization?						
	…Customers have scopes to use others identity information to open any type of utility account in your organization?						
	…Customers have scopes to use others identity information to operate utility account in your organization?						

continued on following page

Table 3. Continued

Sector	Question: To what extent you think…	Answer					
		Always	Most of the time	Sometimes	Mostly Not	Never	N/A
Criminal Purpose	…Identity thieves have scopes to interact with your organization hiding personal information for criminal purpose by using others identity information?						
	…Identity thieves have scopes to do any transaction in your organization hiding personal information for criminal purpose by using others identity information?						

Table 4. Identity theft control/prevention methods for EC: External preventive measurement. (Question 3)

Sector	Question: To what extent do you think it will prevent identity theft in your organization, if your government enforces strict laws...	Answer						
		Completely	Mostly	Some	Mostly Not	Nothing	N/A
Control on Organization	...To identify identity thieves?							
	...To control identity thieves?							
	...To punish identity thieves?							
	...For organizations to protect employees' information?							
	...For organizations to protect employees' privacy?							
	...For organizations to protect employees' informational security?							
	...For organizations to protect customers' information?							
	...For organizations to protect customers' privacy?							
	...For organizations to protect customers' informational security?							

Table 5. Identity theft control/prevention methods for EC: Internal preventive measurement. (Question 4)

Sector	Question: To what extent do you think using software/ technology will protect/ control...	Answer					
		Completely	Mostly	Some	Mostly Not	Nothing	N/A
Technical management	...Stealing information of employees from your information databases?						
	...Stealing information of business from your local network systems?						
	...Stealing information of customers from your information databases?						
	...Stealing information of customers during transaction?						
	...Your system from Internet hackers?						
	...Your system from any unauthorized use of your information databases?						
	...Your system from any unauthorized access in your information databases?						
	...Your system from any unauthorized access in customers' transaction?						
	...Your system from any unauthorized access in your local network systems?						

Table 6. Identity theft control/prevention methods for EC: Internal preventive measurement. (Question 5)

Sector	Question: To what extent do you think it will prevent identity theft in your organization; If your organization…	Answer					
		Completely	Mostly	Some	Mostly Not	Nothing	N/A
Managerial policy	…Trains your employees to develop their ethical values to use your employees' information databases with professionalism and confidentiality?						
	…Trains your employees to develop their ethical values to use your business information systems with professionalism and confidentiality?						
	…Trains your employees to develop their ethical values to use your customers' information databases with professionalism and confidentiality?						
	…Trains your employees to develop their ethical values to serve your customers transactions with professionalism and confidentiality?						
	…Rewards your employees for ethical values/honesty?						
	…Rewards your employees to identify any suspicious transaction of customers?						

Table 7. Identity theft control/prevention methods for EC: Internal preventive measurement. (Question 6)

Sector	Question: To what extent do you think any data management techniques to safely preserve information can protect…	Answer					
		Completely	Mostly	Some	Mostly Not	Nothing	N/A
Data management	…Employees' information databases from identity theft?						
	…Customers' information databases from identity theft?						
	…Customers' transactions from identity theft?						
	…Your business information systems from identity theft?						

Table 8. Identity theft control/prevention methods for EC: Internal preventive measurement. (Question 7)

Sector	Question: To what extent do you think it will prevent identity theft in your organization, if your organization controls/screens your ill-motived employees...	Answer					
		Completely	Mostly	Some	Mostly Not	Nothing	N/A
Control over employees	...To get access into employee information databases?						
	...To get access into customer information databases?						
	...To get access into your local business systems which involves confidential information?						
	...So that they cannot steal information from employee information databases?						
	...So that they cannot steal information from customer information databases?						
	...So that they cannot steal information from your local business systems?						
	...So that they cannot steal information from customer transaction?						

Table 9. Identity theft control/prevention methods for EC: Internal preventive measurement. (Question 8)

Sector	Question: To what extent do you think it will prevent identity theft in your organization, if your organization…	Answer					
		Completely	Mostly	Some	Mostly Not	Nothing	N/A
Risk management tool	…Attempts to identify any suspicious transaction of customers?						
	…Checks more carefully to identify any suspicious transaction of customers?						
	…Trains your employees to identify any suspicious transaction of customers?						
	…Verifies any discrepancy in customers' transactions?						
	…Verifies credit card information of any customer if the purchase involves a large amount of money?						
	…Verifies credit card information of a customer if he/she uses a credit card several times within a very short time?						

Table 10. Cost of product/service. (Question 9)

Sector	Question: To what extent do you think the implementation of different identity theft control/prevention techniques related to collection sources and application sources, and ultimately control/ prevention of identity theft will increase/ decrease product/service cost …	Answer					
		Significantly increase	Somewhat increase	Neither increase nor decrease	Somewhat decrease	Significantly decrease	Do not know
Cost of product / service	…For implementation of different identity theft control/ prevent techniques related to collection sources, cost of product/service will….						
	…For implementation of different identity theft control/ prevent techniques related to application sources, cost of product/service will….						

Table 11. Operational performance. (Question 10)

Sector	Question: To what extent do you think implementation of different identity theft control/prevention techniques related to collection sources and application sources, and ultimately control/ prevention of identity theft will increase/decrease operational performance in the following tasks…	Answer					
		Significantly increase	**Somewhat increase**	**Neither increase nor decrease**	**Somewhat decrease**	**Significantly decrease**	**Do not know**
Operational performance	..Due to protection of collection sources of identity theft your overall processing of order time will…						
	…Due to protection of collection sources of identity theft customers download time will…						
	…Due to protection of collection sources of identity theft customers overall placement of order time will…						
	…Due to protection of collection sources of identity theft customers' complexity in placing an order will…						
	…Due to protection of application sources of identity theft your overall processing of order time will…						
	…Due to protection of application sources of identity theft customers download time will…						
	…Due to protection of application sources of identity theft customers overall placement of order time will…						
	…Due to protection of application sources of identity theft customers' complexity in placing an order…						

Table 12. Trust. (Question 11)

Sector	Question: To what extent do you think implementation of different identity theft control/prevention techniques related to collection sources and application sources, and ultimately control/prevention of identity theft will increase/ decrease trust in your organization...	Answer					
		Significantly increase	Somewhat increase	Neither increase nor decrease	Somewhat decrease	Significantly decrease	Do not know
Trust	...Due to protection of collection sources of identity theft customers' feeling safe to interact with your organization will...						
	...Due to protection of collection sources of identity theft customers' secured feeling to interact with your organization will...						
	...Due to protection of collection sources of identity theft customers privacy feeling to interact with your organization will...						
	...Due to protection of collection sources of identity theft customers perception of trust to interact with your organization will...						
	...Due to protection of application sources of identity theft customers' safe feeling to interact with your organization will...						
	...Due to protection of application sources of identity theft customers' secured feeling to interact with your organization will...						
	...Due to protection of application sources of identity theft customers privacy feeling to interact with your organization will...						
	...Due to protection of application sources of identity theft customers perception of trust to interact with your organization will...						

Chapter 8
The Influence of Trust in the UTAUT Model

Eduardo Esteva-Armida
Instituto Tecnologico y de Estudios Superiores de Monterrey, Mexico

Alberto Rubio-Sanchez
University of the Incarnate Word, USA

ABSTRACT

This chapter tests the appropriateness of the Unified Theory of Acceptance and Use of Technology (UTAUT) model in the context of end user consumption by means of an online survey with 475 respondents (24% response rate). The study shows which factors have the greatest impact on the adoption process of VoIP technology in the US market in addition to the interactions of the main variables in the model (Performance Expectancy, Effort Expectancy, Social Influence, and Behavioral Intention to Adopt) and whether Trust can improve the predictive value of the UTAUT model to explain intention to adopt. Partial Least Squares (PLS) is used to evaluate the interactions of the main variables. The model includes four moderator variables (Gender, Age, Experience, and Voluntariness of Use). The results support most of the relationships identified in the original UTAUT model. More specifically, Performance Expectancy appears to have the strongest influence on the Intention of a consumer to adopt a new technology. The study provides information about whether the inclusion of Trust can generate good results for industry.

DOI: 10.4018/978-1-4666-4856-2.ch008

ADOPTION PROCESS FOR VoIP: THE UTAUT MODEL

In recent years, consumer research has used different models to find the variables that help consumers make decisions as to whether to adopt a new technology or not. Some of the more popular models used for this purpose are: Technology Acceptance Model (TAM), Theory of Reasoned Action (TRA), Theory of Planned Behavior (TPB), and Innovations Diffusion Theory, among others. Recently, Venkatesh, Morris, Davis, & Davis 2003) tried to unify the different constructs of all these models in one unique model, and with this in mind developed the Unified Theory of Acceptance and Use of Technology (UTAUT). It is the objective of this study to test the usefulness of this model in the context of end user consumption, a task not specifically attempted by Venkatesh, et al. 2003. The setting for this test is Voice over Internet Protocol (VoIP) technology.

What Exactly is VoIP?

VoIP, or Internet phone service, is a technology that substitutes for the regular phone service and allows the making of phone calls using broadband internet connection. The analog voice signals used (in simple words, the voice of people when they talk by phone) are converted into digital packets. These packets can be transferred via cable lines (internet) and later, they are reconverted into analog voice signals. The decreased use of slower options services (like dial-up) and the increasing availability of speedier services (such as ISDN, DSL, ADSL, cable, etc.) is one of the reasons why the use of VoIP is increasing among commercial and private users.

The commercial market has tried to exploit this new technology with different approaches. Each provider has chosen the terms they think better accord with their marketing strategy. VoIP, Broadband phone, Internet phone and Digital voice are different names used for the same concept, depending on the marketing strategy selected by each service provider. All of them use the same core technology and need only a high speed internet connection (DSL or cable) to work. If there is a difference it is related to the kind of calling devices utilized (McIver, 2007).

The Adoption Process

As with any new technology, consumers' adoption process of VoIP has been slow (Harbert, 2005). VoIP phones are not free of some disadvantages so suppliers need information about what factors are more important to customers. Suppliers can then develop strategies to increase the speed of the adoption process in order to maximize their profits. It was the intention of this study that as a by-product of testing the UTAUT model, information would be developed that is useful to the companies and end-users of VoIP.

In summary, the primary objective of this study is to test the usefulness of the UTAUT model in the context of en user consumption, specifically the use of VoIP technology. In the process, the study will show which factors have the greatest impact in the adoption process of VoIP technology in the US market.

Estimation of the UTAUT model was made using Partial Least Squares (PLS) as a technique to measure the relationships between variables, the effect of the interactive effects and the level in which the variance of the dependent variables is explained by the model. PLS is a relatively new procedure that is becoming popular because of its minimal demands of measurement scales, sample sizes, and residual distributions (Chin, Marcolin & Newsted, 1996). The applications of this technique to the field of consumer behavior, and specifically, to the adoption process for end user consumption is in its infancy, so this study will provide some guidelines to its use in this context.

The UTAUT Model

With the intention to formulate a comprehensive model that considered the variables included in previous theory aimed at explaining adoption behavior, Venkatesh, et al. 2003) developed a way to test each of the constructs from eight pre-existing models: Theory of reasoned action (Fishbein & Ajzen, 1975), technology acceptance model (Davis, 1989), motivational model (Calder & Staw, 1975; Davis et al., 1992; Venkatesh & Speier, 1999), theory of planned behavior (Ajzen, 1991), combined TAM and TPB (Mathieson, 1991; Taylor & Todd, 1995), model of PC utilization (Thompson et al., 1991), innovation diffusion theory (Rogers, 1983), and social cognitive theory (Bandura, 1977). They presented a summary of prior model comparison studies and an empirical synthesis of the different models. Finally, with the variables that showed the biggest impact, they described a new model called Unified Theory or Acceptance and Use of Technology (UTAUT). According to the authors, this model accounted for up to 70 percent of the variance (adjusted R^2) in usage intention and it is a definitive model that summarizes what is known and forms a basis for direct future research in this area. Considering a theoretical point of view, UTAUT gives a perspective on how the variables related to intention and behavior change over time. But the main contribution of UTAUT is by unifying the theoretical perspectives common in the adoption literature and incorporating moderators to consider dynamic impacts, namely organizational context, user experience, and demographic characteristics such as age and gender. Because most of the key relationships in the model are moderated, the study of these variables is an important added value of UTAUT (Venkatesh et al., 2003).

Although it is a relatively new model, UTAUT has shown that one of its most important advantages is its generalizability. Since the formulation of this model, researchers have applied it in different fields and conducted qualitative and quantitative studies using UTAUT, such as business to business electronic marketplaces (Wang et al., 2006), mobile services and devices (Park et al., 2007; Carlsson et al., 2006; Rao & Troshani, 2007), short message services (Baron et al., 2006), tablet PCs (Garfield, 2005; Anderson et al., 2006), and web-based course management software (Marchewka, Liu & Kostiwa, 2007). All of these studies have validated this model and found that UTAUT variables have a strong power to explain the constructs intention of use and use behavior.

UTAUT claims that three main factors (Performance Expectancy, Effort Expectancy, and Social Influence) determine the intention toward using a new technology while facilitating conditions and the Behavioral Intention toward using relate to the use behavior. At the same time, some variables moderate these relationships, namely Gender, Age, Experience and Voluntariness of Use. The relations are described in Figure 1 and the main variables and moderators are defined as follows.

Performance Expectancy is defined as the degree to which an individual believes that using the system will help him or her increasing job performance. In UTAUT, this variable captures the constructs of perceived usefulness (TAM and C-TAM-TPB), extrinsic motivation (MM), job-fit (MPCU), relative advantage (IDT), and outcome expectations (SCT). This construct is the strongest predictor of intention and it is moderated by Gender and Age (Venkatesh et al., 2003).

Effort Expectancy is defined as the degree of ease associated with the use of the system. This variable captures the constructs of perceived

Figure 1. Unified theory of acceptance and use of technology (UTAUT) (Adapted from Venkatesh et al., 2003.)

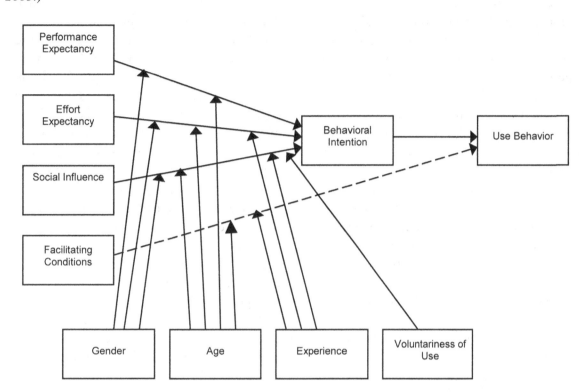

ease of use (TAM), complexity (MPCU), and ease of use (IDT). Effort Expectancy is moderated by Gender, Age, and Experience, becoming non significant with periods of extended usage when users learn to effectively operate the new technology (Venkatesh et al., 2003).

Social Influence is related to the degree to which an individual perceives that other people believe he or she should use the new technology (Venkatesh et al., 2003). In the previous models, this variable is represented as subjective norm (TRA, TPB and C-TAM-TPB), social factors (MPCU), and image (IDT). But, independently of the label, each variable explains that the individual's behavior is influenced by their own perceptions about how other people react to their use of the new technology. Social Influence is moderated by Gender, Age, Experience, and Voluntariness of Use.

Facilitating conditions is defined as the degree to which an individual thinks that an organization and technical infrastructure exists to support him or her in the use of the new technology. This variable captures the constructs of perceived behavioral control (TPB and C-TAM-TPB), facilitating conditions (MPCU), and compatibility (IDT). Facilitating conditions is a construct that relates to intention and use behavior, especially when Effort Expectancy is not present. However, research shows that variables related to the support infrastructure are included in Effort Expectancy constructs. Normally, this construct captures the idea of the ease in which some technology can be used (Venkatesh, 2000). For that reason, even though this construct can be significant in some of the previous studied models, it is expected that in UTAUT model, when Effort Expectancy is included, it will be non-significant in predicting intention. Facilitating conditions is moderated by Age and Experience.

In addition to the main variables, the UTAUT model includes four moderating variables that were mentioned in previous lines: Age, Gender, Experience and Voluntariness of Use. Even though these variables were not included in the original 8 models that were used as starting point to build the UTAUT, findings related them to one or more of these models, so they were included in UTAUT as moderators.

Age has been mentioned as related to the Theory of Planned Behavior. Morris and Venkatesh's (2000) research found that attitude toward behavior is higher in younger workers and perceived behavioral control was more important for older ones. On the other hand, older women show more influence from subjective norm.

Gender is mentioned as an important moderator in findings related to Technology Acceptance Model and Theory of Planned Behavior. Using TPB, Venkatesh et al. (2000) report difference in gender results. When they evaluated attitude toward behavior, men were more salient than woman but subjective norm and perceived behavioral control were more salient in women. In TAM, Venkatesh and Morris (2000) findings report stronger results in men when they measure perceived usefulness and in women when they measure ease of use. In both studies, when they measured subjective norm, they found stronger relationships related to women in early stages of experience.

Experience, as the rest of the variables, was not explicitly included in the original models. But late findings relate this variable in almost all the models with significant differences according to the level of experience of respondents. Karahanna et al. 1999) reported that with more experience, attitude toward behavior was more salient and subjective norm was less salient. Similar results were found with Theory of Planned Behavior (Morris & Venkatesh, 2000).

Using the Technology Acceptance Model, some research (Davis et al., 1989; Szajna, 1996) found that ease of use is not significant when experience level increases. Taylor & Todd (1995) used experience in the Combined TAM-TPB model and found that perceived usefulness, attitude toward behavior, and perceived behavioral control were perceives as more important with more experience. On the other hand, subjective norm was considered less important when experience increased. With the Model of PC some results (Thompson et al., 1994) provide evidence that complexity, affected use, social factors and facilitation conditions were considered more important with less experience and concern about long-term consequences were considered more important with higher levels of experience.

Finally, Voluntariness of Use was not included in the original models, but some late research gave this variable some importance as a moderator. In relation to Theory of Reasoned Action and Theory of Planned Behavior, Hartwick and Barki (1994) found that subjective norm was more salient if system use was seeing as less voluntary.

The UTAUT Model + Trust

Trust is an important element for successful business, too. It is hard for companies to be optimistic about their long-run existence if they fail to obtain consumers´ trust. In business environments, trust is a key factor to decrease customer's perceptions about risk and uncertainty (McKnight et al., 2002). The reason why trust is important is related to the needs of people to control or, at least feel that they can understand the social environment where they interact. In that sense, trust is seen as a faith or confidence that the other party will fulfill obligations set forth in an exchange (Gundlach & Murphy, 1993).

There is little information about how trust can affect the UTAUT model, but some of the previous literature has shown that trust can be related not only with behavioral intention to adopt but also with some of the equivalent variables included in UTAUT. For example, Wu and Chen (2005) found that trust has a positive impact on perceived usefulness, perceived behavioral control, and subjective norm. In a similar way, Pavlou (2003) showed significant relationships between trust and perceived usefulness and perceived ease of use. This study has the intention to evaluate whether trust can improve the UTAUT model as a predictor of performance expectancy, effort expectancy, and behavioral intention to adopt. For that purpose, a distinction in the concept of trust is necessary. Research has shown that two different constructs of trust can be used to evaluate related but different factors: customer trust in companies or vendors, and customer trust in the technology itself (Gefen et al., 2003). For that reason, in order to distinguish the possible relationship between trust with the UTAUT constructs and to measure the possible impact in intention to adopt, it is necessary to manage both types of trust separately.

For the purpose of this research, the UTAUT model including trust will be evaluated to compare the results with the original UTAUT model. In the modified model, trust is related to performance expectancy, effort expectancy, facilitating conditions and behavioral intention. Because social influence is defined as the individual's perceptions about how other people see them using the new technology, the relationship between trust and social influence is not considered relevant. The relationships between constructs in the model adding trust can be seen in Figure 2. Three different models are tested separately adding trust: first, using the variable Trust in the VOIP company provider, second, using Trust in the VOIP technology, and third, including both measures of Trust.

Finally, there is one more consideration in applying the model. In order to test the models and measure intention and use behavior, the sample needs to be tested in two different moments: previous to adoption (to measure intention), and after adoption (to measure use behavior). In this research, the main objective is to test the original model and the model adding trust in order to measure what factors have the highest influence on end-use consumers´ intention to adopt this new technology. In order to meet this objective non-users of VOIP technology were the target. That means measurement of use behavior is not including in this research.

Based on the previous discussion, 6 hypotheses were developed:

H1: Performance Expectancy will positively affect Behavioral Intention to Adopt VoIP Technology.

H2: Effort Expectancy will positively affect Behavioral Intention to Adopt VoIP Technology.

H3: Social Influence will positively affect Behavioral Intention to Adopt VoIP Technology.

H4a: Trust in company will positively affect Performance expectancy.

H4b: Trust in company will positively affect Effort expectancy.

H4c: Trust in company will positively affect Behavioral intention to adopt.

H5a: Trust in technology will positively affect Performance expectancy.

H5b: Trust in technology will positively affect Effort expectancy.

H5c: Trust in technology will positively affect Behavioral intention to adopt.

H6a: The impact of Performance Expectancy on Behavioral Intention to Adopt VoIP Technology will be moderated by Gender and Age.

H6b: The impact of Effort Expectancy on Behavioral Intention to Adopt VoIP Technol-

Figure 2. UTAUT adapted for VOIP acceptance including trust.
* Two different constructs will be tested: Trust in Company (Provider) and Trust in Technology

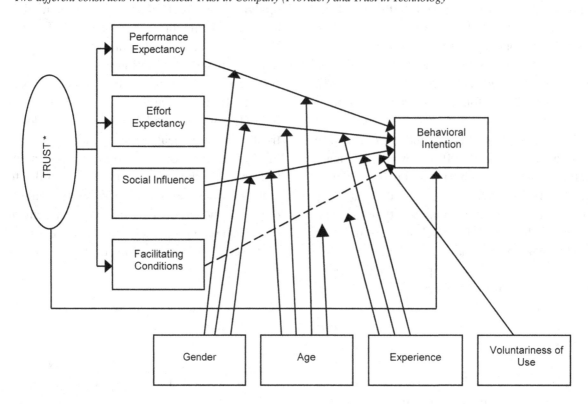

ogy will be moderated by Gender, Age, and Experience.

H6c: The impact of Social Influence on Behavioral Intention to Adopt VoIP Technology will be moderated by Gender, Age, Experience, and Voluntariness of Use.

METHODOLOGY AND SAMPLE

In recent years, online research has increased in popularity for different reasons. According to McDaniel and Gates (2005) part of the success of online survey is related to the finding that the online population is very similar to the general population, for example, in gender distribution (as reported by the U. S. Census), marital status, age distribution, and the average online household. Research has also shown that when the issue under investigation is of equal interest for both populations (internet and overall target population), quality of the information provided by Internet surveys is similar to that using mail or telephone surveys (Coderre, Mathieu, & St-Laurent, 2004). Another important aspect in favor of online surveys is the higher cooperation and survey completion rates. For these reasons, an online survey was selected for this study.

An online questionnaire was prepared to collect information from customers living in U. S. related to their habits regarding use of VoIP services. The advantages of using online questionnaire as a method to collect data are related to reduced costs, rapid deployment, real-time reporting, high response rates, speed of data collection, and decreased data entry error (Ilieva et al., 2002; Wharton et al., 2003; McDaniel & Gates, 2005; Gaide, 2005). In other words, using an online questionnaire allows the researcher to reach many respondents in a short period of time and at a lower cost than other methods.

Sample

A distribution list provided by a research agency was used in order to obtain an actual sample. This company is a well known market research agency that remains committed to providing the most responsive and highest quality electronic communications channels available. It has delivered more than 6 million completed surveys and has supported many of successful studies ranging from small, targeted audiences to large, generalized populations. The company works with panels of over 3.2 million members in seven different countries and it has been a member of CASRO (Council of American Research Organizations) since 2001.

Because this study sets out to test intention to adopt, the main characteristic of the sample was that subjects were not VoIP users. It was important that all of them were phone and internet users, or at least had the intention to be users in the short-term. Otherwise, probability to be VoIP user would be low, not necessarily because of the technology itself, but also because of the previous life style of the subject. The distribution list included 2000 possible respondents and 475 usable answers were received.

Instrument

The main variables of the models (Performance Expectancy, Effort Expectancy, Social Influence, Facilitating Conditions, Trust in Company, Trust in VOIP Technology and Behavioral Intention toward using VoIP technology) were measured with previously tested scales. Each of these items was constructed as a Likert scale with five response categories (anchored by Strongly Disagree - Strongly Agree). A Likert scale is appropriate when the research needs to measure

the respondents´ attitude toward constructs (McDaniel & Gates, 2005). In this study, that is precisely the object of measurement: attitudes and perceptions about VoIP technology. Cronbach's Alpha was used to ensure satisfactory levels of internal consistency of the scale items. Questions with a good level of reliability from previous research were selected. After reviews by experts and a pretest the final questionnaire consisted of 44 items (Appendix A).

Variables

The original UTAUT model includes four independent variables: Performance Expectancy, Effort Expectancy, Social Influence, and facilitating conditions. These factors affect a dependent variable: Behavioral Intention. Finally, four extra variables moderate the relationship between independent and dependent variables: Gender, Age, Experience and Voluntariness of Use. The modified UTAUT model adds two independent variables: Trust in Provider and Trust in Company. Items used to measure these variables were adapted from Venkatesh et al. (2003), and can be seen in the final survey in Appendix A.

Procedures

As stated above, the method of collecting data was an online survey. Participation was voluntary. The format used in the web page was developed so access was easy, even for respondents with slow internet speeds.

Partial Least Squares (PLS) was used to evaluate the relationships in the model. PLS is a component-based structural equation modeling technique similar to regression, but it also models the structural paths and measurement paths (Chin, Marcolin, & Newsted, 1996). The objective of PLS is to predict or analyze some dependent variables from a group of independent variables (predictors). This process is achieved by extracting from the predictors a group of orthogonal factors (latent variables) which have the best predictive power. Its goal is to predict one variable (Y) from another (X) describing the common structure underlying these variables.

There were two reasons to use this technique. First, this technique was used in the original UTAUT model, so in order to compare results with that model, it was necessary to use PLS. Second, PLS procedure is a new technique which is becoming popular because of its minimal demands on measurement scales, sample size, and residual distributions. Some advantages that PLS offers are: modeling of multiple dependent and independent variables, handling multicollinearity in independent variables, handling range of variables (nominal, ordinal, continuous), usefulness with small samples, among others (Chin, Marcolin, & Newsted, 1996). The software used to perform all the analyses related to Partial Least Squares was Smart PLS 2.0.

RESULTS

The sample for this study consisted of 475 respondents out of 2000 contacts. This represented a response rate of 23.8%. Table 1 shows the demographic characteristics related to Age, Gender, Education, Marital Status, Ethnicity, and Income. Even with some differences, the sample shows a good distribution compared to the target population. Most of the United States was represented in the sample (except Alaska and Delaware). Female respondents were a majority (55%) and the median age was 26 (51% and 35 for US population). The sample is younger than the US population, but there is no significant difference when it comes to gender. Regarding education, the sample has a higher level than the United States sample. This is congruent with a study published by the Stanford Institute for the

Quantitative Study of Society (Nie & Erbring, 2000). This study reports that internet users have relatively higher levels of education than the overall US population. Marital status in the sample is similar to the general population. In the sample, 59% of respondents lived with a partner (includes married, living with a partner, civil union or civil partnership), compared to 54% for the general population. The White/Caucasian respondents were overrepresented in the sample (84% compared with 75% in the United States population).

Item Reliability

The relationships among constructs were analyzed through structural equation modeling using the Partial Least Squares technique (PLS). According to Hulland 1999: a PLS model should be analyzed and interpreted in two steps: 1) the assessment of the reliability and validity of the measurement model, 2) the assessment of the structural model. This process allows researchers to have reliable and valid measures before making any conclusions about the relationships of the constructs. The model can be evaluated with individual item reliability, convergent validity of the measures related to constructs, and discriminant validity.

In PLS, individual item reliability is evaluated with the loadings of the measures and their constructs. The rule of thumb dictates that items with loadings of 0.7 are deemed reliable. But in many studies it is common to find some items below 0.7 (especially when new items or new scales are being developed). In these contexts, items with loadings of less than 0.5 should be dropped (Hulland, 1999). Five item loadings fell below 0.5 (EE1, FC3, FC4, TC4, and TT2) and were eliminated. Final loadings, after eliminating items with low loadings, are shown in Table 2. All of them, except one, have loadings above 0.7.

Table1. Demographic and descriptive statistics

Gender	n	%
Female	263	55%
Male	212	45%
Age	**n**	**%**
Less than 20	3	1%
20-29	83	17%
30-39	128	27%
40-49	100	21%
50-59	91	19%
60 or more	70	15%
Education	**n**	**%**
High school or less	44	9%
Some college or technical school	127	26.5%
College or technical school graduate	174	37%
Graduate school	128	27%
Prefer not to answer	2	0.5%
Marital status	**n**	**%**
Living with partner	280	59%
Single	189	40%
Prefer not to answer	6	1%
Ethnicity	**n**	**%**
Caucasian / White	400	84%
Asian / Asian American	23	5%
African American / Black	16	3.5%
Spanish / Hispanic / Hispanic origin	13	3%
Native American	3	0.5%
Other	5	1%
Prefer not to answer	15	3%
Income	**n**	**%**
Less than 25,000	39	8%
25,000 – 49,999	127	27%
50,000 – 74,999	107	23%
75,000 – 99,999	62	13%
100,000 or more	98	20%
Prefer not to answer	42	9%

Table 2. Cronbach's alpha, internal consistency (IC) and Average variance extracted (AVE) for assessment of convergent validity

Items	Loading	Cronbach's	IC	AVE
Performance Expectancy				
PE1	0.71	0.92	0.90	0.64
PE2	0.85			
PE3	0.88			
PE4	0.81			
PE5	0.74			
Effort Expectancy				
EE2	0.88	0.95	0.92	0.79
EE3	0.87			
EE4	0.91			
Social Influence				
SI1	0.85	0.95	0.92	0.75
SI2	0.90			
SI3	0.87			
SI4	0.85			
Facilitating Conditions				
FC1	0.71	0.75	0.72	0.57
FC2	0.80			
Behavioral Intention				
BI1	0.83	0.98	0.87	0.70
BI2	0.85			
BI3	0.83			
Trust in Company				
TC1	0.92	0.90	0.91	0.69
TC2	0.89			
TC3	0.88			
TC5	0.63			
TC6	0.78			
Trust in Technology				
TT1	0.70	0.88	0.83	0.61
TT3	0.82			
TT4	0.83			

Table 3. Correlation matrix among constructs for assessment of discriminant validity

	PE	EE	SI	FC	BI	TC	TT
PE	.80						
EE	.46	.89					
SI	.56	.21	.87				
FC	.43	.65	.36	.75			
BI	.57	.30	.63	.49	.84		
TC	.20	.28	.08	.25	.18	.83	
TT	.40	.45	.25	.39	.33	.57	.78

Convergent Validity

When multiple measures are used for a construct, it is important not only to have individual reliability, but also to assess the extent to which the measures show convergent validity. In order to evaluate convergent validity, Table 2 presents two measures: Cronbach's alpha and the internal consistency measure (IC in Table 2) developed by Fornell and Larcker (1981). The rule of thumb for both of them is 0.7 or higher (Nunnally, 1978). The seven constructs in this research meet this requirement.

The Average Variance Extracted (AVE) is evaluated, too. The rule of thumb for AVE is a value equal or higher than 0.5, otherwise, the validity of each indicator and the whole construct is questionable. The constructs in this study meet this conservative requirement, too.

Discriminant Validity

In order to assess discriminant validity, the Average Variance Extracted (AVE) was used. This test requires that AVE be greater than the variance shared between the construct and other constructs in the model. Table 3 shows the correlations between different constructs (in the lower left off-diagonal elements) and the square roots of the AVE values (along the diagonal). For every scale in this study, the diagonal elements show greater values than the off-diagonal elements, which indicate adequate discriminant validity.

UTAUT Model Analysis

When PLS structural models are used, the respective loadings for each construct can be interpreted as loadings in a principal component factor analysis. In that sense, paths are interpreted as standardized beta weights in a regression analysis (Agarwal & Karahanna, 2000).

LISREL and other covariance structure analysis modeling tools include parameter estimation procedures which attempt to reproduce the observed covariance matrix with minimum differences. The main goal of PLS is to minimize the error (in other words, the maximization of variance explained) in all endogenous variables. For this purpose, the PLS model determines the R^2 values for the endogenous constructs (dependent variables). The main difference with this discrepancy in objectives between the modeling tools like LISREL and PLS is that no proper overall goodness-of-fit measures exist for models estimated using PLS. In that sense, the R^2 values are the normal tool used with this technique and reported by researchers (Hulland, 1999).

In this research, the constructs were considered as reflective. According to Hulland

Figure 3. Unified theory of acceptance and use of technology (UTAUT) (Adapted from Venkatesh et al., 2003)

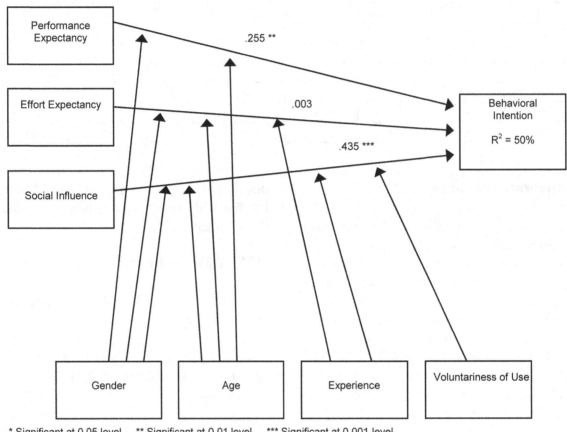

(1999), reflective indicators "are believed to reflect the unobserved, underlying construct, with the construct giving rise to (or causing) the observed measures" (Hulland, 1999, p. 201). They were measured using at least three indicators (the only exception was the variable Facilitating Conditions, which after eliminating the items with low loadings was measured with two indicators). However, as discussed earlier, in the UTAUT model Facilitating Conditions is related to Use Behavior. Since this research was done with non users of VoIP technology, Use Behavior is not measured. For that reason, this variable was not included in the estimation.

The model to be tested was adapted from the original UTAUT model (Venkatesh et al., 2003). The loadings for variables in the model and the variance explained for Behavioral Intention (given by the R-square value) are shown in Figure 2. Only the loadings related to Behavioral Intention are shown in Figure 3.

Path coefficients in the UTAUT model were calculated using the entire sample. Then significance of the structural coefficients was calculated using the bootstrapping method (Efron & Gong, 1983). Bootstrapping is the practice of estimating properties of an estimator by measuring those properties when sampling from an approximating distribution. PLS

Table 4. Structural UTAUT model parameter estimates

Variable	PLS estimate	Standard deviation
Dependent Variable: Behavioral Intention		
Age	0.0006	0.0883
EE * Age	0.0485	0.0986
EE * Experience	0.0014	0.0936
EE * Gender	-0.0211	0.0802
Effort Expectancy	0.0030	0.0859
Experience	-0.1330	0.0876
Gender	-0.0069	0.0786
PE * Age	-0.0768	0.1287
PE * Gender	0.0321	0.1170
Performance Expectancy	0.2550	0.1184
SI * Age	0.0457	0.1214
SI * Experience	0.0562	0.0989
SI * Gender	-0.0554	0.1149
SI * Voluntariness of Use	-0.0316	0.0927
Social Influence	0.4349	0.1087
Voluntariness of Use	-0.1197	0.0905

software uses bootstrapping to calculate t values and standard errors. In this study, these parameters were computed on the basis of 500 bootstrapping runs. The rest of the parameter estimates in the structural model and the standard deviations are shown in Table 4. Since there are no indirect effects in this model, the parameters shown in this table are equivalents to the total effects in Behavioral Intention.

Figure 3 shows significant relationships in two out of three paths, at least at the 0.01 level. R-square value for the endogenous variable (Behavioral Intention) is 50%.

This value is very similar to the 48% in the original model used by Venkatesh et al. 2003. (see Table 4)

The second model to be analyzed is the model including the variable Trust in company. In this model, Trust in company is related to Performance expectancy and Effort expectancy.

This relationship converts these variables in endogenous variables, and that means that PLS will generate not only the R-square value for Behavioral intention but also the explained variances for Performance expectancy and Effort expectancy. The loadings for variables in the model and the variance explained for Behavioral intention, Performance expectancy and Effort expectancy are shown in Figure 4. Four out of six paths are significant at least at the 0.05 level and one of the two non significant at that level (Trust in company – Behavioral intention) is significant at 0.07. The R-square value for Behavioral intention remains in the same level as in the first model (50%). R-square value for Performance expectancy is 6%, and 4% for Effort expectancy.

The rest of parameters estimates in the structural model and the standard deviations are shown in Table 5. This table shows the

Figure 4. UTAUT model + trust in company (Adapted from Venkatesh et al., 2003)

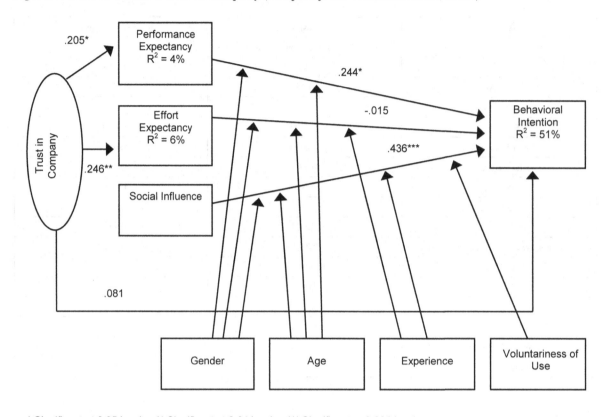

* Significant at 0.05 level   ** Significant at 0.01 level   *** Significant at 0.001 level.

total effects for each relationship. Since only Trust in company has indirect effects based in the relationships between Trust in company to Performance expectancy (0.2428 * 0.2050) and Trust in company to Effort expectancy (-0.0151 * 0.2463), the value for Trust in company in the table (0.1270) is bigger than the path showed in Figure 4 (0.081). For the rest of the variables, direct effects are the same as total effects.

The third model to be analyzed is the model including the variable Trust in technology. In this model, Trust in technology is related to Performance expectancy and Effort expectancy. In a similar way to the previous model, these variables are endogenous variables, so R-square values are generated for both of them and for Behavioral intention. The loadings

for variables in the model and the variance explained for Behavioral intention, Performance expectancy and Effort expectancy are shown in Figure 5.

In this model, five out of six paths are significant at least at the 0.05 level. The R-square value for Behavioral intention is 51%, for Performance expectancy is 16% and for Effort expectancy is 14%. Compared with the previous model, this model shows some improvement in the variance explained for the three exogenous variables. This improvement is small for Behavioral intention, but bigger for Performance expectancy and Effort expectancy. The directions of the paths are unchanged compared with the previous model. The rest of parameters estimates in the structural model and the stan-

Table 5. Structural UTAUT model + Trust in company parameter estimates

Variable	PLS Estimate	Standard Deviation
Dependent Variable: Behavioral Intention		
Age	-0.0056	0.0888
EE * Age	0.0472	0.0983
EE * Experience	0.0055	0.0995
EE * Gender	-0.0144	0.0887
Effort expectancy	-0.0151	0.0957
Experience	-0.1411	0.0875
Gender	-0.0147	0.0780
PE * Age	-0.0826	0.1345
PE * Gender	0.0288	0.1219
Performance expectancy	0.2438	0.1302
SI * Age	0.0491	0.1260
SI * Experience	0.0555	0.0947
SI * Gender	-0.0508	0.1140
SI * Voluntariness of use	-0.0258	0.0923
Social influence	0.4357	0.1111
Trust in company	0.1270	0.0897
Voluntariness of use	-0.1155	0.0946
Dependent variable: Performance expectancy		
Trust in company	0.2050	0.1144
Dependent variable: Effort expectancy		
Trust in company	0.2463	0.1178

dard deviations are shown in Table 6. This table shows the total effects for each relationship. Since only Trust in technology has indirect effects based in the relationships between Trust in technology and Performance expectancy (0.2310 * 0.3997), and Trust in technology and Effort expectancy (-0.0255 * 0.3780), the value for Trust in technology in the table (0.1788) is bigger than the path showed in Figure 5 (0.096). For the rest of the variables, direct effects are the same as total effects.

Given these results we can conclude that hypothesis 1 should be accepted since Performance expectancy is positively related to Behavioral intention. Performance Expectancy is significantly and positively related to Behavioral Intention to Adopt but only in the absence of Trust variables in the model. Strong support was provided for Hypothesis 3. The relationship between Social Influence and Behavioral Intention is, as predicted, positive and significant.

The relationships between Trust in company and Performance expectancy or Effort expectancy are positive and significant but the relationship with Behavioral intention is weaker (significance level: 0.07).

The results for Trust in Technology are stronger that Trust in company and the relationships with the three variables are significant and support hypotheses H5a, H5b and H5c.

Figure 5. UTAUT model + trust in technology (Adapted from Venkatesh et al., 2003)

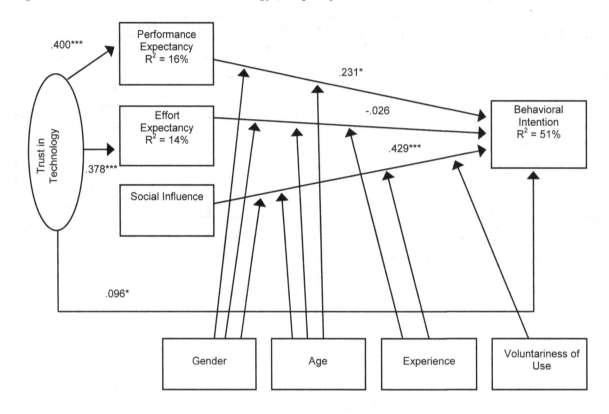

* Significant at 0.05 level   ** Significant at 0.01 level   *** Significant at 0.001 level.

The results show that the first order interactions for the four moderator variables with the main variables are not significant. Since the first order interactions are not significant, it is not expected than higher order interactions would be significant either. Hence, there is no support for hypotheses H6a, H46 or H6c.

DISCUSSION

The present study evaluates the significance of one integrated model that captures the essential elements of eight previously established models: UTAUT model (Venkatesh et al., 2003). The original model was tested using information systems technologies. In order to evaluate it in a different context, this study uses VoIP technology as a technology to be adopted for end-use consumers.

Companies providing this service require plenty of information in order to attract and convince consumers to adopt it. These companies need to penetrate not only the business market where they have been successful, but the end-consumer market, where they are fighting a more complicated battle. For that reason, this study worked with potential adopters of VoIP technology.

The results generated in this work using the UTAUT model are congruent with the original study made by Venkatesh et al. 2003. In both, Performance Expectancy has an influence in the Behavioral Intention to Adopt a technology

Table 6. Structural UTAUT model + Trust in technology parameter estimates

Variable	PLS Estimate	Standard Deviation
Dependent Variable: Behavioral Intention		
Age	-0.0025	0.0864
EE * Age	0.0443	0.0961
EE * Experience	0.0024	0.0966
EE * Gender	-0.0244	0.0943
Effort expectancy	-0.0255	0.0931
Experience	-0.1388	0.0911
Gender	-0.0134	0.0807
PE * Age	-0.0799	0.1352
PE * Gender	0.0347	0.1244
Performance expectancy	0.2310	0.1310
SI * Age	0.0434	0.1221
SI * Experience	0.0609	0.1001
SI * Gender	-0.0553	0.1166
SI * Voluntariness of use	-0.0230	0.0916
Social influence	0.4289	0.1155
Trust in technology	0.1788	0.0955
Voluntariness of use	-0.1145	0.0901
Dependent Variable: Performance Expectancy		
Trust in technology	0.3997	0.1019
Dependent Variable: Effort Expectancy		
Trust in technology	0.3780	0.1009

(called information system technology or VoIP technology). Both studies were able to account around for 50% of the variance in Behavioral Intention to Adopt. The significance of the relationship between Effort Expectancy and Behavioral Intention to Adopt is not clear in either study. The results in this study show a weak and non significant relationship.

The only difference between both studies is presented by the relationship between Social Influence and Behavioral Intention to Adopt. In the original study, this relationship is not as strong and significant as that in the present research. One possible explanation can be related to the differences in characteristics of the sample. The

study of Venkatesh et al. (2000) was done with professionals in four organizations and the technology evaluated was something that is useful for their work. In comparison, the sample for this research was done with more heterogeneous respondents and the technology is something that they can use in daily life. The respondents' disposition to accept other person's influence in the decision to adopt these technologies may be different and stronger than in the sample used in the original study.

When Trust in company was added to the original model (Figure 4) the results were consistent with the original model. Performance expectancy and Social influence remained as a positive and significant relationship. Trust in company showed a positive and significant relationship with Performance expectancy and Social influence and, at a lower level, with Behavioral intention to adopt. Actually, the path estimate for this last relationship increased (from 0.0807 to 0.1270) thanks to the indirect effects generated by the relationship between Trust in company with the other two variables. The only difference in the process was presented in Effort expectancy. Consistent with the original model, the relationship between Effort expectancy with Behavioral intention when Trust in company is incorporated to the model is not significant, but the difference this time is that the relationship turned negative (in the original model it was positive). But since the values in both models are close to zero, this is not necessarily important. Finally, with Trust in company in the model, the explained variance for Behavioral intention to adopt increases marginally from 50 to 51%.

When Trust in technology was added to the original model (Figure 5), the results are consistent with the previous models. The relationship between Performance expectancy and Social influence with Behavioral intention to adopt is positive and significant and the relationship between Effort expectancy and Behavioral intention to adopt is close to zero and non significant. The relationship between Trust in technology with Performance expectancy, Effort expectancy and Behavioral intention to adopt is bigger and more significant than the relationship between these variables with Trust in company. Actually, while the variance explained for Behavioral intention to adopt is not different to that presented in Trust in company (the difference is smaller than 1 point); in Performance expectancy and Effort expectancy there is a considerable difference (4 vs. 16% and 6 vs. 14%, respectively).

Implications

The Unified Theory of Acceptance and Use of Technology (UTAUT) model has been the subject of attention in different researches lately (Anderson et al., 2006; Carlsson et al., 2006; Marchewka et al., 2007; Park et al., 2007). But despite the claim that it is "an important model in IS literature (it) has not been tested in many different settings and contexts yet" (Li & Kishore, 2006). One such important context is end-use consumption. Accumulation of knowledge related to different applications of UTAUT model is basic in order to evaluate the capacity of this model to explain and predict intention and use behavior in the adoption process. That was one of the goals of this study.

The results in this research provide support for almost all of the relationships specified in the model. Future research will be necessary to validate the relationship between Effort Expectancy and Behavioral Intention to Adopt. Questions could be addressed to the sample, the model or to the scales used to measure one or both of these variables. This opens possibilities for future research.

Another noteworthy aspect of testing the model is the effect of the moderator variables. In the past, other researchers had found it difficult to evaluate and provide support for moderators in the model (Anderson et al, 2006; Li & Kishore, 2006; Marchewka et al., 2007). This study found the same problem. Even though the moderator variables Gender, Age, Experience and Voluntariness of Use show some relationship with other variables in the model, none of them was statistically significant. Research will need to be cautious in future research regarding these relationships.

This research supports some variables that can generate an impact for the providers of VoIP services. Performance Expectancy and

Social Influence are important variables that affect the intention to adopt a new technology for consumers. Managers should allocate resources to communicate to their consumers all the characteristics of their product and business that are relevant to specific variables. For example, if they want to impact Performance Expectancy, they should communicate the useful characteristics of Internet phones (lower cost, portability, store incoming calls, send voice mails, 3 way calling, caller ID, call forwarding, call waiting, etc.). Consumers can be swayed if they can understand the advantages provided by this technology

The most important limitation in most empirical applications is the sample. Since the sample used in this research was an internet sample, some issues need to be addressed. Even though the demographic data of the sample are consistent with the population; there is not large body of scientific research regarding the representativeness of internet samples. If, as some believe, samples drawn in cyberspace do not correctly represent the general population, then generalizations of results are problematic. During the process of collecting data, there is little control over who answers the survey or over the reliability of the data included in the answers. So even if the topic used in this study is directly related to the people that use the internet, which gives some support to the sampling process, the results should be taken with caution and be supported with future research that includes a national representation.

A second limitation that can affect the comparison of results between this study and the original research of Venkatesh et al. (2003) is related to the model itself. Since the intention of this work was to compare the intention to adopt

of non users of VoIP technology and the budget and time constrain did not permit a longitudinal study, the model used in this process was condensed version from the original model. When two variables of the model are not considered, the results can change due to the differences in the variables considered in the process. Future research should consider the possibility of a longitudinal study that can follow the process from intention to adopt through the use behavior of the respondents.

A third limitation can be related with the kind of technology used for research purposes. In the original study, the technology used was some that is needed for work in four different organizations. Since this study is applied to the possibilities that consumers adopt VoIP technology as a daily life technology (for regular and home calls, not for work purposes), some results could be different. The UTAUT model was created to explain organization adoption, and used for information technologies. The motivation for adopting and using the VoIP technology could be related to different variables (cost, opinion of other persons living in the household, capacity of persuasion of the providers, type of advertising or promotions, etc.). Future research should consider these differences in more detail.

A fourth limitation is related to the scales used to measure the variables in the model. Since this study uses the UTAUT original model as reference, it was assumed that the scales used in the model are adequate. But there is not enough literature supporting the strength of these scales. Future research should validate the scales and that validation could lead to new approaches to the model.

REFERENCES

Agarwal, R., & Karahanna, E. (2000). Time flies when you're having fun: Cognitive absorption and beliefs about information technology usage. *Management Information Systems Quarterly*, *24*(4), 665–694. doi:10.2307/3250951

Ajzen, I. (1991). The theory of planned behavior. *Organizational Behavior and Human Decision Processes*, *50*, 179–211. doi:10.1016/0749-5978(91)90020-T

Anderson, J. E., Schwager, P. H., & Kerns, R. L. (2006). The drivers for acceptance of tablet PCs by faculty in a college of business. *Journal of Information Systems Education*, *17*(4), 429–440.

Bandura, A. (1977). Self-efficacy: Toward a unifying theory of behavioral change. *Psychological Review*, *84*(2), 191–215. doi:10.1037/0033-295X.84.2.191 PMID:847061

Baron, S., Patterson, A., & Harris, K. (2006). Beyond technology acceptance: Understanding consumer practice. *International Journal of Service Industry Management*, *17*(2), 111–135. doi:10.1108/09564230610656962

Calder, B. J., & Staw, B. M. (1975). Self-perception of intrinsic and extrinsic motivation. *Journal of Personality and Social Psychology*, *31*(4), 599–605. doi:10.1037/h0077100 PMID:1159610

Carlsson, C., Carlsson, J., Hyvönen, K., Puhakainen, J., & Walden, P. (2006). Adoption of mobile devices/services – Searching for answers with the UTAUT. In *Proceedings of the 39th Hawaii International Conference on Systems Sciences.* IEEE.

Chin, W. W., Marcolin, B. L., & Newsted, P. R. (1996). A partial least squares latent variable modeling approach for measuring interaction effects: Results from a Montecarlo simulation study and voice mail emotion/adoption study. In *Proceedings of the 17th International Conference on Information Systems,* (pp. 21-41). IEEE.

Coderre, F., Mathieu, A., & St-Laurent, N. (2004). Comparison of the quality of qualitative data obtained through telephone, postal and email surveys. *International Journal of Market Research*, *46*(3), 347–357.

Davis, F. D. (1989). Perceived usefulness, perceived ease of use, and user acceptance of information technology. *Management Information Systems Quarterly*, *13*(3), 319–340. doi:10.2307/249008

Davis, F. D., Bagozzi, R. P., & Warshaw, P. R. (1989). User acceptance of computer technology: A comparison of two theoretical models. *Management Science*, *35*(8), 982–1003. doi:10.1287/mnsc.35.8.982

Efron, B., & Gong, G. (1983). A leisurely look at the bootstrap, the jackknife, and cross-validation. *The American Statistician*, *37*(1), 36–48.

Fishbein, M., & Ajzen, I. (1975). *Belief, attitude, intention and behavior: An introduction to theory and research.* Reading, MA: Addison-Wesley.

Fornell, C., & Larcker, D. F. (1981). Evaluating structural equation models with unobservable variables and measurement error. *JMR, Journal of Marketing Research*, *18*(1), 39–50. doi:10.2307/3151312

Gaide, S. (2005). Evaluating distance education programs with online surveys. *Distance Education Report*, *9*(20), 4–5.

Garfield, M. J. (2005). Acceptance of ubiquitous computing. *Information Systems Management*, *22*(4), 24–31. doi:10.1201/1078.10580530/45520.22.4.20050901/90027.3

Gefen, D., Karahanna, E., & Straub, D. (2003). Trust and TAM in online shopping: An integrated model. *Management Information Systems Quarterly*, *27*(1), 51–90.

Gundlach, G. T., & Murphy, P. E. (1993). Ethical and legal foundations of relational marketing exchanges. *Journal of Marketing*, *57*(4), 35–46. doi:10.2307/1252217

Harbert, T. (2005). VoIP for the masses. *Electronic Business*, *31*(5), 26–28.

Hartwick, J., & Barki, H. (1994). Explaining the role of user participation in information system use. *Management Science*, *40*(4), 440–465. doi:10.1287/mnsc.40.4.440

Hulland, J. (1999). Use of partial least squares (PLS) in strategic management research: A review of four recent studies. *Strategic Management Journal*, *20*(2), 195–204. doi:10.1002/(SICI)1097-0266(199902)20:2<195::AID-SMJ13>3.0.CO;2-7

Ilieva, J., Baron, S., & Healey, N. M. (2002). Online surveys in marketing research: Pros and cons. *International Journal of Market Research*, *44*(3), 361–382.

Karahanna, E., Straub, D. W., & Chervany, N. L. (1999). Information technology adoption across time: A cross-sectional comparison of pre-adoption and post-adoption beliefs. *Management Information Systems Quarterly*, *23*(2), 183–213. doi:10.2307/249751

Li, J. P., & Kishore, R. (2006). How robust is the UTAUT instrument? A multigroup invariance analysis in the context of acceptance and use of online community weblog systems. In *Proceedings of the 2006 ACM SIGMIS CPR Conference on Computer Personnel Research,* (pp. 183-189). ACM.

Marchewka, J. T., Liu, C., & Kostiwa, K. (2007). An application of the UTAUT model for understanding student perceptions using course management software. *Communications of the IIMA*, *7*(2), 93–104.

Mathieson, K. (1991). Predicting user intentions: Comparing the technology acceptance model with the theory of planned behavior. *Information Research Systems*, *2*(3), 173–191. doi:10.1287/isre.2.3.173

McDaniel, C., & Gates, R. (2005). *Marketing research*. Hoboken, NJ: John Wiley & Sons, Inc.

McIver, R. (2007). *VoIP 101: Voice over IP for beginners.* Retrieved September 25, 2010, from http://ezinearticles.com/?VoIP-101:-Voice-over-IP-for-Beginnersandid=20911

McKnight, D. H., Choudhury, V., & Kacmar, C. (2002). Developing and validating trust measures for e-commerce: An integrative typology. *Information Systems Research*, *13*(3), 334–359. doi:10.1287/isre.13.3.334.81

Morris, M. G., & Venkatesh, V. (2000). Age differences in technology adoption decisions: Implications for a changing workforce. *Personnel Psychology*, *53*(2), 375–403. doi:10.1111/j.1744-6570.2000.tb00206.x

Nie, N. H., & Erbring, L. (2000). *Internet and society: A preliminary report.* Stanford, CA: Stanford Institute for the Quantitative Study of Society.

Nunally, J. C. (1978). *Psychometric theory* (2nd ed.). New York: McGraw-Hill.

Park, J. K., Yang, S., & Lehto, X. (2007). Adoption of mobile technologies for Chinese consumers. *Journal of Electronic Commerce Research*, *8*(3), 196–206.

Rao, S., & Troshani, I. (2007). A conceptual framework and propositions for the acceptance of mobile services. *Journal of Theoretical and Applied Electronic Commerce Research*, *2*(2), 61–73.

Rogers, E. M. (1983). *Diffusion of innovations.* New York: The Free Press.

Szajna, B. (1996). Empirical evaluation of the revised technology acceptance model. *Management Science*, *42*(1), 85–92. doi:10.1287/mnsc.42.1.85

Taylor, S., & Todd, P. (1995). Assessing IT usage: The role of prior experience. *Management Information Systems Quarterly*, *19*(4), 561–570. doi:10.2307/249633

Thompson, R. L., Higgins, C. A., & Howell, J. M. (1991). Personal computing: Toward a conceptual model of utilization. *Management Information Systems Quarterly*, *15*(1), 125–143. doi:10.2307/249443

Thompson, R. L., Higgins, C. A., & Howell, J. M. (1994). Influence of experience on personal computer utilization: Testing a conceptual model. *Journal of Management Information Systems*, *11*(1), 167–187.

Venkatesh, V. (2000). Determinants of perceived ease if use: Integrating perceived behavioral control, computer anxiety and enjoyment into the technology acceptance model. *Information Systems Research*, *11*(4), 342–365. doi:10.1287/isre.11.4.342.11872

Venkatesh, V., Morris, M., Davis, G., & Davis, F. (2003). User acceptance of information technology: Toward a unified view. *Management Information Systems Quarterly*, *27*(3), 425–478.

Venkatesh, V., & Morris, M. G. (2000). Why don't men ever stop to ask for directions? Gender, social influence, and their role in technology acceptance and usage behavior. *Management Information Systems Quarterly*, *24*(1), 155–139. doi:10.2307/3250981

Venkatesh, V., Morris, M. G., & Ackerman, P. L. (2000). A longitudinal field investigation of gender differences in individual technology adoption decision-making processes. *Organizational Behavior and Human Decision Processes*, *83*(1), 33–60. doi:10.1006/obhd.2000.2896 PMID:10973782

Venkatesh, V., & Speir, C. (1999). Computer technology training in the workplace: A longitudinal investigation of the effect of mood. *Organizational Behavior and Human Decision Processes*, *79*(1), 1–28. doi:10.1006/obhd.1999.2837 PMID:10388607

Wharton, C. M., Hampl, J. S., Hall, R., & Winham, D. H. (2003). PCs or paper-and-pencil: Online surveys for data collection. *Journal of the American Dietetic Association*, *103*(11), 1458–1460. doi:10.1016/j.jada.2003.09.004 PMID:14626248

Wu, I., & Chen, J. (2005). An extension of trust and TAM model with TPB in the initial adoption of on-line tax: An empirical study. *International Journal of Human-Computer Studies*, *62*, 784–808. doi:10.1016/j.ijhcs.2005.03.003

APPENDIX

Items Used to Measure Performance Expectancy

1. I would find the internet phone useful in my daily activities.
2. Using internet phone would enable me to accomplish tasks more quickly.
3. Using internet phone could increase my efficiency.
4. If I use internet phone, my phone calls will be more productive.
5. Using internet phone, I will have more tools for improving my communication with other people.

Items Used to Measure Effort Expectancy

1. It would be easy for me to become skillful at using internet phone.
2. I would find internet phone easy to use.
3. Learning to operate internet phone would be easy for me.

Items Used to Measure Social Influence

1. People who influence my behavior think that I should use internet phone.
2. People who are important to me think that I should use internet phone.
3. My family says that I should use internet phone.
4. My friends tell me that using internet phone could be good for me.

Items Used to Measure Facilitating Conditions

1. I have the resources necessary to use internet phone.
2. I have the knowledge necessary to use internet phone.

Items Used to Measure Behavioral Intention to Adopt

1. I intent to use internet phone in the next 12 months.
2. I predict I would use internet phone in the next 12 months.
3. I plan to use Internet phone in the next 12 months.

Items Used to Measure Trust in Company

1. The company will be trustworthy.
2. The company will want to be known as one that keeps promises and commitments.
3. I trust this company will keep my best interest in mind.
4. This company will have more to lose than gain by not delivering on its promises.
5. This company's behavior will meet my expectations.

Items Used to Measure Trust in Technology

1. The technology will be trustworthy.
2. I think this technology will work well.
3. This technology will meet my expectations.

Chapter 9
Technology–Related Risks in Virtual and Traditional Information Systems Projects

April Reed
East Carolina University, USA

ABSTRACT

Technology is important to software development projects; however, virtual projects are more dependent on technology than traditional co-located projects due to communication and collaboration needs. Two research studies in this chapter sought to determine whether seven technology-related risks pose a greater danger to virtual projects than traditional projects and to determine if technology-related risks have a high impact on project success. Results indicate that two technology-related risks exhibited a significantly greater impact on virtual IT projects: (1) inexperience with the company and its processes and (2) inadequate technical resources. Project managers need to be aware that traditional project risks can have a greater impact on virtual projects. Additionally, technology-related risks in the second study were found to have low levels of impact on project success. Results indicate in cases where a majority of team members are experienced with the application, development technology, and project technology, the risk of technology-related issues seems to lessen.

DOI: 10.4018/978-1-4666-4856-2.ch009

INTRODUCTION

The use of virtual Information Systems (IS) and Information Technology (IT) project teams has continued to grow and change the way we work (Berry, 2011; Brandt, England, & Ward, 2011). Several factors have influenced this growth, including the increased use of outsourcing and off-shoring, as well as a shortage of skilled resources in particularly narrow specialties and a need to access those resources wherever they reside (Aspray, Mayadas, & Vardi, 2006; Barkhi, Amiri, & James, 2006; Jones, Oyung, & Pace, 2005). An IS/IT project team is a group of technology professionals working together towards a common goal such as software development, to create a unique product, service or result (PMI, 2013). A team is considered virtual when its' members are not co-located but reside in different locations where they must rely heavily on Information Communication and Technology (ICT) tools in order to communicate across distances. For these teams, face-to-face communication is either limited or non-existent. Dube and Pare (2001) in their research indicated there are a wide range of collaborative technologies that can be used to support these types of teams, such as video-conferencing, intranet, collaborative software, etc., especially for global virtual teams (Dube & Pare, 2001). Such technologies and their associated risks are the main focus of this paper.

Although the concept of 24 by 7 work and better access to expertise are aspects that make virtual teams potentially beneficial, these teams can have their own issues. Dube and Pare (2001) reviewed literature on virtual teams and found some of the "key challenges" that face virtual project leaders to be communication and technology. Oshri et al. (2008) in their research on globally distributed teams found the management of dispersed teams to be more challenging than the management of traditional co-located teams (Oshri, Kotlarshy, & Willcocks, 2008). Berry (2011) acknowledged a higher level of complexity in managing virtual teams than traditional face-to-face teams while at the same time recognizing they share some common characteristics and dynamics of teams in general (Berry, 2011).

Two similar research studies will be referenced here. The first study considers whether technology related risks are greater for virtual IS/IT projects than for traditional co-located IS/IT projects. The second study re-visits the analysis of the same set of risk factors several years later to determine if they still cause issues for virtual IS/IT projects. The research is based in the following two factors: (1) Technology-related risks are recognized as threats to Information Systems and Information Technology projects in general; (2) Virtual Information Systems and Information Technology projects by their nature are compelled to supplement or replace face-to-face communication, and typically they do this by leveraging the use of technology. In the Background section that follows, I discuss each of these two factors in greater depth. Additional details about the two studies are outlined in the Methodology section.

BACKGROUND

Technology-Related Risks

Project risk has been researched previously; however, much of that research focused on traditional co-located projects. In this research, technology was found to be a major category of risk. Boehm (1991), one of the first to rank risk factors, referenced technology as "straining computer-science capabilities" (Boehm, 1991). A few years later, Barki et al. (1993) conducted a large study which identified risks (uncertainty factors) that were grouped into five areas, the first being "technological newness" (Barki, Rivard, & Talbot, 1993). Within that category, the following specific risks which were related to issues with technology implementation on a project were recognized: need for new software, need for new hardware, and technical complexity. Likewise, several years later a Delphi study revealed "introduction of new technology" as one of a universal set of risk factors (Keil, Cule, Lyytinen, & Schmidt, 1998). Finally, Wallace (1999) conducted a survey whose results revealed six categories of risk. "New technology" was found to be a specific risk in the Project Complexity category (Wallace, 1999). Project risk, especially technology-related risk, has not been researched as thoroughly for virtual projects. Instead, much of the prior literature in this area has focused on investigating virtual team characteristics, such as trust, conflict and communication (Andres, 2006; Jones, Oyung, & Pace, 2005; Kirkman & Mathieu, 2005; Lipnack & Stamps, 1997).

Technology-related risks in software development projects are likely to involve communication and collaboration, particularly the tools necessary to accomplish communication at a distance. However, technology related risk can also reference other tools, such as those necessary for application development. Additionally included are tools used by project management practitioners to oversee the project and to facilitate team collaboration, such as Project Management Information Systems (PMIS) or scheduling software. Software goes hand in hand with hardware especially when software must be run on specific hardware, such as hand-held devices, tablets, or even specific operating systems.

Virtual Projects Leverage Technology for Communication

Many virtual projects use some form of technology, specifically Information and Communication Technologies (ICTs), to facilitate or enhance communication among team members as they perform various tasks such as exchange of documents via email, team meetings via videoconferences, joint creation and finalizing of requirement documents via configuration management software, and scheduling via joint online calendars. While any project may use these tools, heavier reliance on technology for communication is a characteristic of virtual projects. Table 1 lists a wide variety of ICTs used to keep virtual project teams functioning effectively.

METHODOLOGY

The research reported in this article is a subset of two larger studies that sought to identify critical risk factors for virtual software development projects. The primary research tool was a survey, chosen after a review of prior literature on research methods used to study risk for traditional software projects. There were several prior researchers who identified project risk factors by using a survey as the research tool, including Boehm (1991), Barki (1993), and Wallace (1999).

The research process consisted of several steps. First, a review of the literature was conducted to identify project risk factors from literature. Prior literature also uncovered a survey questionnaire by Wallace (1999) which was key to the development of the questionnaire for this research study. The next step was face-to-face interviews, which were conducted with project management practitioners using the first version

Table 1. Virtual Team Technology Tools (Hamblen, 2009; Kroenke, 2010; Merriam-Webster, n.d.; Robb, 2002; Malhotra & Majchrzak, 2005)

Name of Feature	Description of Technology (in context of this research)
Configuration Management/Version Control Software	Software system that allows multiple users to update the same software and/or data files without confusion, typically by providing separate pre-and post-release versions, rigorous version control, and built-in audit trails. Configuration management may also apply to hardware.
Content Management Software	While Content Management systems are often used to allow users to update Web information using a simple interface rather than HTML code and then have that information propagated automatically throughout a site, such systems can also be used to control the process of document development, particularly within a virtual project where many team members contribute to a single document (document sharing). In this case, such features as pre-and post-release versions, rigorous version control, and built-in audit trails are particularly important.
E-mail	Transmitting messages electronically between computers on a network, typically the Internet.
Instant messaging	Pop-up messaging that allows immediate access to fellow team members.
Groupware	Software that enables users to work collaboratively on projects or files via a network. Groupware often includes the capability for synchronous or asynchronous discussion.
Shared Calendars	A function that allows group members to see availability on other members' calendars for the purpose of scheduling meetings.
Blog (Web-log)	An online journal, which uses technology to publish information over the Internet.
Wikis	A common-knowledge base maintained by its users; processed on Web sites that allow multiple users to add, remove and edit content.
Web conferencing	Presentations or meetings that are broadcast over the internet either live or videotaped.
Video conferencing	Interactive synchronous telecommunication systems and equipment that allow participants at two or more locations to interact via two-way video and audio transmissions, usually used for conducting virtual meetings.
Skype	A service provider using Voice-over-Internet protocol (VoIP), to provide free or low-cost voice, video, and instant message capabilities through the Internet.
Voice Over IP (VOIP)	Communications technology for carrying voice telephone traffic over a data network such as the Internet.
Presence management	"Buddy list" icon or picture indicating who is currently logged on. Often used in concert with another tool, such as Instant Messaging.
Project Management tools	Software supporting electronic generation and synchronization of timelines, budget tools, issue logs, status reports, and responsibility matrices. An example is Microsoft Project Manager.

of the questionnaire. Open-ended questions in the questionnaire were used to validate the list of risks identified from the literature and to identify additional risk factors from the practitioner point of view. Rich data was collected from the practitioners as they described the major challenges they encountered in a specific project. Some of the pertinent project manager insights are shared later in this document. Interviews were followed by an electronically facilitated focus group session, which was held to identify any risk factors that may have been missed, as well as to validate those found in the literature review and the face-to-face interviews. The large amount of data collected from these steps went through an iterative process of sorting and combining to produce a comprehensive list of 55 potential risk factors. Prior to mass distribution, the questionnaire was modified to remove the open ended questions and to include the complete list of 55 risk factors. It was also pilot tested.

The second research study began with a few modifications and additions to the original survey questionnaire to enhance the validity of the results. However, the 55 risk factors remained unchanged and were included in the second survey. In this study, only participants on virtual project teams were invited to complete the survey. Traditional software development projects were not a focus since even in 2007, when the original version of the survey was conducted, it was difficult to find participants who developed software using strictly traditional co-located teams. Although the potential participant pool was not exactly the same, the survey was completed by project management practitioners with many coming from the Project Management Institute membership. Seven of the 55 potential risk factors in the study are relevant to the current topic of technology-related risk and are reported upon here.

HYPOTHESES

Prior literature as well as data from the face-to-face interviews and focus group led to the following seven hypotheses.

H1: Technical Connectivity Issues are More Likely to Pose a Risk for Virtual Projects than for Traditional Co-Located Projects

For virtual project teams, where daily face-to-face communication is not an option, technology forms the thread that links team members together. Technology is used for communicating, collaborating, and coordinating virtually everything, including one-on-one questions, task status, requirements, procedures, meetings, schedules, etc. With its heightened importance on virtual teams, it is possible that the risk of technical connectivity issues plays a greater role in the workings of a virtual project team. Walther et al. (2005) in their research concluded

that distributed groups were impacted negatively by several aspects of a distributed environment, including restricted communication media (Walther, Bunz, & Bazarova, 2005). Recognition of this risk factor also arose from our interviews and focus group. One project manager in the face-to-face interview portion of this research identified connectivity as one of two major issues on a particular virtual project. The project consisted of remote team members who could not access the LAN because the Virtual Private Networks (VPNs) were in conflict. This made sharing of files and information very difficult. In this project manager's view, connectivity issues translated into a loss of time, negatively affecting the success of the project.

H2: A Lack of Appropriately Skilled Resources is a Greater Risk for a Virtual Project than a Traditional Co-Located Project

Virtual software project team members generally require a variety of skills, depending not only on the nature of the project, but also on the nature of the technologies used for team communication. These skills can include technical work-enabling tools such as Microsoft Project, web conferencing, Groupware, Skype, and many more software usage abilities, which may likely be required on a daily basis (Cusumano, 2008). Despite the lack of agreement among stakeholders on exactly what skills are most important in an IT project, there is agreement in the prior research that lack of expertise is a risk for traditional projects (Jiang, Klein, & Wang, 2007). Boehm (1991) identified issues with the expertise of the team in general as a risk. Barki et al. (1993) identified several risks related to lack of expertise, such as lack of the team's expertise in general or with the development tools, the tasks, or the application, and the user's lack of experience. Keil et al. (1998)

identified the risk of the team having a lack of knowledge and/or skills required for the project. Wallace (1999) identified team members' insufficient knowledge in general as a risk. Jiang, Klein, Beck, and Wang (2007) found lack of application development domain knowledge and lack of system development skills both had negative effects on project performance, but that this could be mitigated through organizational technology learning (Jiang, Klein, Beck, & Wang, 2007).

H3: Resource Inexperience with the Company and its Processes is a Greater Risk for a Virtual Project than a Traditional Co-Located Project

Prior literature refers to the team members' general lack of knowledge on traditional projects, which is likely to include processes and procedures. This was usually identified separately from technical expertise. However, in this study, this risk factor includes a wide variety of inexperience such as lack of knowledge with software development processes and procedures. Barki et al. (1993) referenced general expertise separate from development or application expertise. Keil et al. (1998) identified the team members' lack of required knowledge. Wallace (1999) referenced insufficient knowledge among the team members as an added project risk. Gefen, Wyss, and Lichtenstein (2008) demonstrated that a prior business relationship with a vendor is related to lowering risk and improving the monetary aspects of software development outsourcing contracts (Gefen, Wyss, & Lichtenstein, 2008).

In a face-to-face interview early in this research study, a project manager identified this risk as a major issue on a virtual project where most team members were consultants from different organizations. A lack of understanding of the company environments required for developing and testing the system was a problem. Furthermore, team members had little understanding of the processes and terminology of the company or the company's industry. The project manager was able to resolve some of these issues with training. However, in the end this experienced project manager summarized his feelings of frustration by saying, "Companies are using virtual projects because it's quick, easy and cheap, but they aren't giving these people any training to know how to work with virtual teams."

H4: Inadequate Technical Resources, i.e. Hardware, Software, Processing Availability, etc. is a Greater Risk for a Virtual Project than a Traditional Co-Located Project

Barki et al. (1993) identified resource insufficiency as a risk within the environment category for traditional projects. During the face-to-face interview portion of this research, a project manager identified lack of computer capacity to run test cycles as a major project issue. When a special type of test environment is needed, for example using "time machines" to emulate dates in the year 2000 for Y2K testing, lack of availability of this special environment can bring project progress to a halt. Similarly, projects requiring large volumes of testing can create situations where it is difficult to gain sufficient access to enough CPU time slots to test properly.

H5: Risks Involving Hardware New to the Organization are Greater for a Virtual Project than a Traditional Co-Located Project

New hardware on a project can come in the form of new equipment to be used in the development process for the project or new hardware to be used as a part of the final delivered product at project completion. Virtual project environments depend on more technology for communications than traditional projects. Since face-to-face communication is not available on a virtual project, hardware is needed for activities such as videoconferencing, Skype and wikis which imposes an extra requirement on the virtual process. Lyytinen et al. (1996) listed technology new to the organization as a common issue uncovered during the risk identification process on a project (Lyytinen, Mathiassen, & Ropponen, 1996). Barki et al. (1993) included technological newness on projects as a major category of risk. Within that category, new hardware and technical complexity were specifically identified as potential individual risks. Keil et al. (1998) were very specific in identifying not just new technology, but the introduction of new technology as a risk. Wallace (1999) also identified new technology as a potential risk for a project.

During the interview process, one project manager identified the learning curve with new technology as a major issue on their project. An office relocation included setting up new IT infrastructure. Once established in the new office, the project team was required to implement a software system. During implementation, the team determined the system could not be set up on the hardware that had been selected by those who set up the IT infrastructure. The client perceived the problems with the software implementation as a failure of the project team, when in fact the problem resulted from compatibility issues with new technology hardware at the new office site.

H6: Risks Involving Software New to the Organization are Greater for a Virtual Project than a Traditional Co-Located Project

The risk of new software is very similar to the risk of new hardware. However, coordination and collaboration in a virtual project environment are very dependent on software such as groupware, web conferencing or configuration management software. It can be assumed that most companies have some type of computer and even networking capabilities. However, not all companies have access to software for web conferencing, configuration management, or even project scheduling software. Although traditional co-located projects may use these types of software, a virtual project is more likely to depend on them. Barki et al. (1993) identified new software as a risk on projects. Unlike many other researchers, they were careful to list software risk separate from hardware risk. Lyytinen et al. (1996) summed up the high level of risk that can be associated with technology by referring to it as an indisputable source of risk. These researchers attributed much of the criticality of technology risk to the rapid rate of change associated with technology. An example of issues with new technology software was shared by one project manager interviewed about a project to integrate new Asset Management software into existing software. The new software would be web based and would need to be integrated into an Oracle database. Some of the software was new to the organization, while other pieces were already in use. The project manager believed that lack of knowledge among the project team and lack of access to knowledgeable personnel using the database software, as well as the newness of the Asset Management software, all contributed to the failure of this project.

H7: Risks Involving Unidentified Technical Constraints are Greater for a Virtual Project than a Traditional Co-Located Project

Being required to use technology that is incompatible is another technology-related risk. In this case, company standards may impose technical constraints or they may be a result of hardware or software choices. Barki et al. (1993) referenced this type of risk as hardware imposed constraints. Al-Rousan, Sulaiman, and Abdul Salam (2009) referred to technical infrastructure risk as that resulting from "inhomogeneity and immaturity of used components" or a "hard to predict operational environment" (Al-Rousan, Sulaiman, & Abdul Salam, 2009). Similar to the previous two risk factors, the problematic technology may be used in the process of running the project or as a part of the final product delivery. Either way, being forced to work within unforeseen constraints can be costly if additional resources must be purchased to resolve the situation or if constraints cause project schedule delays. One project manager, when interviewed, indicated that he experienced a major blow to a project when during the course of the project the team was notified that the software had already been purchased and they would be required to adjust the project around the new software.

H8: Technology-Related Risks will Generally Result in a High Impact on the Successful Completion of a Project for Virtual Information Systems Projects

As evidenced in the hypotheses above, technology presents challenges on projects. This hypothesis is from the second research study and focuses more on the degree of impact from the seven technology-related risks overall on the successful completion of projects in a virtual environment. The data for this analysis will be extracted solely from the second research study and will therefore refer only to virtual software development projects and not to traditional co-located projects. In general, technology-related risks are directly related to communication on virtual teams as indicated earlier. It is common knowledge that communication is important to organizations and hence to virtual teams. In fact, several researchers have listed technology as a key factor in virtual team effectiveness (Andres, 2006; Berry, 2011; Brandt, England, & Ward, 2011; Dube & Pare, 2001).

Brandt (2011) references communication among a few other factors that are important to project outcome; he indicates they have "key differences that may be critical for success for virtual teams" (Brandt, England, & Ward, 2011). Since face-to-face communication is not often available on virtual projects, technology is used to facilitate communication. Brandt (2011) acknowledged that communication methods used on co-located teams are "generally not effective" with virtual teams. Dube and Pare (2001), in their research on global virtual teams, also found technology to be one of the key issues. Specifically, they found issues with incompatibility of hardware/software, as well as, unreliability or unavailability. Some of these issues are particularly prevalent for global teams; i.e., connectivity in developing countries. Another issue was the appropriate use of technology, i.e., using the right technological tool for the task. Andres (2006) found that technology-mediated communication can have a significant impact on virtual team group effectiveness. These findings from the prior literature lead me to propose that technology is likely to be of high importance to project success, and I expect technology-related risk factors to be rated as "high impact" in the survey results.

Table 2. Project characteristics

Demographic	Categories	Research Study 1	Research Study 2
Project Environment	Virtual Projects	69%	100%
	Co-located Projects	31%	0%
Project Type	New Development	48%	39%
	Package Installation	17%	18%
	Software Upgrade	24%	25%
	Other	11%	18%
Project Cost	<$100K	22%	18%
	>$100K to $500K	30%	27%
	>$500K to $1M	10%	14%
	>$1M	33%	41%
Project Duration	0 to 6 months	19%	23%
	>6 months to 1 year	34%	35%
	1 to 2 years	27%	29%
	>2 years	20%	13%
Project Team Site Locations	1 to 2 locations	20%	11%
	3 to 5 locations	57%	49%
	> 5 locations	23%	40%

SURVEY POPULATION AND DEMOGRAPHICS

For the first research study, most survey participants were contacted through a list purchased from a major project management website and through solicitation of an international association, the Project Management Institute (PMI). Using multiple sources insured that the survey was not skewed by a particular project management philosophy. Participants were either invited to take the survey or were self-selected when they accessed the survey through a website link. A total of 154 IS/IT practitioners, i.e. project managers/leaders and systems analysts completed the survey. Participants were asked to base their answers on a recent virtual software project if possible. If virtual project experience was not an option, participants were asked to substitute a recent co-located project. This approach resulted in replies based on actual project experiences, as opposed to student team experiences. Furthermore, having participants base risk ratings on actual project experiences with a specific project, rather than on general opinion, leads to a more reliable result, in accordance with Flanagan's critical incident technique (Flanagan, 1954).

The second research study was also conducted through a survey questionnaire which was developed by modifying the original questionnaire. Modifications focused on improving the quality of the results by collecting more open-ended answers instead of multiple choice selections to aid in the subsequent statistical analysis. For example, when asked about the project manager's years of experience, the first survey offered multiple choice selections with groupings of years, while the second survey collected a numeric value. Additional questions were added to the second survey to explore certain areas in more detail. The participants for this survey were from the PMI Information Systems Community of Practice (ISCoP), the PMI website survey page, project managers from a Fortune 500 company, and some project management groups on LinkedIn.

Demographics from the original survey indicate a majority of the projects on which the participants based their responses were virtual projects (69%), although about a third of the projects were traditional co-located projects.

Table 3. Survey respondent background

Demographic	Categories	Research Study 1	Research Study 2
Participant's Role on Team	Project Manager/Leader	64%	69%
	Team Lead	17%	20%
	Team Member	6%	3%
	Other	12%	8%
Project Manager Experience	>10 years	31%	35%
	>5 to 10 years	29%	35%
	>2 to 5 years	18%	22%
	1 to 2 years	10%	9%
	Not the Project Manager	12%	

Table 4. Organization characteristics

Total Number of Employees in Organization	Large (>20K)	31%
	Medium (1K to 20K)	42%
	Small (<1K)	27%
Industry	IT Services	14%
	Finance/Banking	13%
	Manufacturing	13%
	Business Consulting	8%
	Insurance/Real Estate	8%

Table 2 contains information on other characteristics of the study projects. The types of projects varied, with the majority of the projects in both studies being New Development. Project costs and duration varied widely, as did the number of team members on the project. Approximately 61% in the first study and 64% in the second study of the projects were six months to two years in duration. Finally, the number of project team site locations is a validation of how distributed the project teams were. The overall majority, 80% in the first study and 89% in the second study, of the project teams had team members in more than three locations. This is consistent with the definition of a virtual or distributed team. Since project team members resided in different locations, face-to-face communication would have been difficult to achieve in all situations. Therefore, some form of ICTs was likely needed to run the project.

Demographics from the second research study have been included as a column in the demographic tables where possible. In some instances, the questions in the second research study were redesigned and the results were not comparable to the original study. In those cases, additional results were not included.

Table 3 provides background on the research participants' roles in their projects. Although most managed the project (64% and 69%), a small percentage were team members. For those who managed, the majority were knowledgeable, with more than five years of experience in both studies (60% and 70% respectively).

Organization characteristics, shown in Table 4, indicate a range of organization sizes, measured by the number of employees, as well as a broad spectrum of industries, with the largest three industries each representing just 14% or less of the total responses.

Table 5 shows demographics on various aspects of the project teams' experience. These percentages provide a profile of the level of overall experience with the application being

Table 5. Team member experience level

Demographic	Categories	Research Study 1	Research Study 2
Experience with the Business Application	>5 years	22%	43%
	>2to 5 years	34%	36%
	1 to 2 years	18%	11%
	<1 year	15%	8%
	No experience	11%	2%
Experience with the Development Technology	>5 years	18%	41%
	>2to 5 years	44%	47%
	1 to 2 years	22%	7%
	<1 year	9%	4%
	No experience	8%	1%
Experience with the Project Technology	>5 years	16%	26%
	>2to 5 years	41%	35%
	1 to 2 years	18%	11%
	<1 year	11%	14%
	No experience	14%	14%

developed or modified, the technology, i.e., programming languages, etc. used to develop the application for the project and the technologies, i.e., ICTs used to manage the project. The participant responses show that 56% in the first study and 79% in the second study had a good knowledge of the business application, with more than two years of experience. However, over half of the team members had more than two years of experience with both the tools to develop and those to manage the project in both studies, (62% and 88%) and (57% and 61%) respectively.

RESULTS AND DISCUSSION

Original Research Study

Hypothesis 1 through 7 report on results from the original research study only. Survey participants were asked to rate each of the risk factors on the degree of impact each risk had on the successful completion of their particular project. Success was defined as being completed within a reasonable percentage of the estimated time schedule, budget, and requested requirements. Each risk

factor was rated by using a three-point Likert scale. In the ratings a "1" indicated the risk factor had no impact on the project or simply did not occur during the course of the project. A "2" indicated the risk factor had a minor impact on the successful completion of the project. A "3" indicated the risk factor had a major impact on the successful completion of the project. Since the participants were from both virtual projects and traditional co-located projects, significant differences in effect between these two groups indicate areas where technology in virtual projects has a significantly different and more severe effect. The technology related risk factors and participant response percentages are listed in Table 6. They will be discussed sequentially.

H1: Technical Connectivity Issues are More Likely to Pose a Risk for Virtual Projects than for Traditional Co-Located Projects

This hypothesis is not supported. The results of the survey show no significant differences between the risk impact for this risk factor on a virtual project versus a traditional co-located project, as indicated by a very high p-value of

Table 6. Technology related risk factors

Risk Factors	Virtual Projects			Traditional Projects			
	No Impact or Did Not Occur	Minor Impact	Major Impact	No Impact or Did Not Occur	Minor Impact	Major Impact	p-value
Technical connectivity issues hinder communication	31.78	53.27	14.95	34.04	48.94	17.02	0.8783
Lack of appropriately skilled resources	41.12	39.25	19.63	55.32	29.79	14.89	0.2651
Resource inexperience with company and its processes	38.32	34.58	27.1	55.32	36.17	8.51	*0.0240
Inadequate technical resources, i.e., hardware, processing availability	47.66	40.19	12.15	72.34	21.28	6.38	*0.0179
Technology hardware new to the organization	57.94	28.04	14.02	63.83	29.79	6.38	0.3959
Technology software new to the organization	36.45	39.25	24.3	47.83	39.13	13.04	0.2239
Unidentified technical constraints	40.19	38.32	21.5	48.94	40.43	10.64	0.2544

0.8783 (well above 0.05). In fact, there were minimal differences in the response percentages from participants in virtual projects versus those working on traditional co-located projects in each of the three impact categories, as shown in Table 6. These results contradict the suggestion in our face-to-face interviews that connectivity is a more significant problem for virtual projects. It may be possible that virtual projects put extra effort into insuring effective communication links. It may also be true that, while technical connectivity may at one time have been a major problem, the increasing effectiveness of technical communications has limited the scope of the problem. These possibilities are supported by the fact that fewer than 15% of virtual project survey participants rated this factor as having a major impact. Nonetheless, this risk factor does have a negative impact on projects. Results show 68% of virtual projects and 66% of co-located projects had some level of negative impact from technical connectivity

issues. This may be a result of the increasing technical complexity of software and hardware, as well as the increasing diverse nature of the building blocks used to construct systems. In any case, it is a subject worthy of future study.

H2: A Lack of Appropriately Skilled Resources is a Greater Risk for a Virtual Project than a Traditional Co-Located Project

This hypothesis is not supported. Survey results for this risk factor showed no significant difference in impact between virtual and traditional projects. Perhaps this is because one advantage of a virtual project is the availability of a vast pool of skilled resources where location is not a barrier. An argument could be made that the risk of a lack of skilled resources in a virtual environment simply does not exist. Thus the ability for organizations implementing virtual projects to hire team members with needed

Figure 1. Major impact response percentages

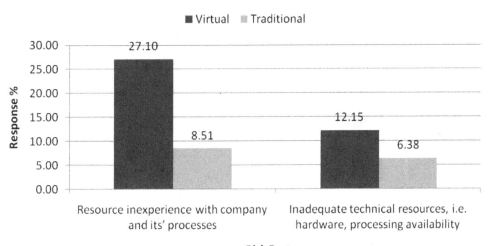

Major Impact

■ Virtual   ▓ Traditional

technical skills may weigh against the increased reliance on technical skills by such projects. If the skills in question are needed for technology tools necessary to collaborate, coordinate or communicate with virtual project team members, perhaps technically savvy team members can learn to use the tools on their own, thus mitigating the risk. This risk may also have been mitigated by the use of training, either formal or informal. Thus I posit that the project risk from a lack of appropriate skills is a function of three primary characteristics: the amount of reliance within the project on technical skills, the difficulty in staffing the project with people possessing appropriate skills, and the difficulty in learning those skills. While technical skills, particularly as they relate to communication, may be more important on a virtual project, the study suggests that this fact is likely offset by the fact that for virtual projects, either appropriate training is a higher priority or it is generally easier to hire team members with either exactly the skills needed or the ability to pick up new tools quickly and independently.

Although differences were not statistically significant between the two types of projects, a notable percentage of all participants found the lack of appropriately skilled resources to pose a project risk (59% of virtual projects, and 45% of traditional projects).

H3: Resource Inexperience with the Company and its Processes is a Greater Risk for a Virtual Project than a Traditional Co-Located Project

This hypothesis is supported. For this risk factor, the difference in the risk impact level between virtual and traditional co-located projects is significant, as indicated by a p-value of 0.024 (<0.05). Furthermore, a major impact is much more likely to occur in a virtual environment, 27.1%, versus only 8.1% in a traditional project environment (See Figures 1 and 2). Lack of knowledge of processes, such as how to promote code or set up a beta test or even get a logon ID for an application can halt or delay a project. This negative effect is demonstrably greater for

Figure 2. Minor impact response percentages

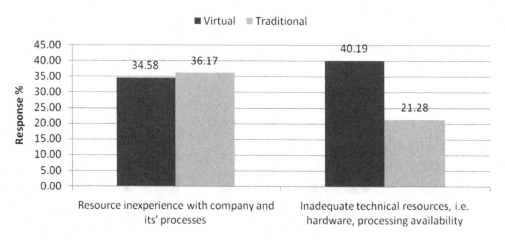

virtual projects. Virtual project managers need to be aware that resource inexperience with the organization and its processes is more likely to have a negative impact on their project.

H4: Inadequate Technical Resources, i.e. Hardware, Software, Processing Availability, etc. are a Greater Risk for a Virtual Project than a Traditional Co-Located Project

This hypothesis is supported. The availability of technical resources, either hardware or software or both, i.e., laptops, version management software, scheduling software, etc., showed a significant difference in impact between virtual and traditional co-located projects. Interestingly, there was little major impact in virtual or traditional projects. This type of problem tends to be seen as minor by study participants. However, that minor impact was significantly greater on virtual projects (p=0.018). Perhaps this is because the virtual team, with less resource experience with the company, takes longer to gain

access to the appropriate resources, as indicated by the prior risk factor. Or, it may be that virtual projects are more dependent on such resources and so their lack has a greater impact. In any case, project leaders and managers should be aware that insufficient technical resources are more likely to slow down a virtual project. To maximize project members' productivity, steps should be taken as part of a project's risk management program to insure that when technical resources are inadequate, the problem surfaces and is addressed quickly.

H5: Risks Involving Hardware New to the Organization are Greater for a Virtual Project than a Traditional Co-Located Project

This hypothesis is not supported. The survey results showed no significant difference in the impact of using new hardware between virtual and traditional projects. This is likely because the new hardware needed to support a virtual development environment is generally anticipated and provided, while new hardware needed in the final delivered project is the same regardless of whether the project team is virtual or not. For instance, if a new project involves installing a new set of scanners, the project environment is a moot point and the issues related to acquiring, installing and training for the scanners are the same regardless of the project environment. Although differences were not statistically significant between the two types of projects, a notable percentage of all participants found hardware new to the organization to pose a project risk (42% of virtual projects, and 36% of traditional projects). This traditional project risk factor applies to both types of projects.

H6: Risks Involving Software New to the Organization are Greater for a Virtual Project than a Traditional Co-Located Project

This hypothesis is not supported. As in the case of new hardware, the differences between virtual and traditional projects were not statistically significant. Also as in the case of hardware, a notable percentage of all participants found software new to the organization to pose a project risk (64% of virtual projects, and 53% of traditional projects). This traditional project risk factor is important for both types of projects.

H7: Risks Involving Unidentified Technical Constraints are Greater on For a Virtual Project than a Traditional Co-Located Project

This hypothesis is not supported. The survey results show there was no significant difference in the impact of this risk based on project environment. This is likely because the technologies used more heavily in a virtual environment to enhance communications are stable enough and user friendly enough that they pose no signifi-

cantly greater risk to these projects. Nonetheless, a notable percentage of all participants found unidentified technical constraints to pose a project risk (60% of virtual projects, and 51% of traditional projects). This traditional project risk factor is also important for virtual projects.

Research Study 2

In the second research study the same 55 risk factors were used and the question regarding degree of impact was the same; however, the Likert scale was changed to a seven-point scale instead of a three-point scale. Again, survey participants were asked to rate each of the risk factors on the degree of impact each risk had on the successful completion of their particular project. In the Likert scale ratings a "1" indicated "no impact", the mid-range at "4" was labeled as "moderate impact" while the highest scale of "7" was labeled "major impact". Although the other numbers in-between 1 and 7 were shown, they were not labeled.

H8: Technology-Related Risks will Generally Result in a High Impact on the Successful Completion of a Project for Virtual Information Systems/ Information Technology Projects

This hypothesis is not supported. To display the results, the Likert scales for the second research study were combined into four groups. The Likert scale of "1" remained alone and represented "no impact", scales of 2 and 3 were combined, scales of 3 and 4 were combined and scales of 6 and 7 representing "high impact" were combined. Table 7 shows the seven technology-related risk factors sorted by the percentage of participants rating the risk in the "high impact" range, i.e. selecting the Likert scale number of 6 or 7. Figure 3 is a graph of

Table 7. Technology-related risk factor percentages on virtual projects sorted by high impact level

Risk Factors	No Impact 1	2 & 3	4 & 5	High Impact 6 & 7
Technology software new to the organization	34.11	28.01	23.16	14.72
Unidentified technical constraints	27.34	36.15	23.02	13.49
Lack of appropriately skilled resources	27.29	34.83	24.60	13.29
Resource inexperience with company and its' processes	36.80	33.21	21.54	8.44
Technology hardware new to the organization	51.35	24.96	15.44	8.26
Inadequate technical resources, i.e. hardware, processing availability	37.70	34.83	19.57	7.90
Technical connectivity issues hinder communication	39.32	35.19	17.59	7.90

Figure 3. Graph of technology-related risk factor percentages on virtual projects

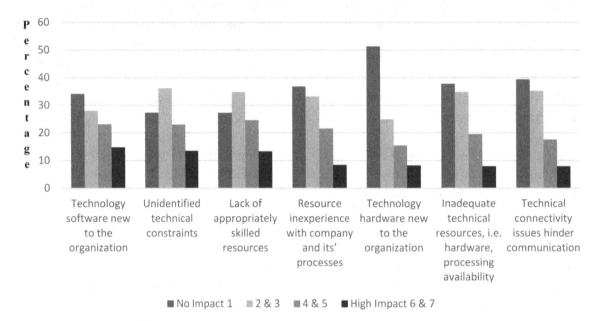

the percentages in Table 7. The results were interesting and unexpected.

The results of the second survey show for each of the seven technology-related risk factors the predominant impact levels were in the "minor impact" or "no impact" range. In other words, the percentage of participants selecting the "high impact" levels of 6 or 7 or the moderate impact levels of 4 or 5 were lower than the percentage of participants selecting the "minor impact" levels of 2 or 3 and most importantly

the "no impact" level of 1. The graph in Figure 3 clearly shows this and highlights the fact that the "no impact" level was selected by the highest percentage of respondents for five of the seven technology-related risk factors. Only the risk of unidentified technical constraints and lack of appropriately skilled resources had more of a minor impact than any other levels according to the respondents.

These results may have occurred overall because the majority of the respondents for the second research study reported the technical team members were experienced with the development and project technology as indicated in Table 5 in the demographics section. A high number of participants reported technical team members were experienced with the development technology (88% with more than two years of experience). Additionally, more than half of the participants indicated team members were experienced with the project technology (61% with more than two years of experience). It is expected that technology savvy team members would not see technology as so much of a threat if they are experienced since they may feel they have the skills and the knowledge to resolve many issues. Three of the risks are likely to be lessened by team members possessing technology expertise: (1) technology hardware new to the organization, (2) technology software new to the organization and (3) inadequate technical resources such as hardware and processing availability. Issues like software or hardware new to the organization may have less of an impact since experienced team members should be comfortable with training themselves or may have related technical expertise to help them overcome such obstacles. When faced with inadequate technical resources, team members with technology experience are more likely to develop alternatives.

The risk of technical connectivity issues hindering communication may have lessened over time as indicated earlier due to technological advances. Today, connectivity can be provided in a wide variety of methods and from many sources which results in alternatives when connectivity issues occur. The only exception is global teams in developing countries where connectivity can still be an issue. The results for the risk of resource inexperience with the company and its processes may have been minor overall because a large majority of the participants reported their team members were

experienced with the business application (79% with more than two years of experience). Expertise with the business application that is the focus of the project implies experience with the organization where the business application is used. Participants who have been around more than two years are very likely to be familiar with organizational processes or at a minimum know who to contact within the organization for assistance.

Finally, the two risks that were reported to have a predominately minor impact may have received that ranking because those types of issues are often beyond the control of the team members. For instance, when the risk from unidentified technical constraints surfaces there is generally little a project manager can do to change the constraints. However, if the project team consists of technically experienced members their expertise may make it more likely for them to design a technical solution. However, there are some constraints that have no easy solution such as software that won't run on the current hardware. These often require additional significant expenditures for items such as more hardware or procuring services from expert consultants. In the case of risk from the lack of appropriately skilled resources, team member technical expertise is unlikely to provide a solution. Instead, additional team members may need to be brought onto the project with the appropriate skill set. That solution is generally a problem when the skill set is difficult to find, is in short supply in the marketplace or is prohibitively expensive.

Overall, these results indicate the seven technology related risk factors in this study had a predominately "minor" or "no" impact on the successful completion of the project. This was unexpected but was understandable once the demographics on team member experience were reviewed. This leads us to propose in cases where a majority of team members have experience of more than two years with the application, the development technology and the project technology the risk of technology-related issues is lessened to a minor impact and many times to "no impact" on successful project outcomes. It is possible that technology alone is not the issue but instead technology-related risks when combined with other risk categories may create higher levels of impact. Nydegger and Nydegger (2010) in their research indicated how important it was not to use technology as the "scapegoat," but instead to determine the real culprit (Nydegger & Nydegger, 2010).

LIMITATIONS AND FUTURE WORK

This research was limited in scope to software development projects. Other types of IS/IT projects, such as network installation or hardware upgrades, might uncover different results. Similarly, including end users in the study along with IT project managers, experienced systems analysts, and IT project leaders may yield different results. Survey results also may have been influenced by self-reporting bias in areas such as the cost and duration of the project. Also, although we attempted with our survey technique to work against this, the self-selection method of obtaining survey participants may have caused some degree of bias. Finally, it is not known what type of technology was used by the survey participants. Future studies of technology-related risk might delve more deeply into the types of technologies being used, as well as whether they are part of the goal project itself, being used only for development, or being used primarily for communication during development. In addition, further research is needed into the two risks identified here as greater on virtual projects to determine specifically the types of technical connectivity and

inadequate technical resource issues that occur, as well as the context in which they are most likely to develop.

CONCLUSION

One clear implication of this research is the increasingly broad and varied nature of technology-related risk. Many of the risks previously identified by the literature, including the lack of appropriate skills, inexperience with the company and its processes, new software, and technical constraints, have all broadened in recent years to include the communication technology needed to support a virtual project's development environment. Beyond this, the contributions of the original research study fall into two broad categories. First, we identified from the literature and from our own interviews and focus group a set of seven technology-related project risk factors. Since all seven technology-related risks were found to have a negative impact on project success for both project types, they should be considered in risk management plans without regard to the virtual or traditional nature of the project. Second, two of the risk factors isolated and studied here were found to be a significantly greater threat to virtual project teams than to traditional co-located project teams: (1) Resource inexperience with the company and its processes; and (2) Inadequate technical resources, i.e., hardware, processing availability. Resource inexperience with the organization has the most dramatic difference in major impact between the two project types. However, both risk factors should be considered carefully, especially for organizations or individuals moving from traditional project management into virtual project management. Experienced IT project managers may approach managing virtual projects in the same way they manage traditional IT projects. This can be a lethal mistake simply because, as this research has demonstrated, there are cases where the impact of a particular risk can be much greater on a virtual project. Thus, I conclude that technology-related risks today are broader and more complex than previously demonstrated and that some of these risks pose an even greater hazard in virtual project environments.

In the second research study the contribution of the analysis of technology-related risks in virtual project environments was the realization that the impact of this type of risk is sometimes minor and often there is no impact. These results were unexpected and this is unlikely to occur in all instances as indicated by results from the original research study. However, over time and in specific situations technology-related risk factors were found here to have low levels of impact. In cases where a majority of team members have experience of more than two years with the application, the development technology and the project technology, the risk of technology-related issues seems to lessen. Further research is needed in this area to validate these results.

REFERENCES

Al-Rousan, T., Sulaiman, S., & Abdul Salam, R. (2009). Risk analysis and web project management. *Journal of Software*, *4*(6), 614–621. doi:10.4304/jsw.4.6.614-621

Andres, H. P. (2006). The impact of communication medium on virtual team group process. *Information Resources Management Journal*, *19*(2), 1–17. doi:10.4018/irmj.2006040101

Aspray, W., Mayadas, F., & Vardi, M. (2006). *Globalization and offshoring of software: A report of the ACM job migration task force. Association for Computing Machinery*. ACM.

Barkhi, R., Amiri, A., & James, T. L. (2006). A study of communication and coordination in collaborative software development. *Journal of Global Information Technology Management*, *9*(1), 44–61.

Barki, H., Rivard, S., & Talbot, J. (1993). Towards an assessment of software development risk. *Journal of Management Information Systems*, *10*(2), 203–225.

Berry, G. R. (2011). Enahnacing effectivness on virtual teams: Understanding why traditional team skills are insufficient. *Journal of Business Communication*, *48*(2), 186–206. doi:10.1177/0021943610397270

Boehm, B. (1991). Software risk management: Principles and practices. *IEEE Software*, *8*(1), 32–41. doi:10.1109/52.62930

Brandt, V., England, W., & Ward, S. (2011). Virtual teams. *Research Technology Management*, *54*(6), 62–63.

Cummings, J. N., & Kiesler, S. (2008). *Who collaborates successfully? Prior experience reduces collaboration barriers in distributed interdisciplinary research*. San Diego, CA: ACM. doi:10.1145/1460563.1460633

Cusumano, M. A. (2008). Managing software development in globally distributed teams. *Communications of the ACM*, *51*(2), 15–17. doi:10.1145/1314215.1314218

Dube, L., & Pare, G. (2001). Global virtual teams. *Communications of the ACM*, *44*(12), 71–73. doi:10.1145/501317.501349

Flanagan, J. C. (1954). The critical incident technique. *Psychological Bulletin*, *51*(4), 327–358. doi:10.1037/h0061470 PMID:13177800

Gefen, D., Wyss, S., & Lichtenstein, Y. (2008). Business familiarity as risk mitigation in software development outsoucing contracts. *Management Information Systems Quarterly*, *32*(3), 531–551.

Hamblen, M. (2009, October 14). *Collaboration tools worth the investment, survey says*. Retrieved January 11, 2010, from www.infoworld.com/d/mobilize/collaboration-tools-worth-the-investment-survey-says-000

Jiang, J., Klein, G., Beck, P., & Wang, E. T. (2007). Lack of skill risks to organizational technology learning and software project performance. *Information Resources Management Journal*, *20*(3), 32–45. doi:10.4018/irmj.2007070103

Jiang, J., Klein, G., & Wang, E. T. (2007). Relationship of skill expectation gap between IS employees and their managers with user satisfaction. *Information Resources Management Journal*, *20*(3), 63–75. doi:10.4018/irmj.2007070105

Jones, R., Oyung, R., & Pace, L. (2005). *Working virtually: Challenges of virtual teams*. Hershey, PA: Idea Group Inc. doi:10.4018/978-1-59140-585-6

Keil, M., Cule, P. E., Lyytinen, K., & Schmidt, R. C. (1998). A framework for identifying software project risks. *Communications of the ACM*, *41*(11), 76–83. doi:10.1145/287831.287843

Kirkman, B., & Mathieu, J. (2005). The dimensions and antecedents of virtuality. *Journal of Management, 31*(5), 700–718. doi:10.1177/0149206305279113

Kroenke, D. M. (2010). *Experiencing MIS* (2nd ed.). Upper Saddle River, NJ: Pearson Education, Inc.

Lipnack, J., & Stamps, J. (1997). *Virtual teams: Reaching across space, time, and organizations with technology*. Hoboken, NJ: John Wiley & Sons, Inc.

Lyytinen, K., Mathiassen, L., & Ropponen, J. (1996). A framework for software risk management. *Journal of Information Technology, 11*, 275–285. doi:10.1057/jit.1996.2

Majchrzak, A., Malhotra, A., Stamps, J., & Lipnack, J. (2004). Can absence make a team grow stronger? *Harvard Business Review, 82*(5), 131–137. PMID:15146742

Malhotra, A., & Majchrzak, A. (2005, Winter). Virtual workspace technologies. *MIT Sloan Management Review*, 11-14.

Merriam-Webster. (n.d.). *Merriam-Webster online dictionary*. Retrieved January 15, 2010, from http://www.merriam-webster.com/dictionary/email

Mohan, B. K. (2006, November). Globalization and offshoring of software: A report of the ACM job migration task force. *ACM,* 2-2.

Nydegger, R., & Nydegger, L. (2010). Challenges in managing virtual teams. *Journal of Business & Economics Research, 8*(3), 69–82.

Oshri, I., Kotlarshy, J., & Willcocks, L. (2008). Missing links: Building critical social ties for global collaborative teamwork. *Communications of the ACM, 51*(4), 76–81. doi:10.1145/1330311.1330327

PMI. (2013). *A guide to the project management body of knowledge (PMBOK guide)* (5th ed.). Newtown Square, PA: Project Management Institute.

Robb, D. (2002). Collaboration gets it together. *Computerworld, 36*(50), 29–30.

Wallace, L. (1999). *The development of an instrument to measure software project risk*. Atlanta, GA: Georgia State University College of Business Administration.

Walther, J. B., Bunz, U., & Bazarova, N. (2005). The rules of virtual groups. In *Proceedings of the 38th Hawaii International Conference on System Sciences*. IEEE.

Chapter 10
A Likelihood Ratio–Based Forensic Text Comparison in SMS Messages:
A Fused System with Lexical Features and N-Grams

Shunichi Ishihara
The Australian National University, Australia

ABSTRACT

This chapter is built on two studies: Ishihara (2011) "A Forensic Authorship Classification in SMS Messages: A Likelihood Ratio-Based Approach Using N-Grams" and Ishihara (2012) "A Forensic Text Comparison in SMS Messages: A Likelihood Ratio Approach with Lexical Features." They are two of the first Likelihood Ratio (LR)-based forensic text comparison studies in forensic authorship analysis. The author attribution was modelled using N-grams in the former, whereas it was modelled using so-called lexical features in the latter. In the current study, the LRs obtained from these separate experiments are fused using a logistic regression fusion technique, and the author reports how much improvement in performance the fusion brings to the LR-based forensic text comparison system. The performance of the fused system is assessed based on the magnitude of the fused LRs using the log-likelihood-ratio cost (C_{llr}). The strength of the fused LRs is graphically presented in Tippett plots and compared with those of the original LRs. The chapter demonstrates that the fused system outperforms the original systems.

DOI: 10.4018/978-1-4666-4856-2.ch010

1. PREAMBLE

This research is an extended study from two of the first likelihood ratio (LR) based forensic authorship analysis studies (Ishihara 2011, 2012). In Ishihara (2011), each author's attribution was modelled based on the sequence of word occurrence by means of the N-grams whereas in Ishihara (2012), it was represented in terms of word- and character-based lexical features. The LRs were also calculated differently in these studies: Doddington's (2001) formula in the former and Aitken and Lucy's multivariate LR formulae (Aitken and Lucy 2004) in the latter.

One of the advantages of the LR approach is that the LRs derived from different evidence types (e.g. voice and fingerprint) or features (e.g. syntactic features and morphology-based features) can be combined to produce overall LRs. This is significantly important as most cases involve many different types of evidence. It is straightforward to combine multiple LRs from different evidence types or features by applying Bayes' Theorem, providing they are NOT correlated. If they are correlated, the technique called fusion needs to be employed (refer to §6 for the details of fusion).

In the current study, we fuse the LRs obtained from Ishihara (2011) and those from Ishihara (2012) in order to see how the system performance will improve or deteriorate by the fusion. We fuse (not combine by means of Bayes' Theorem) the two sets of the LRs because the features which were used to calculate these LRs can be judged that they are correlated to a certain degree.

2. GENERAL INTRODUCTION

Due to a continuous increase in the use of mobile phones, the short message service (SMS) is more and more becoming a common medium of communication. Unfortunately, its convenience, low cost and high visual anonymity can be exploited, with SMS messages sometimes used in, for example, communication between drug dealers and buyers, or illicit acts such as, extortion, fraud, scams, hoaxes, false reports of terrorist threats, and many more. SMS messages have been reportedly used as evidence in some legal cases (Cellular-news 2006, Grant 2007, 2010), and it is not difficult to predict that the use of SMS messages as evidence will increase.

That being said, there is a large amount of research on forensic authorship analysis in other electronically-generated texts, such as emails (De Vel et al. 2001, Iqbal et al. 2008), whereas forensic authorship analysis studies specifically focusing on SMS messages are conspicuously sparse (Grant 2010, Mohan et al. 2010).

The forensic sciences are experiencing a paradigm shift in the evaluation and presentation of evidence (Saks and Koehler 2005). This paradigm shift has already happened in forensic DNA comparison. Saks and Koehler (2005) fervently suggest that other forensic comparison sciences should follow forensic DNA comparison, which adopts the LR framework for the evaluation of evidence. The use of the LR framework has been advocated in the main textbooks on the evaluation of forensic evidence (e.g. Robertson and Vignaux 1995) and by forensic statisticians (e.g. Aitken and Stoney 1991, Aitken and Taroni 2004). (e.g. Aitken and Stoney 1991, Aitken and Taroni 2004). However, despite the fact that the LR framework has started making inroads in other fields of forensic comparison sciences, such as forensic voice comparison (Morrison 2009) – which is perhaps the closest to our field – we are somewhat behind in this trend in forensic authorship analysis.

Like the previous studies that the current study is based on, the validity of the fused system is assessed using the log-likelihood-ratio-cost function (C_{llr}) which was originally developed for use in automatic speaker recognition systems (Brümmer and du Preez 2006), and subsequently adopted in forensic voice comparison (Morrison 2011). The strength of LRs (= strength of evidence) obtained in this study is graphically presented using Tippett plots, and compared with those of the original LRs.

3. FORENSIC AUTHORSHIP ANALYSIS

3.1. Profiling, Identification and Verification

Forensic authorship analysis can be broadly classified into the subfields of *authorship profiling*, *authorship identification* and *authorship verification*. In order to clarify where a series of LR-based studies stand, commonly-held descriptions of the tasks of these subfields are concisely given below:

- *Authorship profiling* summarises socio-linguistic characteristics, such as gender, age, occupation, educational and cultural background, of the unknown author (offender) of the (illicit) document in question (Stamatatos 2009).
- The task of (forensic) *authorship identification* is to identify the most likely author (suspect) of a given (incriminating) document from a group of candidate authors (suspects) (Iqbal et al. 2013).
- The task of (forensic) *authorship verification* is to determine or verify if a target author (suspect) did or did not write a specific (incriminating) document (Halteren 2007).

Using the conventional terminology, the current study is related to forensic authorship *verification*. When a suspect is prosecuted, a forensic expert can perform authorship verification for it "to be determined if a suspect did or did not write a specific, probably incriminating, text" (Halteren 2007).

3.2. Role of Forensic Expert

Commonly-held views about forensic authorship analysis have been summarised above. However, it is important to explicitly state here that the forensic scientist as a witness is NOT in a position, either legally or logically, to identify, confirm, decide or even verify if two samples (one associated with the offender and the other with a suspect) are from the same person or different people (Robertson and Vignaux 1995). This is the task of the trier of fact, who can be the judge, the panel of judges, or the jury, depending on the legal system of a country. That is, the ultimate decision as to, for example, whether the author of a document in question is a suspect or not, does not lie with the forensic expert, but with the court. When a forensic scientist presents evidence, it is important that he/she should not violate the province of the trier of fact, and he/she should not even be asked his/her opinion on the likelihood that, for example, it is the suspect who wrote the text in question (Doheny 1996).

So, what is the role of the forensic scientist? Aitken and Stoney (1991), Aitken and Taroni (2004) and Robertson and Vignaux (1995) state that the role of forensic scientist is to estimate the strength of evidence. That is to say,

... the task of forensic scientist is to provide the court with a strength-of-evidence statement in answer to the question: How much more likely are the observed differences/similarities between the known and questioned samples to

arise under the hypothesis that they have the same origin than under the hypothesis that they have different origins? (Morrison 2009).

The strength of evidence which is the main concern of forensic scientists is technically termed as likelihood ratio (LR).

4. LIKELIHOOD-RATIO APPROACH

It has been stressed above that the task of the forensic expert is to provide the court with a strength-of-evidence statement by estimating the LR (Aitken 1995, Aitken and Stoney 1991, Aitken and Taroni 2004, Robertson and Vignaux 1995). What, then, is the LR?

4.1. Likelihood Ratio

The LR is the probability that the evidence would occur if an assertion is true, relative to the probability that the evidence would occur if the assertion is not true (Robertson and Vignaux 1995). Thus, the LR can be expressed in (1).

$$LR = \frac{p(E|H_p)}{p(E|H_d)} \quad (1)$$

For forensic authorship analysis, it will be the probability of observing the difference (referred to as the evidence, E) between the group of texts written by the offender and that written by the suspect if they have come from the same author (H_p) (i.e. if the prosecution hypothesis is true) relative to the probability of observing the same evidence (E) if they have been produced by different authors (H_d) (i.e. if the defence hypothesis is true). The relative strength of the given evidence with respect to the competing hypotheses (H_p vs. H_d) is reflected in the magnitude of the LR. The more the LR deviates from unity (LR = 1; logLR = 0), the greater support for either the prosecution hypothesis (LR > 1; logLR > 0) or the defence hypothesis (LR < 1; logLR < 0). The LR is a component of Bayes' Theorem. In terms of this theorem, the task of the trier of fact is the delivery of posterior odds. Please note that $\log_{10}LR$ is used in this study in which case the neutral point is $\log_{10}LR = 0$.

Table 1. Verbal equivalents of LRs and Log$_{10}$ LRs (Champod and Evett 2000)

LR	Log$_{10}$ LR	Possible Verbal Equivalent	
>10000	>4	Very strong ...	
1000 to 10,000	3 to 4	Strong ...	Support for the prosecution hypothesis
100 to 1000	2 to 3	Moderately strong ...	
10 to 100	1 to 2	Moderate ...	
1 to 10	0 to 1	Limited ...	
1 to 0.1	0 to -1	Limited ...	
0.1 to 0.01	-1 to -2	Moderate ...	Support for the defence hypothesis
0.01 to 0.001	-2 to -3	Moderately strong...	
0.001 to 0.0001	-3 to -4	Strong ...	
<0.0001	<-4	Very strong ...	

4.2. Verbal Equivalents of Likelihood Ratios

An LR is a continuous value to quantify the strength of evidence. The numerical form of an LR is not readily interpretable. Thus, in order to aid the court to interpret LR values, some verbal interpretations of the ranges of LR values have been proposed. The one proposed by Champod and Evett (2000) is given in Table 1.

For example, although the LR of 1000 and that of 5 both support the prosecution hypothesis, the former provides "moderately strong" support for the hypothesis whereas the latter provides only "limited support". Unless one obtains the LR of 0, any LR value supports either hypothesis. However, Table 1 indicates that the evidence of which LR value falls in the range between LR = 0.1 and LR = 10 (or $Log_{10}LR = -1$ and $Log_{10}LR = 1$) is not of much use as evidence (although some people argue that there isn't such a thing as useless evidence). In this study, whenever appropriate, we verbally express the strength of evidence based on Table 1.

5. RELATED STUDIES

In this section, the experimental settings of Ishihara (2011, 2012) will be explained in detail. The main differences between these two experiments are the type of features and the formulae used to calculate LRs. These differences are explained in §5.4 and §5.5.

5.1. Scenario

The scenario that Ishihara (2011, 2012) simulated is as follows: the police authority obtained a set of incriminating messages written by an offender while another set of messages were obtained from a suspect. The relevant parties would like to know whether these two sets of messages were actually written by the same author or different authors. Needless to say, the task of the forensic expert is to provide the court with a strength-of-evidence statement (in other words, LR) so as to assist the trier of fact to make a decision as to whether the suspect is guilty or not.

5.2. Database

The SMS corpus compiled by the National University of Singapore (the NUS SMS corpus)[1] was used in Ishihara (2011, 2012). A new version of the NUS SMS corpus has been released almost monthly, and we used *version 2011.05.11* which contains 38193 messages from 228 authors. 69% of the total messages were written by native speakers of English; 30% by non-native; 1% unknown. Male authors account for 71%; female for 16%; unknown for 13%. The average length of a message is 13.8 words (sd = 13.5; max = 231; min = 1).

5.3. Selection of Messages

Two message types of author pairs – same-author pairs and different-author pairs – are necessary to assess a forensic text comparison system. The same author pairs are used for so-called *Same Author Comparison* (SA comparison) where two groups of messages produced by the same author are expected to receive the desired LR value given the same-origin, whereas the different author pairs are for *mutatis mutandis*, *Different Author Comparison* (DA comparison). Thus, we need two groups of messages from each of the authors.

Ishihara (2011, 2012) also investigated how the performance of the system and the strength of evidence (= LR) are influenced by the sample

Table 2. Dataset (DS) configuration: sample size (N) = the number of words included in each message group; auths. = the number of authors appearing in the DS; SA = number of SA comparisons; DA = number of DA comparisons.

DS+N	auths.	SA	DA
DS200	85	85	14280
DS1000	43	43	3612
DS2000	34	34	2244
DS3000	24	24	1104

size, i.e. the number of message words used for modelling. It can be safely predicted that the more messages we use, the better the performance will be. However, each SMS message is essentially short, and it is forensically unrealistic to conduct experiments using thousands of messages to model an author's attribute. Thus, as shown in Table 2, we created 4 different datasets (DS) in which the number of words appearing in each message group is different (N = 200, 1000, 2000 and 3000 words). For DS200, each message group contains a total of approximately 200 words. Since we cannot perfectly control the number of words appearing in one message, it needs to be *approximately* 200 words.

In order to compile a message group of about 200 words, we added messages one by one from the chronologically sorted messages to the group until the word number reached more than 200 words. As explained earlier, we need two groups of messages from the same author. For one message group, we started from the top of the chronologically sorted messages while for the other of the same author from the bottom so that the two groups of messages from the same author are non-contemporaneous.

The process of message selection and the compilation of datasets are illustrated in Figure 1.

5.4. N-grams: Ishihara (2011)

In Ishihara (2011), each author's attribution was modelled based on the sequence of word occurrence by means of the N-grams. As a pre-process before building N-grams, the SMS messages were tokenised using the *SimpleTokenizer* function of the *opennlp-tools* (version 1.5.05)[2] without any stemming algorithms. The *SimpleTokenizer* provides simple tokenisation based on space and punctuations. In some cases, it is difficult to automatically locate a sentence boundary in SMS messages as the use of upper/lower cases, punctuation, space, etc. do not always conform to the standard orthographic rules. Therefore, the words appearing in the same message were treated as a sequence of words, without parsing them into sentences in this study.

For building N-grams, we used the *ngram-count* and *ngram* functions of the *Speech Technology and Research Laboratory Language Modelling Toolkit (SRLM)[3]* in this study. The *ngram-count* function is used to build an N-gram language model for a group of messages (model group). The resultant N-gram language model should represent the characteristics of this particular group of messages. The *ngram* function is used to calculate log probabilities between the N-gram language model of a given group of messages (model group) and another

Figure 1. A schematic illustration of the selection of messages and the compilation of datasets (DS). x = the number of messages belong to an author (x can be different depending on authors). Messages are all chronologically sorted for each author.

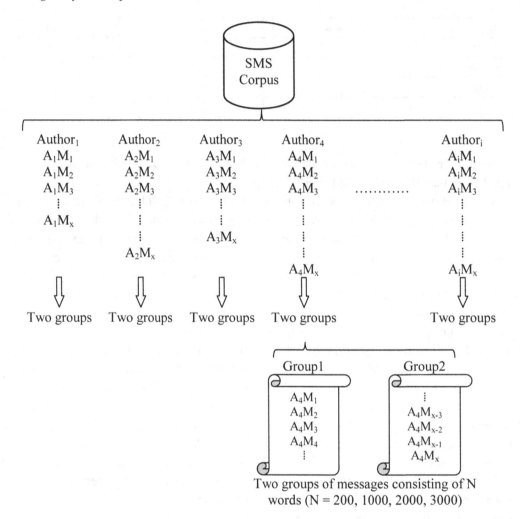

Two groups of messages consisting of N
words (N = 200, 1000, 2000, 3000)

given group of messages (test group). The log probabilities calculated by the *ngram* function show the degree of similarities/differences between the former group of messages which were modelled in the form of the N-grams (model group) and the latter group of messages (test group). The *backoff* technique was used for the calculation of log probabilities (Jurafsky and Martin 2000).

An open-vocabulary N-gram language model (N = 1, 2, 3) was built for each group of messages. The minimal count of N–grams was set as > 9, which is the default setting of the SRLM toolkit. Thus, all N–grams with frequency of < 9 were discounted to 0. The default *Good-Turing* discounting was used for smoothing.

Table 3. List of features

Feature type		Features
vocabulary richness	1.	Yule's K
	2.	Type-token ratio (TTR)
	3.	Honoré's R
lexical: word-based	4.	Average word number per message
	5.	SD of word number
lexical: character based	6.	Average character number per message
	7.	SD of character number
	8.	Upper case ratio
	9.	Digits ratio
	10.	Average character number in a word
	11.	Punctuation character ratio (, . ? ! ;: ' ")
	12.	Special character ratio (< > % ! [ ] { } \ / @ # ~ + - * $ ^ & =)

5.4.1. Likelihood Ratio Calculation: Ishihara (2011)

In Ishihara (2011), a conventional LR was estimated using the formula given in 4) (Doddington 2001).

$$LR_{i.j} = \frac{\log_{10} \dfrac{\Lambda^i_{author}(j)}{\Lambda_{background}(j)}}{N_j} \quad (2)$$

Thus, the $LR_{i,j}$ of the test message group (j) against the model message group (i) is defined to be the log ratio of the similarity between the test message group (j) and the author model (Λ^i_{Author}) of the model message group (i) to the typicality of the test message against the background author model $(\Lambda_{background})$, normalised by the number of words appearing in the test message group (N_j). The background author model was built in the cross-validated manner, using all messages appearing in the NUS SMS corpus, except those in comparison. The configurations of the N-grams for the background author model are the same as those used for the model message group.

5.5. Lexical Features: Ishihara (2012)

Following the results of previous authorship studies (De Vel, et al. 2001, Iqbal et al. 2010, Zheng et al. 2006), and given the general characteristics of SMS messages (Tagg 2009), the features listed in Table 3 are used in Ishihara (2012).

All features listed in Table 3 are, in a broad sense, lexical features. They can be further sub-classified into the features of *vocabulary richness*, *word-based lexical* and *character-based lexical features*. All feature values are normalised. Features related to sentences and paragraphs are not used in this study as in many cases it is difficult to automatically locate a sentence or a paragraph boundary in SMS messages since the use of upper/lower cases, punctuation, space, etc. does not always conform to standard orthographical rules.

Different combinations of features listed in Table 3 are tested to see what combination yields the best results. However, since testing all possible permutations of these features with various dimensions of a feature vector is time-consuming, we systematically selected only some possible combinations. First of all, we tried all possible combinations of two features $[f_1, f_2]$, and selected the five best performing bi-features. Using these five best performing bi-features as bases, we tested the performance of the tri-features $[f_1, f_2, f_3]$ by adding one of the remaining features one by one to these bases. We repeated this process for feature vectors of higher dimensions.

5.5.1. Likelihood Ratio Calculation: Ishihara (2012)

As briefly introduced in §1, It is straightforward to combine multiple LRs from different evidence types or features by applying Bayes' Theorem, providing they are not correlated. This is a significant feature of the LR approach as most cases involve many different types of evidence. However, it is obvious that the features listed in Table 3 are correlated in one way or another, thus a simple combination is inappropriate. Aitken and Lucy (2004) addressed the problem of estimating LRs from correlated variables by deriving the multivariate kernel density LR (MVLR) formulae. Following the initial application of the formulae to the data from glass fragments, it has been successfully applied to forensic voice comparison, in particular with acoustic-phonetic features. Please refer to Aitken and Lucy (2004) for the exposition of the MVLR formulae.

Numerator of MVLR (H_p = true),

$$p\left(\overline{y}_1, \overline{y}_2 | U, C, h\right) = \tag{3}$$

$$\left(2\pi\right)^{-p}\left|D_1\right|^{-1/2}\left|D_2\right|^{-1/2}\left|C\right|^{-1/2}\left(mh^p\right)^{-1}\left|D_1^{-1} + D_2^{-1} + \left(h^2C\right)^{-1}\right|^{-1/2}$$

$$\times \exp\left\{-\frac{1}{2}\left(\overline{y}_1 - \overline{y}_2\right)^T\left(D_1 + D_2\right)^{-1}\left(\overline{y}_1 - \overline{y}_2\right)\right\}$$

$$\times\sum_{i=1}^{m}\exp[-\frac{1}{2}\left(y^* - \overline{x}_i\right)^T\left\{\left(D_1^{-1} + D_2^{-1}\right)^{-1} + \left(h^2C\right)\right\}^{-1}\left(y^* - \overline{x}_i\right)]$$

Denominator of MVLR (H_d = true), $p\left(\overline{y}_1, \overline{y}_2 | U, C, h\right) =$ (4)

$$\left(2\pi\right)^{-p}\left|C\right|^{-1}\left(mh^p\right)^{-2} \times \prod_{l=1}^{2}\left[\left|D_l\right|^{-1/2}\left|D_l^{-1} + \left(h^2C\right)^{-1}\right|^{-1/2}\right.$$

$$\times\sum_{i=1}^{m}\exp\left\{-\frac{1}{2}\left(\overline{y}_l - \overline{x}_i\right)^T\left(D_l + h^2C\right)^{-1}\left(\overline{y}_l - \overline{x}_i\right)\right\}]$$

where m = number of groups (e.g. authors) in the background data;

p = number of assumed correlated variables measured on each object (e.g. message);

n_i = number of objects in each group in the background data;

x_{ij} = measurements constituting the background data = $(x_{ij1}, \ldots, x_{ijp})^T$, i = 1,...,m, j = 1,...,n_i;

$\overline{x}_i$ = within-object means of the background data

$$= \frac{1}{n_i}\sum_{j=1}^{n_i}x_{ij};$$

y_{lj} = measurements constituting offender (l = 1) and suspect (l = 2) data = $(y_{lj1}, \ldots, y_{ljp})^T$, l = 1,2, j = 1,...,$n_l$;

$\overline{y}_l$ = offender (l = 1) and suspect (l = 2) means

$$= \frac{1}{n_l}\sum_{j=1}^{n_l}y_{lj}, l = 1,2.$$

U, C = within-group and between-group variance/covariance matrices;

D_l = offender (l = 1) and suspect (l = 2) variance/covariance matrices = $n_l^{-1}U$, l = 1,2;

h = optimal kernel smoothing parameter = $\left(4/\left(2p + 1\right)\right)^{1/(p+4)}m^{-1/(p+4)}$;

$y^* = \left(D_1^{-1} + D_2^{-1}\right)^{-1}\left(D_1^{-1}\overline{y}_1 + D_2^{-1}\overline{y}_2\right).$

This MVLR formula evaluates the similarity and typicality of the two groups of messages in comparison and allows us to estimate LRs. In the case of Ishihara (2012), it estimates "the probability of observing the difference between the given two groups of messages in comparison when both are coming from the same individual" divided by "the probability of observing the same when they are coming from two separate individuals". Its numerator and denominator are given at (3) and (4) respectively in the formula presented above. This formula also allows us to handle multiple variables (like those given in Table 3) and estimate a single LR from them, discounting the correlation among them. This is an important feature, since many features can be extracted from single evidence, and they naturally have some correlations among them. The features used in Ishihara (2012) are no exception.

5.6. Calibration

A logistic-regression calibration was applied to the derived LRs in Ishihara (2011, 2012) (Brümmer and du Preez 2006). Given two sets of LRs derived from the SA and DA comparison pairs and a decision boundary, calibration is a normalisation procedure involving linear monotonic shifting and scaling of the LRs relative to the decision boundary so as to minimise a cost function.

5.7. Evaluation of Performance

Morrison (2011) argues that classification-accuracy/classification-error rates, such as equal error rate, precision and recall, are inappropriate for use within the LR framework because they implicitly refer to posterior probabilities – which is the province of the trier of fact – rather than LRs – which is the province of forensic scientists – and "they are based on a categorical threshholding, error versus non-error, rather than a gradient strength of evidence … An ap-

propriate metric … is the log-likelihood-ratio cost (C_{llr})", which is a gradient metric based on LRs. See (5) for calculating C_{llr} (Brümmer and du Preez 2006). In (5), N_{Hp} and N_{Hd} are the numbers of SA and of DA comparisons, and LR_i and LR_j are the LRs derived from the SA and DA comparisons, respectively. If the system is producing good quality LRs, all the SA comparisons should produce LRs greater than 1, and the DA comparisons should produce LRs less than 1. In this approach, LRs which support counter-factual hypotheses are given a penalty. The size of this penalty is determined according to how significantly the LRs deviate from the neutral point. That is, an LR supporting a counter-factual hypothesis with greater strength will be penalised more heavily than the ones which have the strength close to the unity, because it is more misleading. The lower the C_{llr} value is, the better the performance.

$$C_{llr} = \frac{1}{2} \left(\frac{1}{N_{H_p}} \sum_{i \text{ for } H_p = true}^{N_{H_p}} \log_2 \left(1 + \frac{1}{LR_i}\right) + \frac{1}{N_{H_d}} \sum_{j \text{ for } H_d = true}^{N_{H_d}} \log_2 \left(1 + LR_j\right) \right) \quad (5)$$

C_{llr} can be split into a discrimination loss (C_{llr_min}) – which is the value achievable after the application of a calibration procedure (see §5.5.1) – and a calibration loss (C_{llr_cal}) ($C_{llr} = C_{llr\_min} + C_{llr\_cal}$). Thus, the C_{llr} can provide an overall evaluation of a system while the C_{llr_min} and C_{llr_cal} can specifically show how the discrimination loss and the calibration loss contributed to the overall performance of the system. The FoCal toolkit[4] is used to calculate C_{llr} in this study. Since C_{llr_min} is the theoretically best C_{llr} value of an optimally calibrated system, the performance of the system was assessed based on the C_{llr_min} values.

Table 4. A comparison in performance between the system with N-grams, the system with lexical features, and the fused system

DS+N	N-grams			Lexical Features				Fusion		
	C_{llr}	C_{llr_min}	C_{llr_cal}	features	C_{llr}	C_{llr_min}	C_{llr_cal}	C_{llr}	C_{llr_min}	C_{llr_cal}
DS200	1.29	**0.96**	0.33	1,2,10,11	0.94	**0.85**	0.08	0.88	**0.83**	0.04
DS1000	0.99	**0.84**	0.14	2,8,10,11	0.72	**0.61**	0.10	0.70	**0.57**	0.13
DS2000	0.87	**0.72**	0.14	2,10,11,12	1.36	**0.54**	0.81	0.59	**0.45**	0.13
DS3000	0.80	**0.62**	0.17	1,2,4,8,11	1.29	**0.46**	0.83	0.50	**0.33**	0.16

DS = Dataset; sample size (N) = the number of words included in each message group; features = best performing feature sets

C_{llr} provides a scale value which shows the overall performance of a system. A Tippett plot is a graphical presentation which provides more detailed information about the derived LRs. A more detailed explanation of Tippett plots is given in §7 where Tippett plots are presented.

6. LOGISTIC REGRESSION FUSION

Aitken and Lucy's multivariate LR formulae (Aitken and Lucy 2004) generate a single LR from multiple features, taking their correlations into consideration. However, if you would like to obtain an overall LR from the LRs derived from different evidence types or features which are correlated, a fusion technique needs to be employed. Although there are some different fusion techniques available, we used the logistic regression fusion (6) in this study as it is a robust technique and its validity is tested in many LR based forensic comparison systems (Morrison 2013). Logistic-regression fusion enables us to combine parallel sets of LRs from different forensic comparison systems, with the output being calibrated LRs.

$$\log(\text{fused LR}) = \alpha + \beta_1 s_1 + \beta_2 s_2 + \dots + \beta_n s_n \tag{6}$$

where s_1, s_2, ..., s_n are the LRs from the first to the nth systems, and β_1, β_2, ... β_n are the logistic regression coefficient weights (Morrison 2013:16-17). In the current study, these weights were intrinsically calculated. For fusion, as well, we used FoCal Toolkit[4] which performs fusion and calibration simultaneously (Brümmer and du Preez 2006).

7. FUSED RESULTS AND DISCUSSIONS

The results of the three systems in comparison are given in Table 4. Since C_{llr_min} is the theoretically best C_{llr} value of an optimally calibrated system, the performance of the system is assessed based on the C_{llr_min} values.

The results given in Table 4 show that the fused system achieved the best result in all datasets (DS). This can be seen in Table 4 that all C_{llr_min} values of the fused system are smaller than those of the other systems. The improvement in performance is greater as the sample size of the DS increases. For example, in terms of the C_{llr_min} values, the fused system (C_{llr_min} = 0.83) improved by 0.02 from the system with lexical features (C_{llr_min} = 0.85) for DS200 whereas the fused system (C_{llr_min} = 0.62) improved by 0.13 from the system with lexical features (C_{llr_min} = 0.46) for DS3000.

Figure 2. Tippett plots showing the LRs of the three different systems

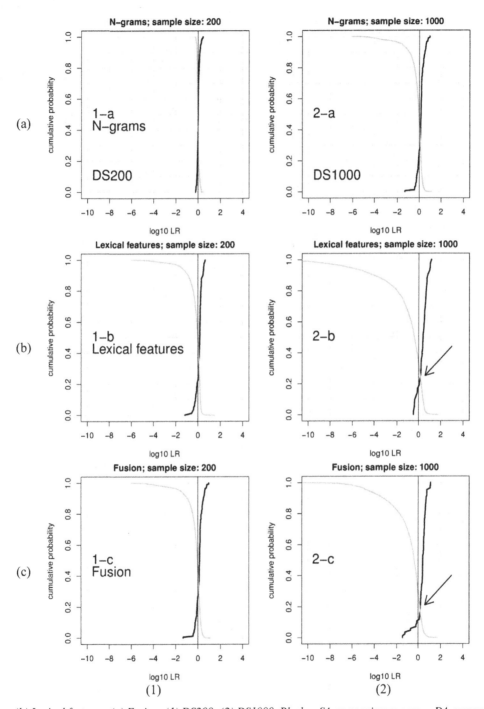

(a) N-gram; (b) Lexical features; (c) Fusion; (1) DS200; (2) DS1000. Black = SA comparisons; grey = DA comparisons. Arrows = EER

Figure 3. (Continued from Figure 2) Tippett plots showing the LRs of the three different systems

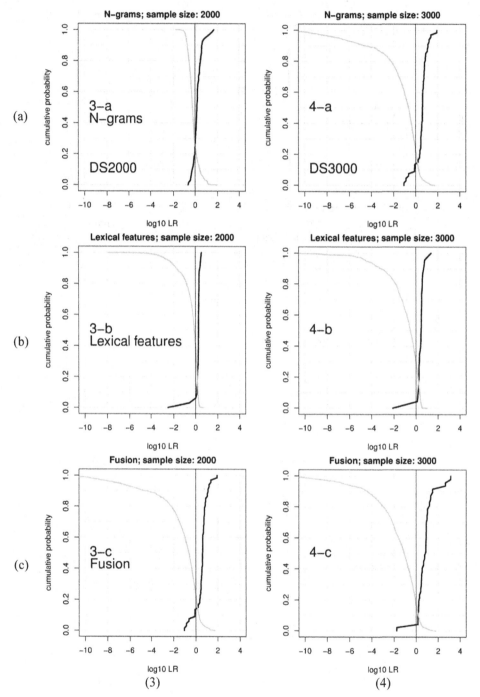

(a) N-gram; (b) Lexical features; (c) Fusion; (3) DS2000; (4) DS3000; Black = SA comparisons; grey = DA comparisons

The calibrated LRs of these three systems are graphically presented as Tippett plots in Figures 2 and 3, in which the $\log_{10}$LRs, which are equal to or greater than the value indicated on the x-axis, are cumulatively plotted separately for the SA (black) and DA (grey) comparisons. In Figures 2 and 3, a logarithmic (base 10) scale is used, in which case the neutral value is $\log_{10}$LR = 0. Tippett plots show how strongly the derived LRs not only support the correct hypothesis but also misleadingly support the contrary-to-fact hypothesis.

It was pointed out earlier that the fused system performed best out of the three systems, but that the degree of the improvement the fusion brought about depends on the sample size, namely the larger the sample size, the greater the improvement. This can be clearly seen in the Tippett plots given in Figures 2 and 3. When the sample size is small, say DS200, although the fusion resulted in an improvement in performance in terms of the C_{llr_min} value, the magnitude of the fused LRs is still fairly weak in that many of the LRs fall in the range between $\log_{10}$LR = -1 and $\log_{10}$LR = 1. For example, Figure 2 1-c which is the Tippett plot of the fused system with DS200 shows that almost all SA LRs and about 90% of the DA LRs are within the range between $\log_{10}$LR = -1 and $\log_{10}$LR = 1. According to Champod and Evett (2000), the LRs which are in the range between $\log_{10}$LR = -1 and $\log_{10}$LR = 1 can provide only limited support for either hypothesis. Practically speaking, the evidence of that degree of strength is not useful as evidence.

Even with DS1000, as far as the Tippett plots are concerned (Figure 2 2), there is no significant difference between the system with lexical features (the second best system of the three) and the fused system in terms of the magnitude of the LRs. However, the clear difference that can be observed between the system with lexical features (Figure 2 2-b) and the fused system (Figure 2 2-c) is the improvement of discriminability (e.g. EER) by c.a. 7%. The EER of the system with lexical features is c.a. 24% (refer to the arrow of Figure 2 2-b) while that of the fused system is c.a. 17% (refer to the arrow of Figure 2 2-c).

When the sample size is large (e.g. DS2000 and DS3000), the effect of the fusion is clearly conceivable in the Tippett plots in that the LRs of the fused system (Figure 3 3-c and Figure 3 4-c) are a lot greater than those of the systems with lexical features and N-grams system (Figure 3 3-a/b and Figure 3 4-a/b). The positive effect of the fusion is great in particular for the DA LRs. For example, as for DS3000, only c.a. 20% of the DA LRs is greater than $\log_{10}$LR = -2 for the system with lexical features (Figure 3 4-b) while as much as c.a. 32% of the DA LRs is greater than $\log_{10}$LR = -2 for the fused system (Figure 3 4-c). According to Champod and Evett (2000), the $\log_{10}$LR = -2 to $\log_{10}$LR = -3 provide "moderately strong support" for the defence hypothesis.

8. CONCLUSION

We fused the LRs derived from the system with lexical features and those derived from the system with N-grams in this study. We demonstrated that the fusion consistently improved the performance of the LR-based forensic text comparison systems regardless of the sample size. However, we also showed that the degree of improvement attributable to the fusion is greater with larger sample sizes.

We pointed out that although the fusion brought positive effects on the system performance regardless of the sample size, when the sample size is small (e.g. DS200 and DS1000), even the LRs of the fused system are still weak, providing only limited support for either hypothesis in many cases. When the sample size is large (e.g. DS2000 and DS3000), the fusion enhanced the magnitude of the LRs greatly.

9. ACKNOWLEDGMENT

This study was financially supported by the ANU Research School of Asia and the Pacific.

REFERENCES

Aitken, C. G. G. (1995). *Statistics and the evaluation of evidence for forensic scientists.* Chichester, UK: John Wiley.

Aitken, C. G. G., & Lucy, D. (2004). Evaluation of trace evidence in the form of multivariate data. *Journal of the Royal Statistical Society. Series C, Applied Statistics*, *53*, 109–122. doi:10.1046/j.0035-9254.2003.05271.x

Aitken, C. G. G., & Stoney, D. A. (1991). *The use of statistics in forensic science.* New York: Ellis Horwood.

Aitken, C. G. G., & Taroni, F. (2004). *Statistics and the evaluation of evidence for forensic scientists.* Chichester, UK: Wiley. doi:10.1002/0470011238

Brümmer, N., & du Preez, J. (2006). Application-independent evaluation of speaker detection. *Computer Speech & Language*, *20*(2-3), 230–275. doi:10.1016/j.csl.2005.08.001

Cellular-News. (2006). SMS as a tool in murder investigations. *Cellular-News*. Retrieved on 10 November 2011 from http://www.cellular-news.com/story/18775.php

Champod, C., & Evett, I. W. (2000). Commentary on A. P. A. Broeders (1999) 'some observations on the use of probability scales in forensic identification', Forensic Linguistics 6(2), 228-41. *International Journal of Speech Language and the Law*, *7*(2), 238–243. doi:10.1558/sll.2000.7.2.238

De Vel, O., Anderson, A., Corney, M., & Mohay, G. (2001). Mining e-mail content for author identification forensics. *SIGMOD Record*, *30*(4), 55–64. doi:10.1145/604264.604272

Doddington, G. (2001). Speaker recognition based on idiolectal differences between speakers. In Proceedings of 2001 Eurospeech (pp. 2521-2524). Academic Press.

Doheny. (1996). R v Doheny. Court of Appeal Criminal Division. No. 95/5297/Y2.

Grant, T. (2007). Quantifying evidence in forensic authorship analysis. *International Journal of Speech Language and the Law*, *14*(1), 1–25.

Grant, T. (2010). Text messaging forensics: txt 4n6: Idiolect free authorship analysis? In A. J. M. Coulthard (Ed.), *The Routledge handbook of forensic linguistics* (pp. 508–522). New York: Routledge.

Halteren, H. V. (2007). Author verification by linguistic profiling: An exploration of the parameter space. *Journal of ACM Transactions on Speech and Language Processing*, *4*(1), 1–17. doi:10.1145/1187415.1187416

Iqbal, F., Binsalleeh, H., Fung, B., & Debbabi, M. (2010). Mining writeprints from anonymous e-mails for forensic investigation. *Digital Investigation*, *7*(1), 56–64. doi:10.1016/j.diin.2010.03.003

Iqbal, F., Binsalleeh, H., Fung, B. C. M., & Debbabi, M. (2013). A unified data mining solution for authorship analysis in anonymous textual communications. *Information Sciences*, 98–112. doi:10.1016/j.ins.2011.03.006

Iqbal, F., Hadjidj, R., Fung, B., & Debbabi, M. (2008). A novel approach of mining write-prints for authorship attribution in e-mail forensics. *Digital Investigation*, *5*(Supplement), S42–S51. doi:10.1016/j.diin.2008.05.001

Ishihara, S. (2011). A forensic authorship classification in SMS messages: A likelihood ratio based approach using n-gram. In *Proceedings of the Australasian Language Technology Workshop 2011* (pp. 47-56). Academic Press.

Ishihara, S. (2012). Probabilistic evaluation of SMS messages as forensic evidence: Likelihood ration based approach with lexical features. *International Journal of Digital Crime and Forensics*, *4*(3), 47–57. doi:10.4018/jdcf.2012070104

Jurafsky, D., & Martin, J. H. (2000). *Speech and language processing: An introduction to natural language processing, computational linguistics, and speech recognition.* Upper Saddle River, NJ: Prentice Hall.

Mohan, A., Baggili, I. M., & Rogers, M. K. (2010). *Authorship attribution of SMS messages using an n-grams approach* (CERIAS Tech Report 2010-11). West Lafayette, IN: Center for Education and Research Information Assurance and Security Purdue University.

Morrison, G. S. (2009). Forensic voice comparison and the paradigm shift. *Science & Justice*, *49*(4), 298–308. doi:10.1016/j.scijus.2009.09.002 PMID:20120610

Morrison, G. S. (2011). Measuring the validity and reliability of forensic likelihood-ratio systems. *Science & Justice*, *51*(3), 91–98. doi:10.1016/j.scijus.2011.03.002 PMID:21889105

Morrison, G. S. (2013). Tutorial on logistic-regression calibration and fusion:converting a score to a likelihood ratio. *The Australian Journal of Forensic Sciences*, *45*(2), 173–197. doi:10.1080/00450618.2012.733025

Robertson, B., & Vignaux, G. A. (1995). *Interpreting evidence: Evaluating forensic science in the courtroom.* Chichester, UK: Wiley.

Saks, M. J., & Koehler, J. J. (2005). The coming paradigm shift in forensic identification science. *Science*, *309*(5736), 892–895. doi:10.1126/science.1111565 PMID:16081727

Stamatatos, E. (2009). A survey of modern authorship attribution methods. *Journal of the American Society for Information Science and Technology*, *60*(3), 538–556. doi:10.1002/asi.21001

Tagg, C. (2009). *A corpus linguistics study of SMS Text messaging.* (PhD Dissertation). The University of Birmingham, Birmingham, UK.

Zheng, R., Li, J. X., Chen, H. C., & Huang, Z. (2006). A framework for authorship identification of online messages: Writing-style features and classification techniques. *Journal of the American Society for Information Science and Technology*, *57*(3), 378–393. doi:10.1002/asi.20316

ENDNOTES

[1] http://wing.comp.nus.edu.sg:8080/SMSCorpus

[2] http://incubator.apache.org/opennlp/

[3] http://www.speech.sri.com/projects/srilm/

[4] https://sites.google.com/site/nikobrummer/focal

Related References

To continue our tradition of advancing information science and technology research, we have compiled a list of recommended IGI Global readings. These references will provide additional information and guidance to further enrich your knowledge and assist you with your own research and future publications.

Acharjya, D. P., & Mary, A. G. (2014). Privacy preservation in information system. In B. Tripathy, & D. Acharjya (Eds.) Advances in secure computing, internet services, and applications (pp. 49-72). Hershey, PA: Information Science Reference. doi: doi:10.4018/978-1-4666-4940-8.ch003

Agamba, J., & Keengwe, J. (2012). Pre-service teachers' perceptions of information assurance and cyber security. [IJICTE]. *International Journal of Information and Communication Technology Education, 8*(2), 94–101. doi:10.4018/jicte.2012040108

Aggarwal, R. (2013). Dispute settlement for cyber crimes in India: An analysis. In R. Khurana, & R. Aggarwal (Eds.), *Interdisciplinary perspectives on business convergence, computing, and legality* (pp. 160–171). Hershey, PA: Business Science Reference. doi:10.4018/978-1-4666-4209-6.ch015

Agwu, E. (2013). Cyber criminals on the internet super highways: A technical investigation of different shades and colours within the Nigerian cyber space. [IJOM]. *International Journal of Online Marketing, 3*(2), 56–74. doi:10.4018/ijom.2013040104

Ahmad, A. (2012). Security assessment of networks. In I. Management Association (Ed.), Wireless technologies: Concepts, methodologies, tools and applications (pp. 208-224). Hershey, PA: Information Science Reference. doi: doi:10.4018/978-1-61350-101-6.ch111

Ahmed, N., & Jensen, C. D. (2012). Security of dependable systems. In L. Petre, K. Sere, & E. Troubitsyna (Eds.), *Dependability and computer engineering: Concepts for software-intensive systems* (pp. 230–264). Hershey, PA: Engineering Science Reference.

Al, M., & Yoshigoe, K. (2012). Security and attacks in wireless sensor networks. In I. Management Association (Ed.), Wireless technologies: Concepts, methodologies, tools and applications (pp. 1811-1846). Hershey, PA: Information Science Reference. doi: doi:10.4018/978-1-61350-101-6.ch706

Al-Ahmad, W. (2011). Building secure software using XP. [IJSSE]. *International Journal of Secure Software Engineering, 2*(3), 63–76. doi:10.4018/jsse.2011070104

Al-Bayatti, A. H., & Al-Bayatti, H. M. (2012). Security management and simulation of mobile ad hoc networks (MANET). In H. Al-Bahadili (Ed.), *Simulation in computer network design and modeling: Use and analysis* (pp. 297–314). Hershey, PA: Information Science Reference. doi:10.4018/978-1-4666-0191-8.ch014

Al-Bayatti, A. H., Zedan, H., Cau, A., & Siewe, F. (2012). Security management for mobile ad hoc network of networks (MANoN). In I. Khalil, & E. Weippl (Eds.), *Advancing the next-generation of mobile computing: Emerging technologies* (pp. 1–18). Hershey, PA: Information Science Reference. doi:10.4018/978-1-4666-0119-2.ch001

Al-Hamdani, W. A. (2011). Three models to measure information security compliance. In H. Nemati (Ed.), *Security and privacy assurance in advancing technologies: New developments* (pp. 351–373). Hershey, PA: Information Science Reference.

Al-Hamdani, W. A. (2014). Secure e-learning and cryptography. In K. Sullivan, P. Czigler, & J. Sullivan Hellgren (Eds.), *Cases on professional distance education degree programs and practices: Successes, challenges, and issues* (pp. 331–369). Hershey, PA: Information Science Reference.

Al-Jaljouli, R., & Abawajy, J. H. (2012). Security framework for mobile agents-based applications. In A. Kumar, & H. Rahman (Eds.), *Mobile computing techniques in emerging markets: Systems, applications and services* (pp. 242–269). Hershey, PA: Information Science Reference. doi:10.4018/978-1-4666-0080-5.ch009

Al-Jaljouli, R., & Abawajy, J. H. (2014). Mobile agents security protocols. In I. Management Association (Ed.), Crisis management: Concepts, methodologies, tools and applications (pp. 166-202). Hershey, PA: Information Science Reference. doi: doi:10.4018/978-1-4666-4707-7.ch007

Al-Suqri, M. N., & Akomolafe-Fatuyi, E. (2012). Security and privacy in digital libraries: Challenges, opportunities and prospects. [IJDLS]. *International Journal of Digital Library Systems*, 3(4), 54–61. doi:10.4018/ijdls.2012100103

Alavi, R., Islam, S., Jahankhani, H., & Al-Nemrat, A. (2013). Analyzing human factors for an effective information security management system. [IJSSE]. *International Journal of Secure Software Engineering*, 4(1), 50–74. doi:10.4018/jsse.2013010104

Alazab, A., Abawajy, J. H., & Hobbs, M. (2013). Web malware that targets web applications. In L. Caviglione, M. Coccoli, & A. Merlo (Eds.), *Social network engineering for secure web data and services* (pp. 248–264). Hershey, PA: Information Science Reference. doi:10.4018/978-1-4666-3926-3.ch012

Alazab, A., Hobbs, M., Abawajy, J., & Khraisat, A. (2013). Malware detection and prevention system based on multi-stage rules. [IJISP]. *International Journal of Information Security and Privacy*, 7(2), 29–43. doi:10.4018/jisp.2013040102

Alazab, M., Venkatraman, S., Watters, P., & Alazab, M. (2013). Information security governance: The art of detecting hidden malware. In D. Mellado, L. Enrique Sánchez, E. Fernández-Medina, & M. Piattini (Eds.), *IT security governance innovations: Theory and research* (pp. 293–315). Hershey, PA: Information Science Reference.

Alhaj, A., Aljawarneh, S., Masadeh, S., & Abu-Taieh, E. (2013). A secure data transmission mechanism for cloud outsourced data. [IJCAC]. *International Journal of Cloud Applications and Computing*, 3(1), 34–43. doi:10.4018/ijcac.2013010104

Ali, M., & Jawandhiya, P. (2012). Security aware routing protocols for mobile ad hoc networks. In K. Lakhtaria (Ed.), *Technological advancements and applications in mobile ad-hoc networks: Research trends* (pp. 264–289). Hershey, PA: Information Science Reference. doi:10.4018/978-1-4666-0321-9.ch016

Ali, S. (2012). Practical web application security audit following industry standards and compliance. In J. Zubairi, & A. Mahboob (Eds.), *Cyber security standards, practices and industrial applications: Systems and methodologies* (pp. 259–279). Hershey, PA: Information Science Reference.

Aljawarneh, S. (2013). Cloud security engineering: Avoiding security threats the right way. In S. Aljawarneh (Ed.), *Cloud computing advancements in design, implementation, and technologies* (pp. 147–153). Hershey, PA: Information Science Reference.

Alshaer, H., Muhaidat, S., Shubair, R., & Shayegannia, M. (2014). Security and connectivity analysis in vehicular communication networks. In D. Rawat, B. Bista, & G. Yan (Eds.), *Security, privacy, trust, and resource management in mobile and wireless communications* (pp. 83–107). Hershey, PA: Information Science Reference.

Alzamil, Z. A. (2012). Information security awareness at Saudi Arabians' organizations: An information technology employee's perspective. [IJISP]. *International Journal of Information Security and Privacy*, 6(3), 38–55. doi:10.4018/jisp.2012070102

Anyiwo, D., & Sharma, S. (2011). Web services and e-business technologies: Security issues. In O. Bak, & N. Stair (Eds.), *Impact of e-business technologies on public and private organizations: Industry comparisons and perspectives* (pp. 249–261). Hershey, PA: Business Science Reference. doi:10.4018/978-1-60960-501-8.ch015

Apostolakis, I., Chryssanthou, A., & Varlamis, I. (2011). A holistic perspective of security in health related virtual communities. In I. Management Association (Ed.), Virtual communities: Concepts, methodologies, tools and applications (pp. 1190-1204). Hershey, PA: Information Science Reference. doi: doi:10.4018/978-1-60960-100-3.ch406

Arnett, K. P., Templeton, G. F., & Vance, D. A. (2011). Information security by words alone: The case for strong security policies. In H. Nemati (Ed.), *Security and privacy assurance in advancing technologies: New developments* (pp. 154–159). Hershey, PA: Information Science Reference.

Arogundade, O. T., Akinwale, A. T., Jin, Z., & Yang, X. G. (2011). A unified use-misuse case model for capturing and analysing safety and security requirements. [IJISP]. *International Journal of Information Security and Privacy*, 5(4), 8–30. doi:10.4018/jisp.2011100102

Arshad, J., Townend, P., Xu, J., & Jie, W. (2012). Cloud computing security: Opportunities and pitfalls. [IJGHPC]. *International Journal of Grid and High Performance Computing*, 4(1), 52–66. doi:10.4018/jghpc.2012010104

Asim, M., & Petkovic, M. (2012). Fundamental building blocks for security interoperability in e-business. In E. Kajan, F. Dorloff, & I. Bedini (Eds.), *Handbook of research on e-business standards and protocols: Documents, data and advanced web technologies* (pp. 269–292). Hershey, PA: Business Science Reference. doi:10.4018/978-1-4666-0146-8.ch013

Askary, S., Goodwin, D., & Lanis, R. (2012). Improvements in audit risks related to information technology frauds. [IJEIS]. *International Journal of Enterprise Information Systems*, 8(2), 52–63. doi:10.4018/jeis.2012040104

Aurigemma, S. (2013). A composite framework for behavioral compliance with information security policies. [JOEUC]. *Journal of Organizational and End User Computing*, 25(3), 32–51. doi:10.4018/joeuc.2013070103

Avalle, M., Pironti, A., Pozza, D., & Sisto, R. (2011). JavaSPI: A framework for security protocol implementation. [IJSSE]. *International Journal of Secure Software Engineering*, 2(4), 34–48. doi:10.4018/jsse.2011100103

Axelrod, C. W. (2012). A dynamic cyber security economic model: incorporating value functions for all involved parties. In M. Gupta, J. Walp, & R. Sharman (Eds.), *Threats, countermeasures, and advances in applied information security* (pp. 462–477). Hershey, PA: Information Science Reference. doi:10.4018/978-1-4666-0978-5.ch024

Ayanso, A., & Herath, T. (2012). Law and technology at crossroads in cyberspace: Where do we go from here? In A. Dudley, J. Braman, & G. Vincenti (Eds.), *Investigating cyber law and cyber ethics: Issues, impacts and practices* (pp. 57–77). Hershey, PA: Information Science Reference.

Baars, T., & Spruit, M. (2012). Designing a secure cloud architecture: The SeCA model. [IJISP]. *International Journal of Information Security and Privacy*, 6(1), 14–32. doi:10.4018/jisp.2012010102

Bachmann, M. (2011). Deciphering the hacker underground: First quantitative insights. In T. Holt, & B. Schell (Eds.), *Corporate hacking and technology-driven crime: Social dynamics and implications* (pp. 105–126). Hershey, PA: Information Science Reference. doi:10.4018/978-1-61350-323-2.ch112

Bachmann, M., & Smith, B. (2012). Internet fraud. In Z. Yan (Ed.), *Encyclopedia of cyber behavior* (pp. 931–943). Hershey, PA: Information Science Reference. doi:10.4018/978-1-4666-0315-8.ch077

Bai, Y., & Khan, K. M. (2011). Ell secure information system using modal logic technique. [IJSSE]. *International Journal of Secure Software Engineering*, 2(2), 65–76. doi:10.4018/jsse.2011040104

Bandeira, G. S. (2014). Criminal liability of organizations, corporations, legal persons, and similar entities on law of portuguese cybercrime: A brief discussion on the issue of crimes of "false information," the "damage on other programs or computer data," the "computer-software sabotage," the "illegitimate access," the "unlawful interception," and "illegitimate reproduction of the protected program". In I. Portela, & F. Almeida (Eds.), *Organizational, legal, and technological dimensions of information system administration* (pp. 96–107). Hershey, PA: Information Science Reference.

Barjis, J. (2012). Software engineering security based on business process modeling. In K. Khan (Ed.), *Security-aware systems applications and software development methods* (pp. 52–68). Hershey, PA: Information Science Reference. doi:10.4018/978-1-4666-1580-9.ch004

Bedi, P., Gandotra, V., & Singhal, A. (2013). Innovative strategies for secure software development. In H. Singh, & K. Kaur (Eds.), *Designing, engineering, and analyzing reliable and efficient software* (pp. 217–237). Hershey, PA: Information Science Reference. doi:10.4018/978-1-4666-2958-5.ch013

Belsis, P., Skourlas, C., & Gritzalis, S. (2011). Secure electronic healthcare records management in wireless environments. [JITR]. *Journal of Information Technology Research*, 4(4), 1–17. doi:10.4018/jitr.2011100101

Bernik, I. (2012). Internet study: Cyber threats and cybercrime awareness and fear. [IJCWT]. *International Journal of Cyber Warfare & Terrorism*, 2(3), 1–11. doi:10.4018/ijcwt.2012070101

Bhatia, M. S. (2011). World war III: The cyber war. [IJCWT]. *International Journal of Cyber Warfare & Terrorism*, 1(3), 59–69. doi:10.4018/ijcwt.2011070104

Blanco, C., Rosado, D., Gutiérrez, C., Rodríguez, A., Mellado, D., & Fernández-Medina, E. et al. (2011). Security over the information systems development cycle. In H. Mouratidis (Ed.), *Software engineering for secure systems: Industrial and research perspectives* (pp. 113–154). Hershey, PA: Information Science Reference.

Bobbert, Y., & Mulder, H. (2012). A research journey into maturing the business information security of mid market organizations. In W. Van Grembergen, & S. De Haes (Eds.), *Business strategy and applications in enterprise IT governance* (pp. 236–259). Hershey, PA: Business Science Reference. doi:10.4018/978-1-4666-1779-7.ch014

Boddington, R. (2011). Digital evidence. In D. Kerr, J. Gammack, & K. Bryant (Eds.), *Digital business security development: Management technologies* (pp. 37–72). Hershey, PA: Business Science Reference.

Bossler, A. M., & Burruss, G. W. (2011). The general theory of crime and computer hacking: Low self-control hackers? In T. Holt, & B. Schell (Eds.), *Corporate hacking and technology-driven crime: Social dynamics and implications* (pp. 38–67). Hershey, PA: Information Science Reference. doi:10.4018/978-1-61350-323-2.ch707

Bouras, C., & Stamos, K. (2011). Security issues for multi-domain resource reservation. In D. Kar, & M. Syed (Eds.), *Network security, administration and management: Advancing technology and practice* (pp. 38–50). Hershey, PA: Information Science Reference. doi:10.4018/978-1-60960-777-7.ch003

Bracci, F., Corradi, A., & Foschini, L. (2014). Cloud standards: Security and interoperability issues. In H. Mouftah, & B. Kantarci (Eds.), *Communication infrastructures for cloud computing* (pp. 465–495). Hershey, PA: Information Science Reference.

Brodsky, J., & Radvanovsky, R. (2011). Control systems security. In T. Holt, & B. Schell (Eds.), *Corporate hacking and technology-driven crime: Social dynamics and implications* (pp. 187–204). Hershey, PA: Information Science Reference.

Brooks, D. (2013). Security threats and risks of intelligent building systems: Protecting facilities from current and emerging vulnerabilities. In C. Laing, A. Badii, & P. Vickers (Eds.), *Securing critical infrastructures and critical control systems: Approaches for threat protection* (pp. 1–16). Hershey, PA: Information Science Reference.

Bülow, W., & Wester, M. (2012). The right to privacy and the protection of personal data in a digital era and the age of information. In C. Akrivopoulou, & N. Garipidis (Eds.), *Human rights and risks in the digital era: Globalization and the effects of information technologies* (pp. 34–45). Hershey, PA: Information Science Reference. doi:10.4018/978-1-4666-0891-7.ch004

Canongia, C., & Mandarino, R. (2014). Cybersecurity: The new challenge of the information society. In I. Management Association (Ed.), Crisis management: Concepts, methodologies, tools and applications (pp. 60-80). Hershey, PA: Information Science Reference. doi: doi:10.4018/978-1-4666-4707-7.ch003

Cao, X., & Lu, Y. (2011). The social network structure of a computer hacker community. In H. Nemati (Ed.), *Security and privacy assurance in advancing technologies: New developments* (pp. 160–173). Hershey, PA: Information Science Reference.

Cardholm, L. (2014). Identifying the business value of information security. In T. Tsiakis, T. Kargidis, & P. Katsaros (Eds.), *Approaches and processes for managing the economics of information systems* (pp. 157–180). Hershey, PA: Business Science Reference. doi:10.4018/978-1-4666-4983-5.ch010

Cardoso, R. C., & Gomes, A. (2012). Security issues in massively multiplayer online games. In M. Cruz-Cunha (Ed.), *Handbook of research on serious games as educational, business and research tools* (pp. 290–314). Hershey, PA: Information Science Reference. doi:10.4018/978-1-4666-0149-9.ch016

Carpen-Amarie, A., Costan, A., Leordeanu, C., Basescu, C., & Antoniu, G. (2012). Towards a generic security framework for cloud data management environments. [IJDST]. *International Journal of Distributed Systems and Technologies*, 3(1), 17–34. doi:10.4018/jdst.2012010102

Caushaj, E., Fu, H., Sethi, I., Badih, H., Watson, D., Zhu, Y., & Leng, S. (2013). Theoretical analysis and experimental study: Monitoring data privacy in smartphone communications. [IJITN]. *International Journal of Interdisciplinary Telecommunications and Networking*, 5(2), 66–82. doi:10.4018/jitn.2013040106

Cepheli, Ö., & Kurt, G. K. (2014). Physical layer security in wireless communication networks. In D. Rawat, B. Bista, & G. Yan (Eds.), *Security, privacy, trust, and resource management in mobile and wireless communications* (pp. 61–81). Hershey, PA: Information Science Reference.

Chakraborty, P., & Raghuraman, K. (2013). Trends in information security. In K. Buragga, & N. Zaman (Eds.), *Software development techniques for constructive information systems design* (pp. 354–376). Hershey, PA: Information Science Reference. doi:10.4018/978-1-4666-3679-8.ch020

Chandrakumar, T., & Parthasarathy, S. (2012). Enhancing data security in ERP projects using XML. [IJEIS]. *International Journal of Enterprise Information Systems*, 8(1), 51–65. doi:10.4018/jeis.2012010104

Chapple, M. J., Striegel, A., & Crowell, C. R. (2011). Firewall rulebase management: Tools and techniques. In M. Quigley (Ed.), *ICT ethics and security in the 21st century: New developments and applications* (pp. 254–276). Hershey, PA: Information Science Reference. doi:10.4018/978-1-60960-573-5.ch013

Chen, L., Hu, W., Yang, M., & Zhang, L. (2011). Security and privacy issues in secure e-mail standards and services. In H. Nemati (Ed.), *Security and privacy assurance in advancing technologies: new developments* (pp. 174–185). Hershey, PA: Information Science Reference.

Chen, L., Varol, C., Liu, Q., & Zhou, B. (2014). Security in wireless metropolitan area networks: WiMAX and LTE. In D. Rawat, B. Bista, & G. Yan (Eds.), *Security, privacy, trust, and resource management in mobile and wireless communications* (pp. 11–27). Hershey, PA: Information Science Reference.

Cherdantseva, Y., & Hilton, J. (2014). Information security and information assurance: Discussion about the meaning, scope, and goals. In I. Portela, & F. Almeida (Eds.), *Organizational, legal, and technological dimensions of information system administration* (pp. 167–198). Hershey, PA: Information Science Reference.

Cherdantseva, Y., & Hilton, J. (2014). The 2011 survey of information security and information assurance professionals: Findings. In I. Portela, & F. Almeida (Eds.), *Organizational, legal, and technological dimensions of information system administration* (pp. 243–256). Hershey, PA: Information Science Reference.

Chowdhury, M. U., & Ray, B. R. (2013). Security risks/vulnerability in a RFID system and possible defenses. In N. Karmakar (Ed.), *Advanced RFID systems, security, and applications* (pp. 1–15). Hershey, PA: Information Science Reference. doi:10.4018/978-1-4666-4707-7.ch084

Cofta, P., Lacohée, H., & Hodgson, P. (2011). Incorporating social trust into design practices for secure systems. In H. Mouratidis (Ed.), *Software engineering for secure systems: Industrial and research perspectives* (pp. 260–284). Hershey, PA: Information Science Reference.

Conway, M. (2012). What is cyberterrorism and how real is the threat? A review of the academic literature, 1996 – 2009. In P. Reich, & E. Gelbstein (Eds.), *Law, policy, and technology: Cyberterrorism, information warfare, and internet immobilization* (pp. 279–307). Hershey, PA: Information Science Reference.

Corser, G. P., Arslanturk, S., Oluoch, J., Fu, H., & Corser, G. E. (2013). Knowing the enemy at the gates: Measuring attacker motivation. [IJITN]. *International Journal of Interdisciplinary Telecommunications and Networking*, *5*(2), 83–95. doi:10.4018/jitn.2013040107

Crosbie, M. (2013). Hack the cloud: Ethical hacking and cloud forensics. In K. Ruan (Ed.), *Cybercrime and cloud forensics: Applications for investigation processes* (pp. 42–58). Hershey, PA: Information Science Reference.

Curran, K., Carlin, S., & Adams, M. (2012). Security issues in cloud computing. In L. Chao (Ed.), *Cloud computing for teaching and learning: Strategies for design and implementation* (pp. 200–208). Hershey, PA: Information Science Reference. doi:10.4018/978-1-4666-0957-0.ch014

Czosseck, C., Ottis, R., & Talihärm, A. (2011). Estonia after the 2007 cyber attacks: Legal, strategic and organisational changes in cyber security. [IJCWT]. *International Journal of Cyber Warfare & Terrorism*, *1*(1), 24–34. doi:10.4018/ijcwt.2011010103

Czosseck, C., & Podins, K. (2012). A vulnerability-based model of cyber weapons and its implications for cyber conflict. [IJCWT]. *International Journal of Cyber Warfare & Terrorism*, *2*(1), 14–26. doi:10.4018/ijcwt.2012010102

da Silva, F. A., Moura, D. F., & Galdino, J. F. (2012). Classes of attacks for tactical software defined radios. [IJERTCS]. *International Journal of Embedded and Real-Time Communication Systems*, *3*(4), 57–82. doi:10.4018/jertcs.2012100104

Dabcevic, K., Marcenaro, L., & Regazzoni, C. S. (2013). Security in cognitive radio networks. In T. Lagkas, P. Sarigiannidis, M. Louta, & P. Chatzimisios (Eds.), *Evolution of cognitive networks and self-adaptive communication systems* (pp. 301–335). Hershey, PA: Information Science Reference. doi:10.4018/978-1-4666-4189-1.ch013

Dahbur, K., Mohammad, B., & Tarakji, A. B. (2013). Security issues in cloud computing: A survey of risks, threats and vulnerabilities. In S. Aljawarneh (Ed.), *Cloud computing advancements in design, implementation, and technologies* (pp. 154–165). Hershey, PA: Information Science Reference.

Dark, M. (2011). Data breach disclosure: A policy analysis. In M. Dark (Ed.), *Information assurance and security ethics in complex systems: Interdisciplinary perspectives* (pp. 226–252). Hershey, PA: Information Science Reference.

Das, S., Mukhopadhyay, A., & Bhasker, B. (2013). Today's action is better than tomorrow's cure - Evaluating information security at a premier indian business school. [JCIT]. *Journal of Cases on Information Technology*, *15*(3), 1–23. doi:10.4018/jcit.2013070101

Dasgupta, D., & Naseem, D. (2014). A framework for compliance and security coverage estimation for cloud services: A cloud insurance model. In S. Srinivasan (Ed.), *Security, trust, and regulatory aspects of cloud computing in business environments* (pp. 91–114). Hershey, PA: Information Science Reference. doi:10.4018/978-1-4666-5788-5.ch005

De Fuentes, J. M., González-Tablas, A. I., & Ribagorda, A. (2011). Overview of security issues in vehicular ad-hoc networks. In M. Cruz-Cunha, & F. Moreira (Eds.), *Handbook of research on mobility and computing: Evolving technologies and ubiquitous impacts* (pp. 894–911). Hershey, PA: Information Science Reference. doi:10.4018/978-1-60960-042-6.ch056

De Groef, W., Devriese, D., Reynaert, T., & Piessens, F. (2013). Security and privacy of online social network applications. In L. Caviglione, M. Coccoli, & A. Merlo (Eds.), *Social network engineering for secure web data and services* (pp. 206–221). Hershey, PA: Information Science Reference. doi:10.4018/978-1-4666-3926-3.ch010

Denning, D. E. (2011). Cyber conflict as an emergent social phenomenon. In T. Holt, & B. Schell (Eds.), *Corporate hacking and technology-driven crime: Social dynamics and implications* (pp. 170–186). Hershey, PA: Information Science Reference.

Desai, A. M., & Mock, K. (2013). Security in cloud computing. In A. Bento, & A. Aggarwal (Eds.), *Cloud computing service and deployment models: Layers and management* (pp. 208–221). Hershey, PA: Business Science Reference.

Dionysiou, I., & Ktoridou, D. (2012). Enhancing dynamic-content courses with student-oriented learning strategies: The case of computer security course. [IJCEE]. *International Journal of Cyber Ethics in Education, 2*(2), 24–33. doi:10.4018/ijcee.2012040103

Disterer, G. (2012). Attacks on IT systems: Categories of motives. In T. Chou (Ed.), *Information assurance and security technologies for risk assessment and threat management: Advances* (pp. 1–16). Hershey, PA: Information Science Reference.

Dougan, T., & Curran, K. (2012). Man in the browser attacks. [IJACI]. *International Journal of Ambient Computing and Intelligence, 4*(1), 29–39. doi:10.4018/jaci.2012010103

Dubey, R., Sharma, S., & Chouhan, L. (2013). Security for cognitive radio networks. In M. Ku, & J. Lin (Eds.), *Cognitive radio and interference management: Technology and strategy* (pp. 238–256). Hershey, PA: Information Science Reference.

Dunkels, E., Frånberg, G., & Hällgren, C. (2011). Young people and online risk. In E. Dunkels, G. Franberg, & C. Hallgren (Eds.), *Youth culture and net culture: Online social practices* (pp. 1–16). Hershey, PA: Information Science Reference.

Dunkerley, K., & Tejay, G. (2012). The development of a model for information systems security success. In Z. Belkhamza, & S. Azizi Wafa (Eds.), *Measuring organizational information systems success: New technologies and practices* (pp. 341–366). Hershey, PA: Business Science Reference. doi:10.4018/978-1-4666-0170-3.ch017

Dunkerley, K., & Tejay, G. (2012). Theorizing information security success: Towards secure e-government. In V. Weerakkody (Ed.), *Technology enabled transformation of the public sector: Advances in e-government* (pp. 224–235). Hershey, PA: Information Science Reference. doi:10.4018/978-1-4666-1776-6.ch014

Eisenga, A., Jones, T. L., & Rodriguez, W. (2012). Investing in IT security: How to determine the maximum threshold. [IJISP]. *International Journal of Information Security and Privacy, 6*(3), 75–87. doi:10.4018/jisp.2012070104

Eyitemi, M. (2012). Regulation of cybercafés in Nigeria. In I. Management Association (Ed.), Cyber crime: Concepts, methodologies, tools and applications(pp. 1305-1313). Hershey, PA: Information Science Reference. doi: doi:10.4018/978-1-61350-323-2.ch606

Ezumah, B., & Adekunle, S. O. (2012). A review of privacy, internet security threat, and legislation in Africa: A case study of Nigeria, South Africa, Egypt, and Kenya. In J. Abawajy, M. Pathan, M. Rahman, A. Pathan, & M. Deris (Eds.), *Internet and distributed computing advancements: Theoretical frameworks and practical applications* (pp. 115–136). Hershey, PA: Information Science Reference. doi:10.4018/978-1-4666-0161-1.ch005

Farooq-i-Azam, M., & Ayyaz, M. N. (2014). Embedded systems security. In I. Management Association (Ed.), Software design and development: Concepts, methodologies, tools, and applications (pp. 980-998). Hershey, PA: Information Science Reference. doi:doi:10.4018/978-1-4666-4301-7.ch047

Fauzi, A. H., & Taylor, H. (2013). Secure community trust stores for peer-to-peer e-commerce applications using cloud services. [IJEEI]. *International Journal of E-Entrepreneurship and Innovation*, 4(1), 1–15. doi:10.4018/jeei.2013010101

Fenz, S. (2011). E-business and information security risk management: Challenges and potential solutions. In E. Kajan (Ed.), *Electronic business interoperability: Concepts, opportunities and challenges* (pp. 596–614). Hershey, PA: Business Science Reference. doi:10.4018/978-1-60960-485-1.ch024

Fernandez, E. B., Yoshioka, N., Washizaki, H., Jurjens, J., VanHilst, M., & Pernu, G. (2011). Using security patterns to develop secure systems. In H. Mouratidis (Ed.), *Software engineering for secure systems: Industrial and research perspectives* (pp. 16–31). Hershey, PA: Information Science Reference.

Flores, A. E., Win, K. T., & Susilo, W. (2011). Secure exchange of electronic health records. In A. Chryssanthou, I. Apostolakis, & I. Varlamis (Eds.), *Certification and security in health-related web applications: Concepts and solutions* (pp. 1–22). Hershey, PA: Medical Information Science Reference.

Fonseca, J., & Vieira, M. (2014). A survey on secure software development lifecycles. In I. Management Association (Ed.), Software design and development: Concepts, methodologies, tools, and applications (pp. 17-33). Hershey, PA: Information Science Reference. doi: doi:10.4018/978-1-4666-4301-7.ch002

Fournaris, A. P., Kitsos, P., & Sklavos, N. (2013). Security and cryptographic engineering in embedded systems. In M. Khalgui, O. Mosbahi, & A. Valentini (Eds.), *Embedded computing systems: Applications, optimization, and advanced design* (pp. 420–438). Hershey, PA: Information Science Reference. doi:10.4018/978-1-4666-3922-5.ch021

Franqueira, V. N., van Cleeff, A., van Eck, P., & Wieringa, R. J. (2013). Engineering security agreements against external insider threat. [IRMJ]. *Information Resources Management Journal*, 26(4), 66–91. doi:10.4018/irmj.2013100104

French, T., Bessis, N., Maple, C., & Asimakopoulou, E. (2012). Trust issues on crowd-sourcing methods for urban environmental monitoring. [IJDST]. *International Journal of Distributed Systems and Technologies*, 3(1), 35–47. doi:10.4018/jdst.2012010103

Fu, Y., Kulick, J., Yan, L. K., & Drager, S. (2013). Formal modeling and verification of security property in Handel C program. [IJSSE]. *International Journal of Secure Software Engineering*, 3(3), 50–65. doi:10.4018/jsse.2012070103

Furnell, S., von Solms, R., & Phippen, A. (2011). Preventative actions for enhancing online protection and privacy. [IJITSA]. *International Journal of Information Technologies and Systems Approach*, 4(2), 1–11. doi:10.4018/jitsa.2011070101

Gaivéo, J. (2011). SMEs e-business security issues. In M. Cruz-Cunha, & J. Varajão (Eds.), *Innovations in SMEs and conducting e-business: Technologies, trends and solutions* (pp. 317–337). Hershey, PA: Business Science Reference. doi:10.4018/978-1-60960-765-4.ch018

Gaivéo, J. M. (2013). Security of ICTs supporting healthcare activities. In M. Cruz-Cunha, I. Miranda, & P. Gonçalves (Eds.), *Handbook of research on ICTs for human-centered healthcare and social care services* (pp. 208–228). Hershey, PA: Medical Information Science Reference. doi:10.4018/978-1-4666-3986-7.ch011

Gelbstein, E. E. (2013). Designing a security audit plan for a critical information infrastructure (CII). In C. Laing, A. Badii, & P. Vickers (Eds.), *Securing critical infrastructures and critical control systems: Approaches for threat protection* (pp. 262–285). Hershey, PA: Information Science Reference.

Gódor, G., & Imre, S. (2012). Security aspects in radio frequency identification systems. In D. Saha, & V. Sridhar (Eds.), *Next generation data communication technologies: Emerging trends* (pp. 187–225). Hershey, PA: Information Science Reference.

Gogolin, G. (2011). Security and privacy concerns of virtual worlds. In B. Ciaramitaro (Ed.), *Virtual worlds and e-commerce: Technologies and applications for building customer relationships* (pp. 244–256). Hershey, PA: Business Science Reference.

Gogoulos, F. I., Antonakopoulou, A., Lioudakis, G. V., Kaklamani, D. I., & Venieris, I. S. (2014). Trust in an enterprise world: A survey. In M. Cruz-Cunha, F. Moreira, & J. Varajão (Eds.), *Handbook of research on enterprise 2.0: Technological, social, and organizational dimensions* (pp. 199–219). Hershey, PA: Business Science Reference.

Goldman, J. E., & Ahuja, S. (2011). Integration of COBIT, balanced scorecard and SSE-CMM as an organizational & strategic information security management (ISM) framework. In M. Quigley (Ed.), *ICT ethics and security in the 21st century: New developments and applications* (pp. 277–309). Hershey, PA: Information Science Reference. doi:10.4018/978-1-60960-573-5.ch014

Goldschmidt, C., Dark, M., & Chaudhry, H. (2011). Responsibility for the harm and risk of software security flaws. In M. Dark (Ed.), *Information assurance and security ethics in complex systems: Interdisciplinary perspectives* (pp. 104–131). Hershey, PA: Information Science Reference.

Grahn, K., Karlsson, J., & Pulkkis, G. (2011). Secure routing and mobility in future IP networks. In M. Cruz-Cunha, & F. Moreira (Eds.), *Handbook of research on mobility and computing: Evolving technologies and ubiquitous impacts* (pp. 952–972). Hershey, PA: Information Science Reference. doi:10.4018/978-1-60960-042-6.ch059

Greitzer, F. L., Frincke, D., & Zabriskie, M. (2011). Social/ethical issues in predictive insider threat monitoring. In M. Dark (Ed.), *Information assurance and security ethics in complex systems: Interdisciplinary perspectives* (pp. 132–161). Hershey, PA: Information Science Reference. doi:10.4018/978-1-61350-323-2.ch506

Grobler, M. (2012). The need for digital evidence standardisation. [IJDCF]. *International Journal of Digital Crime and Forensics*, 4(2), 1–12. doi:10.4018/jdcf.2012040101

Guo, J., Marshall, A., & Zhou, B. (2014). A multi-parameter trust framework for mobile ad hoc networks. In D. Rawat, B. Bista, & G. Yan (Eds.), *Security, privacy, trust, and resource management in mobile and wireless communications* (pp. 245–277). Hershey, PA: Information Science Reference.

Gururajan, R., & Hafeez-Baig, A. (2011). Wireless handheld device and LAN security issues: A case study. In D. Kerr, J. Gammack, & K. Bryant (Eds.), *Digital business security development: Management technologies* (pp. 129–151). Hershey, PA: Business Science Reference. doi:10.4018/978-1-61350-101-6.ch402

Ha, H. (2012). Online security and consumer protection in ecommerce an Australian case. In K. Mohammed Rezaul (Ed.), *Strategic and pragmatic e-business: Implications for future business practices* (pp. 217–243). Hershey, PA: Business Science Reference. doi:10.4018/978-1-4666-1619-6.ch010

Hagen, J. M. (2012). The contributions of information security culture and human relations to the improvement of situational awareness. In C. Onwubiko, & T. Owens (Eds.), *Situational awareness in computer network defense: Principles, methods and applications* (pp. 10–28). Hershey, PA: Information Science Reference. doi:10.4018/978-1-4666-0104-8.ch002

Hai-Jew, S. (2011). The social design of 3D interactive spaces for security in higher education: A preliminary view. In A. Rea (Ed.), *Security in virtual worlds, 3D webs, and immersive environments: Models for development, interaction, and management* (pp. 72–96). Hershey, PA: Information Science Reference.

Halder, D., & Jaishankar, K. (2012). Cyber crime against women and regulations in Australia. In I. Management Association (Ed.), Cyber crime: Concepts, methodologies, tools and applications (pp. 757-764). Hershey, PA: Information Science Reference. doi: doi:10.4018/978-1-61350-323-2.ch404

Halder, D., & Jaishankar, K. (2012). Cyber victimization of women and cyber laws in India. In I. Management Association (Ed.), Cyber crime: Concepts, methodologies, tools and applications (pp. 742-756). Hershey, PA: Information Science Reference. doi: doi:10.4018/978-1-61350-323-2.ch403

Halder, D., & Jaishankar, K. (2012). Definition, typology and patterns of victimization. In I. Management Association (Ed.), Cyber crime: Concepts, methodologies, tools and applications (pp. 1016-1042). Hershey, PA: Information Science Reference. doi: doi:10.4018/978-1-61350-323-2.ch502

Hamlen, K., Kantarcioglu, M., Khan, L., & Thuraisingham, B. (2012). Security issues for cloud computing. In H. Nemati (Ed.), *Optimizing information security and advancing privacy assurance: New technologies* (pp. 150–162). Hershey, PA: Information Science Reference.

Harnesk, D. (2011). Convergence of information security in B2B networks. In E. Kajan (Ed.), *Electronic business interoperability: Concepts, opportunities and challenges* (pp. 571–595). Hershey, PA: Business Science Reference. doi:10.4018/978-1-60960-485-1.ch023

Harnesk, D., & Hartikainen, H. (2011). Multi-layers of information security in emergency response. [IJISCRAM]. *International Journal of Information Systems for Crisis Response and Management, 3*(2), 1–17. doi:10.4018/jiscrm.2011040101

Hawrylak, P. J., Hale, J., & Papa, M. (2013). Security issues for ISO 18000-6 type C RFID: Identification and solutions. In I. Association (Ed.), *Supply chain management: Concepts, methodologies, tools, and applications* (pp. 1565–1581). Hershey, PA: Business Science Reference.

He, B., Tran, T. T., & Xie, B. (2014). Authentication and identity management for secure cloud businesses and services. In S. Srinivasan (Ed.), *Security, trust, and regulatory aspects of cloud computing in business environments* (pp. 180–201). Hershey, PA: Information Science Reference. doi:10.4018/978-1-4666-5788-5.ch011

Henrie, M. (2012). Cyber security in liquid petroleum pipelines. In J. Zubairi, & A. Mahboob (Eds.), *Cyber security standards, practices and industrial applications: Systems and methodologies* (pp. 200–222). Hershey, PA: Information Science Reference.

Herath, T., Rao, H. R., & Upadhyaya, S. (2012). Internet crime: How vulnerable are you? Do gender, social influence and education play a role in vulnerability? In I. Management Association (Ed.), Cyber crime: Concepts, methodologies, tools and applications (pp. 1-13). Hershey, PA: Information Science Reference. doi: doi:10.4018/978-1-61350-323-2.ch101

Hilmi, M. F., Pawanchik, S., Mustapha, Y., & Ali, H. M. (2013). Information security perspective of a learning management system: An exploratory study. [IJKSR]. *International Journal of Knowledge Society Research, 4*(2), 9–18. doi:10.4018/jksr.2013040102

Hommel, W. (2012). Security and privacy management for learning management systems. In I. Management Association (Ed.), Virtual learning environments: Concepts, methodologies, tools and applications (pp. 1151-1170). Hershey, PA: Information Science Reference. doi: doi:10.4018/978-1-4666-0011-9.ch602

Hoops, D. S. (2012). Lost in cyberspace: Navigating the legal issues of e-commerce. [JECO]. *Journal of Electronic Commerce in Organizations, 10*(1), 33–51. doi:10.4018/jeco.2012010103

Houmb, S., Georg, G., Petriu, D., Bordbar, B., Ray, I., Anastasakis, K., & France, R. (2011). Balancing security and performance properties during system architectural design. In H. Mouratidis (Ed.), *Software engineering for secure systems: Industrial and research perspectives* (pp. 155–191). Hershey, PA: Information Science Reference.

Huang, E., & Cheng, F. (2012). Online security cues and e-payment continuance intention. [IJEEI]. *International Journal of E-Entrepreneurship and Innovation, 3*(1), 42–58. doi:10.4018/jeei.2012010104

Ifinedo, P. (2011). Relationships between information security concerns and national cultural dimensions: Findings in the global financial services industry. In H. Nemati (Ed.), *Security and privacy assurance in advancing technologies: New developments* (pp. 134–153). Hershey, PA: Information Science Reference.

Inden, U., Lioudakis, G., & Rückemann, C. (2013). Awareness-based security management for complex and internet-based operations management systems. In C. Rückemann (Ed.), *Integrated information and computing systems for natural, spatial, and social sciences* (pp. 43–73). Hershey, PA: Information Science Reference.

Islam, S., Mouratidis, H., Kalloniatis, C., Hudic, A., & Zechner, L. (2013). Model based process to support security and privacy requirements engineering. [IJSSE]. *International Journal of Secure Software Engineering, 3*(3), 1–22. doi:10.4018/jsse.2012070101

Itani, W., Kayssi, A., & Chehab, A. (2012). Security and privacy in body sensor networks: Challenges, solutions, and research directions. In M. Watfa (Ed.), *E-healthcare systems and wireless communications: Current and future challenges* (pp. 100–127). Hershey, PA: Medical Information Science Reference.

Jansen van Vuuren, J., Grobler, M., & Zaaiman, J. (2012). Cyber security awareness as critical driver to national security. [IJCWT]. *International Journal of Cyber Warfare & Terrorism, 2*(1), 27–38. doi:10.4018/ijcwt.2012010103

Jansen van Vuuren, J., Leenen, L., Phahlamohlaka, J., & Zaaiman, J. (2012). An approach to governance of CyberSecurity in South Africa. [IJCWT]. *International Journal of Cyber Warfare & Terrorism, 2*(4), 13–27. doi:10.4018/ijcwt.2012100102

Jensen, J., & Groep, D. L. (2012). Security and trust in a global research infrastructure. In J. Leng, & W. Sharrock (Eds.), *Handbook of research on computational science and engineering: Theory and practice* (pp. 539–566). Hershey, PA: Engineering Science Reference.

Johnsen, S. O. (2014). Safety and security in SCADA systems must be improved through resilience based risk management. In I. Management Association (Ed.), Crisis management: Concepts, methodologies, tools and applications (pp. 1422-1436). Hershey, PA: Information Science Reference. doi: doi:10.4018/978-1-4666-4707-7.ch071

Johnston, A. C., Wech, B., & Jack, E. (2012). Engaging remote employees: The moderating role of "remote" status in determining employee information security policy awareness. [JOEUC]. *Journal of Organizational and End User Computing, 25*(1), 1–23. doi:10.4018/joeuc.2013010101

Jung, C., Rudolph, M., & Schwarz, R. (2013). Security evaluation of service-oriented systems using the SiSOA method. In K. Khan (Ed.), *Developing and evaluating security-aware software systems* (pp. 20–35). Hershey, PA: Information Science Reference.

Kaiya, H., Sakai, J., Ogata, S., & Kaijiri, K. (2013). Eliciting security requirements for an information system using asset flows and processor deployment. [IJSSE]. *International Journal of Secure Software Engineering, 4*(3), 42–63. doi:10.4018/jsse.2013070103

Kalloniatis, C., Kavakli, E., & Gritzalis, S. (2011). Designing privacy aware information systems. In H. Mouratidis (Ed.), *Software engineering for secure systems: Industrial and research perspectives* (pp. 212–231). Hershey, PA: Information Science Reference.

Kamoun, F., & Halaweh, M. (2012). User interface design and e-commerce security perception: An empirical study. [IJEBR]. *International Journal of E-Business Research, 8*(2), 15–32. doi:10.4018/jebr.2012040102

Kamruzzaman, J., Azad, A. K., Karmakar, N. C., Karmakar, G., & Srinivasan, B. (2013). Security and privacy in RFID systems. In N. Karmakar (Ed.), *Advanced RFID systems, security, and applications* (pp. 16–40). Hershey, PA: Information Science Reference.

Kaosar, M. G., & Yi, X. (2011). Privacy preserving data gathering in wireless sensor network. In D. Kar, & M. Syed (Eds.), *Network security, administration and management: Advancing technology and practice* (pp. 237–251). Hershey, PA: Information Science Reference. doi:10.4018/978-1-60960-777-7.ch012

Kar, D. C., Ngo, H. L., Mulkey, C. J., & Sanapala, G. (2011). Advances in security and privacy in wireless sensor networks. In H. Nemati (Ed.), *Security and privacy assurance in advancing technologies: New developments* (pp. 186–213). Hershey, PA: Information Science Reference. doi:10.4018/978-1-61350-101-6.ch810

Karadsheh, L., & Alhawari, S. (2011). Applying security policies in small business utilizing cloud computing technologies. [IJCAC]. *International Journal of Cloud Applications and Computing, 1*(2), 29–40. doi:10.4018/ijcac.2011040103

Karokola, G., Yngström, L., & Kowalski, S. (2012). Secure e-government services: A comparative analysis of e-government maturity models for the developing regions–The need for security services. [IJEGR]. *International Journal of Electronic Government Research, 8*(1), 1–25. doi:10.4018/jegr.2012010101

Kassim, N. M., & Ramayah, T. (2013). Security policy issues in internet banking in Malaysia. In I. Management Association (Ed.), IT policy and ethics: Concepts, methodologies, tools, and applications (pp. 1274-1293). Hershey, PA: Information Science Reference. doi: doi:10.4018/978-1-4666-2919-6.ch057

Kayem, A. V. (2013). Security in service oriented architectures: Standards and challenges. In I. Association (Ed.), *Digital rights management: Concepts, methodologies, tools, and applications* (pp. 50–73). Hershey, PA: Information Science Reference.

K.C, A., Forsgren, H., Grahn, K., Karvi, T., & Pulkkis, G. (2013). Security and trust of public key cryptography for HIP and HIP multicast. [IJDTIS]. *International Journal of Dependable and Trustworthy Information Systems*, 2(3), 17–35. doi: doi:10.4018/jdtis.2011070102

Kelarev, A. V., Brown, S., Watters, P., Wu, X., & Dazeley, R. (2011). Establishing reasoning communities of security experts for internet commerce security. In J. Yearwood, & A. Stranieri (Eds.), *Technologies for supporting reasoning communities and collaborative decision making: Cooperative approaches* (pp. 380–396). Hershey, PA: Information Science Reference.

Kerr, D., Gammack, J. G., & Boddington, R. (2011). Overview of digital business security issues. In D. Kerr, J. Gammack, & K. Bryant (Eds.), *Digital business security development: Management technologies* (pp. 1–36). Hershey, PA: Business Science Reference.

Khan, K. M. (2011). A decision support system for selecting secure web services. In I. Management Association (Ed.), Enterprise information systems: Concepts, methodologies, tools and applications (pp. 1113-1120). Hershey, PA: Business Science Reference. doi: doi:10.4018/978-1-61692-852-0.ch415

Khan, K. M. (2012). Software security engineering: Design and applications. [IJSSE]. *International Journal of Secure Software Engineering*, 3(1), 62–63. doi:10.4018/jsse.2012010104

Kilger, M. (2011). Social dynamics and the future of technology-driven crime. In T. Holt, & B. Schell (Eds.), *Corporate hacking and technology-driven crime: Social dynamics and implications* (pp. 205–227). Hershey, PA: Information Science Reference.

Kirwan, G., & Power, A. (2012). Hacking: Legal and ethical aspects of an ambiguous activity. In A. Dudley, J. Braman, & G. Vincenti (Eds.), *Investigating cyber law and cyber ethics: Issues, impacts and practices* (pp. 21–36). Hershey, PA: Information Science Reference.

Kline, D. M., He, L., & Yaylacicegi, U. (2011). User perceptions of security technologies. [IJISP]. *International Journal of Information Security and Privacy*, 5(2), 1–12. doi:10.4018/jisp.2011040101

Kolkowska, E., Hedström, K., & Karlsson, F. (2012). Analyzing information security goals. In M. Gupta, J. Walp, & R. Sharman (Eds.), *Threats, countermeasures, and advances in applied information security* (pp. 91–110). Hershey, PA: Information Science Reference. doi:10.4018/978-1-4666-0978-5.ch005

Korhonen, J. J., Hiekkanen, K., & Mykkänen, J. (2012). Information security governance. In M. Gupta, J. Walp, & R. Sharman (Eds.), *Strategic and practical approaches for information security governance: Technologies and applied solutions* (pp. 53–66). Hershey, PA: Information Science Reference. doi:10.4018/978-1-4666-0197-0.ch004

Korovessis, P. (2011). Information security awareness in academia. [IJKSR]. *International Journal of Knowledge Society Research*, 2(4), 1–17. doi:10.4018/jksr.2011100101

Koskosas, I., & Sariannidis, N. (2011). Project commitment in the context of information security. [IJITPM]. *International Journal of Information Technology Project Management*, 2(3), 17–29. doi:10.4018/jitpm.2011070102

Kotsonis, E., & Eliakis, S. (2013). Information security standards for health information systems: The implementer's approach. In I. Management Association (Ed.), User-driven healthcare: Concepts, methodologies, tools, and applications (pp. 225-257). Hershey, PA: Medical Information Science Reference. doi: doi:10.4018/978-1-4666-2770-3.ch013

Krishna, A. V. (2014). A randomized cloud library security environment. In S. Dhamdhere (Ed.), *Cloud computing and virtualization technologies in libraries* (pp. 278–296). Hershey, PA: Information Science Reference.

Kruck, S. E., & Teer, F. P. (2011). Computer security practices and perceptions of the next generation of corporate computer users. In H. Nemati (Ed.), *Pervasive information security and privacy developments: Trends and advancements* (pp. 255–265). Hershey, PA: Information Science Reference.

Kumar, M., Sareen, M., & Chhabra, S. (2011). Technology related trust issues in SME B2B E-Commerce. [IJICTHD]. *International Journal of Information Communication Technologies and Human Development*, *3*(4), 31–46. doi:10.4018/jicthd.2011100103

Kumar, P., & Mittal, S. (2012). The perpetration and prevention of cyber crime: An analysis of cyber terrorism in India. [IJT]. *International Journal of Technoethics*, *3*(1), 43–52. doi:10.4018/jte.2012010104

Kumar, P. S., Ashok, M. S., & Subramanian, R. (2012). A publicly verifiable dynamic secret sharing protocol for secure and dependable data storage in cloud computing. [IJCAC]. *International Journal of Cloud Applications and Computing*, *2*(3), 1–25. doi:10.4018/ijcac.2012070101

Kumar, S., & Dutta, K. (2014). Security issues in mobile ad hoc networks: A survey. In D. Rawat, B. Bista, & G. Yan (Eds.), *Security, privacy, trust, and resource management in mobile and wireless communications* (pp. 176–221). Hershey, PA: Information Science Reference.

Lawson, S. (2013). Motivating cybersecurity: Assessing the status of critical infrastructure as an object of cyber threats. In C. Laing, A. Badii, & P. Vickers (Eds.), *Securing critical infrastructures and critical control systems: Approaches for threat protection* (pp. 168–189). Hershey, PA: Information Science Reference.

Leitch, S., & Warren, M. (2011). The ethics of security of personal information upon Facebook. In M. Quigley (Ed.), *ICT ethics and security in the 21st century: New developments and applications* (pp. 46–65). Hershey, PA: Information Science Reference. doi:10.4018/978-1-60960-573-5.ch003

Li, M. (2013). Security terminology. In A. Miri (Ed.), *Advanced security and privacy for RFID technologies* (pp. 1–13). Hershey, PA: Information Science Reference. doi:10.4018/978-1-4666-3685-9.ch001

Ligaarden, O. S., Refsdal, A., & Stølen, K. (2013). Using indicators to monitor security risk in systems of systems: How to capture and measure the impact of service dependencies on the security of provided services. In D. Mellado, L. Enrique Sánchez, E. Fernández-Medina, & M. Piattini (Eds.), *IT security governance innovations: Theory and research* (pp. 256–292). Hershey, PA: Information Science Reference.

Lim, J. S., Chang, S., Ahmad, A., & Maynard, S. (2012). Towards an organizational culture framework for information security practices. In M. Gupta, J. Walp, & R. Sharman (Eds.), *Strategic and practical approaches for information security governance: Technologies and applied solutions* (pp. 296–315). Hershey, PA: Information Science Reference. doi:10.4018/978-1-4666-0197-0.ch017

Lin, X., & Luppicini, R. (2011). Socio-technical influences of cyber espionage: A case study of the GhostNet system. [IJT]. *International Journal of Technoethics*, *2*(2), 65–77. doi:10.4018/jte.2011040105

Lindström, J., & Hanken, C. (2012). Security challenges and selected legal aspects for wearable computing. [JITR]. *Journal of Information Technology Research*, *5*(1), 68–87. doi:10.4018/jitr.2012010104

Maheshwari, H., Hyman, H., & Agrawal, M. (2012). A comparison of cyber-crime definitions in India and the United States. In I. Management Association (Ed.), Cyber crime: Concepts, methodologies, tools and applications (pp. 714-726). Hershey, PA: Information Science Reference. doi: doi:10.4018/978-1-61350-323-2.ch401

Malcolmson, J. (2014). The role of security culture. In I. Portela, & F. Almeida (Eds.), *Organizational, legal, and technological dimensions of information system administration* (pp. 225–242). Hershey, PA: Information Science Reference.

Mantas, G., Lymberopoulos, D., & Komninos, N. (2011). Security in smart home environment. In A. Lazakidou, K. Siassiakos, & K. Ioannou (Eds.), *Wireless technologies for ambient assisted living and healthcare: Systems and applications* (pp. 170–191). Hershey, PA: Medical Information Science Reference.

Maple, C., Short, E., Brown, A., Bryden, C., & Salter, M. (2012). Cyberstalking in the UK: Analysis and recommendations. [IJDST]. *International Journal of Distributed Systems and Technologies*, *3*(4), 34–51. doi:10.4018/jdst.2012100104

Maqousi, A., & Balikhina, T. (2011). Building security awareness culture to serve e-government initiative. In A. Al Ajeeli, & Y. Al-Bastaki (Eds.), *Handbook of research on e-services in the public sector: E-government strategies and advancements* (pp. 304–311). Hershey, PA: Information Science Reference.

Martin, N., & Rice, J. (2013). Spearing high net wealth individuals: The case of online fraud and mature age internet users. [IJISP]. *International Journal of Information Security and Privacy*, *7*(1), 1–15. doi:10.4018/jisp.2013010101

Martino, L., & Bertino, E. (2012). Security for web services: Standards and research issues. In L. Jie-Zhang (Ed.), *Innovations, standards and practices of web services: Emerging research topics* (pp. 336–362). Hershey, PA: Information Science Reference.

Massonet, P., Michot, A., Naqvi, S., Villari, M., & Latanicki, J. (2013). Securing the external interfaces of a federated infrastructure cloud. In I. Management Association (Ed.), IT policy and ethics: Concepts, methodologies, tools, and applications (pp. 1876-1903). Hershey, PA: Information Science Reference. doi: doi:10.4018/978-1-4666-2919-6.ch082

Maumbe, B., & Owei, V. T. (2013). Understanding the information security landscape in South Africa: Implications for strategic collaboration and policy development. In B. Maumbe, & C. Patrikakis (Eds.), *E-agriculture and rural development: Global innovations and future prospects* (pp. 90–102). Hershey, PA: Information Science Reference.

Mazumdar, C. (2011). Enterprise information system security: A life-cycle approach. In I. Management Association (Ed.), Enterprise information systems: Concepts, methodologies, tools and applications (pp. 154-168). Hershey, PA: Business Science Reference. doi: doi:10.4018/978-1-61692-852-0.ch111

McCune, J., & Haworth, D. A. (2012). Securing America against cyber war. [IJCWT]. *International Journal of Cyber Warfare & Terrorism*, *2*(1), 39–49. doi:10.4018/ijcwt.2012010104

Melvin, A. O., & Ayotunde, T. (2011). Spirituality in cybercrime (Yahoo Yahoo) activities among youths in south west Nigeria. In E. Dunkels, G. Franberg, & C. Hallgren (Eds.), *Youth culture and net culture: Online social practices* (pp. 357–380). Hershey, PA: Information Science Reference.

Miller, J. M., Higgins, G. E., & Lopez, K. M. (2013). Considering the role of e-government in cybercrime awareness and prevention: Toward a theoretical research program for the 21st century. In I. Association (Ed.), *Digital rights management: Concepts, methodologies, tools, and applications* (pp. 789–800). Hershey, PA: Information Science Reference.

Millman, C., Whitty, M., Winder, B., & Griffiths, M. D. (2012). Perceived criminality of cyber-harassing behaviors among undergraduate students in the United Kingdom. [IJCBPL]. *International Journal of Cyber Behavior, Psychology and Learning*, 2(4), 49–59. doi:10.4018/ijcbpl.2012100104

Minami, N. A. (2012). Employing dynamic models to enhance corporate IT security policy. [IJATS]. *International Journal of Agent Technologies and Systems*, 4(2), 42–59. doi:10.4018/jats.2012040103

Mirante, D. P., & Ammari, H. M. (2014). Wireless sensor network security attacks: A survey. In I. Management Association (Ed.), Crisis management: Concepts, methodologies, tools and applications (pp. 25-59). Hershey, PA: Information Science Reference. doi: doi:10.4018/978-1-4666-4707-7.ch002

Mishra, A., & Mishra, D. (2013). Cyber stalking: A challenge for web security. In J. Bishop (Ed.), *Examining the concepts, issues, and implications of internet trolling* (pp. 32–42). Hershey, PA: Information Science Reference. doi:10.4018/978-1-4666-2803-8.ch004

Mishra, S. (2011). Wireless sensor networks: Emerging applications and security solutions. In D. Kar, & M. Syed (Eds.), *Network security, administration and management: Advancing technology and practice* (pp. 217–236). Hershey, PA: Information Science Reference. doi:10.4018/978-1-60960-777-7.ch011

Mitra, S., & Padman, R. (2012). Privacy and security concerns in adopting social media for personal health management: A health plan case study. [JCIT]. *Journal of Cases on Information Technology*, 14(4), 12–26. doi:10.4018/jcit.2012100102

Modares, H., Lloret, J., Moravejosharieh, A., & Salleh, R. (2014). Security in mobile cloud computing. In J. Rodrigues, K. Lin, & J. Lloret (Eds.), *Mobile networks and cloud computing convergence for progressive services and applications* (pp. 79–91). Hershey, PA: Information Science Reference.

Mohammadi, S., Golara, S., & Mousavi, N. (2012). Selecting adequate security mechanisms in e-business processes using fuzzy TOPSIS. [IJFSA]. *International Journal of Fuzzy System Applications*, 2(1), 35–53. doi:10.4018/ijfsa.2012010103

Mohammed, L. A. (2012). ICT security policy: Challenges and potential remedies. In I. Management Association (Ed.), Cyber crime: Concepts, methodologies, tools and applications (pp. 999-1015). Hershey, PA: Information Science Reference. doi: doi:10.4018/978-1-61350-323-2.ch501

Molok, N. N., Ahmad, A., & Chang, S. (2012). Online social networking: A source of intelligence for advanced persistent threats. [IJCWT]. *International Journal of Cyber Warfare & Terrorism*, 2(1), 1–13. doi:10.4018/ijcwt.2012010101

Monteleone, S. (2011). Ambient intelligence: Legal challenges and possible directions for privacy protection. In C. Akrivopoulou, & A. Psygkas (Eds.), *Personal data privacy and protection in a surveillance era: Technologies and practices* (pp. 201–221). Hershey, PA: Information Science Reference.

Moralis, A., Pouli, V., Grammatikou, M., Kalogeras, D., & Maglaris, V. (2012). Security standards and issues for grid computing. In N. Preve (Ed.), *Computational and data grids: Principles, applications and design* (pp. 248–264). Hershey, PA: Information Science Reference. doi:10.4018/978-1-4666-0879-5.ch708

Mouratidis, H., & Kang, M. (2011). Secure by design: Developing secure software systems from the ground up. [IJSSE]. *International Journal of Secure Software Engineering*, 2(3), 23–41. doi:10.4018/jsse.2011070102

Murthy, A. S., Nagadevara, V., & De', R. (2012). Predictive models in cybercrime investigation: An application of data mining techniques. In J. Wang (Ed.), *Advancing the service sector with evolving technologies: Techniques and principles* (pp. 166–177). Hershey, PA: Business Science Reference. doi:10.4018/978-1-4666-0044-7.ch011

Nabi, S. I., Al-Ghmlas, G. S., & Alghathbar, K. (2012). Enterprise information security policies, standards, and procedures: A survey of available standards and guidelines. In M. Gupta, J. Walp, & R. Sharman (Eds.), *Strategic and practical approaches for information security governance: Technologies and applied solutions* (pp. 67–89). Hershey, PA: Information Science Reference. doi:10.4018/978-1-4666-0197-0.ch005

Nachtigal, S. (2011). E-business and security. In O. Bak, & N. Stair (Eds.), *Impact of e-business technologies on public and private organizations: Industry comparisons and perspectives* (pp. 262–277). Hershey, PA: Business Science Reference. doi:10.4018/978-1-60960-501-8.ch016

Namal, S., & Gurtov, A. (2012). Security and mobility aspects of femtocell networks. In R. Saeed, B. Chaudhari, & R. Mokhtar (Eds.), *Femtocell communications and technologies: Business opportunities and deployment challenges* (pp. 124–156). Hershey, PA: Information Science Reference. doi:10.4018/978-1-4666-0092-8.ch008

Naqvi, D. E. (2011). Designing efficient security services infrastructure for virtualization oriented architectures. In H. Nemati (Ed.), *Pervasive information security and privacy developments: Trends and advancements* (pp. 149–171). Hershey, PA: Information Science Reference.

Neto, A. A., & Vieira, M. (2011). Security gaps in databases: A comparison of alternative software products for web applications support. [IJSSE]. *International Journal of Secure Software Engineering*, 2(3), 42–62. doi:10.4018/jsse.2011070103

Ngugi, B., Mana, J., & Segal, L. (2011). Evaluating the quality and usefulness of data breach information systems. [IJISP]. *International Journal of Information Security and Privacy*, 5(4), 31–46. doi:10.4018/jisp.2011100103

Nhlabatsi, A., Bandara, A., Hayashi, S., Haley, C., Jurjens, J., & Kaiya, H. ... Yu, Y. (2011). Security patterns: Comparing modeling approaches. In H. Mouratidis (Ed.), *Software engineering for secure systems: Industrial and research perspectives* (pp. 75-111). Hershey, PA: Information Science Reference. doi: doi:10.4018/978-1-61520-837-1.ch004

Nicho, M. (2013). An information governance model for information security management. In D. Mellado, L. Enrique Sánchez, E. Fernández-Medina, & M. Piattini (Eds.), *IT security governance innovations: Theory and research* (pp. 155–189). Hershey, PA: Information Science Reference.

Nicho, M., Fakhry, H., & Haiber, C. (2011). An integrated security governance framework for effective PCI DSS implementation. [IJISP]. *International Journal of Information Security and Privacy*, 5(3), 50–67. doi:10.4018/jisp.2011070104

Nobelis, N., Boudaoud, K., Delettre, C., & Riveill, M. (2012). Designing security properties-centric communication protocols using a component-based approach. [IJDST]. *International Journal of Distributed Systems and Technologies*, 3(1), 1–16. doi:10.4018/jdst.2012010101

Ohashi, M., & Hori, M. (2011). Security management services based on authentication roaming between different certificate authorities. In M. Cruz-Cunha, & J. Varajao (Eds.), *Enterprise information systems design, implementation and management: Organizational applications* (pp. 72–84). Hershey, PA: Information Science Reference.

Okubo, T., Kaiya, H., & Yoshioka, N. (2012). Analyzing impacts on software enhancement caused by security design alternatives with patterns. [IJSSE]. *International Journal of Secure Software Engineering*, 3(1), 37–61. doi:10.4018/jsse.2012010103

Oost, D., & Chew, E. K. (2012). Investigating the concept of information security culture. In M. Gupta, J. Walp, & R. Sharman (Eds.), *Strategic and practical approaches for information security governance: Technologies and applied solutions* (pp. 1–12). Hershey, PA: Information Science Reference. doi:10.4018/978-1-4666-0197-0.ch001

Otero, A. R., Ejnioui, A., Otero, C. E., & Tejay, G. (2013). Evaluation of information security controls in organizations by grey relational analysis. [IJDTIS]. *International Journal of Dependable and Trustworthy Information Systems*, 2(3), 36–54. doi:10.4018/jdtis.2011070103

Ouedraogo, M., Mouratidis, H., Dubois, E., & Khadraoui, D. (2011). Security assurance evaluation and IT systems' context of use security criticality. [IJHCR]. *International Journal of Handheld Computing Research*, 2(4), 59–81. doi:10.4018/jhcr.2011100104

Pal, S. (2013). Cloud computing: Security concerns and issues. In A. Bento, & A. Aggarwal (Eds.), *Cloud computing service and deployment models: Layers and management* (pp. 191–207). Hershey, PA: Business Science Reference.

Palanisamy, R., & Mukerji, B. (2012). Security and privacy issues in e-government. In M. Shareef, N. Archer, & S. Dutta (Eds.), *E-government service maturity and development: Cultural, organizational and technological perspectives* (pp. 236–248). Hershey, PA: Information Science Reference.

Pan, Y., Yuan, B., & Mishra, S. (2011). Network security auditing. In D. Kar, & M. Syed (Eds.), *Network security, administration and management: Advancing technology and practice* (pp. 131–157). Hershey, PA: Information Science Reference. doi:10.4018/978-1-60960-777-7.ch008

Patel, A., Taghavi, M., Júnior, J. C., Latih, R., & Zin, A. M. (2012). Safety measures for social computing in wiki learning environment. [IJISP]. *International Journal of Information Security and Privacy*, 6(2), 1–15. doi:10.4018/jisp.2012040101

Pathan, A. K. (2012). Security management in heterogeneous distributed sensor networks. In S. Bagchi (Ed.), *Ubiquitous multimedia and mobile agents: Models and implementations* (pp. 274–294). Hershey, PA: Information Science Reference.

Paul, C., & Porche, I. R. (2011). Toward a U.S. army cyber security culture. [IJCWT]. *International Journal of Cyber Warfare & Terrorism*, 1(3), 70–80. doi:10.4018/ijcwt.2011070105

Pavlidis, M., Mouratidis, H., & Islam, S. (2012). Modelling security using trust based concepts. [IJSSE]. *International Journal of Secure Software Engineering*, 3(2), 36–53. doi:10.4018/jsse.2012040102

Pendegraft, N., Rounds, M., & Stone, R. W. (2012). Factors influencing college students' use of computer security. In H. Nemati (Ed.), *Optimizing information security and advancing privacy assurance: New technologies* (pp. 225–234). Hershey, PA: Information Science Reference.

Petkovic, M., & Ibraimi, L. (2011). Privacy and security in e-health applications. In C. Röcker, & M. Ziefle (Eds.), *E-health, assistive technologies and applications for assisted living: Challenges and solutions* (pp. 23–48). Hershey, PA: Medical Information Science Reference. doi:10.4018/978-1-60960-469-1.ch002

Picazo-Sanchez, P., Ortiz-Martin, L., Peris-Lopez, P., & Hernandez-Castro, J. C. (2013). Security of EPC class-1. In P. Lopez, J. Hernandez-Castro, & T. Li (Eds.), *Security and trends in wireless identification and sensing platform tags: Advancements in RFID* (pp. 34–63). Hershey, PA: Information Science Reference.

Pieters, W., Probst, C. W., Lukszo, Z., & Montoya, L. (2014). Cost-effectiveness of security measures: A model-based framework. In T. Tsiakis, T. Kargidis, & P. Katsaros (Eds.), *Approaches and processes for managing the economics of information systems* (pp. 139–156). Hershey, PA: Business Science Reference. doi:10.4018/978-1-4666-4983-5.ch009

Pirim, T., James, T., Boswell, K., Reithel, B., & Barkhi, R. (2011). Examining an individual's perceived need for privacy and security: Construct and scale development. In H. Nemati (Ed.), *Pervasive information security and privacy developments: Trends and advancements* (pp. 1–13). Hershey, PA: Information Science Reference.

Podhradsky, A., Casey, C., & Ceretti, P. (2012). The bluetooth honeypot project: Measuring and managing bluetooth risks in the workplace. [IJITN]. *International Journal of Interdisciplinary Telecommunications and Networking*, 4(3), 1–22. doi:10.4018/jitn.2012070101

Pomponiu, V. (2011). Security in e-health applications. In C. Röcker, & M. Ziefle (Eds.), *E-health, assistive technologies and applications for assisted living: Challenges and solutions* (pp. 94–118). Hershey, PA: Medical Information Science Reference. doi:10.4018/978-1-60960-469-1.ch005

Pomponiu, V. (2014). Securing wireless ad hoc networks: State of the art and challenges. In I. Management Association (Ed.), Crisis management: Concepts, methodologies, tools and applications (pp. 81-101). Hershey, PA: Information Science Reference. doi: doi:10.4018/978-1-4666-4707-7.ch004

Pope, M. B., Warkentin, M., & Luo, X. R. (2012). Evolutionary malware: Mobile malware, botnets, and malware toolkits. [IJWNBT]. *International Journal of Wireless Networks and Broadband Technologies*, 2(3), 52–60. doi:10.4018/ijwnbt.2012070105

Prakash, S., Vaish, A., & Coul, N, G, S., Srinidhi, T., & Botsa, J. (2013). Child security in cyberspace through moral cognition. [IJISP]. *International Journal of Information Security and Privacy*, 7(1), 16–29. doi:10.4018/jisp.2013010102

Pye, G. (2011). Critical infrastructure systems: Security analysis and modelling approach. [IJCWT]. *International Journal of Cyber Warfare & Terrorism*, 1(3), 37–58. doi:10.4018/ijcwt.2011070103

Rahman, M. M., & Rezaul, K. M. (2012). Information security management: Awareness of threats in e-commerce. In M. Gupta, J. Walp, & R. Sharman (Eds.), *Threats, countermeasures, and advances in applied information security* (pp. 66–90). Hershey, PA: Information Science Reference. doi:10.4018/978-1-4666-0978-5.ch004

Rak, M., Ficco, M., Luna, J., Ghani, H., Suri, N., Panica, S., & Petcu, D. (2012). Security issues in cloud federations. In M. Villari, I. Brandic, & F. Tusa (Eds.), *Achieving federated and self-manageable cloud infrastructures: Theory and practice* (pp. 176–194). Hershey, PA: Business Science Reference. doi:10.4018/978-1-4666-1631-8.ch010

Ramachandran, M., & Mahmood, Z. (2011). A framework for internet security assessment and improvement process. In M. Ramachandran (Ed.), *Knowledge engineering for software development life cycles: Support technologies and applications* (pp. 244–255). Hershey, PA: Information Science Reference. doi:10.4018/978-1-60960-509-4.ch013

Ramachandran, S., Mundada, R., Bhattacharjee, A., Murthy, C., & Sharma, R. (2011). Classifying host anomalies: Using ontology in information security monitoring. In R. Santanam, M. Sethumadhavan, & M. Virendra (Eds.), *Cyber security, cyber crime and cyber forensics: Applications and perspectives* (pp. 70–86). Hershey, PA: Information Science Reference.

Ramamurthy, B. (2014). Securing business IT on the cloud. In S. Srinivasan (Ed.), *Security, trust, and regulatory aspects of cloud computing in business environments* (pp. 115–125). Hershey, PA: Information Science Reference. doi:10.4018/978-1-4666-5788-5.ch006

Raspotnig, C., & Opdahl, A. L. (2012). Improving security and safety modelling with failure sequence diagrams. [IJSSE]. *International Journal of Secure Software Engineering*, *3*(1), 20–36. doi:10.4018/jsse.2012010102

Reddy, A., & Prasad, G. V. (2012). Consumer perceptions on security, privacy, and trust on e-portals. [IJOM]. *International Journal of Online Marketing*, *2*(2), 10–24. doi:10.4018/ijom.2012040102

Richet, J. (2013). From young hackers to crackers. [IJTHI]. *International Journal of Technology and Human Interaction*, *9*(3), 53–62. doi:10.4018/jthi.2013070104

Rjaibi, N., Rabai, L. B., Ben Aissa, A., & Mili, A. (2013). Mean failure cost as a measurable value and evidence of cybersecurity: E-learning case study. [IJSSE]. *International Journal of Secure Software Engineering*, *4*(3), 64–81. doi:10.4018/jsse.2013070104

Roberts, L. D. (2012). Cyber identity theft. In I. Management Association (Ed.), Cyber crime: Concepts, methodologies, tools and applications (pp. 21-36). Hershey, PA: Information Science Reference. doi: doi:10.4018/978-1-61350-323-2.ch103

Rodríguez, J., Fernández-Medina, E., Piattini, M., & Mellado, D. (2011). A security requirements engineering tool for domain engineering in software product lines. In N. Milanovic (Ed.), *Non-functional properties in service oriented architecture: Requirements, models and methods* (pp. 73–92). Hershey, PA: Information Science Reference. doi:10.4018/978-1-60566-794-2.ch004

Roldan, M., & Rea, A. (2011). Individual privacy and security in virtual worlds. In A. Rea (Ed.), *Security in virtual worlds, 3D webs, and immersive environments: Models for development, interaction, and management* (pp. 1–19). Hershey, PA: Information Science Reference.

Rowe, N. C., Garfinkel, S. L., Beverly, R., & Yannakogeorgos, P. (2011). Challenges in monitoring cyber-arms compliance. [IJCWT]. *International Journal of Cyber Warfare & Terrorism*, *1*(2), 35–48. doi:10.4018/ijcwt.2011040104

Rwabutaza, A., Yang, M., & Bourbakis, N. (2012). A comparative survey on cryptology-based methodologies. [IJISP]. *International Journal of Information Security and Privacy*, *6*(3), 1–37. doi:10.4018/jisp.2012070101

Sadkhan, S. B., & Abbas, N. A. (2014). Privacy and security of wireless communication networks. In J. Rodrigues, K. Lin, & J. Lloret (Eds.), *Mobile networks and cloud computing convergence for progressive services and applications* (pp. 58–78). Hershey, PA: Information Science Reference.

Saedy, M., & Mojtahed, V. (2011). Machine-to-machine communications and security solution in cellular systems. [IJITN]. *International Journal of Interdisciplinary Telecommunications and Networking*, *3*(2), 66–75. doi:10.4018/jitn.2011040105

San Nicolas-Rocca, T., & Olfman, L. (2013). End user security training for identification and access management. [JOEUC]. *Journal of Organizational and End User Computing*, *25*(4), 75–103. doi:10.4018/joeuc.2013100104

Satoh, F., Nakamura, Y., Mukhi, N. K., Tatsubori, M., & Ono, K. (2011). Model-driven approach for end-to-end SOA security configurations. In N. Milanovic (Ed.), *Non-functional properties in service oriented architecture: Requirements, models and methods* (pp. 268–298). Hershey, PA: Information Science Reference. doi:10.4018/978-1-60566-794-2.ch012

Saucez, D., Iannone, L., & Bonaventure, O. (2014). The map-and-encap locator/identifier separation paradigm: A security analysis. In M. Boucadair, & D. Binet (Eds.), *Solutions for sustaining scalability in internet growth* (pp. 148–163). Hershey, PA: Information Science Reference.

Schell, B. H., & Holt, T. J. (2012). A profile of the demographics, psychological predispositions, and social/behavioral patterns of computer hacker insiders and outsiders. In I. Management Association (Ed.), Cyber crime: Concepts, methodologies, tools and applications (pp. 1461-1484). Hershey, PA: Information Science Reference. doi: doi:10.4018/978-1-61350-323-2.ch705

Schmidt, H. (2011). Threat and risk-driven security requirements engineering. [IJMCMC]. *International Journal of Mobile Computing and Multimedia Communications*, *3*(1), 35–50. doi:10.4018/jmcmc.2011010103

Schmidt, H., Hatebur, D., & Heisel, M. (2011). A pattern-based method to develop secure software. In H. Mouratidis (Ed.), *Software engineering for secure systems: Industrial and research perspectives* (pp. 32–74). Hershey, PA: Information Science Reference.

Seale, R. O., & Hargiss, K. M. (2011). A proposed architecture for autonomous mobile agent intrusion prevention and malware defense in heterogeneous networks. [IJSITA]. *International Journal of Strategic Information Technology and Applications*, *2*(4), 44–54. doi:10.4018/jsita.2011100104

Sen, J. (2013). Security and privacy challenges in cognitive wireless sensor networks. In N. Meghanathan, & Y. Reddy (Eds.), *Cognitive radio technology applications for wireless and mobile ad hoc networks* (pp. 194–232). Hershey, PA: Information Science Reference. doi:10.4018/978-1-4666-4221-8.ch011

Sen, J. (2014). Security and privacy issues in cloud computing. In A. Ruiz-Martinez, R. Marin-Lopez, & F. Pereniguez-Garcia (Eds.), *Architectures and protocols for secure information technology infrastructures* (pp. 1–45). Hershey, PA: Information Science Reference.

Sengupta, A., & Mazumdar, C. (2011). A mark-up language for the specification of information security governance requirements. [IJISP]. *International Journal of Information Security and Privacy*, *5*(2), 33–53. doi:10.4018/jisp.2011040103

Shaqrah, A. A. (2011). The influence of internet security on e-business competence in Jordan: An empirical analysis. In I. Management Association (Ed.), Global business: Concepts, methodologies, tools and applications (pp. 1071-1086). Hershey, PA: Business Science Reference. doi: doi:10.4018/978-1-60960-587-2.ch413

Shareef, M. A., & Kumar, V. (2012). Prevent/control identity theft: Impact on trust and consumers' purchase intention in B2C EC. [IRMJ]. *Information Resources Management Journal*, *25*(3), 30–60. doi:10.4018/irmj.2012070102

Sharma, K., & Singh, A. (2011). Biometric security in the e-world. In H. Nemati, & L. Yang (Eds.), *Applied cryptography for cyber security and defense: Information encryption and cyphering* (pp. 289–337). Hershey, PA: Information Science Reference.

Sharma, R. K. (2014). Physical layer security and its applications: A survey. In D. Rawat, B. Bista, & G. Yan (Eds.), *Security, Privacy, Trust, and Resource Management in Mobile and Wireless Communications* (pp. 29–60). Hershey, PA: Information Science Reference.

Shaw, R., Keh, H., & Huang, N. (2011). Information security awareness on-line materials design with knowledge maps. [IJDET]. *International Journal of Distance Education Technologies*, *9*(4), 41–56. doi:10.4018/jdet.2011100104

Shebanow, A., Perez, R., & Howard, C. (2012). The effect of firewall testing types on cloud security policies. [IJSITA]. *International Journal of Strategic Information Technology and Applications*, *3*(3), 60–68. doi:10.4018/jsita.2012070105

Shen, Y., Li, Y., Wu, L., Liu, S., & Wen, Q. (2014). Data protection in the cloud era. In Y. Shen, Y. Li, L. Wu, S. Liu, & Q. Wen (Eds.), *Enabling the new era of cloud computing: Data security, transfer, and management* (pp. 132–154). Hershey, PA: Information Science Reference.

Shen, Y., Li, Y., Wu, L., Liu, S., & Wen, Q. (2014). Enterprise security monitoring with the fusion center model. In Y. Shen, Y. Li, L. Wu, S. Liu, & Q. Wen (Eds.), *Enabling the new era of cloud computing: Data security, transfer, and management* (pp. 116–131). Hershey, PA: Information Science Reference.

Shore, M. (2011). Cyber security and anti-social networking. In I. Management Association (Ed.), Virtual communities: Concepts, methodologies, tools and applications (pp. 1286-1297). Hershey, PA: Information Science Reference. doi: doi:10.4018/978-1-60960-100-3.ch412

Siddiqi, J., Alqatawna, J., & Btoush, M. H. (2011). Do insecure systems increase global digital divide? In I. Management Association (Ed.), Global business: Concepts, methodologies, tools and applications (pp. 2102-2111). Hershey, PA: Business Science Reference. doi: doi:10.4018/978-1-60960-587-2.ch717

Simpson, J. J., Simpson, M. J., Endicott-Popovsky, B., & Popovsky, V. (2012). Secure software education: A contextual model-based approach. In K. Khan (Ed.), *Security-aware systems applications and software development methods* (pp. 286–312). Hershey, PA: Information Science Reference. doi:10.4018/978-1-4666-1580-9.ch016

Singh, S. (2012). Security threats and issues with MANET. In K. Lakhtaria (Ed.), *Technological advancements and applications in mobile ad-hoc networks: Research trends* (pp. 247–263). Hershey, PA: Information Science Reference. doi:10.4018/978-1-4666-0321-9.ch015

Sockel, H., & Falk, L. K. (2012). Online privacy, vulnerabilities, and threats: A manager's perspective. In I. Management Association (Ed.), Cyber crime: Concepts, methodologies, tools and applications (pp. 101-123). Hershey, PA: Information Science Reference. doi: doi:10.4018/978-1-61350-323-2.ch108

Spruit, M., & de Bruijn, W. (2012). CITS: The cost of IT security framework. [IJISP]. *International Journal of Information Security and Privacy*, *6*(4), 94–116. doi:10.4018/jisp.2012100105

Srinivasan, C., Lakshmy, K., & Sethumadhavan, M. (2011). Complexity measures of cryptographically secure boolean functions. In R. Santanam, M. Sethumadhavan, & M. Virendra (Eds.), *Cyber security, cyber crime and cyber forensics: Applications and perspectives* (pp. 220–230). Hershey, PA: Information Science Reference.

Srivatsa, M., Agrawal, D., & McDonald, A. D. (2012). Security across disparate management domains in coalition MANETs. In I. Management Association (Ed.), Wireless technologies: Concepts, methodologies, tools and applications (pp. 1494-1518). Hershey, PA: Information Science Reference. doi: doi:10.4018/978-1-61350-101-6.ch521

Stojanovic, M. D., Acimovic-Raspopovic, V. S., & Rakas, S. B. (2013). Security management issues for open source ERP in the NGN environment. In I. Association (Ed.), *Enterprise resource planning: Concepts, methodologies, tools, and applications* (pp. 789–804). Hershey, PA: Business Science Reference. doi:10.4018/978-1-4666-4153-2.ch046

Stoll, M., & Breu, R. (2012). Information security governance and standard based management systems. In M. Gupta, J. Walp, & R. Sharman (Eds.), *Strategic and practical approaches for information security governance: Technologies and applied solutions* (pp. 261–282). Hershey, PA: Information Science Reference. doi:10.4018/978-1-4666-0197-0.ch015

Sundaresan, M., & Boopathy, D. (2014). Different perspectives of cloud security. In S. Srinivasan (Ed.), *Security, trust, and regulatory aspects of cloud computing in business environments* (pp. 73–90). Hershey, PA: Information Science Reference. doi:10.4018/978-1-4666-5788-5.ch004

Takabi, H., Joshi, J. B., & Ahn, G. (2013). Security and privacy in cloud computing: Towards a comprehensive framework. In X. Yang, & L. Liu (Eds.), *Principles, methodologies, and service-oriented approaches for cloud computing* (pp. 164–184). Hershey, PA: Business Science Reference. doi:10.4018/978-1-4666-2854-0.ch007

Takabi, H., Zargar, S. T., & Joshi, J. B. (2014). Mobile cloud computing and its security and privacy challenges. In D. Rawat, B. Bista, & G. Yan (Eds.), *Security, privacy, trust, and resource management in mobile and wireless communications* (pp. 384–407). Hershey, PA: Information Science Reference.

Takemura, T. (2014). Unethical information security behavior and organizational commitment. In T. Tsiakis, T. Kargidis, & P. Katsaros (Eds.), *Approaches and processes for managing the economics of information systems* (pp. 181–198). Hershey, PA: Business Science Reference. doi:10.4018/978-1-4666-4983-5.ch011

Talib, S., Clarke, N. L., & Furnell, S. M. (2011). Establishing a personalized information security culture. [IJMCMC]. *International Journal of Mobile Computing and Multimedia Communications*, 3(1), 63–79. doi:10.4018/jmcmc.2011010105

Talukder, A. K. (2011). Securing next generation internet services. In R. Santanam, M. Sethumadhavan, & M. Virendra (Eds.), *Cyber security, cyber crime and cyber forensics: Applications and perspectives* (pp. 87–105). Hershey, PA: Information Science Reference.

Tchepnda, C., Moustafa, H., Labiod, H., & Bourdon, G. (2011). Vehicular networks security: Attacks, requirements, challenges and current contributions. In K. Curran (Ed.), *Ubiquitous developments in ambient computing and intelligence: Human-centered applications* (pp. 43–55). Hershey, PA: Information Science Reference. doi:10.4018/978-1-60960-549-0.ch004

Tereshchenko, N. (2012). US foreign policy challenges of non-state actors' cyber terrorism against critical infrastructure. [IJCWT]. *International Journal of Cyber Warfare & Terrorism*, 2(4), 28–48. doi:10.4018/ijcwt.2012100103

Thurimella, R., & Baird, L. C. (2011). Network security. In H. Nemati, & L. Yang (Eds.), *Applied cryptography for cyber security and defense: Information encryption and cyphering* (pp. 1–31). Hershey, PA: Information Science Reference.

Thurimella, R., & Mitchell, W. (2011). Cloak and dagger: Man-in-the-middle and other insidious attacks. In H. Nemati (Ed.), *Security and privacy assurance in advancing technologies: New developments* (pp. 252–270). Hershey, PA: Information Science Reference.

Tiwari, S., Singh, A., Singh, R. S., & Singh, S. K. (2013). Internet security using biometrics. In I. Management Association (Ed.), IT policy and ethics: Concepts, methodologies, tools, and applications (pp. 1680-1707). Hershey, PA: Information Science Reference. doi: doi:10.4018/978-1-4666-2919-6.ch074

Tomaiuolo, M. (2012). Trust enforcing and trust building, different technologies and visions. [IJCWT]. *International Journal of Cyber Warfare & Terrorism*, *2*(4), 49–66. doi:10.4018/ijcwt.2012100104

Tomaiuolo, M. (2014). Trust management and delegation for the administration of web services. In I. Portela, & F. Almeida (Eds.), *Organizational, legal, and technological dimensions of information system administration* (pp. 18–37). Hershey, PA: Information Science Reference.

Touhafi, A., Braeken, A., Cornetta, G., Mentens, N., & Steenhaut, K. (2011). Secure techniques for remote reconfiguration of wireless embedded systems. In M. Cruz-Cunha, & F. Moreira (Eds.), *Handbook of research on mobility and computing: Evolving technologies and ubiquitous impacts* (pp. 930–951). Hershey, PA: Information Science Reference. doi:10.4018/978-1-60960-042-6.ch058

Traore, I., & Woungang, I. (2013). Software security engineering – Part I: Security requirements and risk analysis. In K. Buragga, & N. Zaman (Eds.), *Software development techniques for constructive information systems design* (pp. 221–255). Hershey, PA: Information Science Reference. doi:10.4018/978-1-4666-3679-8.ch012

Tripathi, M., Gaur, M., & Laxmi, V. (2014). Security challenges in wireless sensor network. In D. Rawat, B. Bista, & G. Yan (Eds.), *Security, privacy, trust, and resource management in mobile and wireless communications* (pp. 334–359). Hershey, PA: Information Science Reference.

Trösterer, S., Beck, E., Dalpiaz, F., Paja, E., Giorgini, P., & Tscheligi, M. (2012). Formative user-centered evaluation of security modeling: Results from a case study. [IJSSE]. *International Journal of Secure Software Engineering*, *3*(1), 1–19. doi:10.4018/jsse.2012010101

Tsiakis, T. (2013). The role of information security and cryptography in digital democracy: (Human) rights and freedom. In C. Akrivopoulou, & N. Garipidis (Eds.), *Digital democracy and the impact of technology on governance and politics: New globalized practices* (pp. 158–174). Hershey, PA: Information Science Reference.

Tsiakis, T., Kargidis, T., & Chatzipoulidis, A. (2013). IT security governance in e-banking. In D. Mellado, L. Enrique Sánchez, E. Fernández-Medina, & M. Piattini (Eds.), *IT security governance innovations: Theory and research* (pp. 13–46). Hershey, PA: Information Science Reference.

Turgeman-Goldschmidt, O. (2011). Between hackers and white-collar offenders. In T. Holt, & B. Schell (Eds.), *Corporate hacking and technology-driven crime: Social dynamics and implications* (pp. 18–37). Hershey, PA: Information Science Reference.

Tvrdíková, M. (2012). Information system integrated security. In M. Gupta, J. Walp, & R. Sharman (Eds.), *Strategic and practical approaches for information security governance: Technologies and applied solutions* (pp. 158–169). Hershey, PA: Information Science Reference. doi:10.4018/978-1-4666-0197-0.ch009

Uffen, J., & Breitner, M. H. (2013). Management of technical security measures: An empirical examination of personality traits and behavioral intentions. [IJSODIT]. *International Journal of Social and Organizational Dynamics in IT*, *3*(1), 14–31. doi:10.4018/ijsodit.2013010102

Vance, A., & Siponen, M. T. (2012). IS security policy violations: A rational choice perspective. [JOEUC]. *Journal of Organizational and End User Computing*, *24*(1), 21–41. doi:10.4018/joeuc.2012010102

Veltsos, C. (2011). Mitigating the blended threat: Protecting data and educating users. In D. Kar, & M. Syed (Eds.), *Network security, administration and management: Advancing technology and practice* (pp. 20–37). Hershey, PA: Information Science Reference. doi:10.4018/978-1-60960-777-7.ch002

Venkataraman, R., Pushpalatha, M., & Rao, T. R. (2014). Trust management and modeling techniques in wireless communications. In D. Rawat, B. Bista, & G. Yan (Eds.), *Security, privacy, trust, and resource management in mobile and wireless communications* (pp. 278–294). Hershey, PA: Information Science Reference.

Venkataraman, R., & Rao, T. R. (2012). Security issues and models in mobile ad hoc networks. In K. Lakhtaria (Ed.), *Technological advancements and applications in mobile ad-hoc networks: Research trends* (pp. 219–227). Hershey, PA: Information Science Reference. doi:10.4018/978-1-4666-0321-9.ch013

Viney, D. (2011). Future trends in digital security. In D. Kerr, J. Gammack, & K. Bryant (Eds.), *Digital business security development: Management technologies* (pp. 173–190). Hershey, PA: Business Science Reference.

Vinod, P., Laxmi, V., & Gaur, M. (2011). Metamorphic malware analysis and detection methods. In R. Santanam, M. Sethumadhavan, & M. Virendra (Eds.), *Cyber security, cyber crime and cyber forensics: Applications and perspectives* (pp. 178–202). Hershey, PA: Information Science Reference.

von Solms, R., & Warren, M. (2011). Towards the human information security firewall. [IJCWT]. *International Journal of Cyber Warfare & Terrorism*, *1*(2), 10–17. doi:10.4018/ijcwt.2011040102

Wall, D. S. (2011). Micro-frauds: Virtual robberies, stings and scams in the information age. In T. Holt, & B. Schell (Eds.), *Corporate hacking and technology-driven crime: Social dynamics and implications* (pp. 68–86). Hershey, PA: Information Science Reference.

Wang, H., Zhao, J. L., & Chen, G. (2012). Managing data security in e-markets through relationship driven access control. [JDM]. *Journal of Database Management*, *23*(2), 1–21. doi:10.4018/jdm.2012040101

Warren, M., & Leitch, S. (2011). Protection of Australia in the cyber age. [IJCWT]. *International Journal of Cyber Warfare & Terrorism*, *1*(1), 35–40. doi:10.4018/ijcwt.2011010104

Weber, S. G., & Gustiené, P. (2013). Crafting requirements for mobile and pervasive emergency response based on privacy and security by design principles. [IJISCRAM]. *International Journal of Information Systems for Crisis Response and Management*, *5*(2), 1–18. doi:10.4018/jiscrm.2013040101

Wei, J., Lin, B., & Loho-Noya, M. (2013). Development of an e-healthcare information security risk assessment method. [JDM]. *Journal of Database Management*, *24*(1), 36–57. doi:10.4018/jdm.2013010103

Weippl, E. R., & Riedl, B. (2012). Security, trust, and privacy on mobile devices and multimedia applications. In I. Management Association (Ed.), Cyber crime: Concepts, methodologies, tools and applications (pp. 228-244). Hershey, PA: Information Science Reference. doi: doi:10.4018/978-1-61350-323-2.ch202

White, G., & Long, J. (2012). Global information security factors. In H. Nemati (Ed.), *Optimizing information security and advancing privacy assurance: New technologies* (pp. 163–174). Hershey, PA: Information Science Reference.

White, S. C., Sedigh, S., & Hurson, A. R. (2013). Security concepts for cloud computing. In X. Yang, & L. Liu (Eds.), *Principles, methodologies, and service-oriented approaches for cloud computing* (pp. 116–142). Hershey, PA: Business Science Reference. doi:10.4018/978-1-4666-2854-0.ch005

Whyte, B., & Harrison, J. (2011). State of practice in secure software: Experts' views on best ways ahead. In H. Mouratidis (Ed.), *Software engineering for secure systems: Industrial and research perspectives* (pp. 1–14). Hershey, PA: Information Science Reference.

Wu, Y., & Saunders, C. S. (2011). Governing information security: Governance domains and decision rights allocation patterns. [IRMJ]. *Information Resources Management Journal*, *24*(1), 28–45. doi:10.4018/irmj.2011010103

Yadav, S. B. (2011). SEACON: An integrated approach to the analysis and design of secure enterprise architecture–based computer networks. In H. Nemati (Ed.), *Pervasive information security and privacy developments: Trends and advancements* (pp. 309–331). Hershey, PA: Information Science Reference.

Yadav, S. B. (2012). A six-view perspective framework for system security: Issues, risks, and requirements. In H. Nemati (Ed.), *Optimizing information security and advancing privacy assurance: New technologies* (pp. 58–90). Hershey, PA: Information Science Reference.

Yamany, H. F., Allison, D. S., & Capretz, M. A. (2013). Developing proactive security dimensions for SOA. In I. Management Association (Ed.), IT policy and ethics: Concepts, methodologies, tools, and applications (pp. 900-922). Hershey, PA: Information Science Reference. doi: doi:10.4018/978-1-4666-2919-6.ch041

Yan, G., Rawat, D. B., Bista, B. B., & Chen, L. (2014). Location security in vehicular wireless networks. In D. Rawat, B. Bista, & G. Yan (Eds.), *Security, privacy, trust, and resource management in mobile and wireless communications* (pp. 108–133). Hershey, PA: Information Science Reference.

Yaokumah, W. (2013). Evaluating the effectiveness of information security governance practices in developing nations: A case of Ghana. [IJITBAG]. *International Journal of IT/Business Alignment and Governance*, *4*(1), 27–43. doi:10.4018/jitbag.2013010103

Yates, D., & Harris, A. (2011). International ethical attitudes and behaviors: Implications for organizational information security policy. In M. Dark (Ed.), *Information assurance and security ethics in complex systems: Interdisciplinary perspectives* (pp. 55–80). Hershey, PA: Information Science Reference.

Yau, S. S., Yin, Y., & An, H. (2011). An adaptive approach to optimizing tradeoff between service performance and security in service-based systems. [IJWSR]. *International Journal of Web Services Research*, *8*(2), 74–91. doi:10.4018/jwsr.2011040104

Zadig, S. M., & Tejay, G. (2012). Emerging cybercrime trends: Legal, ethical, and practical issues. In A. Dudley, J. Braman, & G. Vincenti (Eds.), *Investigating cyber law and cyber ethics: Issues, impacts and practices* (pp. 37–56). Hershey, PA: Information Science Reference.

Zafar, H., Ko, M., & Osei-Bryson, K. (2012). Financial impact of information security breaches on breached firms and their non-breached competitors. [IRMJ]. *Information Resources Management Journal*, *25*(1), 21–37. doi:10.4018/irmj.2012010102

Zapata, B. C., & Alemán, J. L. (2013). Security risks in cloud computing: An analysis of the main vulnerabilities. In D. Rosado, D. Mellado, E. Fernandez-Medina, & M. Piattini (Eds.), *Security engineering for cloud computing: Approaches and tools* (pp. 55–71). Hershey, PA: Information Science Reference. doi:10.4018/978-1-4666-4301-7.ch045

Zboril, F., Horacek, J., Drahansky, M., & Hanacek, P. (2012). Security in wireless sensor networks with mobile codes. In M. Gupta, J. Walp, & R. Sharman (Eds.), *Threats, countermeasures, and advances in applied information security* (pp. 411–425). Hershey, PA: Information Science Reference. doi:10.4018/978-1-4666-0978-5.ch021

Zhang, J. (2012). Trust management for VANETs: Challenges, desired properties and future directions. [IJDST]. *International Journal of Distributed Systems and Technologies*, *3*(1), 48–62. doi:10.4018/jdst.2012010104

Zhang, Y., He, L., Shu, L., Hara, T., & Nishio, S. (2012). Security issues on outlier detection and countermeasure for distributed hierarchical wireless sensor networks. In A. Pathan, M. Pathan, & H. Lee (Eds.), *Advancements in distributed computing and internet technologies: Trends and issues* (pp. 182–210). Hershey, PA: Information Science Publishing.

Zheng, X., & Oleshchuk, V. (2012). Security enhancement of peer-to-peer session initiation. In M. Gupta, J. Walp, & R. Sharman (Eds.), *Threats, countermeasures, and advances in applied information security* (pp. 281–308). Hershey, PA: Information Science Reference. doi:10.4018/978-1-4666-0978-5.ch015

Zineddine, M. (2012). Is your automated healthcare information secure? In M. Watfa (Ed.), *E-healthcare systems and wireless communications: Current and future challenges* (pp. 128–142). Hershey, PA: Medical Information Science Reference.

Compilation of References

Acoca, B. (2008). Online identity theft. *The OECD Observer. Organisation for Economic Co-Operation and Development*, (268): 12–13.

Acquisti, A. (2002). *Protecting privacy with economic: Economic incentives for preventive technologies in ubiquitous computing environment*. Paper presented at the Workshop on Socially-informed Design of Privacy-enhancing Solutions in Ubiquitous Computing. New York, NY.

Acree, R. K., Ullah, N., Karia, A., Rahmeh, J. T., & Abraham, J. A. (1993). An object-oriented approach for implementing algorithm-based fault tolerance. In *Proceedings of the 12th Annual International Phoenix Computers and Communications Conference* (pp. 210-216). Academic Press.

Adlakha, V., & Arsham, H. (1992). A simulation technique for estimation in perturbed stochastic activity networks. *Simulation*, *58*(2), 258–267. doi:10.1177/003754979205800406

Agarwal, R., & Karahanna, E. (2000). Time flies when you're having fun: Cognitive absorption and beliefs about information technology usage. *Management Information Systems Quarterly*, *24*(4), 665–694. doi:10.2307/3250951

Aitken, C. G. G. (1995). *Statistics and the evaluation of evidence for forensic scientists*. Chichester, UK: John Wiley.

Aitken, C. G. G., & Lucy, D. (2004). Evaluation of trace evidence in the form of multivariate data. *Journal of the Royal Statistical Society. Series C, Applied Statistics*, *53*, 109–122. doi:10.1046/j.0035-9254.2003.05271.x

Aitken, C. G. G., & Stoney, D. A. (1991). *The use of statistics in forensic science*. New York: Ellis Horwood.

Ajzen, I. (1991). The theory of planned behavior. *Organizational Behavior and Human Decision Processes*, *50*, 179–211. doi:10.1016/0749-5978(91)90020-T

Alba, J., Lynch, J., Weitz, B., Janiszweski, C., Lutz, R., Sawyer, A., & Wood, S. (1997). Interactive home shopping: Consumer, retailer, and manufacturer incentives to participate in electronic marketplaces. *Journal of Marketing*, *61*(3), 38–53. doi:10.2307/1251788

Alder, G. S., Noel, T. W., & Ambrose, M. L. (2006). Clarifying the effects of internet monitoring on job attitudes: The mediating role of employee trust. *Information & Management*, *43*(7), 894–903. doi:10.1016/j.im.2006.08.008

Al-Rousan, T., Sulaiman, S., & Abdul Salam, R. (2009). Risk analysis and web project management. *Journal of Software*, *4*(6), 614–621. doi:10.4304/jsw.4.6.614-621

Altman, I. (1975). *The environment and social behaviour: Privacy, personal space, territory, and crowding*. Monterey, CA: Brooks/Cole.

AMA Survey. (2001). *Workplace monitoring and surveillance*. Retrieved from http://www.amanet.org/research/pdfs/ems_short2001.pdf

AMA Survey. (2003). *Email rules, policies and practices survey.* Retrieved from http://www.amanet.org/research/pdfs/email_policies_practices.pdf

AMA Survey. (2005). *Electronic monitoring and surveillance survey.* Retrieved from http://www.amanet.org/research/pdfs/ems_summary05.pdf

Anderson, J. E., Schwager, P. H., & Kerns, R. L. (2006). The drivers for acceptance of tablet PCs by faculty in a college of business. *Journal of Information Systems Education*, *17*(4), 429–440.

Anderson, K. B., Durbin, E., & Salinger, M. A. (2008). Identity theft. *The Journal of Economic Perspectives*, *22*(2), 171–192. doi:10.1257/jep.22.2.171

Anderson, R. (2001). *Why information security is hard-an economic perspective.* Cambridge, UK: University of Cambridge Computer Laboratory. doi:10.1109/ACSAC.2001.991552

Andres, H. P. (2006). The impact of communication medium on virtual team group process. *Information Resources Management Journal*, *19*(2), 1–17. doi:10.4018/irmj.2006040101

Applegate, L. M., Austin, R. D., & Soule, D. L. (2009). *Corporate information strategy and management: Texts and cases* (8th ed.). New York: McGraw-Hill Companies, Inc.

Arango, C., & Taylor, V. (2009). *The role of convenience and risk in consumers' means of payment (Discussion Papers 09-8).* Ottawa, Canada: Bank of Canada.

Ardichvili, A. A. (2006). Russian orthodoxy worldview and adult learning in the workplace. *Advances in Developing Human Resources*, *8*(3), 373–381. doi:10.1177/1523422306288430

Arsham, H. (1990). Perturbation analysis of general LP models: A unified approach to sensitivity, parametric, tolerance, and more-for-less analysis. *Mathematical and Computer Modelling*, *13*(8), 79–102. doi:10.1016/0895-7177(90)90073-V

Arsham, H. (2005). A computer implementation of the push-and-pull algorithm and its computational comparison with LP simplex method. *Applied Mathematics and Computation*, *170*(1), 36–63. doi:10.1016/j.amc.2004.10.078

Arsham, H. (2007). Construction of the largest sensitivity region for general linear programs. *Applied Mathematics and Computation*, *189*(2), 1435–1447. doi:10.1016/j.amc.2006.12.020

Ashouei, M., & Chatterjee, A. (2009). Checksum-based probabilistic transient-error compensation for linear digital systems. *IEEE Transactions on Very Large Scale Integration Systems*, *17*(10), 1447–1460. doi:10.1109/TVLSI.2008.2004587

Aspray, W., Mayadas, F., & Vardi, M. (2006). *Globalization and offshoring of software: A report of the ACM job migration task force. Association for Computing Machinery.* ACM.

Avison, D., Jones, J., Powell, P., & Wilson, D. (2004). Using and validating the strategic alignment model. *The Journal of Strategic Information Systems*, *13*, 223–246. doi:10.1016/j.jsis.2004.08.002

Awad, N. F., & Ragowsky, A. (2008). Establishing trust in electronic commerce through online word of mouth: An examination across genders. *Journal of Management Information Systems*, *24*(4), 101–121. doi:10.2753/MIS0742-1222240404

Balasubramanian, S., Konana, P., & Menon, N. M. (2003). Customer, satisfaction in virtual environments: A study of online investing. *Management Science*, *7*, 871–889. doi:10.1287/mnsc.49.7.871.16385

Bandura, A. (1977). Self-efficacy: Toward a unifying theory of behavioral change. *Psychological Review*, *84*(2), 191–215. doi:10.1037/0033-295X.84.2.191 PMID:847061

Banerjee, A., & Paul, A. (2008). On path correlation and PERT bias. *European Journal of Operational Research*, *189*(3), 1208–1216. doi:10.1016/j.ejor.2007.01.061

Banerjee, P., Rahmeh, P. J. T., Stunkel, C. B., Nalr, V. S. S., Roy, K., & Abraham, J. A. (1990). Algorithm-based fault tolerance on a hypercube multiprocessor. *IEEE Transactions on Computers, 39*(9), 1132–1145. doi:10.1109/12.57055

Bardram, J. E., Kjaer, R. E., & Pedersen, M. Ö. (2003). Context-aware user authentication – Supporting proximity-based login. In *Proceedings of the Ubiquitous Computing 5th International Conference*. Seattle, WA: Academic Press.

Barfield, W. (2006). *Information privacy as a function of facial recognition technology and wearable computers* (Legal Series Paper 1739). Berkeley, CA: Berkeley Electronic Press. Retrieved from http://law.bepress.com/expresso/eps/1739

Barker, K. J., D'Amato, J., & Sheridon, P. (2008). Credit card fraud: Awareness and prevention. *Journal of Financial Crime, 15*(4), 398–410. doi:10.1108/13590790810907236

Barkhi, R., Amiri, A., & James, T. L. (2006). A study of communication and coordination in collaborative software development. *Journal of Global Information Technology Management, 9*(1), 44–61.

Barki, H., Rivard, S., & Talbot, J. (1993). Towards an assessment of software development risk. *Journal of Management Information Systems, 10*(2), 203–225.

Baron, S., Patterson, A., & Harris, K. (2006). Beyond technology acceptance: Understanding consumer practice. *International Journal of Service Industry Management, 17*(2), 111–135. doi:10.1108/09564230610656962

Barrett-Howard, E., & Tyler, T. R. (1986). Procedural justice as a criterion in allocation decisions. *Journal of Personality and Social Psychology, 50*(2), 296–304. doi:10.1037/0022-3514.50.2.296

Baskerville, R. (1993). Information systems security design methods: Implications for information systems development. *ACM Computing Surveys*. doi:10.1145/162124.162127

Bauer, H. H., Falk, T., & Hammerschmidt, M. (2006). eTransQual: A transaction process-based approach for capturing service quality in online shopping. *Journal of Business Research, 59*, 866–875. doi:10.1016/j.jbusres.2006.01.021

Baylis, J. (1998). *Error-correcting codes: A mathematical introduction*. New York, NY: Chapman and Hall. doi:10.1007/978-1-4899-3276-1

Bélanger, F., & Crossler, R. E. (2011). Privacy in the digital age: A review of information privacy research in information systems. *Management Information Systems Quarterly, 35*(4), 1017–1041.

Bélanger, F., Hiller, J. S., & Smith, W. J. (2002). Trustworthiness in electronic commerce: The role of privacy, security, and site attributes. *The Journal of Strategic Information Systems, 11*(3-4), 245–270. doi:10.1016/S0963-8687(02)00018-5

Bellman, S., Lohse, G., & Eric, J. (1999). Predictors of online buying behavior. *Communications of the ACM, 42*(12), 32–38. doi:10.1145/322796.322805

Berry, G. R. (2011). Enahnacing effectivness on virtual teams: Understanding why traditional team skills are insufficient. *Journal of Business Communication, 48*(2), 186–206. doi:10.1177/0021943610397270

Biernat, J. (2010). Fast fault-tolerant adders. *International Journal of Critical Computer-Based Systems, 1*(1-3), 117–127. doi:10.1504/IJCCBS.2010.031709

Bies, R. J., & Moag, J. F. (1986). Interactional justice: Communication criteria of fairness. In R. J. Lewicki, B. H. Sheppard, & M. H. Bazerman (Eds.), *Research on negotiations in organisations* (Vol. 1, pp. 43–55). Greenwich, CT: JAI Press.

Bistarelli, S., Fioravanti, F., & Peretti, P. (2006). *Defense trees for economic evaluation of security investments. Dipartimento di Scienze, Universita degli, Studi g. d'Annunzio*. D.O.I.

Bluetooth. (2009). *Security*. Retrieved April 4, 2012, from http://www.bluetooth.com/Pages/Simple-Secure-Everywhere.aspx

Bodin, L., Gordon, L. A., & Loeb, M. P. (2008). Information security and risk management. *Communications of the ACM, 51*(4), 64–68. doi:10.1145/1330311.1330325

Boehm, B. (1991). Software risk management: Principles and practices. *IEEE Software, 8*(1), 32–41. doi:10.1109/52.62930

Boronowsky, M., Herzog, O., Knackfuss, P., & Lawo, M. (2005). wearIT@work – Empowering the mobile worker by wearable computing – The first results. In *Proceedings of the AMI@work Forum Day*, (pp. 38-45). Munich, Germany: AMI@work.

Boswald, M., Hagin, C., & Markwiz, W. (1999, June). Methods and standards for privacy and authentication in communications networks: An overview. *International Journal of Electronics and Communications*, 234.

Brandt, V., England, W., & Ward, S. (2011). Virtual teams. *Research Technology Management, 54*(6), 62–63.

Branscum, D. (2000). Guarding online privacy. *Newsweek, 135*(23), 77-78.

Brown, J. S., & Duguid, P. (1998). Organizing knowledge. *California Management Review, 40*(3), 90–111. doi:10.2307/41165945

Brown, J. S., & Duguid, P. (2000). *The social life of information*. Boston, MA: Harvard Business School Press.

Brown, M., & Muchira, R. (2004). Investigating the relationship between internet privacy concerns and online purchase behavior. *Journal of Electronic Commerce Research, 5*(1), 62–70.

Brümmer, N., & du Preez, J. (2006). Application-independent evaluation of speaker detection. *Computer Speech & Language, 20*(2-3), 230–275. doi:10.1016/j.csl.2005.08.001

Buba, N. M. (2000). Waging war against identity theft: Should the United States borrow from the European Union's battalion? *Suffolk Transnational Law Review, 23*, 633.

Cai, S., & Jun, M. (2003). Internet users' perceptions of online service quality: A comparison of online buyers and information searches. *Managing Service Quality, 13*(6), 504–519. doi:10.1108/09604520310506568

Calder, B. J., & Staw, B. M. (1975). Self-perception of intrinsic and extrinsic motivation. *Journal of Personality and Social Psychology, 31*(4), 599–605. doi:10.1037/h0077100 PMID:1159610

California Department of Motor Vehicles. (2002). Retrieved from http://dmv.ca.gov/pubs/vctop/appndxa/civil/civ1798_92.htm

Carlsson, C., Carlsson, J., Hyvönen, K., Puhakainen, J., & Walden, P. (2006). Adoption of mobile devices/services – Searching for answers with the UTAUT. In *Proceedings of the 39th Hawaii International Conference on Systems Sciences*. IEEE.

Cassone, D. (2010). A process to build new product development cycle time predictive models combining fuzzy set theory and probability theory. *International Journal of Applied Decision Sciences, 3*(2), 168–183. doi:10.1504/IJADS.2010.034838

Cavoukian, A. (2009). *Privacy in the clouds*. Toronto: Information and Privacy Commission of Ontario.

Cavusoglu, H., Mishra, B., & Raghunathan, S. (2004). A model for evaluating IT security investments. *Communications of the ACM*. doi:10.1145/1005817.1005828

Cellular-News. (2006). SMS as a tool in murder investigations. *Cellular-News*. Retrieved on 10 November 2011 from http://www.cellular-news.com/story/18775.php

Champod, C., & Evett, I. W. (2000). Commentary on A. P. A. Broeders (1999) 'some observations on the use of probability scales in forensic identification', Forensic Linguistics 6(2), 228-41. *International Journal of Speech Language and the Law, 7*(2), 238–243. doi:10.1558/sll.2000.7.2.238

Chan, Y., Huff, S., Barclay, D., & Copeland, D. (1997). Business strategy orientation. *Information Systems Research, 8*(2), 125–150. doi:10.1287/isre.8.2.125

Chen, Z., & Dongarra, J. (2008). Algorithm-based fault tolerance for fail-stop failures. *IEEE Transactions on Parallel and Distributed Systems, 19*(12), 1628–1641. doi:10.1109/TPDS.2008.58

Chin, W. W., Marcolin, B. L., & Newsted, P. R. (1996). A partial least squares latent variable modeling approach for measuring interaction effects: Results from a Montecarlo simulation study and voice mail emotion/adoption study. In *Proceedings of the 17th International Conference on Information Systems,* (pp. 21-41). IEEE.

Choi, J., Dongarra, J. J., & Walker, D. W. (1996). PB-BLAS: A set of parallel block basic linear algebra subprograms. In *Proceedings of the Conference on Scalable High-Performance Computing* (pp. 534-541). Academic Press.

Ciborra, C. U. (1996). Introduction: What does groupware mean for the organization hosting it? In C. U. Ciborra (Ed.), *Groupware & teamwork.* Chichester, UK: John Wiley & Sons.

Ciborra, C. U. (1997). De Profundis? Deconstructing the concept of strategic alignment. *Scandinavian Journal of Information Systems, 9*(1), 67–82.

Ciborra, C. U. (1998). Crisis and foundations: An inquiry into the nature and limits of models and methods in the information systems discipline. *Scandinavian Journal of Information Systems, 7*(1), 5–16.

Ciborra, C. U. (2002). *The labyrinths of information: Challenging the wisdom of systems.* Oxford, UK: Oxford University Press.

Clarke, R. (1999). Internet privacy concerns confirm the case for intervention. *Communications of the ACM, 42*(2), 60–67. doi:10.1145/293411.293475

Clarke, R. A. (1988). Information technology and dataveillance. *Communications of the ACM, 31*(5), 498–512. doi:10.1145/42411.42413

Coderre, F., Mathieu, A., & St-Laurent, N. (2004). Comparison of the quality of qualitative data obtained through telephone, postal and email surveys. *International Journal of Market Research, 46*(3), 347–357.

Cohen-Charash, Y., & Spector, P. E. (2001). The role of justice in organizations: A meta-analysis. *Organizational Behavior and Human Decision Processes, 86*(2), 278–321. doi:10.1006/obhd.2001.2958

Collier, J. E., & Bienstock, C. C. (2006). Measuring service quality in e-retailing. *Journal of Service Research, 8*(3), 260–275. doi:10.1177/1094670505278867

Collins, J. M. (2001). *Preventing identity theft in the workplace using the four-factor model to secure people, processes, proprietary information, and property (virtual and actual).* Paper presented at the Academy of Criminal Justice Sciences 38th Annual Meeting. Washington, DC.

Collins, J. M. (2003). Business identity theft: The latest twist. *Journal of Forensic Accounting, 1524*(5586), 303–306.

Collins, J. M., & Hoffman, S. K. (2002). *Identity theft: Perpetrator (n = 1,037) profiles and practices: Case study conducted in preparation for grant funding.* Washington, DC: National Institute of Justice, U. S. Department of Justice, Office of Justice Programs.

Copes, H., Kerley, K. R., Huff, R., & Kane, J. (2010). Differentiating identity theft: An exploratory study of victims using a national victimization survey. *Journal of Criminal Justice, 38*(5), 1045–1052. doi:10.1016/j.jcrimjus.2010.07.007

Costello, D., & Lin, S. (2004). *Error control coding fundamentals and applications* (2nd ed.). Upper Saddle River, NJ: Pearson Education.

Cragg, P. B., King, M., & Hussin, H. (2002). IT alignment and firm performance in small manufacturing firms. *The Journal of Strategic Information Systems*, *11*, 109–132. doi:10.1016/S0963-8687(02)00007-0

Craver, C. B. (2006). Privacy issues affecting employers, employees and labour organizations. *Louisiana Law Review*, *66*, 1057–1078.

Culnan, M. J. (1993). How did they get my name? An exploratory investigation of consumer attitudes toward secondary information use. *Management Information Systems Quarterly*, *17*(3), 341–364. doi:10.2307/249775

Cummings, J. N., & Kiesler, S. (2008). *Who collaborates successfully? Prior experience reduces collaboration barriers in distributed interdisciplinary research.* San Diego, CA: ACM. doi:10.1145/1460563.1460633

Cusumano, M. A. (2008). Managing software development in globally distributed teams. *Communications of the ACM*, *51*(2), 15–17. doi:10.1145/1314215.1314218

Czuchra, W. (1999). Optimizing budget spendings for software implementation and testing. *Computers & Operations Research*, *26*(7), 731–747. doi:10.1016/S0305-0548(98)00086-0

D'Urso, S. C. (2006). Who's watching us at work? Toward a structural-perceptual model of electronic monitoring and surveillance in organisations. *Communication Theory*, *16*, 281–303. doi:10.1111/j.1468-2885.2006.00271.x

Daft, R. L. (2000). *Management* (5th ed.). Hinsdale, IL: The Dryden Press.

Dagon, D., Martin, T., & Starner, T. (2004). Mobile phones as computing devices: The viruses are coming! *Pervasive Computing*, *3*(4), 11–15. doi:10.1109/MPRV.2004.21

D'Aquila, N. (1993). Facilitating in-service programs through PERT/CPM: Simultaneous use of these tools can assist nurses in organizing workshops. *Nursing Management*, *24*(2), 92–98. PMID:8265089

Davis, E. S. (2003). A world wide problem on the world wide web: International responses to transnational identity theft via the internet. *Journal of Law and Policy*, *12*, 201–227.

Davis, F. D. (1989). Perceived usefulness, perceived ease of use, and user acceptance of information technology. *Management Information Systems Quarterly*, *13*(3), 319–340. doi:10.2307/249008

Davis, F. D., Bagozzi, R. P., & Warshaw, P. R. (1989). User acceptance of computer technology: A comparison of two theoretical models. *Management Science*, *35*(8), 982–1003. doi:10.1287/mnsc.35.8.982

Davis, G. B. (2002). Anytime/anyplace computing and the future of knowledge work. *Communications of the ACM*, *45*(12), 67–73. doi:10.1145/585597.585617

De Vel, O., Anderson, A., Corney, M., & Mohay, G. (2001). Mining e-mail content for author identification forensics. *SIGMOD Record*, *30*(4), 55–64. doi:10.1145/604264.604272

Devaraj, S., Fan, M., & Kohli, R. (2002). Antecedents of B2C channel satisfaction and preference: Validating e-commerce metrics. *Information Systems Research*, *13*(3), 316–333. doi:10.1287/isre.13.3.316.77

Dinev, T., & Hart, P. (2006). An extended privacy calculus model for e-commerce transactions. *Information Systems Research*, *17*(1), 61–80. doi:10.1287/isre.1060.0080

Dinev, T., Xu, H., Smith, J. H., & Hart, P. (2013). Information privacy and correlates: An empirical attempt to bridge and distinguish privacy-related concepts. *European Journal of Information Systems*, *22*, 295–316. doi:10.1057/ejis.2012.23

Doddington, G. (2001). Speaker recognition based on idiolectal differences between speakers. In Proceedings of 2001 Eurospeech (pp. 2521-2524). Academic Press.

Doheny. (1996). R v Doheny. Court of Appeal Criminal Division. No. 95/5297/Y2.

Dongarra, J. J., & Whaley, R. C. (1995). *A user's guide to the BLACS v1.0* (Tech. Rep. No. CS-95-281). Knoxville, TN: University of Tennessee.

Dotsika, F. (2006). An IT perspective on supporting communities of practice. In E. Coakes, & S. Clarke (Eds.), *Encyclopedia of communities of practice in information and knowledge management* (pp. 257–263). Hershey, PA: Idea Group. doi:10.4018/978-1-59140-556-6.ch045

Douglass, D. B. (2009). An examination of the fraud liability shift in consumer card-based payment systems. *Economic Perspectives*, *33*(1), 43–49.

Dubé, L., Bourhis, A., & Réal Jacob, R. (2006). Towards a typology of virtual communities of practice. *Interdisciplinary Journal of Information, Knowledge, and Management, 1*.

Dube, L., & Pare, G. (2001). Global virtual teams. *Communications of the ACM*, *44*(12), 71–73. doi:10.1145/501317.501349

Duncan, B.D. (2009). An examination of the fraud liability shift in consumer card-based payment systems. *Econ Perspect*, (Q I), 43-49.

Efron, B., & Gong, G. (1983). A leisurely look at the bootstrap, the jackknife, and cross-validation. *The American Statistician*, *37*(1), 36–48.

Ekici, S., Yildirim, S., & Poyraz, M. (2009). A transmission line fault locator based on Elman recurrent networks. *Applied Soft Computing*, *9*(1), 341–347. doi:10.1016/j.asoc.2008.04.011

Elgesem, D. (1999). The structure of rights in directive 95/46/EC on the protection of individuals with regard to the processing of personal data and the free movement of such data. *Ethics and Information Technology*, *1*(4), 283–293. doi:10.1023/A:1010076422893

Elnozahy, E. N., Johnson, D. B., & Zwaenepoel, W. (1992). The performance of consistent checkpointing. In *Proceedings of the 11th Symposium on Reliable Distributed Systems* (pp. 39-47). Academic Press.

European Union Data Protection Directive. (n.d.). Retrieved from http://europa.eu.int/ISPO/legal/en/dataprot/dataprot. html

European Union. (2002). *Directive 95/46/EC: Article 29 WP55*. Retrieved from http://ec.europa.eu/justice_home/fsj/privacy/docs/wpdocs/2002/wpss_en.pdf

Evans, L. (2007). Monitoring technology in the American workplace: Would adopting English privacy standards better balance employee privacy and productivity? *California Law Review*, *95*, 1115–1149.

Farmer, M. (2000). *Agency lists top 10 security threats*. CNET News. Retrieved from http://news.cnet.com

Fassnacht, M., & Koese, I. (2006). Quality of electronic services: Conceptualizing and testing a hierarchical model. *Journal of Service Research*, *9*(1), 19–37. doi:10.1177/1094670506289531

Federal Deposit Insurance Corporation. (2004). Retrieved from www.fdic.gov/consumers/consumer/idtheftstudy/ identity theft.pdf

Federal Trade Commission. (2007). *Consumer fraud and identity theft complaint data: January-December 2006*. Washington, DC: Federal Trade Commission.

Fergerson, J. (2003, June 3). *Five tools you can use to prevent fraud*. Retrieved from http://retailindustry.about.com/library/uc/02/uc_fraud1.htm

Ferreira, L. C., & Dahab, R. (2000). Beyond parasitic authentication. In *Proceedings of the Workshop de Segurança em Informática – Simpósio Brasileiro de Computadores Tolerantes a Falhas*. Curitiba, Brasil: Academic Press.

Fichtman, P. (2001). Preventing credit card fraud and identity theft: A primer for online merchants. *Information Systems Security, 10*(5).

Fishbein, M., & Ajzen, I. (1975). *Belief, attitude, intention and behavior: An introduction to theory and research*. Reading, MA: Addison-Wesley.

Flanagan, J. C. (1954). The critical incident technique. *Psychological Bulletin, 51*(4), 327–358. doi:10.1037/h0061470 PMID:13177800

Flick, U. (1998). *An introduction to qualitative research.* London: Sage Publications.

Foley, L. (2003). *Enhancing law enforcement–Identity theft communication.* Identity Theft Resource Center. Retrieved from http://www.idtheftcenter.org

Fornell, C., & Larcker, D. F. (1981). Evaluating structural equation models with unobservable variables and measurement error. *JMR, Journal of Marketing Research, 18*(1), 39–50. doi:10.2307/3151312

Friedewald, M., Vildjiounaite, E., Punie, Y., & Wright, D. (2007). Privacy, identity and security in ambient intelligence: A scenario analysis. *Telematics and Informatics, 24*, 15–29. doi:10.1016/j.tele.2005.12.005

Froude, J. (2010). *How to choose a firewall.* Retrieved from http://www.inc.com/ss/how-choose-firewall#5

Fung, T. K. F. (2008). Banking with a personalized touch: Examining the impact of website customization on commitment. *Journal of Electronic Commerce Research, 9*(4), 296–309.

Gaide, S. (2005). Evaluating distance education programs with online surveys. *Distance Education Report, 9*(20), 4–5.

Garfield, M. J. (2005). Acceptance of ubiquitous computing. *Information Systems Management, 22*(4), 24–31. doi:10.1201/1078.10580530/45520.22.4.200 50901/90027.3

Garg, A. G., Curtis, J., & Halper, H. (2003). Quantifying the financial impact of of IT security breaches. *Information Management & Computer Security,* 74–84. doi:10.1108/09685220310468646

Gartner Group. (2003, June 2). *Gartner says identity theft is up nearly 80 percent.* Retrieved from http://www3.gartner.com/5_about/press_releases/pr21july2003a.jsp

Gauzente, C. (2004). Web merchants' privacy and security statements: how reassuring are they for consumers? A two-sided approach. *Journal of Electronic Commerce Research, 5*(3), 181–198.

Gefen, D., Karahanna, E., & Straub, D. (2003). Trust and TAM in online shopping: An integrated model. *Management Information Systems Quarterly, 27*(1), 51–90.

Gefen, D., Wyss, S., & Lichtenstein, Y. (2008). Business familiarity as risk mitigation in software development outsoucing contracts. *Management Information Systems Quarterly, 32*(3), 531–551.

Ghosh, A. P. (1998). *E-commerce security – Weak links, best defences.* Hoboken, NJ: John Wiley & Sons.

Gido, J., & Clements, J. (2011). *Successful project management with Microsoft.* New York, NY: South-Western College Pub.

Godfrey, B. (2001). Electronic work monitoring: An ethical model. In *Selected papers from the second Australian institute conference on computer ethics* (pp. 18-21). Academic Press.

Goel, S., & Shawky, H. A. (2009). Estimating the market impact of security breach announcements on firm values. *Information & Management, 46*(7), 404–410. doi:10.1016/j.im.2009.06.005

Gordon, L. A., & Loeb, M. P. (2006). Budgeting process for information security expenditures: Empirical evidence. *Communications of the ACM, 49*(1), 121–125. doi:10.1145/1107458.1107465

Grant, T. (2007). Quantifying evidence in forensic authorship analysis. *International Journal of Speech Language and the Law, 14*(1), 1–25.

Grant, T. (2010). Text messaging forensics: txt 4n6: Idiolect free authorship analysis? In A. J. M. Coulthard (Ed.), *The Routledge handbook of forensic linguistics* (pp. 508–522). New York: Routledge.

Guelzim, T., & Obaidat, M. S. (2011). Pervasive network security. In M. S. Obaidat, M. Denko, & I. Woungang (Eds.), *Pervasive computing and networking* (pp. 159–172). Chichester, UK: John Wiley & Sons. doi:10.1002/9781119970422.ch10

Gundlach, G. T., & Murphy, P. E. (1993). Ethical and legal foundations of relational marketing exchanges. *Journal of Marketing*, *57*(4), 35–46. doi:10.2307/1252217

Gupta, M., Chaturvedi, A. R., Mehta, S., & Valeri, L. (2000). The experimental analysis of information security management issues for online financial services. In *Proceedings of the Twenty First International Conference on Information Systems*, (pp. 667-675). Brisbane, Australia: Academic Press.

Gupta, B., Iyer, L. S., & Weisskirch, R. S. (2010). Facilitating global e-commerce: A comparison of consumers' willingness to disclose personal information online in the U.S., & in India. *Journal of Electronic Commerce Research*, *11*(1), 41–52.

Hair, J. F. Jr, Anderson, R. E., Tatham, R. L., & Black, W. C. (1995). *Multivariate data analysis with readings*. Upper Saddle River, NJ: Prentice Hall.

Hakkarinen, D., & Chen, Z. (2010). Algorithmic Cholesky factorization fault recovery. In *Proceedings of the 24th IEEE International Parallel and Distributed Processing Symposium*. Atlanta, GA: IEEE.

Halteren, H. V. (2007). Author verification by linguistic profiling: An exploration of the parameter space. *Journal of ACM Transactions on Speech and Language Processing*, *4*(1), 1–17. doi:10.1145/1187415.1187416

Hamblen, M. (2009, October 14). *Collaboration tools worth the investment, survey says*. Retrieved January 11, 2010, from www.infoworld.com/d/mobilize/collaboration-tools-worth-the-investment-survey-says-000

Hamidi, H., Vafaei, A., & Monadjemi, A. H. (2009). Algorithm based fault tolerant and checkpointing for high performance computing systems. *Journal of Applied Science*, *9*, 3947–3956. doi:10.3923/jas.2009.3947.3956

Hamidi, H., Vafaei, A., & Monadjemi, A. H. (2010). *A fault-tolerant approach for matrix functions in image processing*. Paper presented at the 6th Iranian Machine Vision and Image Processing Conference. Tehran, Iran.

Hamidi, H., Vafaei, A., & Monadjemi, A. H. (2011). A framework for ABFT techniques in the design of fault-tolerant computing systems. *EURASIP Journal on Advances in Signal Processing*, *1*, 90. doi:10.1186/1687-6180-2011-90

Hamidi, H., Vafaei, A., & Monadjemi, A. H. (2012). Analysis and design of an ABFT and parity-checking technique in high performance computing systems. *Journal of Circuits, Systems, and Computers*, *21*(3). doi:10.1142/S021812661250017X

Harbert, T. (2005). VoIP for the masses. *Electronic Business*, *31*(5), 26–28.

Harris Interactive. (2003). *Poll*. Retrieved from http://www.harrisinteractive.com/harris_poll/index.asp?PID=365

Hartman, J. C., & Schafrick, I. C. (2004). The relevant internal rate of return. *The Engineering Economist*, *49*(2), 139–158. doi:10.1080/00137910490453419

Hartmann-Wendels, T., Mählmann, T., & Versen, T. (2009). Determinants of banks' risk exposure to new account fraud – Evidence from Germany. *Journal of Banking & Finance*, *33*, 347–357. doi:10.1016/j.jbankfin.2008.08.005

Hartwick, J., & Barki, H. (1994). Explaining the role of user participation in information system use. *Management Science*, *40*(4), 440–465. doi:10.1287/mnsc.40.4.440

Hasan, H., & Gould, E. (2001). Support for the sense-making activity of managers. *Decision Support Systems, 1*(31), 71–86. doi:10.1016/S0167-9236(00)00120-2

Hatch, M. (2001). The privatization of big brother: Protecting sensitive personal information from commercial interests in the 21st century. *William Mitchell Law Review, 27*(3), 1457–1502.

Hauenstein, N. M. A., McGonigle, T., & Flinder, S. W. (2001). A meta-analysis of the relationship between procedural justice and distributive justice: Implications for justice research. *Employee Responsibilities and Rights Journal, 13*(1), 39–56. doi:10.1023/A:1014482124497

Hayes, N. (2011). Information technology and the possibilities for knowledge sharing. In *Handbook of organizational learning and knowledge management.* Chichester, UK: John Wiley & Sons.

Helne, C. A. (2005). Predicting workplace deviance from the interaction between organizational justice and personality. *Journal of Managerial Issues, 17*(2), 247–263.

Henderson, J. C., & Venkatraman, N. (1992). Strategic alignment: A model for organizational transformation through information technology. In T. A. Kochan, & M. Ussem (Eds.), *Transforming organizations.* New York, NY: Oxford University Press.

Herreri'as-Velasco, J., Herreri'as-Pleguezuelo, R., & René van Dorp, J. (2011). Revisiting the PERT mean and variance. *European Journal of Operational Research, 210*(2), 448–451. doi:10.1016/j.ejor.2010.08.014

Higgs, S. (1995). Software roundup: Project management for windows. *Byte, 20,* 185–186.

Hoar, S. B. (2001). Identity theft: The crime of the new millennium. *Oregon Law Review, 80,* 1423.

Hoffer, J., Valacich, J., & George, J. (2011). *Essentials of systems analysis and design.* Englewood Cliffs, NJ: Prentice Hall.

Hoofnagle, C. J. (2007). Identity theft: Making the known unknowns known. *Harvard Journal of Law & Technology,* 21.

Horton, R. L. (1976). The structure of perceived risk. *Journal of the Academy of Marketing Science, 4,* 694–706. doi:10.1007/BF02729830

Hsaio, R., & Ormerod, R. (1998). A new perspective on the dynamics of IT-enabled strategic change. *Information Systems Journal, 8*(1), 21–52. doi:10.1046/j.1365-2575.1998.00003.x

Huang, K. H., & Abraham, J. A. (1984). Algorithm-based fault tolerance for matrix operations. *IEEE Transactions on Computers, 33,* 518–528. doi:10.1109/TC.1984.1676475

Hulland, J. (1999). Use of partial least squares (PLS) in strategic management research: A review of four recent studies. *Strategic Management Journal, 20*(2), 195–204. doi:10.1002/(SICI)1097-0266(199902)20:2<195::AID-SMJ13>3.0.CO;2-7

Hutchins, J. P. (Ed.). (2007). *Data breach disclosure laws - State by state.* Washington, DC: American Bar Association.

Hu, X., Wu, G., Wu, Y., & Zhang, H. (2010). The effects of web assurance seals on consumers' initial trust in an online vendor: A functional perspective. *Decision Support Systems, 48,* 407–418. doi:10.1016/j.dss.2009.10.004

IBM. (2006). *Stopping insider attacks: How organizations can protect their sensitive information.* Retrieved from http://www-935.ibm.com/services/us/imc/pdf/gsw00316-usen-00-insider-threats-wp.pdf

Ilieva, J., Baron, S., & Healey, N. M. (2002). Online surveys in marketing research: Pros and cons. *International Journal of Market Research, 44*(3), 361–382.

International Chamber of Commerce (ICC). (2003, August 8). *Crime services CSS foils multibillion internet banking fraud*. Retrieved from http://www.iccwbo.org/ccs/news_archives/2001/fraud.asp

Introna, L. D. (1996). Privacy and the computer: Why we need privacy in the information society. *Metaphilosophy, 28*(3), 259–275. doi:10.1111/1467-9973.00055

Introna, L. D. (2001). Workplace surveillance, privacy and distributive justice. In R. A. Spinello, & H. T. Tavani (Eds.), *Readings in cyberethics* (pp. 519–532). Sudbury, MA: Jones and Barlett.

Iqbal, F., Binsalleeh, H., Fung, B. C. M., & Debbabi, M. (2013). A unified data mining solution for authorship analysis in anonymous textual communications. *Information Sciences*, 98–112. doi:10.1016/j.ins.2011.03.006

Iqbal, F., Binsalleeh, H., Fung, B., & Debbabi, M. (2010). Mining writeprints from anonymous e-mails for forensic investigation. *Digital Investigation, 7*(1), 56–64. doi:10.1016/j.diin.2010.03.003

Iqbal, F., Hadjidj, R., Fung, B., & Debbabi, M. (2008). A novel approach of mining write-prints for authorship attribution in e-mail forensics. *Digital Investigation, 5*(Supplement), S42–S51. doi:10.1016/j.diin.2008.05.001

Ishihara, S. (2011). A forensic authorship classification in SMS messages: A likelihood ratio based approach using n-gram. In *Proceedings of the Australasian Language Technology Workshop 2011* (pp. 47-56). Academic Press.

Ishihara, S. (2012). Probabilistic evaluation of SMS messages as forensic evidence: Likelihood ration based approach with lexical features. *International Journal of Digital Crime and Forensics, 4*(3), 47–57. doi:10.4018/jdcf.2012070104

Jackson, T., Dawson, R., & Wilson, D. (2001). *The cost of email interruption* (Item No. 2134/495). Loughborough, UK: Loughborough University Institutional Repository. Retrieved from http://km.lboro.ac.uk/iii/pdf/JOSIT%202001.pdf

Jackson, J. (1994). Fraud masters: Professional credit card offenders and crime. *Criminal Justice Review, 19*(1), 24–55. doi:10.1177/073401689401900103

Janda, S., Trocchia, P. J., & Gwinner, K. P. (2002). Consumer perceptions of internet retail service quality. *International Journal of Service Industry Management, 13*(5), 412–431. doi:10.1108/09564230210447913

Jarvis, J., & Shier, D. (1990). Netsolve: Interactive software for network optimization. *Operations Research Letters, 9*(3), 275–282. doi:10.1016/0167-6377(90)90073-E

Javelin Strategy and Research. (2006). *Identity fraud survey report*. Retrieved from http://www.javelinstrategy.com/reports/2006IdentityFraudSurveyReport.html

Javelin Strategy and Research. (2010). *The 2010 identity fraud survey report*. Javelin Strategy & Research.

Jiang, J., Klein, G., Beck, P., & Wang, E. T. (2007). Lack of skill risks to organizational technology learning and software project performance. *Information Resources Management Journal, 20*(3), 32–45. doi:10.4018/irmj.2007070103

Jiang, J., Klein, G., & Wang, E. T. (2007). Relationship of skill expectation gap between IS employees and their managers with user satisfaction. *Information Resources Management Journal, 20*(3), 63–75. doi:10.4018/irmj.2007070105

Jones, R., Oyung, R., & Pace, L. (2005). *Working virtually: Challenges of virtual teams*. Hershey, PA: Idea Group Inc. doi:10.4018/978-1-59140-585-6

Jou, J. Y., & Abraham, J. A. (1986). Fault-tolerant matrix arithmetic and signal processing on highly concurrent computing structures. *Proceedings of the IEEE, 74*(5), 732–741. doi:10.1109/ PROC.1986.13535

Jou, J. Y., & Abraham, J. A. (1988). Fault-tolerant FFT networks. *IEEE Transactions on Computers, 37*, 548–561. doi:10.1109/12.4606

Jurafsky, D., & Martin, J. H. (2000). *Speech and language processing: An introduction to natural language processing, computational linguistics, and speech recognition*. Upper Saddle River, NJ: Prentice Hall.

Kallo, G. (1996). The reliability of critical path method (CPM) techniques in the analysis and evaluation of delay claims. *Coastal Engineering*, *38*(1), 35–39.

Kamburowski, J. (1997). New validations of PERT times. *Omega*, *25*(3), 323–328. doi:10.1016/S0305-0483(97)00002-9

Kaplan, R. S., & Norton, D. P. (1993, September-October). Putting the balanced scorecard to work. *Harvard Business Review*.

Kaplan, R.S., & Norton, D.P. (1992, January-February). The balanced scorecard-measures that drive performance. *HBR onPoint*.

Karahanna, E., Straub, D. W., & Chervany, N. L. (1999). Information technology adoption across time: A cross-sectional comparison of pre-adoption and post-adoption beliefs. *Management Information Systems Quarterly*, *23*(2), 183–213. doi:10.2307/249751

Katzan, H. Jr. (2010). Identity analytics and belief structures. *Journal of Business & Economics Research*, *8*(6), 31–40.

Keefer, D., & Verdini, W. (1993). Better estimation of PERT activity time parameters. *Management Science*, *39*(6), 1086–1091. doi:10.1287/mnsc.39.9.1086

Keil, M., Cule, P. E., Lyytinen, K., & Schmidt, R. C. (1998). A framework for identifying software project risks. *Communications of the ACM*, *41*(11), 76–83. doi:10.1145/287831.287843

Keramati, A., Dardick, G., Mojir, N., & Banan, B. (2009). Application of latent moderated structuring (LMS) to rank the effects of intervening variables on the IT and firm performance relationship. *International Journal of Applied Decision Sciences*, *2*(2), 167–188. doi:10.1504/IJADS.2009.026551

Kerzner, H. (2009). *Project management: A systems approach to planning, scheduling, and controlling*. New York, NY: Wiley.

Kim, D. J. (2008). Self-perception-based versus transference-based trust determinants in computer mediated transactions: A cross-cultural comparison study. *Journal of Management Information Systems*, *24*(4), 13–45. doi:10.2753/MIS0742-1222240401

Kim, M., Kim, J.-H., & Lennon, S. J. (2006). Online service attributes available on apparel retail web site: an E-S-QUAL approach. *Managing Service Quality*, *16*(1), 51–77. doi:10.1108/09604520610639964

Kirkman, B., & Mathieu, J. (2005). The dimensions and antecedents of virtuality. *Journal of Management*, *31*(5), 700–718. doi:10.1177/0149206305279113

Knospe, H., & Pohl, H. (2004). RFID security. *Information Security Technical Report*, *9*(4), 39–50. doi:10.1016/S1363-4127(05)70039-X

Komninos, N., Vergados, D., & Dogligeris, C. (2006). Layered security design for mobile ad hoc networks. *Computers & Security*, *25*(2), 121–130. doi:10.1016/j.cose.2005.09.005

Kroenke, D. M. (2010). *Experiencing MIS* (2nd ed.). Upper Saddle River, NJ: Pearson Education, Inc.

Kuklan, H. (1993). Effective project management: An expanded network approach. *Journal of Systems Management*, *44*(1), 12–16.

Kumar, A. A., & Makur, A. (2010). Improved coding-theoretic and subspace-based decoding algorithms for a wider class of DCT and DST codes. *IEEE Transactions on Signal Processing*, *58*(2), 695–708. doi:10.1109/TSP.2009.2031727

Lacoste, J., & Tremblay, P. (2003). Crime innovation: A script analysis of patterns in check forgery. *Crime Prevention Studies*, *16*, 171–198.

Lane, F. S. (2003). *The naked employee: How technology is compromising workplace privacy.* New York, NY: AMACOM.

Lardner, J. (1999). I know what you did last summer and fall. *U.S. News & World Report, 126*(15), 55.

Laudon, K. C., & Laudon, J. P. (2001). *Essentials of management information systems: Organisation and technology in the networked enterprise* (4th ed.). Upper Saddle River, NJ: Prentice Hall.

Laudon, K. C., & Laudon, J. P. (2002). *Management information systems: Managing the digital firm* (7th ed.). Upper Saddle River, NJ: Prentice Hall.

Laudon, K. C., & Traver, C. G. (2010). *E-commerce 2010 – Business technology society* (6th ed.). Upper Saddle River, NJ: Prentice Hall.

Lave, J., & Wenger, E. (1991). *Situated learning: Legitimate peripheral participation.* Cambridge, UK: Cambridge University Press. doi:10.1017/CBO9780511815355

Lease, M. L., & Burke, T. W. (2000). Identity theft: A fast growing crime. *FBI Law Enforcement Bulletin, 69*(8), 8.

Levy, M., Powell, P., & Yetton, P. (2001). SMEs: Aligning IS and the strategic context. *Journal of Information Technology, 16*(3), 133–144. doi:10.1080/02683960110063672

Lewis, J. (2007). *Mastering project management: Applying advanced concepts to systems thinking, control & evaluation, resource allocation.* New York: McGraw-Hill.

Li, J. P., & Kishore, R. (2006). How robust is the UTAUT instrument? A multigroup invariance analysis in the context of acceptance and use of online community weblog systems. In *Proceedings of the 2006 ACM SIGMIS CPR Conference on Computer Personnel Research,* (pp. 183-189). ACM.

Lin, C.-J. (2010). Computing shadow prices/costs of degenerate LP problems with reduced simplex tables. *Expert Systems with Applications, 37*(8), 5848–5855. doi:10.1016/j.eswa.2010.02.021

Lin, C.-J. (2011). A labeling algorithm for the sensitivity ranges of the assignment problem. *Applied Mathematical Modelling, 35*(10), 4852–4864. doi:10.1016/j.apm.2011.03.045

Lin, C.-J., & Wen, U.-P. (2003). Sensitivity analysis of the optimal assignment. *European Journal of Operational Research, 149*(1), 35–46. doi:10.1016/S0377-2217(02)00439-3

Lindström, J. (2009). *Models, methodologies and challenges within information security for senior managements.* (Doctoral thesis). Luleå University of Technology, Luleå, Sweden.

Lindström, J., Samuelsson, S., Harnesk, D., & Hägerfors, A. (2008). The need for improved alignment between actability, strategic planning of IS and information security. In *Proceedings of the 13th International ITA Workshop*, Krakow, Poland (pp. 14-27). ITA.

Lipnack, J., & Stamps, J. (1997). *Virtual teams: Reaching across space, time, and organizations with technology.* Hoboken, NJ: John Wiley & Sons, Inc.

Lipschutz, R. P. (2007). *GoToMeeting™ 3.0 review.* Retrieved September 13, 2010 from http://www.pcmag.com/article2/0,2817,2154128,00.asp

Loiacono, E. T., Watson, R. T., & Goodhue, D. L. (2002). WEBQUAL: A measure of website quality. In K. Evans, & L. Scheer (Eds.), *Marketing educators' conference: Marketing theory and applications* (Vol. 13, pp. 432–437). Academic Press.

London Conference. (2000). *Declining & referring jurisdiction in international litigation.* International Law Association.

LoPucki, L. M. (2001). Human identification theory and the identity theft problem. *Texas Law Review*, *80*(1), 89–135.

Louis Harris and Associates. (1999). *Poll*. Retrieved from http://www.natlconsumersleague.org/FNL-SUM1.PDF

Luftman, J. N. (1996). *Competing in the information age: Strategic alignment in practice*. New York, NY: Oxford University Press.

Lyytinen, K., Mathiassen, L., & Ropponen, J. (1996). A framework for software risk management. *Journal of Information Technology*, *11*, 275–285. doi:10.1057/jit.1996.2

Lyytinen, K., & Yoo, Y. (2002). Issues and challenges in ubiquitous computing. *Communications of the ACM*, *45*(12), 63–65.

Madden, M., Fox, S., Smith, A., & Vitak, J. (2007). *Digital footprints: Online identity management and search in the age of transparency*. Retrieved July 29, 2012, from http://pewresearch.org/pubs/663/digital-footprints

Majchrzak, A., Malhotra, A., Stamps, J., & Lipnack, J. (2004). Can absence make a team grow stronger? *Harvard Business Review*, *82*(5), 131–137. PMID:15146742

Malhotra, A., & Majchrzak, A. (2005, Winter). Virtual workspace technologies. *MIT Sloan Management Review*, 11-14.

Mandebilt, B. D. (2001). Identity theft: A new security challenge. *Security*, *38*(8), 21–24.

Mann, S., Nolan, J., & Wellman, B. (2003). Sousveillance: Inventing and using wearable computing devices for data collection in surveillance environments. *Surveillance & Society*, *1*(3), 331–355.

Marchewka, J. T., Liu, C., & Kostiwa, K. (2007). An application of the UTAUT model for understanding student perceptions using course management software. *Communications of the IIMA*, *7*(2), 93–104.

Margulis, S. T. (2003). On the status and contribution of Westin's and Altman's theories of privacy. *The Journal of Social Issues*, *59*(2), 411–429. doi:10.1111/1540-4560.00071

Martín, M., García, C., Pérez, J., & Sánchez Granero, M. (2012). An alternative for robust estimation in project management. *European Journal of Operational Research*, *220*(2), 443–451. doi:10.1016/j.ejor.2012.01.058

Marx, G., & Sherizen, S. (1991). Monitoring on the job: How to protect privacy as well as property. In T. Forester (Ed.), *Computers in the human context: Information technology, productivity, and people* (pp. 397–406). Cambridge, MA: MIT Press.

Mason, R. (1986). Four ethical issues of the information age. *Management Information Systems Quarterly*, *10*(1), 4–12. doi:10.2307/248873

Mathieson, K. (1991). Predicting user intentions: Comparing the technology acceptance model with the theory of planned behavior. *Information Research Systems*, *2*(3), 173–191. doi:10.1287/isre.2.3.173

Mativat, F., & Tremblay, P. (1997). Counterfeiting credit cards: Displacement effects, suitable offenders, and crime wave patterns. *The British Journal of Criminology*, *37*(2), 165–183. doi:10.1093/oxfordjournals.bjc.a014153

Mayer, R. C., Davis, J. D., & Schoorman, F. D. (1995). An integrative model of organisational trust. *Academy of Management Review*, *20*(3), 709–734.

McCarty, B. (2003). Automated identity theft. IEEE Computer Society, 89-92.

McDaniel, C., & Gates, R. (2005). *Marketing research*. Hoboken, NJ: John Wiley & Sons, Inc.

McIver, R. (2007). *VoIP 101: Voice over IP for beginners*. Retrieved September 25, 2010, from http://ezinearticles.com/?VoIP-101:-Voice-over-IP-for-Beginnersandid=20911

McKnight, D. H., Choudhury, V., & Kacmar, C. (2002). Developing and validating trust measures for e-commerce: An integrative typology. *Information Systems Research, 13*(3), 334–359. doi:10.1287/isre.13.3.334.81

McParland, C., & Connolly, R. (2009). *The role of dataveillance in the organsiation: Some emerging trends*. Paper presented at the Irish Academy of Management Conference. Galway, UK.

Mediati, N. (2010). Do identity-theft protection services work? *PCWorld, 28*(10), 41–43.

Mehrotra, K., Chai, J., & Pillutla, S. (1996). A study of approximating the moments of the job completion time in PERT networks. *Journal of Operations Management, 14*(3), 277–289. doi:10.1016/0272-6963(96)00002-2

Mercuri, R. T. (2002). Analyzing security costs. *Communications of the ACM*. PMID:12238525

Meredith, J., & Mantel, S. Jr. (2008). *Project management: A managerial approach*. New York, NY: Wiley.

Merriam-Webster. (n.d.). *Merriam-Webster online dictionary*. Retrieved January 15, 2010, from http://www.merriam-webster.com/dictionary/email

Miles, M., & Huberman, M. (1994). *An expanded sourcebook – Qualitative data analysis* (2nd ed.). Thousand Oaks, CA: Sage.

Miller, A. R., & Tucker, C. (2009). Privacy protection and technology adoption: The case of electronic medical records. *Management Science, 55*(7), 1077–1093. doi:10.1287/mnsc.1090.1014

Miller, A. R., & Tucker, C. E. (2011). Encryption and the loss of patient data. *Journal of Policy Analysis and Management, 30*(3), 534–556. doi:10.1002/pam.20590 PMID:21774164

Miller, K. W., Voas, J., & Hurlburt, G. F. (2012). BYOD: Security and privacy considerations. *IT Professional, 14*(5), 53–55. doi:10.1109/MITP.2012.93

Mintzberg, H. (1983). *Structure in fives: Designing effective organizations*. Engelwood Cliffs, NJ: Prentice Hall.

Mitrakas, A. (2006). Information security and law in Europe: Risks checked? *Information & Communications Technology Law, 15*(1), 33–53. doi:10.1080/13600830600557984

Mohammad, L. A., & Munir, K. (2009). Security issues in pervasive computing. In V. Godara (Ed.), *Risk assessment and management in pervasive computing: Operation, legal, ethical, and financial perspectives* (pp. 196–217). Hershey, PA: IGI Global.

Mohan, A., Baggili, I. M., & Rogers, M. K. (2010). *Authorship attribution of SMS messages using an n-grams approach* (CERIAS Tech Report 2010-11). West Lafayette, IN: Center for Education and Research Information Assurance and Security Purdue University.

Mohan, B. K. (2006, November). Globalization and offshoring of software: A report of the ACM job migration task force. *ACM*, 2-2.

Moosavie Nia, A., & Mohammadi, K. (2007). A generalized ABFT technique using a fault tolerant neural network. *Journal of Circuits, Systems, and Computers, 16*(3), 337–356. doi:10.1142/S0218126607003708

Morelos-Zaragoza, R. H. (2006). *The art of error correcting coding* (2nd ed.). New York, NY: John Wiley & Sons. doi:10.1002/0470035706

Morris, R. G., II. (2004). *The development of an identity theft offender typology: A theoretical approach*. Retrieved from http://www.shsu.edu/~edu_elc/journal/research%20online/re2004/Robert.pdf

Morris, M. G., & Venkatesh, V. (2000). Age differences in technology adoption decisions: Implications for a changing workforce. *Personnel Psychology*, *53*(2), 375–403. doi:10.1111/j.1744-6570.2000.tb00206.x

Morrison, G. S. (2009). Forensic voice comparison and the paradigm shift. *Science & Justice*, *49*(4), 298–308. doi:10.1016/j.scijus.2009.09.002 PMID:20120610

Morrison, G. S. (2011). Measuring the validity and reliability of forensic likelihood-ratio systems. *Science & Justice*, *51*(3), 91–98. doi:10.1016/j.scijus.2011.03.002 PMID:21889105

Morrison, G. S. (2013). Tutorial on logistic-regression calibration and fusion:converting a score to a likelihood ratio. *The Australian Journal of Forensic Sciences*, *45*(2), 173–197. doi:10.1080/00450618.2012.733025

Mossholder, K. W., Bennett, N., Kemery, E. R., & Wesolowski, M. A. (1998). Relationships between bases of power and work reactions: The mediational role of procedural justice. *Journal of Management*, *24*(4), 533–552. doi:10.1016/S0149-2063(99)80072-5

Mostéfaoui, G. K., Chae, J., Kim, J., & Chung, M. (2004). Context-based security management for heterogenous networks using MAUT and simple heuristics. In *Proceeding of the Workshop on State-of-the-Art in Scientific Computing*. Lyngby, Denmark: Academic Press.

Mouhoub, N., Benhocine, A., & Belouadah, H. (2011). A new method for constructing a minimal PERT network. *Applied Mathematical Modelling*, *35*(9), 4575–4588. doi:10.1016/j.apm.2011.03.031

Munkvold, B. E., & Akselsen, S. E. (2003). *Implementing collaboration technologies in industry: Case examples and lessons learned*. London: Springer. doi:10.1007/978-1-4471-0073-7

Nair, V. S. S., & Abraham, J. A. (1990). Real number codes for fault-tolerant matrix operations on process arrays. *IEEE Transactions on Computers*, 426–435. doi:10.1109/12.54836

Nakasumi, M. (2003). Credit risk management system on e-commerce: Case based reasoning approach. In *Proceedings of the 5th International Conference on Electronic Commerce*, (pp. 438-449). Pittsburgh, PA: ACM.

Nasution, S. (1994). Fuzzy critical path method. *IEEE Transactions on Systems, Man, and Cybernetics*, *24*(1), 48–51. doi:10.1109/21.259685

National Institutes of Health. (1979). Microprocessor-based intelligent machines in patient care. In *Proceeding of the Consensus Development Conference Statement*. Bethesda, MD: Academic Press.

Neuman, W. L. (1997). *Social research methods – Qualitative and quantitative approaches* (3rd ed.). Boston: Allyn and Bacon.

Newell, S., Robertson, M., Scarborough, H., & Swan, J. (2009). *Managing knowledge work and innovation*. Basingstoke, UK: Palgrave Macmillan.

Newman, G. R. (2004). *Identity theft, problem-oriented guides for police (Problem-Specific Guides Series, No. 25)*. Washington, DC: U.S. Department of Justice. doi:10.1037/e379342004-001

Nicholas, J., & Steyn, H. (2008). *Project management for business, engineering, and technology*. New York, NY: Butterworth-Heinemann.

Nichols, R. K., & Lekkas, P. C. (2002). *Wireless security: Models, threats, and solutions*. New York, NY: McGraw-Hill.

Nie, N. H., & Erbring, L. (2000). *Internet and society: A preliminary report*. Stanford, CA: Stanford Institute for the Quantitative Study of Society.

Nord, G. D., McCubbins, T. F., & Horn Nord, J. (2006). Email monitoring in the workplace: Privacy, legislation, and surveillance software. *Communications of the ACM*, *49*(8), 73–77.

Nunally, J. C. (1978). *Psychometric theory* (2nd ed.). New York: McGraw-Hill.

Nydegger, R., & Nydegger, L. (2010). Challenges in managing virtual teams. *Journal of Business & Economics Research*, *8*(3), 69–82.

Oechsner, S., & Wimmer, F. (2007). *Rechtliche stellungnahme zum thema wearIT@work*. Linz, Austria: wearIT@work.

Olavsrud, T. (2012). Cost of data breaches declines. *CIO*. Retrieved from http://www.cio.com/article/702494/Cost_of_Data_Breaches_Declines?page=2&taxonomyId=3154

Olivier, R. (2012). Why the BYOD boom is changing how we think about business it. *Engineering and Technology*, *7*(10), 28.

Oshri, I., Kotlarshy, J., & Willcocks, L. (2008). Missing links: Building critical social ties for global collaborative teamwork. *Communications of the ACM*, *51*(4), 76–81. doi:10.1145/1330311.1330327

Pangboonyanon, V. (2004). *Network-layer security in AODV networks*. Bremen, Germany: University of Bremen.

Parasuraman, A., Zeithaml, V. A., & Malhotra, A. (2005). E-S-QUAL a multiple-item scale for assessing electronic service quality. *Journal of Service Research*, *7*(3), 213–233. doi:10.1177/1094670504271156

Parker, R. B. (1974). A definition of privacy. *Rutgers Law Review*, *27*(1), 275.

Park, J. K., Yang, S., & Lehto, X. (2007). Adoption of mobile technologies for Chinese consumers. *Journal of Electronic Commerce Research*, *8*(3), 196–206.

Pasher, E., Popper, Z., Raz, H., & Lawo, M. (2010). WearIT@work: A wearable computing solution for knowledge-based development. *International Journal of Knowledge-Based Development*, *1*(4), 346–360. doi:10.1504/IJKBD.2010.038043

Patterson, P. G., Johnson, L. W., & Spreng, R. A. (1997). Modeling the determinants of customer satisfaction for business to business professional services. *Academy of Marketing Science Journal*, *25*(1), 4–17. doi:10.1007/BF02894505

Pavlou, P. A., Liang, H., & Xue, Y. (2007). Understanding and mitigating uncertainty in online exchange relationships: A principal–agent perspective. *Management Information Systems Quarterly*, *31*(1), 105–136.

Perl, M. W. (2003). It's not always about the money: Why the state identity theft laws fail to adequately address criminal record identity theft. *The Journal of Criminal Law & Criminology*, *94*(1), 169–208. doi:10.2307/3491307

Phillips, D., & Garcia-Diaz, A. (1990). *Fundamental of network analysis*. Englewood Cliffs, NJ: Prentice-Hall.

Pikänen, O., & Niemelä, M. (2007). Privacy and data protection in emerging RFID-applications. In *Proceedings of the European RFID Forum*. Brussels, Belgium: RFID.

Pirdashti, M., Mohammadi, M., Rahimpour, F., & Kennedy, D. (2008). An AHP-Delphi multi-criteria location planning model with application to whey protein production facility decisions. *International Journal of Applied Decision Sciences*, *1*(2), 245–259. doi:10.1504/IJADS.2008.020326

PMI. (2013). *A guide to the project management body of knowledge (PMBOK guide)* (5th ed.). Newtown Square, PA: Project Management Institute.

Ponemon Institute. LLC. (2010). *2009 annual study: Cost of a data breach understanding financial impact, customer turnover, and preventive solutions*. Ponemon Institute LLC. Retrieved from http://www.ponemon.org/local/upload/fckjail/generalcontent/18/file/US_Ponemon_CODB_09_012209_sec.pdf

Ponemon Institute. LLC. (2011). *2010 annual study: U.S. cost of a data breach compliance pressures, cyber attacks targeting sensitive data drive leading IT organizations to respond quickly and pay more.* Ponemon Institute LLC. Retrieved from http://www.symantec.com/content/en/us/about/media/pdfs/symantec_ponemon_data_breach_costs_report.pdf?om_ext_cid=biz_socmed_twitter_facebook_marketwire_linkedin_2011Mar_worldwide_costofdatabreach

Porter, M. E. (1987). From competitive advantage to corporate strategy. *Harvard Business Review, 12,* 15–31. PMID:17183795

Prakhaber, P. R. (2000). Who owns the online consumer? *Journal of Consumer Marketing, 17*(2), 158–171. doi:10.1108/07363760010317213

Premachandra, I. (2001). An approximation of the activity duration distribution in PERT. *Computers & Operations Research, 28*(5), 443–452. doi:10.1016/S0305-0548(99)00129-X

Privacy & American Business Survey. (n.d.). Retrieved from http://www.pandab.org/id_theftpr.html

Ranganathan, C., & Ganapathy, S. (2002). Key dimensions of business to consumer web sites. *Information & Management, 39,* 457–465. doi:10.1016/S0378-7206(01)00112-4

Rao, S., & Troshani, I. (2007). A conceptual framework and propositions for the acceptance of mobile services. *Journal of Theoretical and Applied Electronic Commerce Research, 2*(2), 61–73.

Ratnasingam, P. (2002). The importance of technology trust in web service security. *Information Management & Computer Security, 10*(5), 255–260. doi:10.1108/09685220210447514

Rexford, J., & Jha, N. K. (1992). Algorithm-based fault tolerance for floating-point operations in massively parallel systems. In *Proceedings of the International Symposium on Circuits and Systems* (pp. 649-652). Academic Press.

Robb, D. (2002). Collaboration gets it together. *Computerworld, 36*(50), 29–30.

Roberds, W., & Schreft, S. L. (2009). Data breaches and identity theft. *Journal of Monetary Economics, 56*(7), 918–929. doi:10.1016/j.jmoneco.2009.09.003

Robertson, B., & Vignaux, G. A. (1995). *Interpreting evidence: Evaluating forensic science in the courtroom.* Chichester, UK: Wiley.

Robinson, S. L., & Rousseau, D. M. (1994). Violating the psychological contract: Not the exception but the norm. *Journal of Organizational Behavior, 15*(3), 245–259. doi:10.1002/job.4030150306

Rogers, E. M. (1983). *Diffusion of innovations.* New York: The Free Press.

Roßnagel, A. (2002). Freiheit im cyberspace. *Informatik-Spektrum, 25*(1), 33–35. doi:10.1007/s002870100204

Ross, S. (1995). Uses, abuses, and alternatives to the net-present-value rule. *Financial Management, 24*(3), 96–102. doi:10.2307/3665561

Ross, S., Westerfield, R., & Jordan, B. (2009). *Fundamentals of corporate finance* (9th ed.). New York: McGraw-Hill Irwin.

Rotter, J. B. (1967). A new scale for the measurement of interpersonal trust. *The American Psychologist, 26,* 443–452. doi:10.1037/h0031464

Rust, R. T., Kannan, P. K., & Peng, N. (2002). The customer economics of internet privacy. *Journal of the Academy of Marketing Science, 30*(4), 455–464. doi:10.1177/009207002236917

Safire, W. (2002). The great unwatched. *The New York Times.* Retrieved from http://query.nytimes.com/gst/fullpage.html?res=9A03E7DB1E3FF93BA25751C0A9649C8B63

Saks, M. J., & Koehler, J. J. (2005). The coming paradigm shift in forensic identification science. *Science*, *309*(5736), 892–895. doi:10.1126/science.1111565 PMID:16081727

Salfner, F., Lenk, M., & Malek, M. (2010). A survey of online failure prediction methods. *ACM Computing Surveys*, *42*(3). doi:10.1145/1670679.1670680

Sambamurthy, V., & Sumbramani, M. (2005). Special issue on information technologies and knowledge management. *MIS Quartely*, *29*(1), 1–7.

Santos, J. (2003). E-service quality: A model of virtual service quality dimensions. *Managing Service Quality*, *13*(3), 233–246. doi:10.1108/09604520310476490

Satzinger, J., Jackson, J., & Burd, S. (2011). *Systems analysis and design in a changing world*. New York, NY: Course Technology.

Sauer, C., Yetton, P. W., Benjamin, R., Ciborra, C. U., Coombs, R., & Craig, J. …Zmud, R. W. (1997). Steps to the future: Fresh thinking on the management of IT-based or organizational transformation. San Francisco, CA: Jossey-Bass.

Saxena, N., Ekberg, J., Kostiainen, K., & Asokan, N. (2006). Secure device pairing based on a visual channel. In *Proceedings of the IEEE Symposium on Security and Privacy* (pp. 306-313). IEEE.

Sbodio, M. L., & Thronicke, W. (2006). Context processing within an open, component-oriented, software framework. In *Proceedings of the 3rd International Forum on Applied Wearable Computing*. Bremen, Germany: Academic Press.

Schaupp, L. C., & Bélanger, F. (2005). A conjoint analysis of online consumer satisfaction. *Journal of Electronic Commerce Research*, *6*(2), 95–111.

Sebastianelli, R., Tamimi, N., & Rajan, M. (2006). *Perceived quality of internet retailers: Does shopping frequency and product type make a difference?* Siena, Italy: EABR & ETLC.

Selmi, M. (2006). Privacy for the working class: Public work and private lives. *Louisiana Law Review*, *66*, 1035–1056.

Semuels, A. (2013, April 8). Monitoring upends balance of power at workplace some say. *Los Angeles Times*. Retrieved from http://www.latimes.com/business/money/la-fi-mo-monitoring-upends-balance-of-power-at-workplace-20130408,0,7425573.story

Shareef, M. A., Archer, N., Fong, W., Rahman, M., & Mann, I. J. (2013). Online buying behavior and perceived trustworthiness. *British Journal of Applied Science & Technology*, *3*(4), 662–683.

Shareef, M. A., Kumar, U., & Kumar, V. (2008). Role of different electronic- commerce (EC) quality factors on purchase decision: A developing country perspective. *Journal of Electronic Commerce Research*, *9*(2), 92–113.

Shipley, M., & Olson, D. (2008). Interval-valued evidence sets from simulated product competitiveness: A Bulgarian winery decision. *International Journal of Applied Decision Sciences*, *1*(4), 397–417. doi:10.1504/IJADS.2008.022977

SHRM. (2005). *Workplace privacy – Poll findings: A study by the society for human resource management and careerjournal.com*. Retrieved from http://www.shrm.org/Research/SurveyFindings/Documents/Workplace%20Privacy%20Poll%20Findings%20-%20A%20Study%20by%20SHRM%20and%20CareerJournal.com.pdf

Slattery, J. (2002). *The problem of business identity theft*. CBS 2. Retrieved from http://www.cbsnewyork.com/investigates/local_story_297105022.html

Slosarik, K. (2002). Identity theft: An overview of the problem. *The Justice Professional*, *15*(4), 329–343. doi:10.1080/0888431022000070458

Smith, H. J., Dinev, T., & Xu, H. (2011). Information privacy research: An interdisciplinary review. *Management Information Systems Quarterly*, *35*(4), 989–1015.

Smith, H. J., Milberg, J. S., & Burke, J. S. (1996). Information privacy: Measuring individuals' concerns about organizational practices. *Management Information Systems Quarterly, 20*(2), 167–196. doi:10.2307/249477

Solove, D. J. (2006). A taxonomy of privacy. *University of Pennsylvania Law Review, 154*(3), 477–564. doi:10.2307/40041279

So, M. W. C., & Sculli, D. (2002). The role of trust, quality, value and risk in conducting e-business. *Industrial Management & Data Systems, 102*(9), 503–512. doi:10.1108/02635570210450181

Sonnenreich, W., Albanese, J., & Stout, B. (2006). Return on security investment (ROSI)- A practical quantitative method. *Journal of Research and Practice in Information Technology.*

Sorbel, J. (2003). *Identity theft and e-commerce web security: A primer for small to medium sized businesses.* GIAC Security Essentials Certification (GSEC), Sans Institute, Practical, Version 1.4b, Option 1.

Spiekermann, S., & Langheinrich, M. (2008). An update on privacy in ubiquitous computing. *Personal and Ubiquitous Computing, 13*(6), 389–390. doi:10.1007/s00779-008-0210-7

Sproule, S., & Archer, N. (2010). Measuring identity theft and identity fraud. *Int J Bus Govern Ethics, 5*(1-2), 51–63. doi:10.1504/IJBGE.2010.029555

Stajano, F. (2010). Security issues in ubiquitous computing. In H. Nakashima, H. Aghajan, & J. C. Augusto (Eds.), *Handbook of ambient intelligence and smart environments, Part III* (pp. 281–314). New York, NY: Springer. doi:10.1007/978-0-387-93808-0_11

Stamatatos, E. (2009). A survey of modern authorship attribution methods. *Journal of the American Society for Information Science and Technology, 60*(3), 538–556. doi:10.1002/asi.21001

Stanton, J. M., & Barnes-Farrell, J. L. (1996). Effects of electronic performance-monitoring on personal control, satisfaction and performance. *The Journal of Applied Psychology, 81,* 738–745. doi:10.1037/0021-9010.81.6.738

Stoneburner, G., Goguen, A., & Feringa, A. (2002). *NIST: National institute of standards and technology.* Retrieved November 10, 2011, from http://ibexsecurity.com/cissp/NIST%20Security%20Guides/sp800-30.pdf

Sullivan, R. J. (2008). Can smart cards reduce payments fraud and identity theft? *Econ Rev Fed Reserv Bank Kans City, 93*(3), 35–62.

Sullivan, R. J. (2010). The changing nature of U.S. card payment fraud: Industry and public policy options. *Econ Rev Fed Reserv Bank Kans City, 95*(2), 101–133.

Sun, H. (2010). Transferring attributes of e-commerce systems into business benefits: A relationship quality perspective. *Journal of Electronic Commerce Research, 11*(2), 92–109.

Szajna, B. (1996). Empirical evaluation of the revised technology acceptance model. *Management Science, 42*(1), 85–92. doi:10.1287/mnsc.42.1.85

Sztompka, P. (1999). *Trust: A sociological theory.* Cambridge, UK: Cambridge University Press.

Tagg, C. (2009). *A corpus linguistics study of SMS Text messaging.* (PhD Dissertation). The University of Birmingham, Birmingham, UK.

Tallau, L. J., Gupta, M., & Sharman, R. (2010). Information security investment decisions: Evaluating the balanced scorecard method. *Int. J. Business Information Systems, 5*(1), 34–57. doi:10.1504/IJBIS.2010.029479

Tavani, H. T. (2004). *Ethics and technology: Ethical issues in an age of information and communication technology.* Chichester, UK: John Wiley & Sons.

Taylor, S., & Todd, P. (1995). Assessing IT usage: The role of prior experience. *Management Information Systems Quarterly, 19*(4), 561–570. doi:10.2307/249633

Thomas, R. K., & Sandhu, R. (2004). Models, protocols, and architectures for secure pervasive computing: Challenges and research directions. In *Proceedings of the Second IEEE Annual Conference on Pervasive Computing and Communications Workshop*, (pp. 164-168). IEEE.

Thompson, R. L., Higgins, C. A., & Howell, J. M. (1991). Personal computing: Toward a conceptual model of utilization. *Management Information Systems Quarterly*, *15*(1), 125–143. doi:10.2307/249443

Thompson, R. L., Higgins, C. A., & Howell, J. M. (1994). Influence of experience on personal computer utilization: Testing a conceptual model. *Journal of Management Information Systems*, *11*(1), 167–187.

Torkzadeh, G., & Dhillon, G. (2002). Measuring factors that influence the success of internet commerce. *Information Systems Research*, *13*(2), 187–204. doi:10.1287/isre.13.2.187.87

Trietsch, D., & Baker, K. (2012). PERT 21: Fitting PERT/CPM for use in the 21st century. *International Journal of Project Management*, *30*(4), 490–502. doi:10.1016/j.ijproman.2011.09.004

Turban, E., King, D., Lee, J., Liang, T. P., & Turban, D. (2010). *Electronic commerce 2010: A managerial perspective* (6th ed.). Upper Saddle River, NJ: Pearson.

Turban, E., Leidner, D., McClean, E., & Wetherbe, J. (2006). *Information technology for management – Transforming organisations in the digital economy* (5th ed.). New York, NY: John Wiley & Sons.

Turmon, M., Granat, R., & Katz, D. (2000). Software-implemented fault detection for high-performance space applications. In *Proceedings of the IEEE International Conference on Dependable Systems and Networks* (pp. 107-116). IEEE.

Turmon, M., Granat, R., Katz, D., & Lou, J. (2003). Tests and tolerances for high-performance software-implemented fault detection. *IEEE Transactions on Computers*, *52*(5), 579–591. doi:10.1109/TC.2003.1197125

Turow, J., Feldman, L., & Metlzer, K. (2005). *Open to exploitation: American shoppers online and offline*. Philadelphia, PA: Annenberg Public Policy Centre, University of Pennsylvania.

U.S. Department of Justice (USDOJ). (2004, March 24). *Identity theft and fraud*. Retrieved from http://www.usdoj.gov/fraud/idtheft.html

U.S. Supreme Court case of Greenwood v. California, 486 U.S. 35, (1988).

Udo, G. J. (2001). Privacy and security concerns as major barriers for e-commerce: A survey study. *Information Management & Computer Security*, *9*(4), 165–174. doi:10.1108/EUM0000000005808

Urban, G. L., Sultan, F., & Qualls, W. J. (2000). Placing trust at the center of your internet strategy. *Sloan Management Review*, *42*(1), 39–48.

Van Dyke, J. (2007). *Reading behind the lines: How identity fraud really happens*. Javelin Strategy & Research.

Veeravalli, V. S. (2009). Fault tolerance for arithmetic and logic unit. In *Proceedings of the IEEE Southeast Conference* (pp. 329-334). IEEE.

Venkatesh, V. (2000). Determinants of perceived ease if use: Integrating perceived behavioral control, computer anxiety and enjoyment into the technology acceptance model. *Information Systems Research*, *11*(4), 342–365. doi:10.1287/isre.11.4.342.11872

Venkatesh, V., & Morris, M. G. (2000). Why don't men ever stop to ask for directions? Gender, social influence, and their role in technology acceptance and usage behavior. *Management Information Systems Quarterly*, *24*(1), 155–139. doi:10.2307/3250981

Venkatesh, V., Morris, M. G., & Ackerman, P. L. (2000). A longitudinal field investigation of gender differences in individual technology adoption decision-making processes. *Organizational Behavior and Human Decision Processes*, *83*(1), 33–60. doi:10.1006/obhd.2000.2896 PMID:10973782

Venkatesh, V., Morris, M., Davis, G., & Davis, F. (2003). User acceptance of information technology: Toward a unified view. *Management Information Systems Quarterly*, *27*(3), 425–478.

Venkatesh, V., & Speir, C. (1999). Computer technology training in the workplace: A longitudinal investigation of the effect of mood. *Organizational Behavior and Human Decision Processes*, *79*(1), 1–28. doi:10.1006/obhd.1999.2837 PMID:10388607

Verbauwhede, I., Hodjat, A., Hwang, D., & Lai, B.-C. (2005). Security for ambient intelligent systems. In W. Weber, J. M. Rabaey, & E. Aarts (Eds.), *Ambient intelligence*. Berlin, Germany: Springer-Verlag. doi:10.1007/3-540-27139-2_10

Viterbi, A. J., & Omura, J. K. (1985). *Principles of digital communication and coding* (2nd ed.). New York, NY: McGraw-Hill.

von Krogh, G. (2011). Knowledge sharing in organizations: The role of communities. In *Handbook of organizational learning and knowledge management*. Chichester, UK: John Wiley & Sons.

Wallace, L. (1999). *The development of an instrument to measure software project risk*. Atlanta, GA: Georgia State University College of Business Administration.

Walther, J. B., Bunz, U., & Bazarova, N. (2005). The rules of virtual groups. In *Proceedings of the 38th Hawaii International Conference on System Sciences*. IEEE.

Wang, H., Lee, M. K. O., & Wang, C. (1998). Consumer privacy concerns about internet marketing. *Communications of the ACM*, *41*(3), 63–70. doi:10.1145/272287.272299

Ward, J., Griffiths, P., & Whitmore, P. (1990). *Strategic planning for information systems*. New York, NY: John Wiley & Sons.

Wasko, M., & Teigland, R. (2006). Distinguishing work groups, virtual teams, and electronic networks of practice. In E. Coakes, & S. Clarke (Eds.), *Encyclopedia of communities of practice in information and knowledge management* (pp. 138–140). Hershey, PA: Idea Group. doi:10.4018/978-1-59140-556-6.ch027

Weber, M. (1971). *Makt og byråkrati: Essays om politikk og klasse, samfunn*. Oslo: Gyldendal.

Weiser, M. (1991). The computer for the 21st century. *Scientific American*, *265*(3), 94–104. doi:10.1038/scientificamerican0991-94

Wenger, E. (2005). *Technology for communities*. CEFRIO. Retrieved September 19, 2010 from http://technologyforcommunities.com/CEFRIO_Book_Chapter_v_5.2.pdf

Wenger, E., White, N., & Smith, J. D. (2009). Digital habitats: Stewarding technology for communities. Portland, OR: CPsquare Publishing.

Wenger, E. (1998). *Communities of practice: Learning, meaning and identity*. New York: Cambridge University Press. doi:10.1017/CBO9780511803932

Wenger, E. (2003). Communities of practice and social learning systems. In *Knowing in organizations: A practice-based apporach*. New York: M.E. Sharpe.

Wenger, E. (2004). Knowledge management as a doughnut: Shaping your knowledge strategy through communities of practice. *Ivey Business Journal*, *1*, 1–8.

Wenger, E., McDermott, R., & Snyder, W. M. (2002). *Cultivation communities of practice*. Cambridge, MA: Harvard Business School Press.

Wen, H. J., Schwieger, D., & Gershuny, P. (2007). Internet usage monitoring in the workplace: Its legal challenges and implementation strategies. *Information Systems Management*, *24*, 185–196. doi:10.1080/10580530701221072

Wharton, C. M., Hampl, J. S., Hall, R., & Winham, D. H. (2003). PCs or paper-and-pencil: Online surveys for data collection. *Journal of the American Dietetic Association*, *103*(11), 1458–1460. doi:10.1016/j.jada.2003.09.004 PMID:14626248

Winston, W. (2003). *Operations research: Applications and algorithms*. Boston, MA: PWS-KENT Pub. Co.

Wolfinbarger, M., & Gilly, M. C. (2003). eTailQ: Dimensionalizing, measuring, and predicting etail quality. *Journal of Retailing*, *79*(3), 183–198. doi:10.1016/S0022-4359(03)00034-4

Wu, I., & Chen, J. (2005). An extension of trust and TAM model with TPB in the initial adoption of online tax: An empirical study. *International Journal of Human-Computer Studies*, *62*, 784–808. doi:10.1016/j.ijhcs.2005.03.003

Wu, S., & Wu, M. (1994). *Systems analysis and design*. New York: West Publishing Company.

Xu, H., Dinev, T., Smith, J. H., & Hart, P. (2011). Information privacy concerns: Linking individual perceptions with institutional privacy assurances. *Journal of the Association for Information Systems*, *12*(12), 798–824.

Yaghoubi, S., Noori, S., Azaron, A., & Tavakkoli-Moghaddam, R. (2011). Resource allocation in dynamic PERT networks with finite capacity. *European Journal of Operational Research*, *215*(3), 670–678.

Yakhchali, S. (2012). A path enumeration approach for the analysis of critical activities in fuzzy networks. *Information Sciences*, *204*, 23–35. doi:10.1016/j.ins.2012.01.025

Yin, R. (2003). *Case study research: Design and methods* (3rd ed.). Thousand Oaks, CA: Sage.

Yoo, B., & Donthu, N. (2001). Developing a scale to measure the perceived quality of an internet shopping site (sitequal). *Quarterly Journal of Electronic Commerce*, *2*(1), 31–46.

Zack, M. (1999). Managing codified knowledge. *Sloan Management Review*, *40*(4), 45–58.

Zhang, P., & von Dran, G. (2002). User expectations and rankings of quality factors in different web site domains. *International Journal of Electronic Commerce*, *6*(2), 9–33.

Zheng, R., Li, J. X., Chen, H. C., & Huang, Z. (2006). A framework for authorship identification of online messages: Writing-style features and classification techniques. *Journal of the American Society for Information Science and Technology*, *57*(3), 378–393. doi:10.1002/asi.20316

Zhou, L., Dai, L., & Zhang, D. (2007). Online shopping acceptance model -- A critical survey of consumer factors in online shopping. *Journal of Electronic Commerce Research*, *8*(1), 41–62.

Zweig, D., & Webster, J. (2002). Where is the line between benign and invasive? An examination of psychological barriers to the acceptance of awareness monitoring system. *Journal of Organizational Behavior*, *23*(5), 605–633. doi:10.1002/job.157

About the Contributors

Hamid Nemati is an Associate Professor of Information Systems at the Information Systems and Operations Management Department of The University of North Carolina at Greensboro. He holds a doctorate from the University of Georgia and a Master of Business Administration from The University of Massachusetts. Before coming to UNCG, he was on the faculty of J. Mack Robinson College of Business Administration at Georgia State University. He also has extensive professional experience as a consultant with a number of major corporations. Dr. Nemati is the Editor-in-Chief of *International Journal of Information Security and Privacy* and the Advances in Information Security and Privacy (AISP) Book Series. His research specialization is in the areas of decision support systems, data warehousing and mining, and information security and privacy. His research articles have appeared in a number of premier journals. He has presented numerous research and scholarly papers nationally and internationally.

* * *

Veena Adlakha is a professor of Operations Management at the Merrick School of Business. She has published her research in several prestigious journals including *Networks, Management Science, Operations Research,* and *OMEGA*. Her current research interests include fixed-charge transportation problem, total quality management, and Web-based education.

Hossein Arsham is the Wright Distinguished Research Professor Emeritus of Decision Science at the Merrick School of Business, University of Baltimore. He is currently teaches graduate courses in Management Science at the Johns Hopkins University Carey Business School.

Regina Connolly is a senior lecturer in Information Systems at Dublin City University Business School, Dublin, Ireland. She was conferred with a PhD in Information Systems from Trinity College Dublin. Her research interests include eCommerce trust and privacy issues, Website service quality evaluation, eGovernment, and IT value evaluation in the public sector. Dr. Connolly has served on the expert eCommerce advisory group for Dublin Chamber of Commerce, which has advised national government on eCommerce strategic planning.

Amanda Eisenga has a Master in Accounting and Taxation and an MBA from Florida Gulf Coast University. She obtained her Bachelor of Science in Accounting from the University of Florida. She is currently pursuing her CPA license. Her research interests are related to security, management, and mitigating risks.

Eduardo Esteva-Armida has more than 25 years of experience as professor in bachelor, master, and continual education courses in Mexico, USA, France, and Peru. He had participated as consulter in marketing with organizations as CKlass, Pollo Loco, Cervecería Cuauhtémoc, Sorteos Tec, and Conductores Monterrey, among others, and he had participated as technical reviewer for marketing publications for International Thompson Editors. Eduardo has a bachelor degree in Communications, an MBA, and a Master in Marketing from Tec de Monterrey, and he has a PhD in Consumer behavior from Purdue University. His research areas of interest are retailing, pricing, and strategic marketing. He is Associate Dean in Business in Tec de Monterrey Campus Guadalajara.

Hodjat Hamidi received BSc, MSc, and PhD in electronic and computer engineering, respectively, from the Mazandaran University, Babol, Iran (1999), Iran University of Science and Technology, Teheran, Iran (2000), and University of Isfahan, Isfahan, Iran (2012). His main research interest areas are fault-tolerant systems (fault-tolerant computing, error control in digital designs) and applications and reliable and secure distributed systems and mathematical aspects of computing.

Claas Hanken is a Professional Service DMS/ECM at Nemetschek Bausoftware. Staff member of the Institute for Information Management Bremen GmbH (ifib) from 2003 to 2011. He acquired the Juristisches Staatsexamen and degree diploma in in law (Dipl.-Jur.) at Universität Osnabrück (Lower Saxony, Germany) in 2000. From 2000 until 2002 he was employed as research assistant at Chemnitz University of Technology (Saxony, Germany). From 1997 on, he participated in several IT-law and e-government related projects. Some of those projects resulted in academic publications (e.g. *E-Procurement in der öffentlichen Verwaltung*, in: Kröger/Hoffmann, *Rechts-Handbuch zum E-Government*, Cologne: Verlag Dr. Otto Schmidt Köln 2005, S. 181-198; Kröger/Hanken, *Casebook Internetrecht*, Berlin/Heidelberg/New York et al: Springer 2003).

Inge Hermanrud (Ph.D, Bodø Graduate School of Business, University of Nordland, Norway) holds an Associate Professor position at Hedmark University College, Norway. Inge teaches introductory courses in change management, strategy, organizational learning, communication and organizational identity, and graduate courses in human resource management. His published work appears in journals like *Informing Science, Journal of Cases in Information Technology,* and *Nordic Journal of Social Research*. Inge`s research focuses on distributed organizations, knowledge sharing among dispersed employees and organizational learning in public organizations. He holds a Master of Philosophy in Public Planning and Community research from University of Tromsø, Norway (1999), and a undergraduate degree from Lillehammer University College, Norway (1996).

Shunichi Ishihara (PhD, MSc, MA) is a senior lecturer at the Department of Linguistics of the School of Culture, History, and Language at the Australian National University. He is a speech scientist and a computational linguist with his main interest in forensic voice/text comparison based on likelihood-ratio framework, individual/gender differences manifested in language use, intonational modeling, computer-assisted language learning/teaching, and speech and language processing. He has been an executive member of the Australasian Speech Science and Technology Association (ASSTA) for more than ten years. He is also a member of the ASSTA's Forensic Speech Science Committee. He is a forensic voice/text comparison case worker.

Travis Jones is an Associate Professor of Finance at Florida Gulf Coast University, where he teaches investment and corporate finance courses, including FGCU's student managed fund. Dr. Jones earned his Ph.D. in Finance from the University of Alabama and is a series 3 certified futures broker and series 65 investment advisor. His research interests include: initial public offerings, finance pedagogy, financial risk management, and real estate. Dr. Jones has published two dozen manuscripts in various finance, economics, and business journals, and is actively involved with the CFA Institute and local CFA society.

Uma Kumar is a Full Professor of Management Science and Technology Management and Director of the Research Centre for Technology Management at Carleton University. She has published over 140 papers in journals and refereed proceedings. Ten papers have won best paper awards at prestigious conferences. She has won Carleton's prestigious Research Achievement Award and, twice, the Scholarly Achievement Award. Recently, she won the teaching excellence award at the Carleton University. She has been the Director of Sprott School's Graduate Programs. She has consulted DND, CIDA, the Federal partners of technology transfer, and the Canadian association of business incubators. Uma has taught in executive MBA program in Hong Kong and in Sprott MBA in Ottawa, Iran, and China. Over last 20 years, she has supervised more than 70 MBA, MMS, and EMBA students' projects. She has also given invited lectures to academics and professionals in Brazil, China, Cuba, and India.

Vinod Kumar is a Professor of Technology and Operations Management of the Sprott School of Business (Director of School, 1995–2005), Carleton University. He received his graduate education from the University of California, Berkeley, and the University of Manitoba. Vinod is a well-known expert sought in the field of technology and operations management. He has published over 150 papers in refereed journals and proceedings. He has won several Best Paper Awards in prestigious conferences, Scholarly Achievement Award of Carleton University for the academic years 1985–1986 and 1987–1988, and Research Achievement Award for the year 1993 and 2001. Vinod has given invited lectures to professional and academic organizations in Australia, Brazil, China, Iran, and India, among others.

John Lindström, PhD, EMBA, CISSP, is a member of the information security research group at Luleå University of Technology. John has previously worked for about 15 years with product development, and technical- and management-consulting in the information security business. John was responsible for the Safety and Security part in the European integrated project wearIT@work during 2005-2009. John is an assistant professor and holds a PhD within information systems sciences on strategic information security.

April H. Reed is an Assistant Professor in the College of Business, MIS department at East Carolina University. She conducts research in the area of IS/IT project management. She is also a PMI certified Project Management Professional (PMP) and has held industry positions as a Systems Analyst and an IT Project Manager. She has published several papers on the topic of risk and virtual software development project teams in IS journals such as *International Journal of Information Technology Project Management, Journal of Computer Information Systems, International Journal of Project Management, Informing Sciences*, and *Journal of Information Technology Management*. She holds a PhD from DePaul University.

Walter Rodriguez is Professor of Computer Information Systems and Director of the Institute for Technological Innovation at Florida Gulf Coast University. He obtained his Ph.D. in engineering project management (interdisciplinary CE/ISE) from University of Florida. He founded and chaired the Engineering Computer Graphics Program at Georgia Tech and was awarded the Harvard Foundation Medal and a Postdoctoral Fellowship (Information Technology) at the Massachusetts Institute of Technology, while holder of the Louis Berger Endowed Chair at Tufts University. Dr. Rodriguez research focuses on visual-based systems development, advanced distributed learning technologies, and e-business operations management and strategy.

Alberto Rubio-Sanchez has 15 years of higher education experience teaching in business programs. His areas of expertise include consumer behavior and marketing research. Currently, Alberto is an associate professor of marketing at the University of the Incarnate Word in San Antonio, Texas. As a consultant, Alberto has collaborated in marketing projects for global companies including Kellogg's de Mexico, Sony de Mexico, Worldwide Technical Services, Biovideo, and local organizations, such as Barrington Baptist Church and Onexpo. His expertise helped the previously mentioned companies to better understand their customer needs in different cultural settings, develop local promotional strategies and improve profitability. Some of Alberto's research has been published in national and international journals and he has been a presenter and panelist in conference and seminars around the world. Alberto has a bachelor's degree in Marketing from the Instituto Tecnologico y de Estudios Superiores de Monterrey. He earned a Master of Science and a Doctor of Philosophy degree in Consumer Behavior from Purdue University as well as a certification in Survey Research.

Mahmud A. Shareef is an Associate Professor and Coordinator (Marketing and Management) of school of business, North South University, Bangladesh. He was visiting faculty in DeGroote School of Business, McMaster University, Canada, during his post-doctorate research. He has done his PhD in Business Administration from Sprott School of Business, Carleton University, Canada. He received his graduate degree from both the Institute of Business Administration, University of Dhaka, Bangladesh, in Business Administration and Carleton University, Ottawa, Canada, in Civil Engineering. His research interest is focused on online consumer behavior and virtual organizational reformation. He has published more than 60 papers addressing consumers' adoption behavior and quality issues of e-commerce and e-government in different refereed conference proceedings and international journals. He has been the recipient of more than 10 academic awards including 3 Best Research Paper Awards in the UK and Canada.

Index